100 Essential Drumset Lessons

ROCK
JAZZ
FUNK
METAL
HIP-HOP
BLUES
COUNTRY
REGGAE
AFRO-CUBAN
and MORE!

By Terry O'Mahoney

PLAYBACK+
Speed • Pitch • Balance • Loop

To access audio visit:
www.halleonard.com/mylibrary

Enter Code
3146-8267-7151-0776

ISBN 978-1-4768-2118-4

7777 W. BLUEMOUND RD. P.O. BOX 13819 MILWAUKEE, WI 53213

In Australia Contact:
Hal Leonard Australia Pty. Ltd.
4 Lentara Court
Cheltenham, Victoria, 3192 Australia
Email: ausadmin@halleonard.com.au

Copyright © 2014 by HAL LEONARD CORPORATION
International Copyright Secured   All Rights Reserved

No part of this publication may be reproduced in any form or by
any means without the prior written permission of the Publisher.

Visit Hal Leonard Online at
www.halleonard.com

Table of Contents

Preface 1
Acknowledgments..................................... 1
Notation Legend 1

Rock/Funk/Metal

Lesson 1: Basic Rock Patterns 2
Lesson 2: Two-Bar Rock Grooves.................... 4
Lesson 3: 16th-Note Rock
         Bass Drum Patterns 6
Lesson 4: Basic Rock Fills................................ 8
Lesson 5: Intermediate Rock Grooves 10
Lesson 6: Intermediate Rock Fills................... 12
Lesson 7: 16th-Note Hi-Hat Rock 14
Lesson 8: Open Hi-Hat Rock 16
Lesson 9: Advanced Rock Fills 18
Lesson 10: Rock Ghost Notes 20
Lesson 11: Rock Cymbal and
         Hi-Hat Variations 22
Lesson 12: Soloing Over a Rock Vamp 24
Lesson 13: Basic Rock Chart Interpretation ... 26
Lesson 14: Basic Funk 28
Lesson 15: Intermediate Funk 30
Lesson 16: Advanced Funk 32
Lesson 17: Linear Drumming......................... 34
Lesson 18: Rudimental Drumset
         Applications #1 36
Lesson 19: Rudimental Drumset
         Applications #2 38
Lesson 20: Basic Double Kick
         (Double Bass Drum)...................... 40
Lesson 21: Intermediate Double Kick
         (Double Bass Drum)...................... 42
Lesson 22: Advanced Double Kick
         (Double Bass Drum)...................... 44
Lesson 23: Basic Blast Beats 46
Lesson 24: Basic Metal/Hard Rock Fills 48
Lesson 25: Intermediate Blast Beats............. 50
Lesson 26: Advanced Blast Beats 52
Lesson 27: Prog Metal................................... 54
Lesson 28: Hand/Foot Solo Patterns #1 56
Lesson 29: Hand/Foot Solo Patterns #2 58

Swing

Lesson 30: Basic Swing Comping Patterns.... 60
Lesson 31: Basic Swing Fills 62
Lesson 32: Intermediate Swing
         Comping Patterns 64
Lesson 33: Intermediate Swing Fills 66
Lesson 34: Advanced Swing
         Comping Patterns 68
Lesson 35: Advanced Swing Fills 70
Lesson 36: Advanced Hi-Hat
         Comping Patterns 72
Lesson 37: Drumset Accent Study #1 74
Lesson 38: Drumset Accent Study #2 76
Lesson 39: Drumset Accent Study #3 78
Lesson 40: Jazz "Two" Feel............................ 80
Lesson 41: Basic Brush Patterns................... 82
Lesson 42: Basic Brush Comping Patterns 84
Lesson 43: Jazz Waltz 86
Lesson 44: Jazz Waltz Fills............................ 88
Lesson 45: Advanced Jazz Waltz Concepts ... 90
Lesson 46: 3/4 Brushes 92
Lesson 47: Basic Soloing Concepts 94
Lesson 48: Basic Trading Fours..................... 96
Lesson 49: Trading Eights............................. 98
Lesson 50: Soloing on a 12-Bar Blues 100
Lesson 51: Soloing on a 32-Bar Jazz Tune... 102
Lesson 52: Soloing Over a
         Jazz Ostinato Vamp................... 104
Lesson 53: Basic Swing Chart
         Interpretation 106
Lesson 54: Intermediate Swing Chart
         Interpretation 108
Lesson 55: Advanced Swing Chart
         Interpretation 110
Lesson 56: Soloing Around
         Rhythmic Figures 112
Lesson 57: Changing Time Feels 114
Lesson 58: Fusion Drumming...................... 116
Lesson 59: Modern Jazz/ECM...................... 118
Lesson 60: Advanced Swing Ride Patterns.. 120

Odd Time

Lesson 61: Odd-Time Rock 122
Lesson 62: Intermediate Odd-Time Rock 124
Lesson 63: Advanced Odd-Time Rock 126
Lesson 64: Odd-Time Jazz 128
Lesson 65: Odd-Time Eighth-Note Meters ... 130
Lesson 66: Odd-Time Play-Along 132
Lesson 67: Odd-Time Soloing
 Play-Alongs 134

Blues/Country/Hip-Hop

Lesson 68: The 12/8 Groove 136
Lesson 69: Blues Drumming 138
Lesson 70: Country Drumming 140
Lesson 71: Shuffle Grooves 142
Lesson 72: Rockabilly and Surf Drumming ... 144
Lesson 73: Basic Hip-Hop 146
Lesson 74: Advanced Hip-Hop 148
Lesson 75: Drum N' Bass/Break Beats 150

World/Advanced Concepts

Lesson 76: Basic Afro-Cuban Grooves 152
Lesson 77: Basic Afro-Cuban/Brazilian/
 Caribbean Fills 154
Lesson 78: Advanced Afro-Cuban/Brazilian/
 Caribbean Fills 156
Lesson 79: Brazilian Grooves 158
Lesson 80: Caribbean/South
 American Grooves 160
Lesson 81: Reggae 162
Lesson 82: Basic African Grooves 164
Lesson 83: New Orleans Drumming 166
Lesson 84: Famous Drum Grooves 168
Lesson 85: Odd Groupings 170
Lesson 86: Basic Metric Superimposition 172
Lesson 87: Intermediate Metric
 Superimposition 174
Lesson 88: Advanced Metric Superimposition
 and Metric Modulation 176
Lesson 89: Beat Placement—Playing Behind,
 On, or Ahead of the Beat 178
Lesson 90: Productive Practicing
 Concepts 180
Lesson 91: Transcribing Drum Grooves 182
Lesson 92: Transcribing Drum Solos 184
Lesson 93: Creating an Original Drumset
 Part for a Song 186
Lesson 94: Miscellaneous Drumming
 Concepts 188
Lesson 95: Polyrhythms 190
Lesson 96: Rock Drumset Solo #1 192
Lesson 97: Jazz Drumset Solo #1 194
Lesson 98: Jazz Drumset Solo #2 196
Lesson 99: Jazz Drumset Solo #3 198
Lesson 100: Jazz Drumset Solo #4 200

About the Author 202

Track Listing

Rock/Funk/Metal

1. Basic Rock
2. Basic Rock—8th Note BD
3. Two-Bar Rock Grooves
4. 16th-Note Rock Bass Drum Patterns
5. 16th-Note Rock Bass Drum Patterns (Part 2)
6. Basic Two-Beat Rock Fills
7. Basic Two-Beat Rock Fills on Toms
8. Intermediate Rock Grooves
9. Intermediate Rock Fills
10. 16th-Note Hi-Hat Rock
11. Open Hi-Hat Rock (8th Notes)
12. Open Hi-Hat Rock (16th Notes)
13. Advanced Rock Fills
14. Advanced Rock Fills (Ensemble Figures)
15. Rock Ghost Notes (Groove w/o Ghost Notes)
16. Rock Ghost Notes
17. Rock Ghost Notes (Common Rock Grooves)
18. Rock Cymbal and Hi-Hat Variations
19. Soloing Over a Rock Vamp—Ex. 1
20. Soloing Over a Rock Vamp—Ex. 1 Play-Along
21. Soloing Over a Rock Vamp—Ex. 2 Play-Along
22. Soloing Over a Rock Vamp—Ex. 3 Play-Along
23. Soloing Over a Rock Vamp—Ex. 4 Play-Along
24. Soloing Over a Rock Vamp—Ex. 5 Play-Along
25. Basic Chart Interpretation—Ex. 1
26. Basic Chart Interpretation—Ex. 1 Play-Along
27. Basic Funk
28. Basic Funk—16th Notes
29. Intermediate Funk—Ride Patterns
30. Intermediate Funk—Ghost Notes
31. Advanced Funk—Displaced Backbeat
32. Advanced Funk—Hi-Hat Shots
33. Linear Drumming
34. Linear Drumming—w/ Backbeat
35. Linear Drumming—Implied Backbeat
36. Rudimental Applications #1—Paradiddle
37. Rudimental Applications #1—Double Paradiddle
38. Rudimental Applications #1—Double Paradiddle Alternate
39. Rudimental Applications #2—6-Stroke Roll
40. Rudimental Applications #2—Paradiddle-Diddle
41. Rudimental Applications #2—5-Stroke Roll
42. Basic Double Kick Warm-Ups
43. Basic Double Kick Grooves
44. Intermediate Double Kick Warm-Ups
45. Intermediate Double Kick—Triplet Grooves
46. Advanced Double Kick—Warm-Ups
47. Advanced Double Kick Grooves
48. Basic Blast Beats
49. Basic Blast Beats Grooves
50. Basic Metal/Hard Rock Fills
51. Basic Metal/Hard Rock Fills—w/ Cymbals
52. Basic Metal/Hard Rock Fills—w/ Double Kick
53. Intermediate Blast Beats—Triplet Grooves
54. Intermediate Blast Beats—Shuffles
55. Advanced Blast Beats—16th/32nd Notes
56. Advanced Blast Beats—16th-Note Triplets/Sextuplets
57. Prog Metal
58. Prog Metal—Mixed Meters
59. Hand/Foot Solo Patterns #1—8th Notes
60. Hand/Foot Solo Patterns #1—Triplets
61. Hand/Foot Solo Patterns #1—16th Notes
62. Hand/Foot Solo Patterns #2—Fives
63. Hand/Foot Solo Patterns #2—Solos

Swing

64. Basic Swing Comping Patterns—8th Notes
65. Basic Swing Comping Patterns—Triplet Partials
66. Basic Swing Fills—Triplets
67. Basic Swing Fills—Triplet Partials
68. Intermediate Swing Comping Patterns (SD/BD)
69. Intermediate Swing Comping Patterns—Offbeat 8th Notes
70. Intermediate Swing Fills
71. Intermediate Swing Fills—Triplet Partials
72. Advanced Swing Comping Patterns
73. Advanced Swing Comping Patterns—Two-Bar Phrases
74. Advanced Swing Fills
75. Advanced Swing Fills—16th Triplets
76. Advanced Hi-Hat Comping Patterns
77. Advanced Hi-Hat Comping Patterns (w/ SD and BD)
78. Drumset Accent Study #1—16th Notes
79. Drumset Accent Study #1—RH Lead
80. Drumset Accent Study #2—Triplets
81. Drumset Accent Study #2—RH Lead
82. Drumset Accent Study #3—Paradiddle
83. Drumset Accent Study #3—Double Paradiddle
84. Jazz Two Feel
85. Jazz Two Feel—AABA Form
86. Jazz Two Feel—A "Broken Two" Feel
87. Jazz Two Feel—Brushes
88. Basic Brush Patterns—Ballad
89. Basic Brush Patterns—Medium Swing
90. Basic Brush Patterns—Bossa Nova
91. Basic Brush Patterns—Sweeping Bossa Nova
92. Basic Brush Comping Patterns
93. Basic Brush Comping Patterns—16th Triplet
94. Basic Brush Comping Patterns—Four Stroke
95. Basic Brush Comping Patterns—8th Notes
96. Basic Brush Comping Patterns—Accents
97. Jazz Waltz—Snare/Bass Comping
98. Jazz Waltz—Quarter-Note Ride
99. Jazz Waltz—Groove Variations
100. Jazz Waltz Fills
101. Jazz Waltz Fills—Triplets
102. Advanced Jazz Waltz Concepts
103. 3/4 Brushes—Quarter Notes
104. 3/4 Brushes—Swing

105. 3/4 Brushes—Uptempo
106. 3/4 Brushes—8th Notes
107. Basic Soloing Concepts—Repetition
108. Basic Soloing Concepts—Varied Pitches
109. Basic Soloing Concepts—Fragmentation
110. Basic Soloing Concepts—Retrograde
111. Basic Soloing Concepts—Rhythmic Displacement
112. Basic Soloing Concepts—Play-Along
113. Basic Trading Fours
114. Basic Trading Fours—Play-Along
115. Basic Trading Eights
116. Basic Trading Eights—Play-Along
117. Soloing on a 12-Bar Blues
118. Soloing on a 12-Bar Blues—Play-Along
119. Soloing on a 12-Bar Blues—Straight 8th Feel Play-Along
120. Soloing on a 12-Bar Blues—Two Choruses Play-Along
121. Soloing on a 32-Bar Swing Tune
122. Soloing on a 32-Bar Swing Tune—Play-Along
123. Soloing Over a Jazz Ostinato/Vamp—One-Bar Vamp
124. Soloing Over a Jazz Ostinato/Vamp—Two-Bar Vamp
125. Soloing Over a Jazz Ostinato/Vamp—One-Bar Play-Along
126. Soloing Over a Jazz Ostinato/Vamp—Two-Bar Play-Along
127. Soloing Over a Jazz Ostinato/Vamp—Syncopated Two-Bar Play-Along
128. Soloing Over a Jazz Ostinato/Vamp—Four-Bar Play-Along
129. Soloing Over a Jazz Ostinato/Vamp—Syncopated Four-Bar Play-Along
130. Basic Swing Chart Interpretation—Ensemble Figures
131. Intermediate Swing Chart Interpretation—Short Backgrounds
132. Intermediate Swing Chart Interpretation—Syncopated Backgrounds Play-Along
133. Advanced Swing Chart Interpretation
134. Advanced Swing Chart Interpretation—Play-Along
135. Soloing Around Rhythmic Figures—Four-Bar Examples
136. Soloing Around Rhythmic Figures—Play-Along
137. Soloing Around Rhythmic Figures—Chart
138. Soloing Around Rhythmic Figures—Play-Along
139. Changing Time Feels—Half-Time Rock
140. Changing Time Feels—16th-Note Hi-Hat
141. Changing Time Feels—Rock to Swing
142. Changing Time Feels—Swing to Bossa Nova
143. Changing Time Feels—Swing to Mambo
144. Changing Time Feels—Swing to Afro-Cuban 6/8
145. Fusion Cross-Stick
146. Fusion—Funk
147. Fusion—Samba
148. Fusion—Odd Meter
149. Modern Jazz/ECM—Straight 8th Feel (Drums Only)
150. Modern Jazz/ECM—Straight 8th Example
151. Modern Jazz/ECM—ECM Swing "2" and "4" Feel
152. Modern Jazz/ECM—"2" Feel Example (Drums Only)
153. Modern Jazz/ECM—Straight 8th Play-Along
154. Modern Jazz/ECM—Swing "2" Feel Play-Along
155. Modern Jazz/ECM—Swing "4" Feel Play-Along
156. Advanced Swing Ride Patterns
157. Advanced Swing Ride Patterns—Tied Notes

Odd Time

158. Odd-Time Rock—3/4
159. Odd-Time Rock—5/4
160. Odd-Time Rock—7/4
161. Intermediate Odd-Time Rock—5/4 Bass, 3 + 2
162. Intermediate Odd-Time Rock—5/4 Bass, 2 + 3
163. Intermediate Odd-Time Rock—7/4 Bass, 2 + 2 + 3
164. Intermediate Odd-Time Rock—7/4 Bass, 2 + 3 + 2
165. Intermediate Odd-Time Rock—7/4 Bass, 3 + 2 + 2
166. Intermediate Odd-Time Rock—5/4, 3 + 2 Play-Along
167. Intermediate Odd-Time Rock—5/4, 2 + 3 Play-Along
168. Intermediate Odd-Time Rock—7/4, 2 + 2 + 3 Play-Along
169. Intermediate Odd-Time Rock—7/4, 2 + 3 + 2 Play-Along
170. Intermediate Odd-Time Rock—7/4, 3 + 2 + 2 Play-Along
171. Advanced Odd-Time Rock—3/4, Two-Bar Phrases
172. Advanced Odd-Time Rock—5/4, 3 + 2 Backbeat
173. Advanced Odd-Time Rock—5/4, 2 + 3 Backbeat
174. Advanced Odd-Time Rock—7/4, 2 + 2 + 3 Backbeat
175. Advanced Odd-Time Rock—7/4, 2 + 3 + 2 Backbeat
176. Advanced Odd-Time Rock—7/4, 3 + 2 + 2 Backbeat
177. Odd-Time Jazz—3/4
178. Odd-Time Jazz—5/4, 3 + 2
179. Odd-Time Jazz—5/4, 2 + 3
180. Odd-Time Jazz—7/4, 2 + 2 + 3
181. Odd-Time Jazz—7/4, 2 + 3 + 2
182. Odd-Time Jazz—7/4, 3 + 2 + 2
183. Eighth-Note Odd Meters—5/8, 3 + 2
184. Eighth-Note Odd Meters—5/8, 2 + 3
185. Eighth-Note Odd Meters—7/8, 2 + 2 + 3
186. Eighth-Note Odd Meters—7/8, 2 + 3 + 2
187. Eighth-Note Odd Meters—7/8, 3 + 2 + 2
188. Odd-Time Play-Along—5/8
189. Odd-Time Play-Along—7/8
190. Odd-Time Play-Along—9/8
191. Odd-Time Play-Along—11/8, 2 + 2 + 2 + 2 + 3
192. Odd-Time Play-Along—11/8, 3 + 3 + 3 + 2
193. Odd-Time Play-Along—13/8, 2 + 2 + 2 + 2 + 2 + 3
194. Odd-Time Play-Along—13/8, 3 + 3 + 3 + 4
195. Odd-Time Play-Along—Mixed Meter
196. Odd-Time Rock Trading Fours—3/4 Play-Along
197. Odd-Time Swing Trading Fours—3/4 Play-Along
198. Odd-Time Rock Trading Fours—5/4 Play-Along
199. Odd-Time Swing Trading Fours—5/4 Play-Along
200. Odd-Time Rock Trading Fours—7/4 Play-Along
201. Odd-Time Swing Trading Fours—7/4 Play-Along
202. Odd-Time Rock Trading Eights—3/4 Play-Along
203. Odd-Time Swing Trading Eights—3/4 Play-Along
204. Odd-Time Rock Trading Eights—5/4 Play-Along
205. Odd-Time Swing Trading Eights—5/4 Play-Along
206. Odd-Time Rock Trading Eights—7/4 Play-Along
207. Odd-Time Swing Trading Eights—7/4 Play-Along

Blues/Country/Hip-Hop

208. The 12/8 Groove
209. The 12/8 Groove—16th-Note Bass Drum
210. Blues Drumming—Straight 8th
211. Blues Drumming—16th Notes

212. Blues Drumming—Syncopated Gooves
213. Blues Drumming—12/8 Blues
214. Blues Drumming—Bo Diddley
215. Blues Drumming—6/4
216. Country Drumming—Train Beat
217. Country Drumming—12/8
218. Country Drumming—Western Swing
219. Country Drumming—Shuffle
220. Shuffle Grooves—Brushes
221. Shuffle Grooves—Jazz Shuffle
222. Shuffle Grooves—Jazz Shuffle with Syncopated Bass Drum
223. Shuffle Grooves—Blues
224. Shuffle Grooves—Quarter-Note Ride
225. Shuffle Grooves—Rock Shuffles
226. Rockabilly
227. Surf
228. Surf—Drum Solo
229. Basic Hip-Hop
230. Basic Hip-Hop—Shuffle
231. Advanced Hip-Hop—Basic Shuffle
232. Advanced Hip-Hop Shuffles with Open Hi-Hats
233. Drum N' Bass/Break Beats—1st Break Beat
234. Drum N' Bass/Break Beats—Four-Bar Phrases
235. Drum N' Bass/Break Beat—Groove Flow

World Music/Advanced Concepts

236. Basic Afro-Cuban Grooves—Mambo
237. Basic Afro-Cuban Grooves—Afro-Cuban 6/8/Bembé
238. Basic Afro-Cuban Grooves—Guaguanco
239. Basic Afro-Cuban Grooves—Mozambique
240. Basic Afro-Cuban Grooves—Cha-Cha-Cha
241. Basic Afro-Cuban Grooves—Songo
242. Basic Afro-Cuban/Brazilian/Caribbean Fills
243. Advanced Afro-Cuban/Brazilian/Caribbean Fills 1
244. Advanced Afro-Cuban/Brazilian/Caribbean Fills 2
245. Brazilian Grooves—Bossa Nova
246. Brazilian Grooves—Samba
247. Brazilian Grooves—Partido Alto
248. Brazilian Grooves—Baião
249. Brazilian Grooves—Marcha
250. Brazilian Grooves—Frevo
251. Caribbean/South American Grooves—Calypso
252. Caribbean/South American Grooves—Soca
253. Caribbean/South American Grooves—Plena/Bomba
254. Caribbean/South American Grooves—Merengue
255. Caribbean/South American Grooves—Tango
256. Caribbean/South American Grooves—Cumbia
257. Caribbean/South American Grooves—Joropo
258. Reggae—One-Drop
259. Reggae—Four-Drop
260. Reggae—Shuffle
261. Reggae—Fills
262. Reggae—One-Drop Play-Along
263. Reggae—Four-Drop Play-Along
264. Reggae—One-Drop Shuffle Play-Along
265. Reggae—Four-Drop Shuffle Play-Along
266. Basic African Grooves—Bikutsi
267. Basic African Grooves—Mangambe
268. Basic African Grooves—Afrobeat
269. Basic African Grooves—Soukous
270. Basic African Grooves—Mbaqanga
271. Basic African Grooves—Juju
272. New Orleans—Ragtime
273. New Orleans—Dirge
274. New Orleans—2nd Line
275. New Orleans—2nd Line w/ Buzzes
276. New Orleans—Jazz 2nd Line
277. Famous Drum Grooves—Swing Tom Solo
278. Famous Drum Grooves—Straight 8th Tom Solo
279. Famous Drum Grooves—Clave Tom Groove
280. Famous Drum Grooves—Disco, Polka, Reggaeton
281. Famous Drum Grooves—Motown
282. Famous Drum Grooves—Mojo
283. Odd Groupings—8th Notes Grouped in Threes
284. Odd Groupings—16th Notes Grouped in Threes
285. Odd Groupings—8th Notes Grouped in Fives
286. Odd Groupings—Triplets Grouped in Fives
287. Odd Groupings—16th Notes Grouped in Fives
288. Odd Groupings—8th Notes Grouped in Sevens
289. Odd Groupings—Triplets Grouped in Sevens
290. Odd Groupings—16th Notes Grouped in Sevens
291. Basic Metric Superimposition—Half Time
292. Basic Metric Superimposition—Double Time
293. Basic Metric Superimposition—Half-Time Swing
294. Basic Metric Superimposition—Double-Time Swing
295. Basic Metric Superimposition—Double Time
296. Basic Metric Superimposition—Double-Time Feel
297. Basic Metric Superimposition—3/4 in 4/4
298. Intermediate Metric Superimposition—5/4
299. Intermediate Metric Superimposition—7/4
300. Intermediate Metric Superimposition—3/8, 5/8
301. Intermediate Metric Superimposition—Swing 5/4, 7/4
302. Advanced Metric Superimposition—3 against 4
303. Advanced Metric Superimposition—6/4 over 4/4
304. Advanced Metric Superimposition—Metric Modulation
305. Advanced Metric Superimposition (2 against 3)
306. Beat Placement—Rock/Swing, Behind/On/Ahead of the Beat
307. Beat Placement—Rock Play-Along
308. Beat Placement—Swing Play-Along
309. Beat Placement—Shuffle Play-Along
310. Miscellaneous Concepts—Brushes to Sticks
311. Polyrhythms—Quarter-Note Triplets/6 against 4 (6:4)
312. Polyrhythms—4 against 3 (4:3)
313. Polyrhythms—7 against 4 (7:4)
314. Rock Drumset Solo #1 (excerpt)
315. Jazz Drumset Solo #1 (excerpt)
316. Jazz Drumset Solo #2 (excerpt)
317. Jazz Drumset Solo #3 (excerpt)
318. Jazz Drumset Solo #4 (excerpt)

Preface

100 Essential Drumset Lessons contains information, examples, exercises, and over 300 audio examples* on a range of topics that every drummer—from the novice to the professional—will find useful. Its educational scope runs the gamut, including basic rock, funk, metal, hip-hop, blues, country, basic swing, advanced swing concepts, fills, technical exercises, metric superimposition, soloing concepts, odd time playing, brush playing, as well as Afro-Cuban, Brazilian, and other world music drumming styles. It also includes advice on productive practicing techniques, transcribing drum parts, creating an original drum part for a song, and five drumset audition solos (suitable for use at all-state auditions, music festivals, or recitals).

(* Most audio examples feature demonstrations of the first few exercises only in each example.)

Acknowledgments

This project would not have been possible without help from a number of different people. I wish to extend my sincerest thanks to Wendy (for her love and patience); Kevin Brunkhorst (Golden Lab Studios) for his technical and musical assistance; Doug Smith (DTT), Alex Whitehead, Tony Genge, and Peter Bull for their musical contributions. I would also like to thank Michael Vosbein (Crescent Cymbals), Neil Larrivee (Vic Firth Drumsticks), Michael Baker, Gene Smith, and Dr. Richard Nemisvari (St. Francis Xavier University). All original compositions by Terry O'Mahoney.

Notation Legend

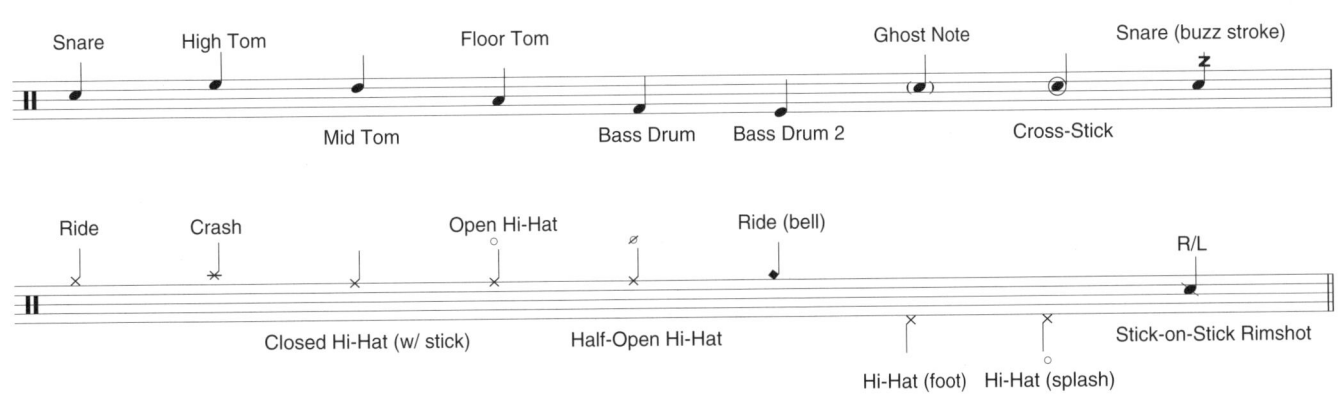

Lesson 1

Basic Rock Patterns

A great place to start drumming is with some basic rock patterns. Most rock drum patterns, also known as grooves, use repetitive patterns in the right hand (on either the hi-hat or the ride cymbal), the left hand (on the snare drum), and the left foot (on the hi-hat). The right foot (playing the bass drum) often plays the most complicated rhythms and frequently changes rhythms during a song.

Playing the drums is similar to building a house; it's done in "layers." Start with eighth notes on the ride cymbal. As you begin practicing, it is important to always count the rhythm that you are playing. Count "1 and 2 and 3 and 4 and" as you play the pattern below on the ride cymbal, like this:

EXAMPLE 1:

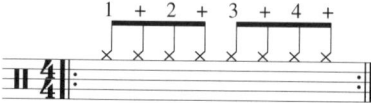

Practice Example 1 until you can play it eight times in a row without any mistakes and without stopping. Next, add the snare drum when you say the words "2" and "4."

EXAMPLE 2:

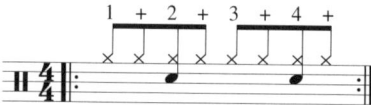

Then add the bass drum on beats 1 and 3.

EXAMPLE 3:

And finally, add the hi-hat by pressing down on the hi-hat pedal with your foot on beats 2 and 4.

EXAMPLE 4:

TRACK 1

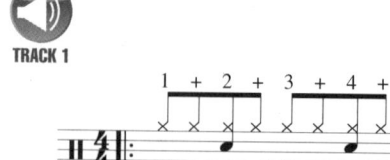

You can repeat this process of building a groove with Exercises 1–24 on the next page. The bass drum variations help to give each song (or part of a song) its own unique feel, energy, and character. The bass drum part often imitates what the bass player is playing, and the following exercises will help to develop your ability to vary the bass drum part using the most common eighth-note patterns while repeating the same ride cymbal, snare drum, and hi-hat rhythms.

Practice each one of these one-measure patterns until they are comfortable and then move on to the next one. After you've mastered all of them, try to start at the top and play straight through the whole page without stopping.

TRACK 2

In addition to playing the right hand on the ride cymbal, you can also play the right hand on the closed hi-hat. Just keep the hi-hat pedal tightly depressed and the hi-hat cymbals tightly together throughout the exercise.

When it's time to play with other musicians, you should realize that drum parts are often not written out and the drummer is expected to be able to just "come up with a drum part" on their own. The ability to improvise a drum part—i.e., instantly make up a drum pattern on the spot—is critical to becoming a good drummer. To practice improvising drum parts yourself, listen to a recording using headphones and try to play along with it using some of the patterns in this lesson. At first, you may not be able to keep up with it, but you'll improve in time. You can also listen to recordings and try to figure out if some of the patterns in this lesson are used in your favorite songs. Once you know which patterns fit with which songs, you will be closer to choosing the best drum pattern for a particular song.

Lesson 2

Two-Bar Rock Grooves

After mastering some basic rock patterns, it is important to realize that not all songs require the drummer to play exactly the same drum pattern (or groove) over and over again. This is a good thing, because doing so might make the song (and the drummer's job) rather boring. Drummers often choose to mix and match drum patterns to make a song less predictable and to allow for more creativity. This often means that drummers group drum patterns for a specific song into two-bar phrases, or sequences, that are used throughout the song. Two-bar drum grooves are often used because the rhythm of the bass drum is meant to match the rhythm played by the bass player in an ensemble. In some cases, this means that beat 1 of the second bar in each two-bar phrase might not have a bass drum note.

Practice the following patterns, paying particular attention to how the second bar of each phrase is different from the first. Try to find songs that use two-bar drum phrases and see how they relate to these exercises. The ride pattern in these exercises may also be played on a closed hi-hat (with the right hand).

TRACK 3

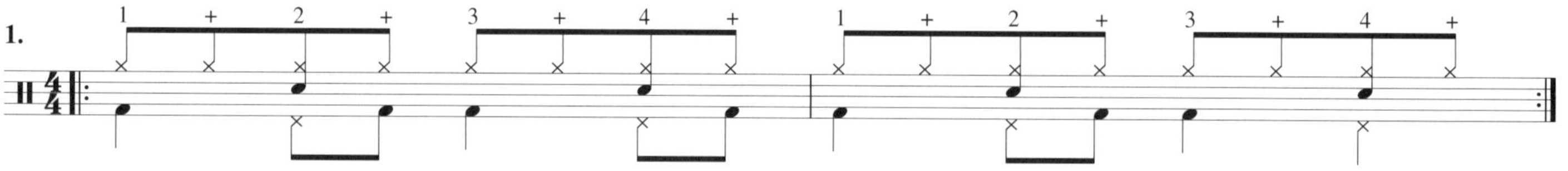

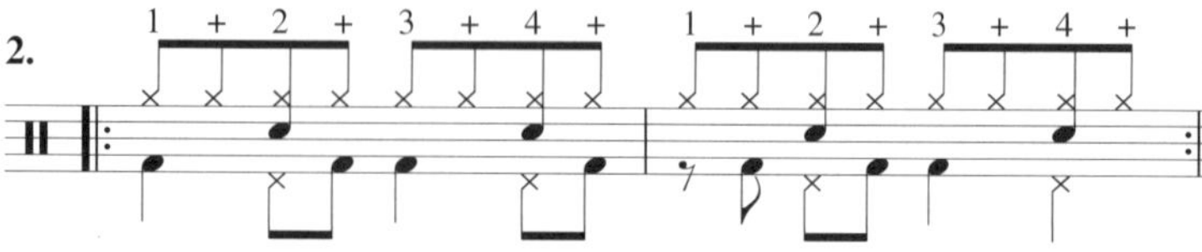

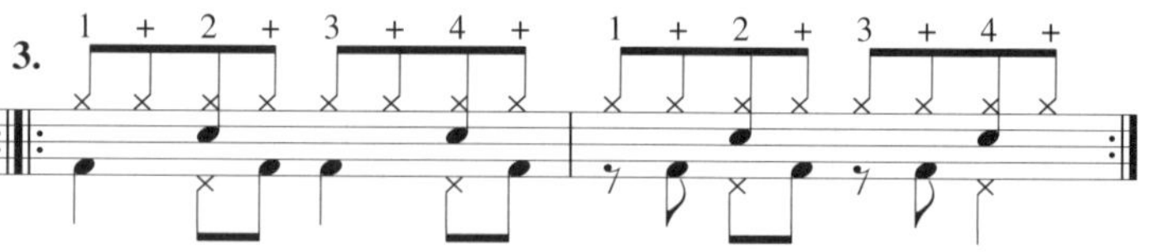

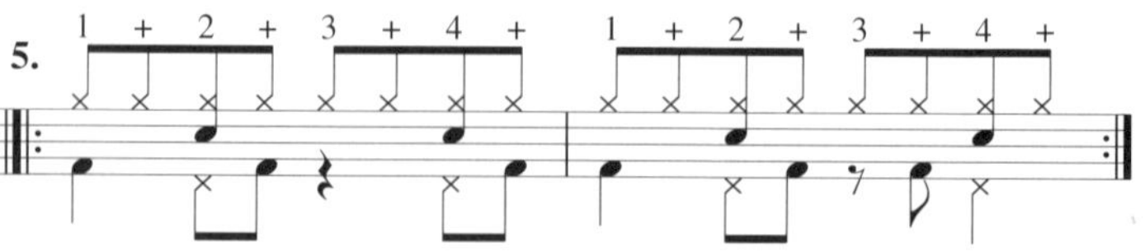

4

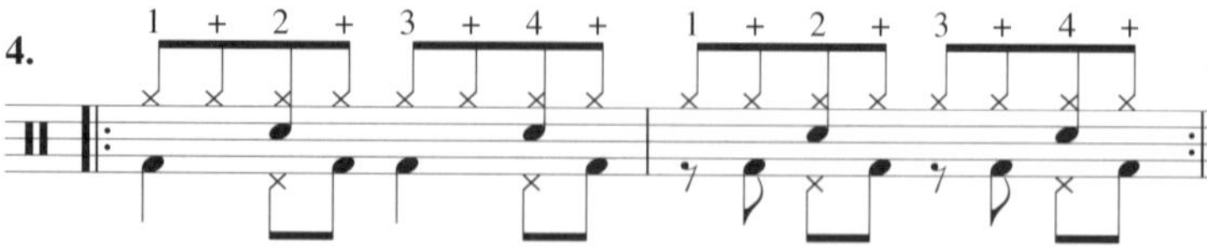

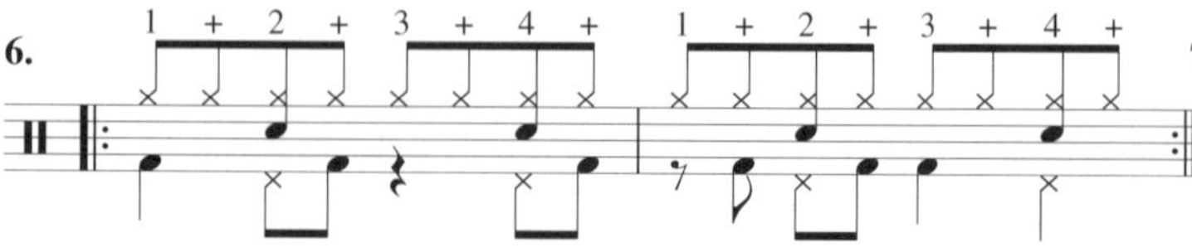

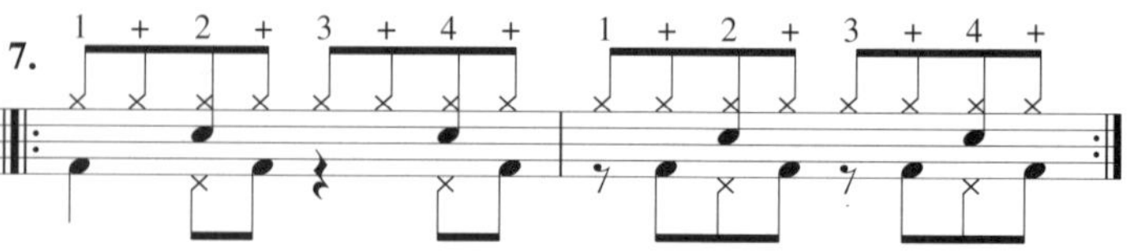

16th-Note Rock Bass Drum Patterns

After mastering eighth-note rock bass drum patterns, the intermediate level of rock patterns begins to incorporate 16th notes in the bass drum. In these exercises, the ride cymbal, hi-hat, and snare drum parts will not change, but the bass drum parts will become more challenging. The exercises below begin to integrate bass drum notes that are played between the eighth notes of the ride cymbal—i.e., on the "e's" and "ah's" of the beat. Notice how each new pattern is different from the one preceding it. Try to master each of these four patterns and see how they will be used to create many different patterns below.

TRACK 4

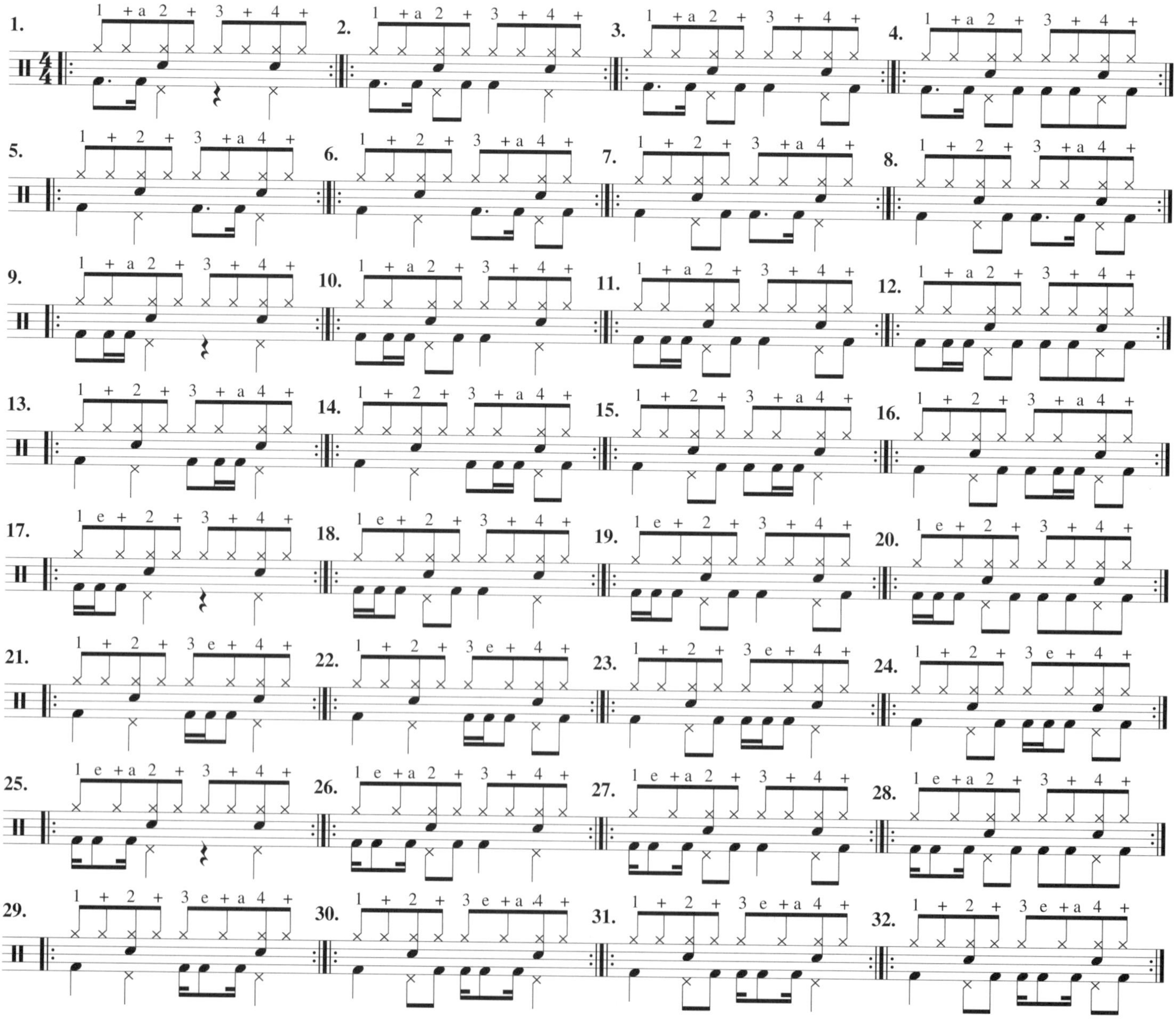

Of course, 16th notes can also be played on other parts of the beat, as in these examples.

TRACK 5

As a creative exercise, try combining some of the new 16th-note bass drum patterns from this lesson with eighth-note patterns you can already play—either by yourself or along with one of your favorite songs.

Lesson 4

Basic Rock Fills

Drummers often play the same rhythmic patterns over and over again in a song (often known as the "beat" of a song or a "groove"). Occasionally, however, they play other short musical passages that break up the routine of the rhythm and add interest and excitement to the music (usually on the snare drum and/or the toms). These passages are known as *fills*. Drum fills are usually improvised, normally found at the end of a musical phrase, can vary in length (usually two or four beats), and, in rock, often end on the first beat of the *next phrase* with a crash cymbal on beat 1 of the bar.

In order to understand where fills are played in most music, you must first understand that most popular music (pop, rock, country, alternative, etc.) is normally organized into four- and eight-bar phrases. It's important to keep track (in your mind) of where you are in the musical phrase in order to put the fill in the right location. One way to keep track of which measure you are playing is to say the number of the bar you are playing on the *downbeat* of each bar.

For example, play this four-bar phrase and count it like this, being sure to say the bold numbers slightly louder than the other beats of the measure to help you keep track:

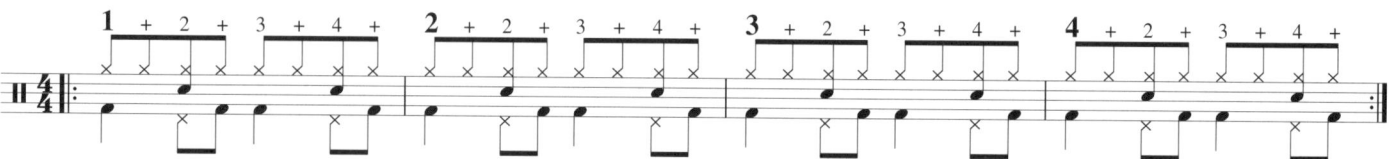

Once you're able to count four bars consistently and keep your place in the music, you can start to add fills.

Exercises 1–8 feature some four-bar patterns with fills that are two beats in length ("two-beat fills") at the end of each phrase. The two-beat fills are substituted for beats 3 and 4 in the fourth bar of the phrase and have a crash cymbal on beat one of the following bar. In rock, fills normally finish with a crash cymbal.

The ride cymbal part may also be played on a closed hi-hat to create a different sound. Try to play the hi-hat on beats 2 and 4 even during the fills to help keep the tempo steady.

TRACK 6

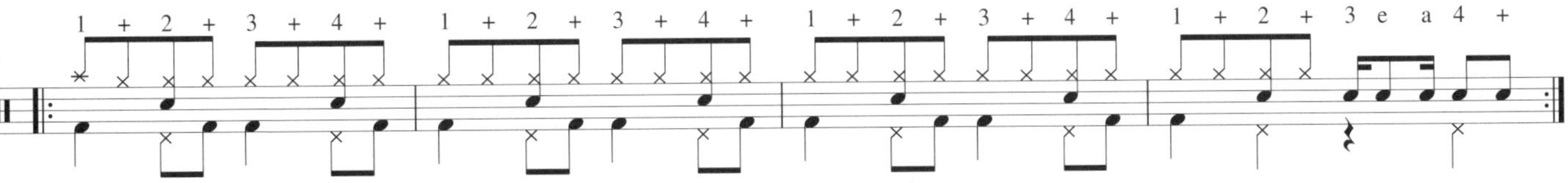

All of the fills are notated on the snare drum. Once you're comfortable with keeping your place in the phrase and with the execution of the fills, try taking the rhythm of the fills and moving them around the toms to create an infinite number of different fills, like this (in this case, we're using line 1):

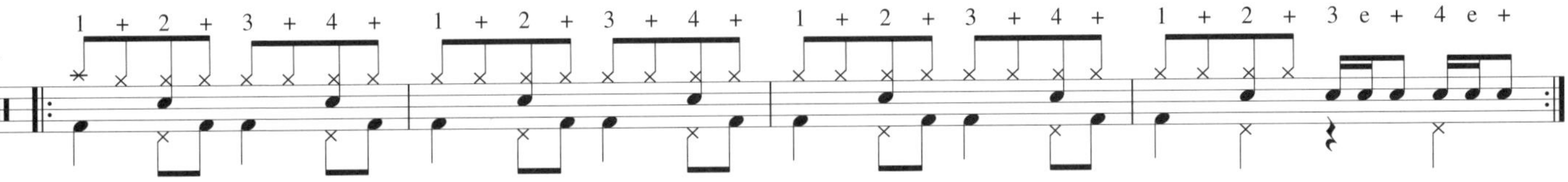

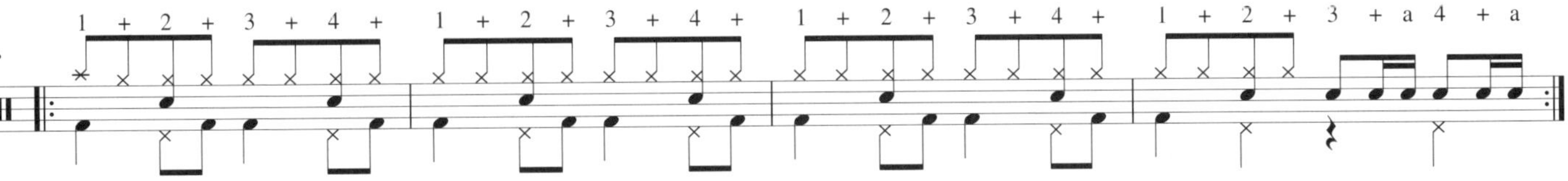

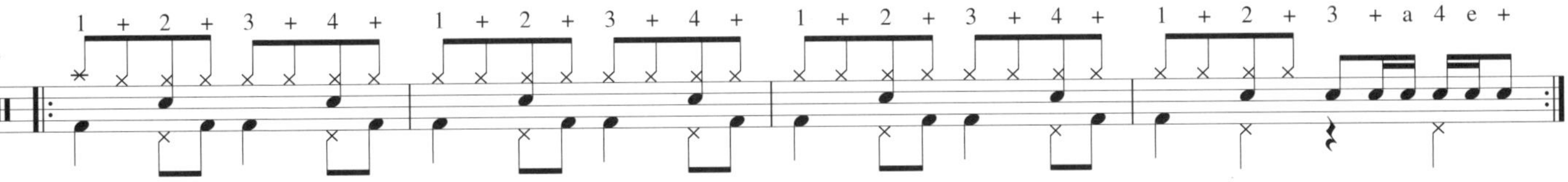

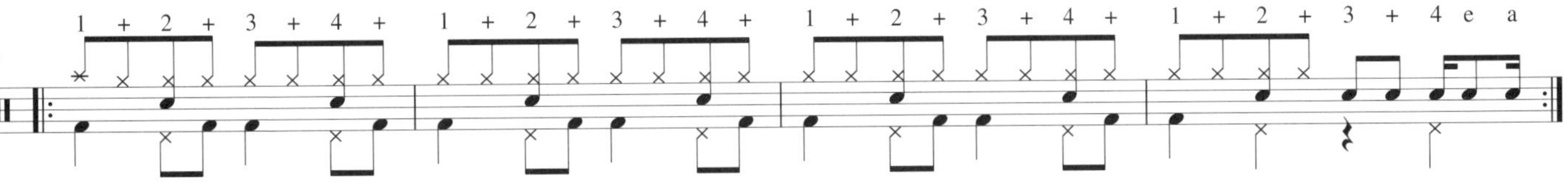

TRACK 7

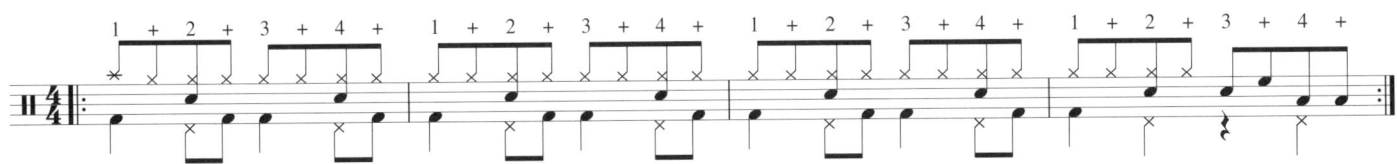

After practicing these exercises for an extended period, you'll eventually develop the ability to "feel" how long a four-bar phrase is and will not have to consciously count each phrase (which is great). This ability to subconsciously feel the length of a phrase is known as *internalization*. It's a useful ability to have; it frees you from having to count every measure and allows you to concentrate on the many others things that are taking place during a performance. For a creative exercise, try improvising two-beat fills along with your favorite song.

Intermediate Rock Grooves

One of the foundations of rock drumming is the snare drum notes on beats 2 and 4 (known as the *backbeat*) with syncopated 16th-note bass drum patterns. The intermediate-level rock patterns in this lesson combine eighth-note and 16th-note bass drum patterns while maintaining the repetitive eighth-note ride cymbal, backbeat snare drum rhythm, and hi-hat patterns found in simpler patterns.

While playing drums, often the speed of the song (also known as the *tempo*) makes it difficult to count each and every 16th note that you intend to play; it's just too much to think about. In those cases, you may want to simplify what you are counting while simultaneously playing complicated rhythms. This allows your mind to concentrate on other things going on in the music—where you are in the form of the song, what kind of fill you intend to play next, etc.

For example, once you're comfortable playing a few 16th-note bass drum patterns, instead of counting all of the bass drum 16th notes, like this…

…try simplifying and counting only the ride cymbal part (while still playing the 16th-note bass drum rhythms), like this:

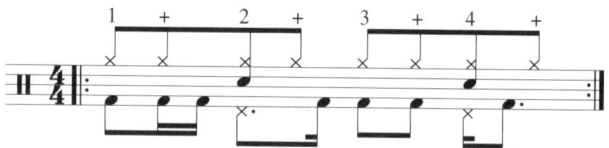

It's OK if you have to count the 16th notes at first. But once you become confident that you are playing the bass drum rhythms correctly, simplify your counting approach by counting only eighth notes (as described above). This will enable you to concentrate on listening to your own performance and assessing your progress. These exercises will only feature the eighth-note ride cymbal counting scheme provided.

TRACK 8

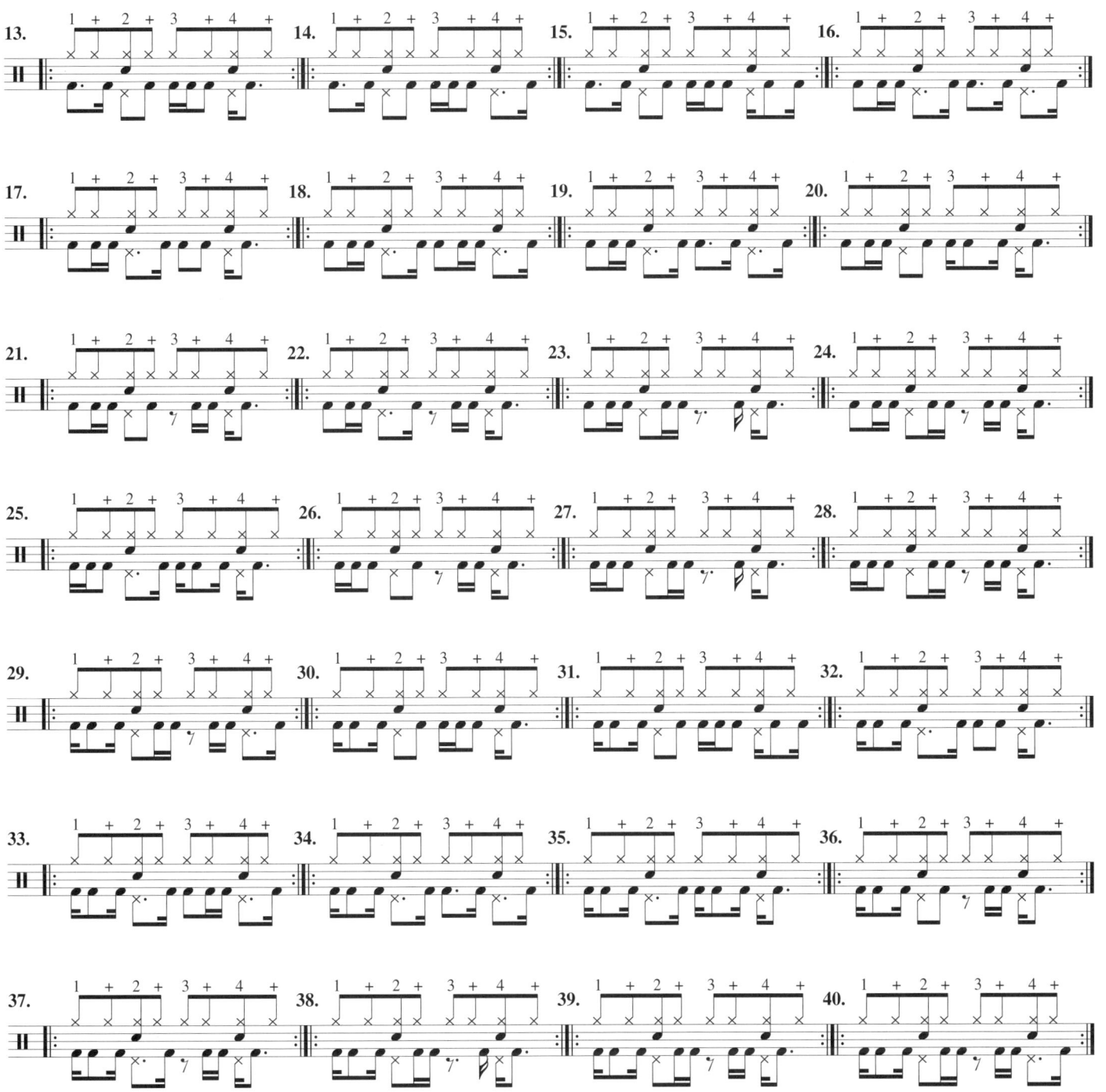

Try playing along with some of your favorite songs (or a metronome) using the eighth-note ride cymbal pattern, snare drum on beats 2 and 4, and hi-hat on beats 2 and 4 while improvising 16th-note patterns on the bass drum. If you can do this successfully, you'll be able to create whatever rock patterns you need. You may also substitute a closed hi-hat for the ride cymbal pattern.

Intermediate Rock Fills

This lesson illustrates four-beat rock fills. We'll also introduce some musical "shorthand"—quicker ways of expressing a musical concept rather than writing out each and every note. In this case, the shorthand method used is four *slash marks* written in the fourth bar of each exercise. Slash marks may have different meanings depending upon the situation. If you're playing a groove, slashes in a bar would mean that you continue the groove you're playing—like a repeat bar. If there are four slashes in the bar and written instructions above the bar (such as *fill* or *solo*), then follow the written directions above the slashes (as is the case in these exercises).

These exercises are organized into four-bar phrases, so you'll play three measures of a basic beat (either the written pattern or one of your choice) followed by the rhythm found in Exercises 1–55 in the fourth bar. Here's the basic beat with shorthand slash marks shown for the fourth bar:

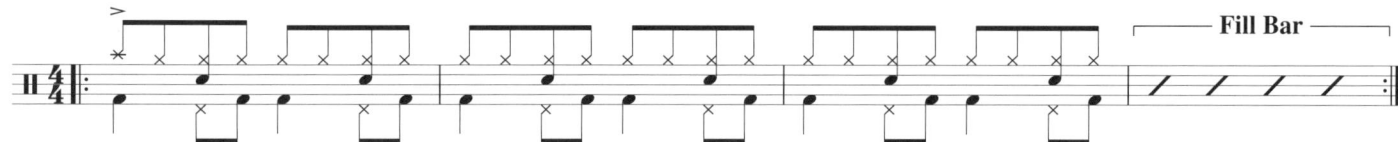

When practicing the following exercises, try these suggestions:

- Learn each fill bar first on the snare drum, and then try as many variations around the drums as you can possibly imagine. Some variations may require double sticking (RR or LL) to work.

- Keep playing the hi-hat on beats 2 and 4 throughout the fill bar.

TRACK 9

You may also substitute a closed hi-hat for the ride cymbal pattern in these exercises.

Lesson 7

16th-Note Hi-Hat Rock

Some rock tunes require a busy, energetic sound that can't be achieved by playing just eighth notes in the ride pattern. In these instances, a 16th-note ride pattern is called for. If the tempo is slow enough, the 16th notes in the ride part can all be played with one hand:

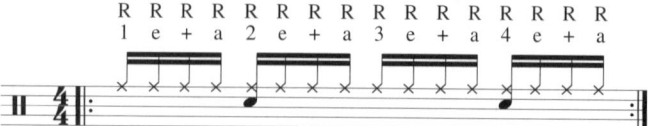

If the tempo is too fast to play with one hand, however, it becomes necessary to play the 16ths with two hands. In this case, the right hand (if you are right-handed) moves between the hi-hat and snare drum, and there are no hi-hat notes on beats 2 and 4:

If you know which hand each bass drum note is aligned with, it will make integrating the bass part easier. For example, all of the bass drum notes on either a "number" or an "and" will be played with the right hand, while all the notes on the "e" or "a" of the beat will be played with the left hand. In these exercises, the left hand never moves off the hi-hat—only the right hand moves to the snare for beats 2 and 4. Remember to keep the hi-hat tightly closed during all of these exercises.

Try playing along with a song that has a 16th-note rock ride pattern (either with two hands or with one hand, if it is slow enough) and improvise different bass drum rhythms.

TRACK 10

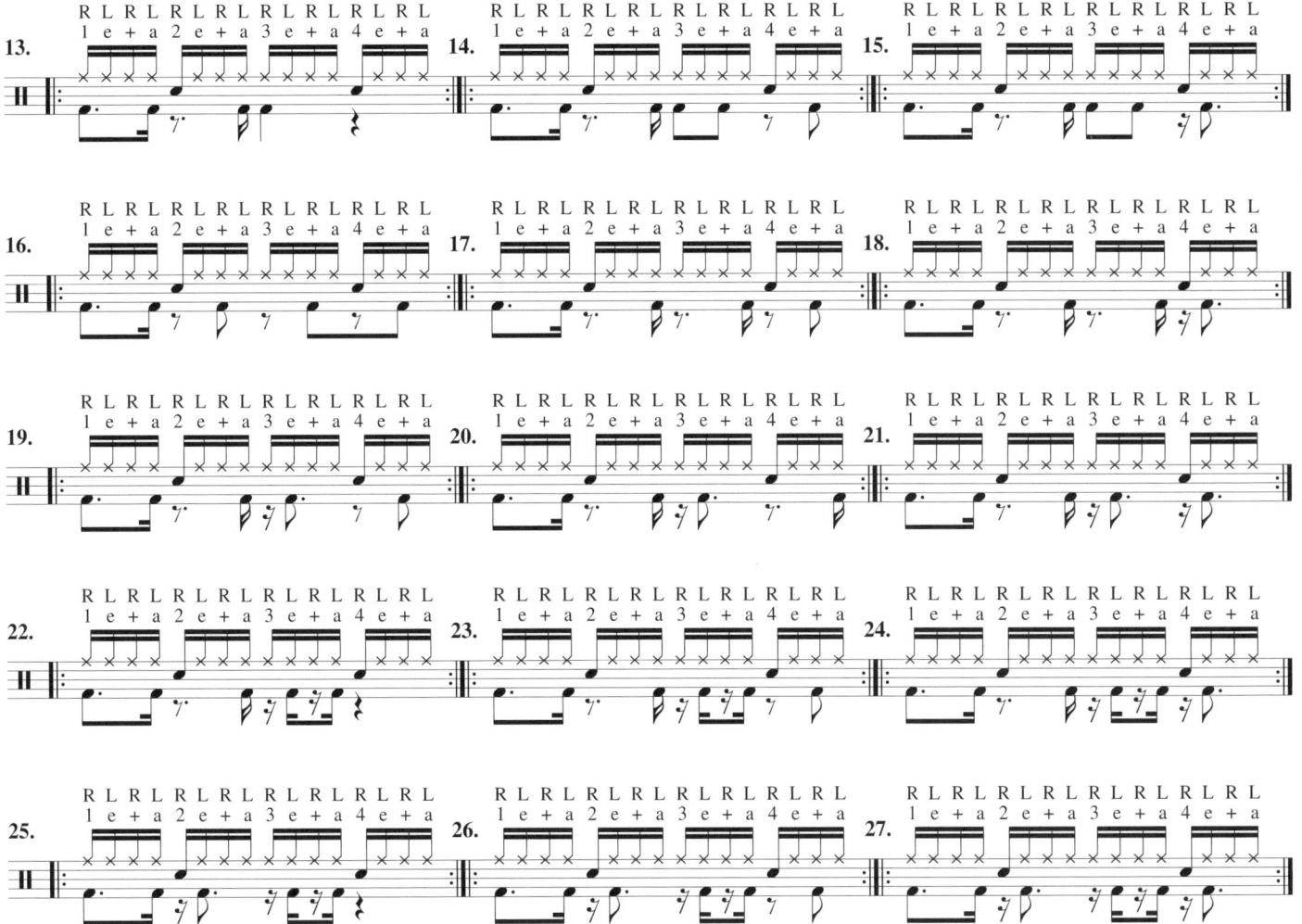

Play each exercise in four-bar phrases and add a fill at the end of each phrase. If you're left-handed, you may reverse all stickings (left hand plays the snare drum notes). In some songs, one part of the song (for example, the verse) may use an eighth-note ride pattern, while another part of the song may need a 16th-note ride pattern (for example, the chorus). Try playing some songs while switching back and forth and see how it affects the song.

Lesson 8

Open Hi-Hat Rock

In addition to playing a ride pattern on the ride cymbal or closed hi-hat, another useful sound is the open hi-hat sound. It's indicated by a small letter "o" above the opened note. The hi-hat should be closed on the note immediately following the opened note. In some cases, a plus sign (+) is used to specify exactly when an open hi-hat note ends. Composers often assume that the drummer knows to close the hi-hat immediately following an open note, but when they want to be very specific, they include a plus sign.

The open hi-hat sound is created by striking the hi-hat with a stick while simultaneously releasing the pressure on the hi-hat footboard. When executing the open hi-hat sound, don't really open the hi-hat all the way; just relax the pressure on the hi-hat footboard enough to allow the cymbals to open (approximately 3/8") and still have their edges touching. You don't want to actually hear the pitch of the cymbal—you just want to hear the "sizzle" of two cymbals vibrating together when struck.

In this first example, the counting scheme, open hi-hat note, and closed hi-hat note are all indicated. You open the hi-hat on the "and" of beat 4 and close it on beat 1 of the next bar. There is a tie (curved line) here to indicate where it opens and where it closes. In future examples, only the "open" sign will be used. Assume that the hi-hat is to be closed on the very next hi-hat note.

TRACK 11

The following exercises use the same bass drum, snare drum, and hi-hat part in order to focus on placing the open hi-hat notes on different beats. Practice these exercises using more difficult bass drum patterns as you start to feel more comfortable with opening the hi-hat on different beats.

The open hi-hat sound may also be used when playing 16th notes on the hi-hat. The same rule applies to 16th-note open hi-hats: open on the first note and close on the very next 16th note. Try these exercises after mastering 16th-note hi-hat patterns without open notes. Knowing which hand plays the open note will help you execute these exercises. Write in the sticking, if necessary.

TRACK 12

Lesson 9

Advanced Rock Fills

The advanced rock fills in this lesson use different combinations of eighth notes, 16th notes, triplets, and sextuplets (six notes per beat). In many songs, fills can vary in length from two beats to two full bars. When practicing the One-Bar Exercises below (1–14), learn each fill bar alone and then try to integrate it into four-bar musical phrases. For example, play the groove below and insert the one-bar fill of your choice in the last bar:

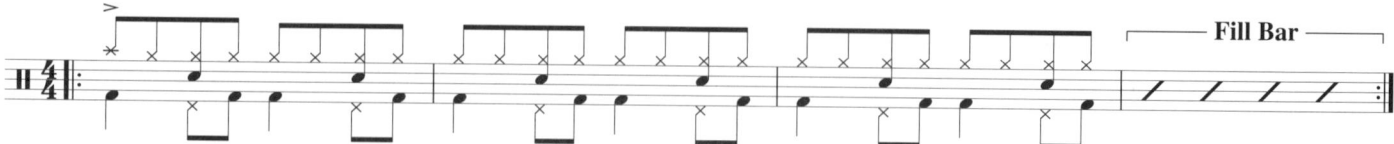

Then combine any two exercises into a two-bar fill at the end of a four-bar phrase:

- Move the rhythms onto any combination of toms.
- Substitute crash cymbals for different notes (particularly on beat 1 of each bar).
- When possible, use *double stops* (both hands play two different drums simultaneously).

ONE-BAR EXERCISES

On the audio, the first four exercises are demonstrated as a one-bar fill in the last measures of a four-bar phrase.

TRACK 13

In addition to improvised fills (which comprise 90 percent of all fills), drummers need to be aware of other circumstances that might influence their fills. In some cases, fills are not really "fills"—they are rhythmic figures played in unison with other instruments, such as an electric guitar. The following five two-bar examples demonstrate how to take a very common rhythm (a dotted quarter-note rhythm repeated over six beats) and embellish it in a number of different ways. The crash cymbal is played in unison with the rhythm of the other instruments, and the drums "fill in" the space between the dotted quarter notes (which are heard on every third eighth note). In situations like this, the drummer has to pay attention to what the other players are doing and decide what to do. Listen to some of your favorite music for this concept and notice how the drummer orchestrates the overall rhythmic figure with different rhythms on various drums. This will help prepare you when you find yourself in a similar situation.

TRACK 14

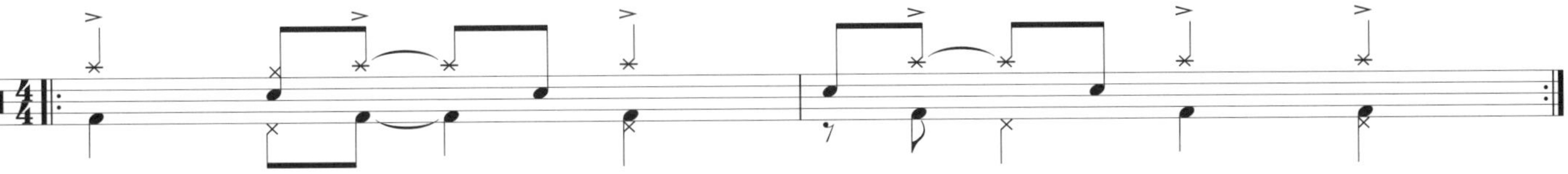

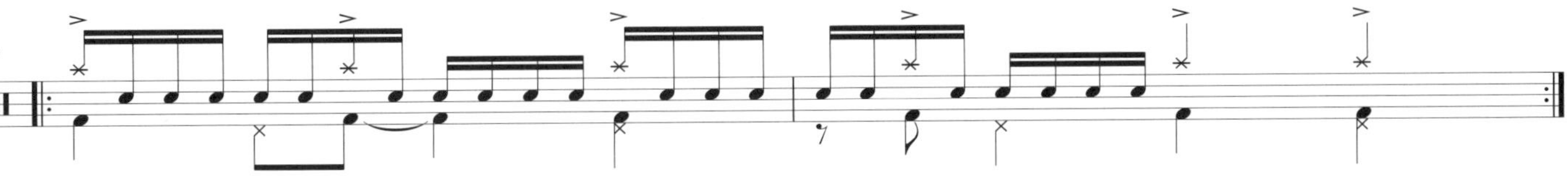

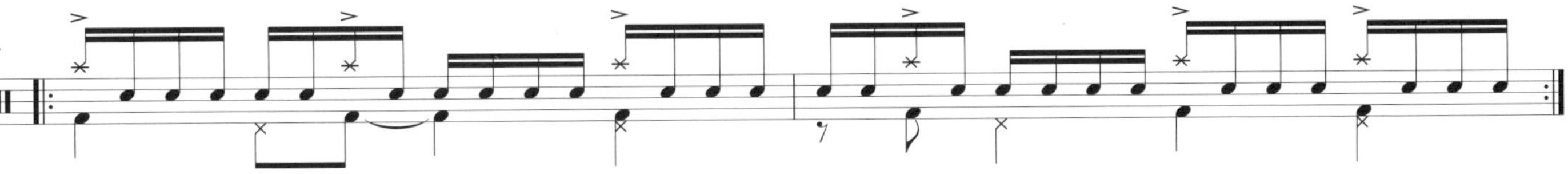

Lesson 10

Rock Ghost Notes

In addition to the snare drum notes on beats 2 and 4 (known as the *backbeat*), there are often other notes that are important to making rock grooves interesting—most notably, *ghost notes*. Commonly found in rock, funk, and many other musical styles, ghost notes are soft, unaccented snare drum notes that add some additional texture and "filler" to a groove. You've probably heard examples of ghost notes but didn't know what to call them or how to execute them.

First, listen to this example without any ghost notes:

TRACK 15

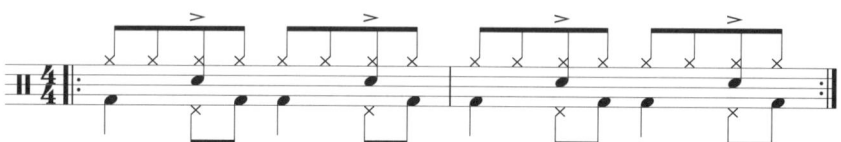

Now listen to this example with ghost notes:

TRACK 16

To execute ghost notes, it's important to develop the ability to play the snare from different stick heights. Raise your stick high for the accented backbeats on 2 and 4 and keep the stick really close to the snare and lightly tap it for the ghost notes. Practice Exercises 1–7 and actually watch your left hand as it plays the snare drum. There should be two very different stick heights. The ride part can also be played on a closed hi-hat. Exercises 1–7 contain the most common ghost notes used in rock.

TRACK 17

These are some additional snare drum and ghost note combinations that may be used in straight eighth-note rock grooves. Learn Exercises 1–18 before proceeding to the final section of the lesson.

Once the ghost notes have been mastered, the next part of the lesson involves something called "component learning." This involves taking the first component (the snare drum ghost notes patterns from 1–18) and combining them with a second component (bass drum patterns 1–32, below) to create new grooves. In some cases, you may wish to write out the "new" exercise in order to make it easier to practice, but your ultimate goal is to be able to mix and match any snare drum ghost note pattern with any bass drum pattern.

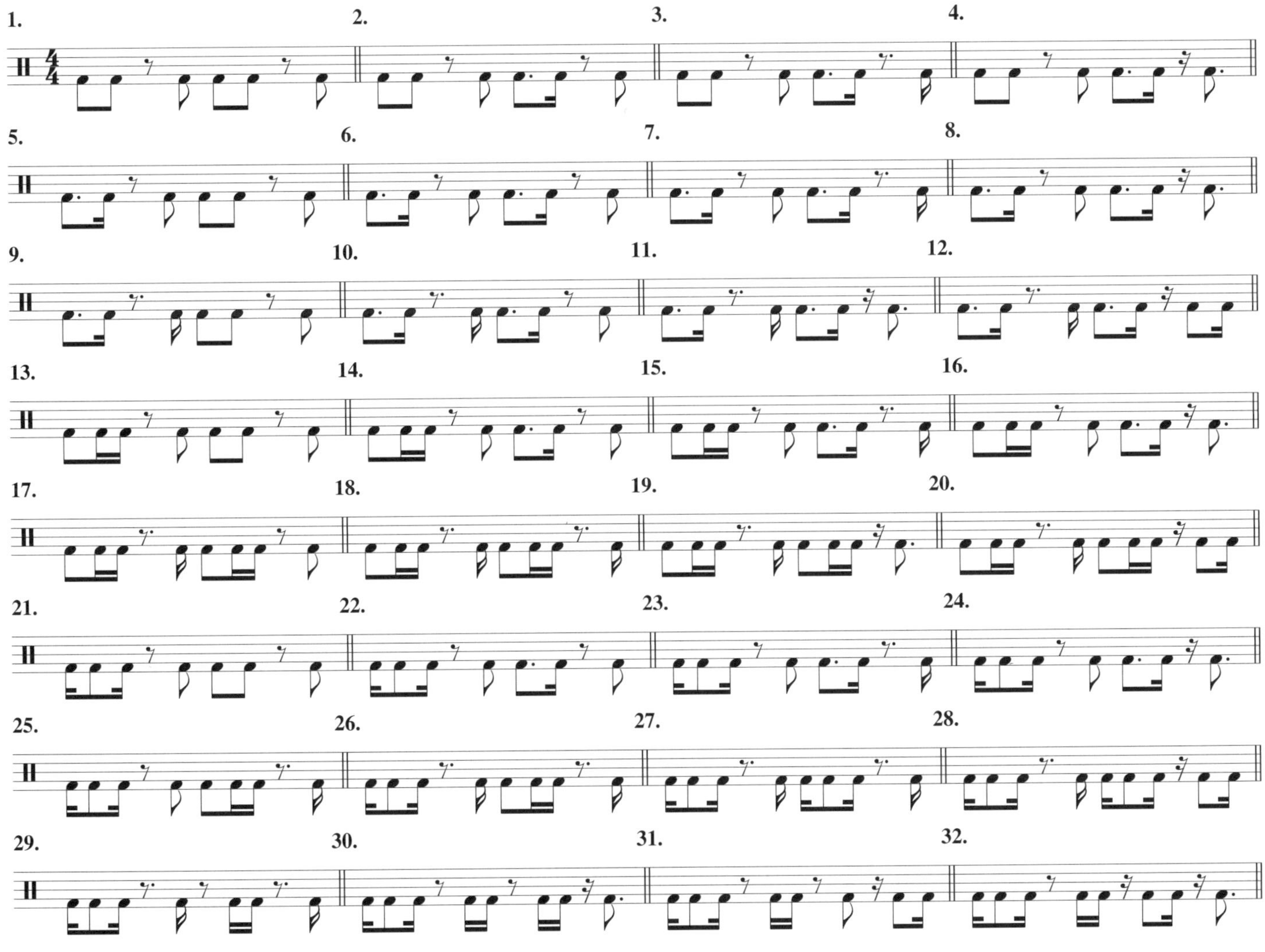

Lesson 11

Rock Cymbal and Hi-Hat Variations

The most common ride pattern used in rock is the eighth-note ride pattern, but there are many more advanced ride patterns as well. You can add some variety by including 16th notes, accents, and notes on the bell of the cymbal. The advanced ride patterns in this lesson can (and should) be applied to any rock grooves you can already play, to enable as much creativity as possible.

For demonstration purposes, all of the ride cymbal patterns in this lesson will be played using this bass drum/snare drum pattern:

Apply the following ride cymbal patterns to any of the bass drum/snare drum patterns at the bottom of the next page (or any other ones you can find or think of yourself).

TRACK 18

When practicing the following exercises, also try these suggestions to further enhance the ride cymbal:

- Substitute the bell of the ride cymbal for any accents.
- Play the ride cymbal rhythm on closed hi-hat (omit the hi-hat notes played with the foot).

When playing the ride pattern on the ride cymbal, the hi-hat can also be altered to create more energy and sound. Combine all of the ride cymbal variations (1–13) in this lesson with each one of these hi-hat and bass drum variations:

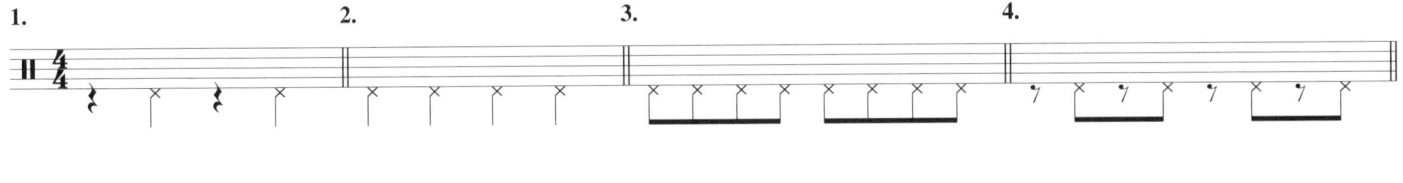

BASS DRUM/SNARE DRUM PATTERNS

As you can see, this lesson creates many possible variations and is very challenging. Like many other lessons and concepts in drumming, it sets various "components" (in this case, the ride cymbal patterns) against a variety of others. The Bass Drum/Snare Drum Patterns (above) are just a few of the possible combinations that would work with this lesson. Find some other examples to use or write your own combinations to continue your progress.

Lesson 12

Soloing Over a Rock Vamp

Soloing over a rock ostinato is a good way to begin soloing on the drums. An *ostinato* (also known as a *vamp*) is a short, repeated musical phrase that is sometimes used to accompany a solo. Many famous rock drummers have soloed over vamps, and it's a good skill to develop as a player. When drummers solo over a vamp, the rest of the band plays the short repeated phrase (sometimes referred to as a *riff*) over and over as the drummer takes a solo.

Solos played over a vamp are used in various places within a song—as an introduction, between soloists, and as endings—and are good ways to transition from one song to the next or provide an interesting vehicle for a soloist. Vamps may be repeated as many times as you want, so you, as the soloist, must be clear about when to end your vamp solo. A band can easily start or develop a vamp by playing something as simple as one chord (Example 1 below) or take a more recognizable riff (played by the guitar or keyboards) and repeat that as a vamp for the drum solo.

When soloing over a vamp, try some of these suggestions:

- Begin your solo by keeping the groove going for a while and slowly add more and more fills until you are playing almost all solo-like fills.

- You don't have to play *every* beat of *every* bar; let the band fill up the space for you sometimes by *not* playing anything on the drums.

- Concentrate on staying in tempo by continuing to play the hi-hat (on beats 2 and 4 or all four beats).

- Put a crash cymbal on beat one of the vamp occasionally to help keep the band together.

- Play the rhythm of the vamp figure occasionally to let the band know you're still with them.

- Have a pre-arranged visual cue to end your solo (by looking at the rest of the band), or…

- Have a pre-arranged musical cue (a rhythm or lick you only play when you want to end your solo) that tells the band that you intend to end your solo soon.

The following example of soloing over a vamp is very straightforward and would be easy to add to any song. The vamp is a two-bar phrase with the other instruments playing a chord on beat 1 of the first bar of the vamp and letting it ring for two measures. There are four bars of a groove to practice "getting into" the vamp and a few bars after the vamp in order to practice finishing your solo. First listen to the example and then use the play-along track to practice.

DEMO TRACK 19   PLAY-ALONG TRACK 20

Example 2 uses a common vamp rhythm (beat 1 and the "and" of beat 2). In this vamp, the drummer often prepares the band to play the "and" of beat 2 by playing either a snare or tom on beat 2 (but not always, as that would be boring and predictable!).

PLAY-ALONG TRACK 21

Use the following play-along tracks to practice some different vamps. Each track begins with four metronome clicks, has four bars of a groove (of your choice), and then the vamp (played eight times). Keep track of how many times you have played the vamp (in your mind) in order to return to the groove. Record yourself in order to assess your progress.

PLAY-ALONG TRACK 22

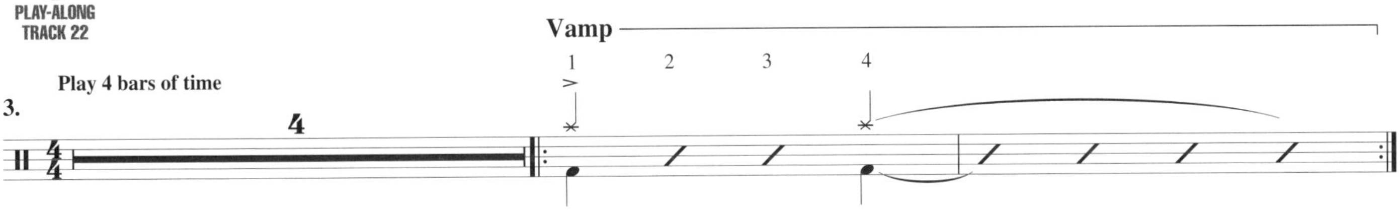

PLAY-ALONG TRACK 23

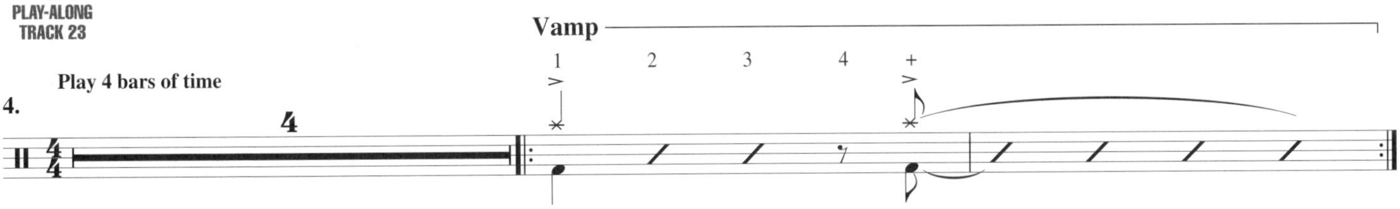

PLAY-ALONG TRACK 24

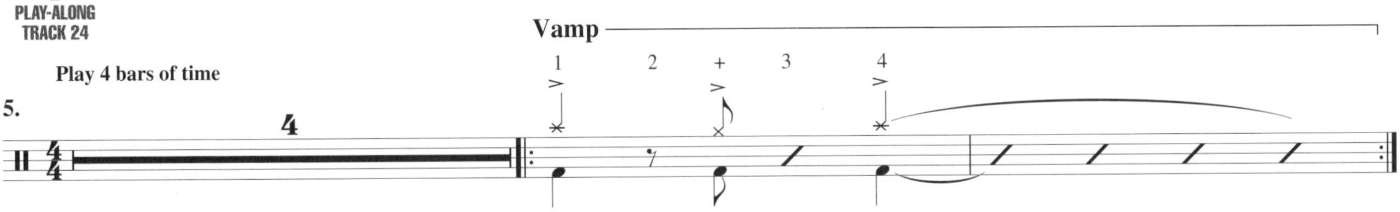

Listen for some other examples of drum solos over vamps; many can be found on live recordings or in concert videos.

Lesson 13

Basic Rock Chart Interpretation

You may be a drummer your whole life and never encounter a "drum chart," but if you do, you'll need to know about how to approach them, what various symbols mean, and basically how to survive the situation. A drum chart differs from a piece of "drum music" in its specificity and purpose. For example, a snare drum etude is a "piece of drum music" for snare drum that is to be played exactly the same way every time by each person that performs it. It normally contains specific rhythms, dynamics, stickings, and other musical directions that ensure that each performance is (more or less) exactly the same. A drum *chart*, on the other hand, is a guide (or suggestion sheet) for a drumset player that contains information a drummer can use to play the tune more accurately and perform certain functions for the band (including fills, tempo changes, different grooves in a different part of the tune, etc.).

Often, the person who wrote the drum chart (the arranger) is not a drummer and may not be familiar with all of the various notational conventions that apply to drumset. Although the situation has improved in the 21st century, there are still many older charts that might require some interpretation, so understanding what drum charts look like and what to do with that information is essential.

Arrangers often assume that drummers know how to play many various grooves (basic rock, swing, funk, numerous Afro-Cuban/Brazilian or Latin grooves, brushes, etc.), so they will often just write the name of the groove they want in the upper left-hand corner of the tune, put a series of slashes (known collectively as *slash marks*) in each measure to indicate that groove, and let the drummer decide what to play. Occasionally, the arranger will notate the exact groove they want you to play. In some cases, this is very helpful because some tunes have very specific grooves that fit that tune. But in other cases, the notated groove is incorrect or awkward. At that point, you have to make a decision: do I play what's on the page or play what I think is a better choice? I would recommend playing what you know is right, unless told to do otherwise by your conductor.

The example chart for this lesson only says "rock" at the top of the chart. Does that mean you start your ride pattern on the closed hi-hats or the ride cymbal? What's the specific bass drum rhythm? What do I play for fills? These are all valid questions, and there are no definitive answers (until you play the chart). With a chart like this, you have to make some decisions on your own and hope it works out the first time. You will have a better idea of exactly what to play after each time you play through the chart.

Here are some helpful suggestions (in no particular order) that will make your chart reading experiences go more smoothly:

- If it's rock, assume you're going to play the snare on beats 2 and 4 (even if it isn't written that way in the music). Assume you're going to play some bass drum pattern that matches the bass player's part, so listen for that and try to emulate the bass part.

- If the fills are notated, you could play them as written, but if that's not possible, substitute your own fills until you're comfortable with the chart. Keep the fills simple and accurate. You can spice them up later. Skip the fills if necessary the first few times through the chart.

- Try to play soft sections (*mp, mf*) with the ride pattern on the closed hi-hats and move to the ride cymbal for the louder sections (*f, ff*).

- Always stop playing time when there are rests written inside the staff.

- Set up your music stand so that you can see the conductor/leader while you are playing. Most drummers put the stand on their left side so they can turn pages, but some drummers put the stand on their right side (by the floor tom) or directly in front of the drumset (this is OK if there are no page turns in the chart).

- If there's time, look the chart over and figure out the "road map" (where the tune starts, stops, repeats, goes to the coda, and ends). This is VERY important.

- Play simply—don't try to play something too technically demanding the first time. Just get through the chart without stopping and/or making too many mistakes.

- Always count measures in your head and keep your place in the chart—at all costs!

- While playing, always look ahead—particularly for fills, rests, changes of tempo, changes of feel (e.g., rock to swing), repeats, coda signs, and endings.

- Try to look at the chart as a series of musical sections—not measure by measure. Normally charts are arranged in eight-bar phrases. If you notice that you're playing an eight-bar phrase, take note of that, keep counting in your head to keep your place, and look ahead to what's coming up. Reading a chart is all about looking ahead and being ready for what comes next.

- Don't forget to *listen* to the music as you're playing. Often, you can intuitively tell when you need to do something because you know how music is supposed to sound.

- If the conductor/leader stops the band during a rehearsal, pay attention to what they are saying (of course), but also use the time, if possible, to study your part some more. For example, if the conductor is speaking specifically to the bass player or another instrumentalist, you can probably use that time to study your chart. Take note of any mistakes you've made so far and try not to let them happen again.

- ALWAYS keep playing until the conductor/leader stops you. You're the drummer—the engine of the band—if you stop, EVERYTHING STOPS!

Listen to the demo for this next example chart and then use the play-along track to practice the chart. It's a rock chart with rehearsal letters (A, B, C, D) to mark different sections of the music and provide a common location for everyone to start again during a rehearsal. It also contains fills in measures 4 and 31, "stops" in measure 8, a drum solo for eight bars beginning in measure 17, and a "cue" (some text about who is playing the melody) that tells you the saxes and trombone enter in measure 25. The song concludes with a fill in measure 31 and a short note on beat 1 of measure 32.

WITH DRUMS TRACK 25   PLAY-ALONG TRACK 26

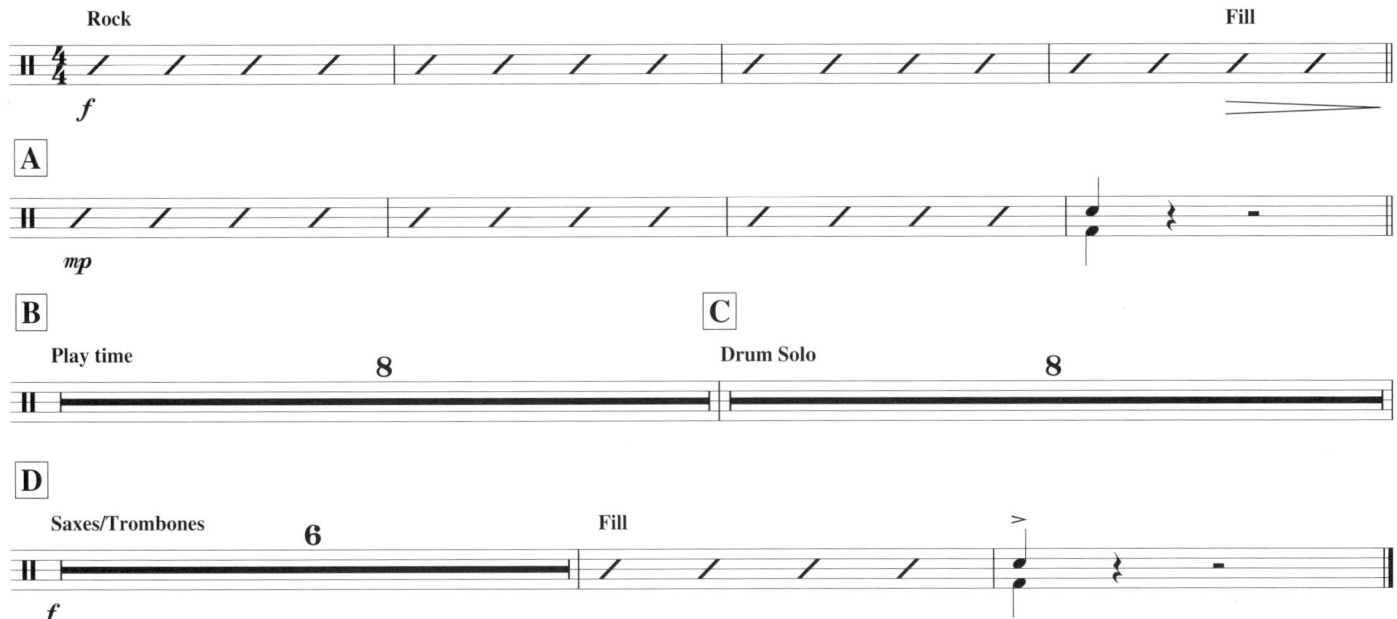

Lesson 14

Basic Funk

Funk is a style of popular dance music that developed in the 1960s and has evolved into numerous branches: New Orleans funk, West Coast funk, linear funk, funk fusion, and others. It was stylistically derived from rhythm and blues and is characterized by a strong emphasis on groove, a strong backbeat on beats 2 and 4 (often using a *rimshot*), an emphasis on rhythmic interaction between the players, use of ghost notes in the drum part, tempos in the range of 96–116 beats per minute (BPM), strong bass lines that are normally played in unison with the bass drum, and syncopated accents played on the hi-hat. In some styles of funk, the backbeat is *displaced*—not played on beats 2 and 4—played one 16th note earlier (on the "ah" of beat 1), one 16th note later (the "e" of beat 2), or even an eighth note earlier or later (on the "and" of beats 1 or 2, respectively). The displaced backbeat is particularly prominent in the style of Joseph "Zigaboo" Modeliste of the Meters and David Garibaldi of Tower of Power. Other important early funk drummers include Clyde Stubblefield, Al Jackson, Earl Palmer, Bernard Purdie, Mike Clark, and Roger Hawkins.

Here are some examples of one-bar funk phrases. The ride pattern may also be played on the ride cymbal with the hi-hat playing on beats 2 and 4 or on all four beats.

TRACK 27

Funk bass players often construct their bass lines in two-bar phrases, so the drums often need to use two-bar bass drum phrasing patterns. Notice that, in many cases, beat 1 of the second bar of each phrase is a rest, which adds to the syncopated character of the music.

Some funk is based on a 16th-note hi-hat groove. Here are some examples of two-bar 16th-note hi-hat funk grooves. You can also create your own grooves by improvising different bass drum rhythms.

TRACK 28

Lesson 15

Intermediate Funk

Funk drumming often includes a variety of different ride rhythms and accent patterns. The following exercises feature common eighth- and 16th-note funk ride pattern variations. To create more variations, you can play the accents on the bell of the ride cymbal. Make the accents clear and noticeably louder than the unaccented ride notes. For maximum flexibility with these ride/accent patterns, superimpose any of these new ride/accent patterns over grooves you already know or simply improvise new grooves using these ride/accent patterns. On the audio, the initial measure of notation (Ride Pattern #1) is not played; audio begins on Exercise 1.

TRACK 29

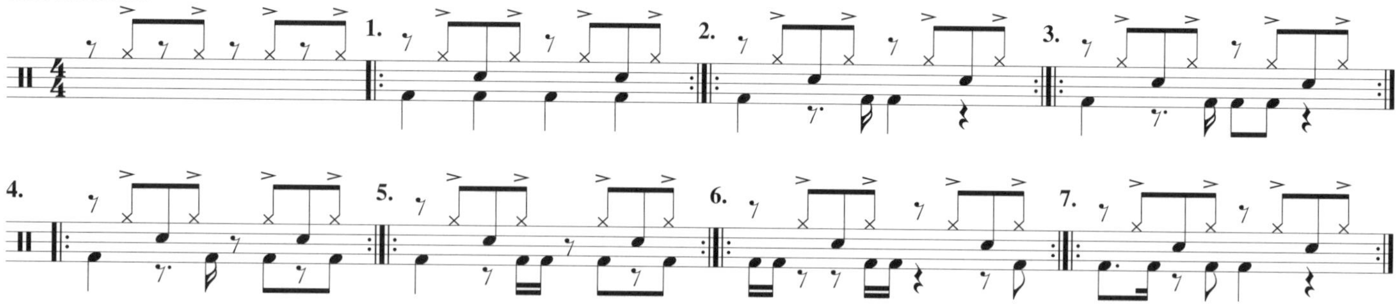

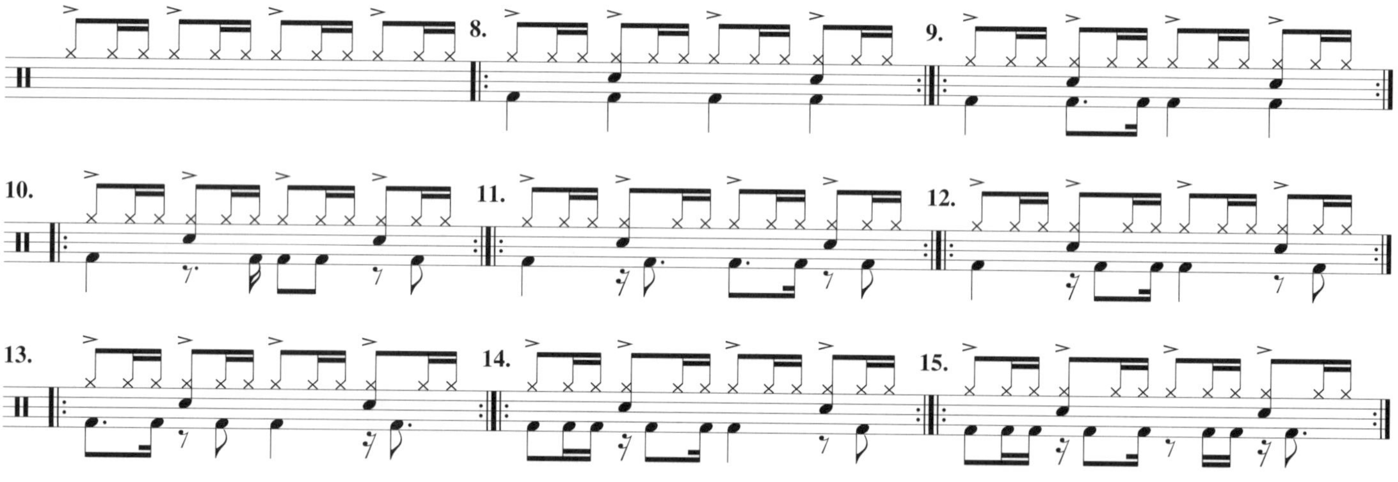

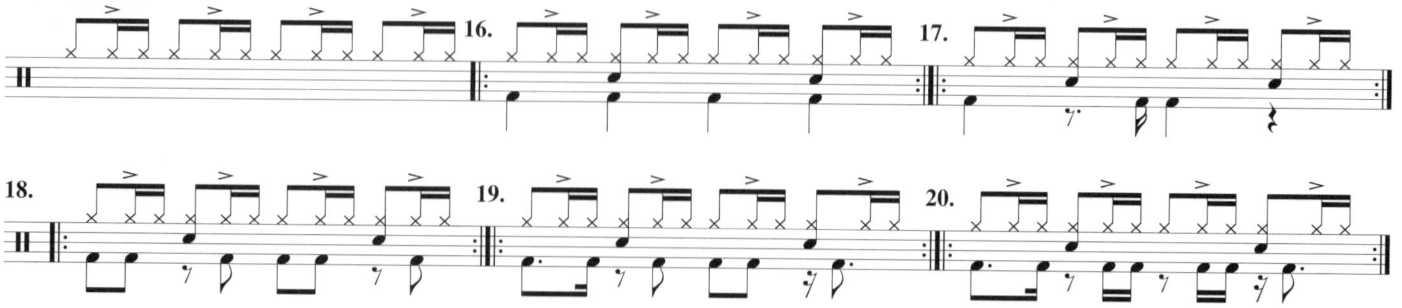

Another important facet of funk drumming is the use of *ghost notes*. Ghost notes are soft, unaccented notes that help fill out a groove. Funk grooves frequently incorporate ghost notes, so it's important to make them very accurate and much softer than the accented backbeat (beats 2 and 4 on the snare). Practice the following grooves slowly and actually watch your left hand to make sure that each ghost note stroke is played from a height of approximately a half inch above the head. This is particularly challenging if you have to play a ghost note immediately following a backbeat. Consciously stop your stick from rebounding higher than a half inch after a backbeat in order to play any subsequent ghost notes at the proper dynamic.

TRACK 30

Lesson 16

Advanced Funk

Some advanced funk drumming patterns make use of a *displaced backbeat*, which means that the snare drum does not play on beats 2 and 4, but is moved to another beat. The exercises below are examples of backbeat displacement to the "and" of beat 2 (one eighth note later than it normally occurs), to the "ah" of beat 1 (one 16th note earlier), and to the "e" of beat 2 (one 16th note later).

TRACK 31

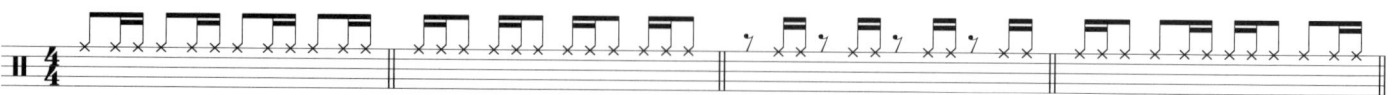

Exercises 1–24 should also be practiced using these alternate ride patterns on either the ride cymbal or hi-hat:

The short, accented open hi-hat sound (sometimes called a "hi-hat shot") is another important characteristic of some funk music. Hi-hat shots are normally found on the "e" or "ah" of the beat. To execute these hi-hat shots, the hi-hat closes on the very next 16th note following the open note and is accompanied by an accented bass drum note. For example, a hi-hat shot on the "ah" of the beat 2 would mean that the hi-hat closes on beat 3. A hi-hat shot on the "e" of beat 2 would close on the "and" of beat 2.

TRACK 32

Lesson 17

Linear Drumming

Linear drumming is a term used to describe a drumming style or approach in which no two limbs play at the same time. Although this is the technical definition, in reality, most linear drum grooves do include the sound of two limbs playing at the same time, though infrequently. The term "linear" almost always refers to drum grooves and not drum fills, because fills are primarily linear by nature.

Linear drumming is a technique or approach—not a specific style—and can be used to create a very "busy" syncopated, sophisticated way to play in rock, funk, and progressive rock genres. In many cases, linear drumming involves the use of almost constant 16th notes broken up between the bass drum, snare, ride, hi-hat, and (occasionally) the toms. Ghost notes are an important part of linear drumming. When practicing linear grooves, be sure to over-emphasize the accents and play the unaccented ghost notes very softly. Drummers frequently develop grooves that contain both linear and non-linear sections to suit the music, and many linear grooves do not include a traditional backbeat. Linear drumming concepts can be heard in the playing of Steve Gadd, Carter Beauford, Gary Chaffee, David Garibaldi, Dave Weckl, Joseph "Zigaboo" Modeliste, Gavin Harrison, and others. Linear drumming is particularly useful and evident in pop, rock, funk, and progressive rock styles where the drummer is given more artistic freedom to create new and unusual grooves.

Here are some examples of completely linear drum grooves—i.e., no two limbs are playing simultaneously.

TRACK 33

It *is* possible to play in a completely linear fashion, but even linear grooves contain some instances where two or more limbs are playing together (also known as *double stops* or *triple stops*.)

Linear drumming is a style that can be studied using a method known as "component learning." By exploring the possible permutations (variations) available by playing 16 16th notes in a bar, you can create an almost infinite number of grooves by using different combinations of each component (or "cell") found in examples 1–26. Using 16th-note combinations in groups of 2-, 3-, or 4-note cells, you can create your own distinctive grooves. Some grooves will sound better than others or be more suitable for specific songs. As a drummer, you must determine what grooves work for you and your musical situation.

Here are some useful linear grooves that include a snare backbeat on beats 2 and 4 using some of the 26 cells.

TRACK 34

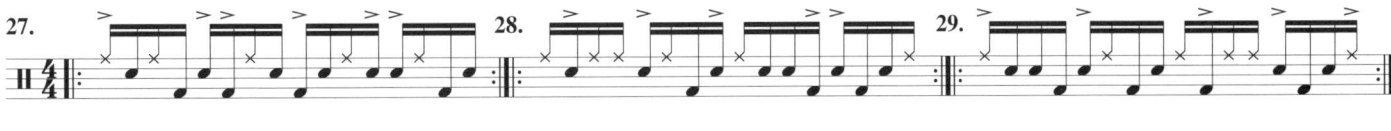

Drummers "Zigaboo" Modeliste and David Garibaldi were early proponents of "implying the backbeat" by moving the snare drum back either one 16th before or after beats 2 or 4 to give the music a great syncopated feel. Here are some linear grooves that are similar to the grooves played by these artists. Notice that there are some double stops in these grooves, but the majority of each groove is linear.

TRACK 35

This lesson is really only an introduction to linear drumming. To truly appreciate and develop this style, listen and transcribe recordings by the previously mentioned drummers. You can create an infinite number of linear drumming grooves by developing your own linear cells (using 16th notes for funk or triplets for swing/shuffle situations), inserting occasional 16th rests, repeating notes on the same limb, changing the accents, adding some open hi-hat notes, and/or adding some double stops. When playing in a linear fashion, however, keep in mind that it is very important to create a groove that enhances the music—not detracts from it.

Lesson 18

Rudimental Drumset Applications #1

Snare drum rudiments are part of the history of drumming and should be a part of every drummer's education. The rudiments (which were created as rote phrases used by military drummers to signal troops in battle and accompany armies as they marched) may be applied to the drumset by orchestrating them in creative ways. All snare drum rudiments can be adapted to drumset in some way, but some are more easily adapted as fills, while others can be adapted as grooves.

The *paradiddle*, whose sticking is R-L-R-R or L-R-L-L, is one of the most versatile rudiments and can be adapted as both fills and grooves. Examples 1–7 are just a few of the ways paradiddles can be adapted as fills and illustrate how paradiddles help you move around the drumset in different (sometimes easier) ways. Practice these fill applications (1–11) by playing three bars of a groove, followed by the exercise measure to create a four-bar phrase.

TRACK 36

By designating the double strokes (R-R or L-L) as bass drum notes and the alternating strokes (R-L or L-R) as hand notes, you can create some interesting hand/foot fill patterns:

Paradiddles also work well as the basis for busy, 16th-note rock/funk grooves. These are just a few of the ways to apply paradiddles as drumset grooves. Always play the unaccented notes very softly (as ghost notes) in these examples to achieve maximum musicality.

The *double paradiddle* is also a very adaptable rudiment. Due to its six-note length, you can adapt the double paradiddle as either triplet or sextuplet fills. Practice fill applications 16–28 by playing three bars of a groove followed by the exercise measure to create a four-bar phrase.

TRACK 37

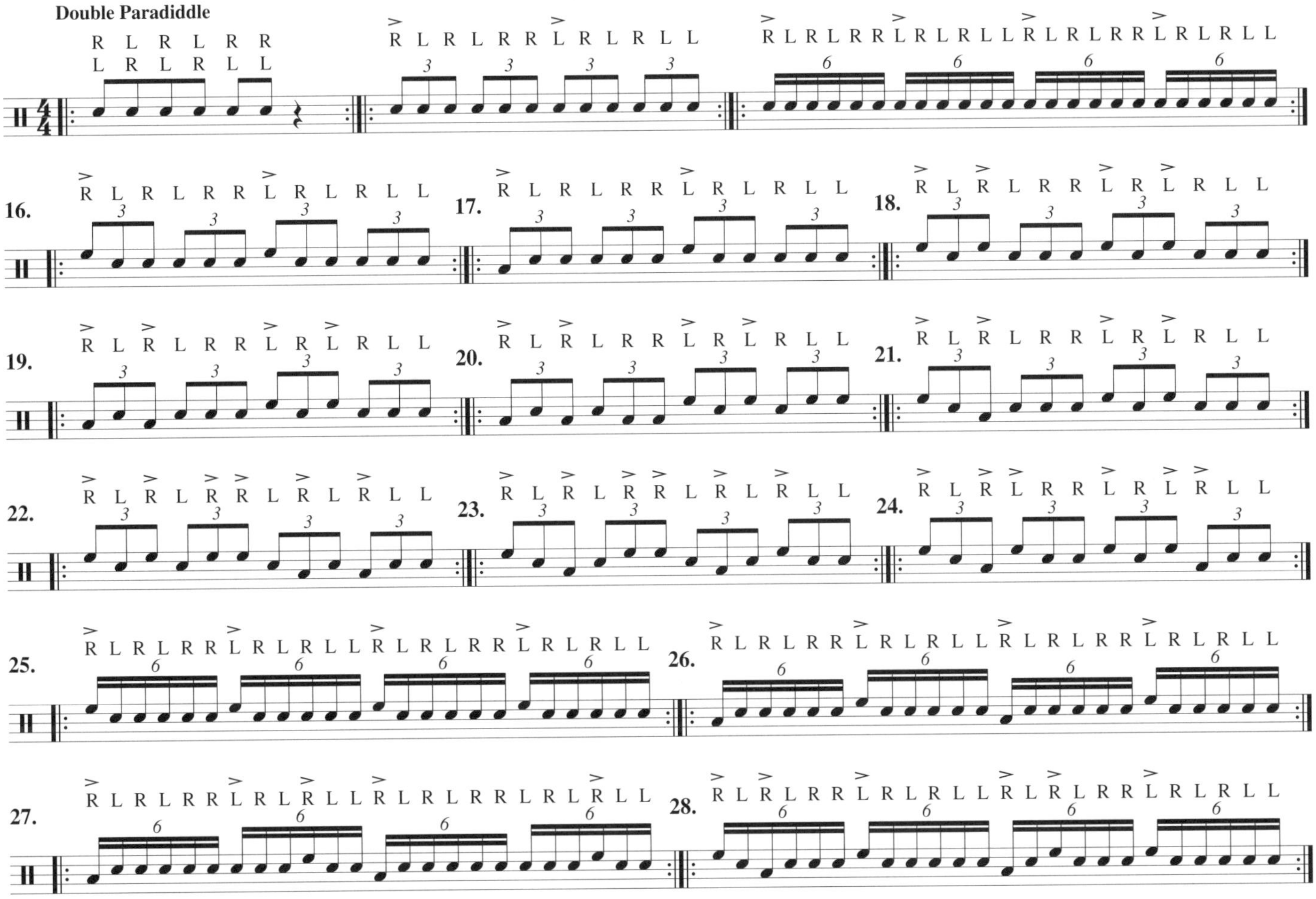

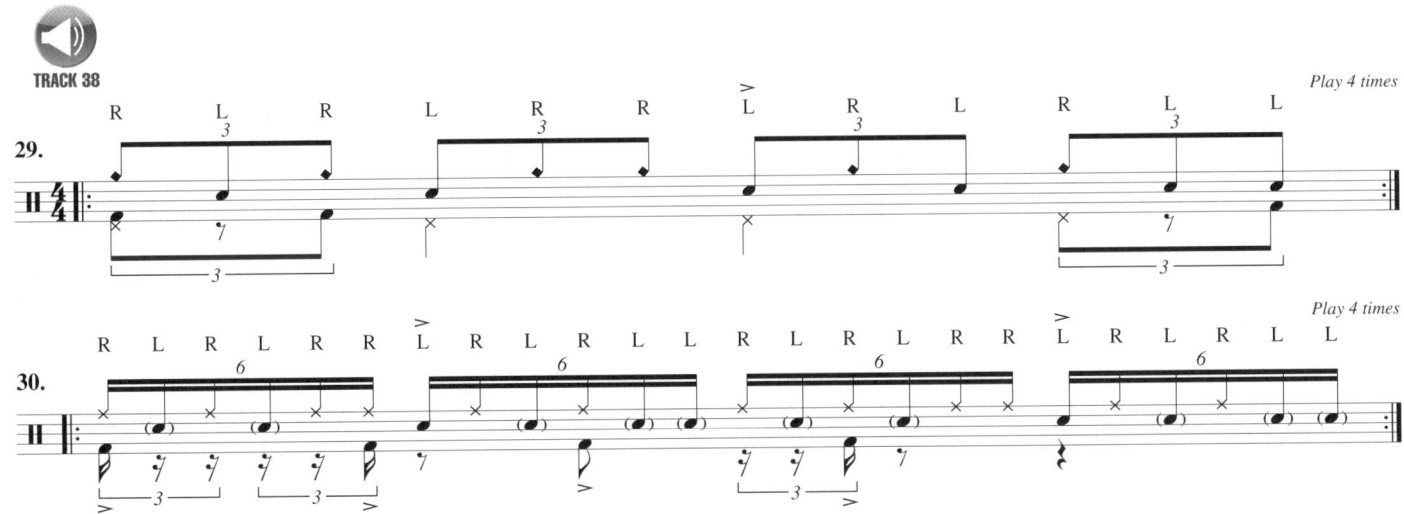

Double paradiddles also work well as a funky, half-time Afro-Cuban 6/8 groove (Ex. 29) or as a half-time shuffle (Ex. 30).

TRACK 38

Lesson 19

Rudimental Drumset Applications #2

The six-stroke roll is a rudiment that can be easily applied to the drumset. It can be written several ways, but it always begins and ends with an accent and may start with either stick (R-LL-RR-L or L-RR-LL-R).

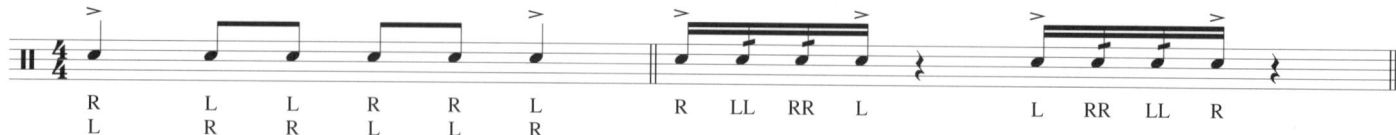

The six-stroke roll may be used as a warm-up exercise beginning with either hand (Examples 1 and 2) or transposed onto the toms or cymbals for fills (Examples 3 and 4).

TRACK 39

The single paradiddle-diddle is also useful for moving around the drumset.

TRACK 40

By substituting two bass drum notes for the double strokes (R-L-R-L-F-F, L-R-L-R-F-F), the double paradiddle becomes an interesting hand/foot fill pattern.

The five-stroke roll is another rudiment that can be adapted in various ways on the drumset.

R R L L R   L L R R L   R R L L R   L L R R L

Five-stroke rolls can:

- be used as fills that resolve to an accented cymbal hit (Example 8)
- end with a stick-on-stick rimshot used by jazz drummers (Example 9)
- create ways to execute 32nd notes around the drums (Example 10)
- add some 16th-note "decorations" to a groove (Example 11)

TRACK 41

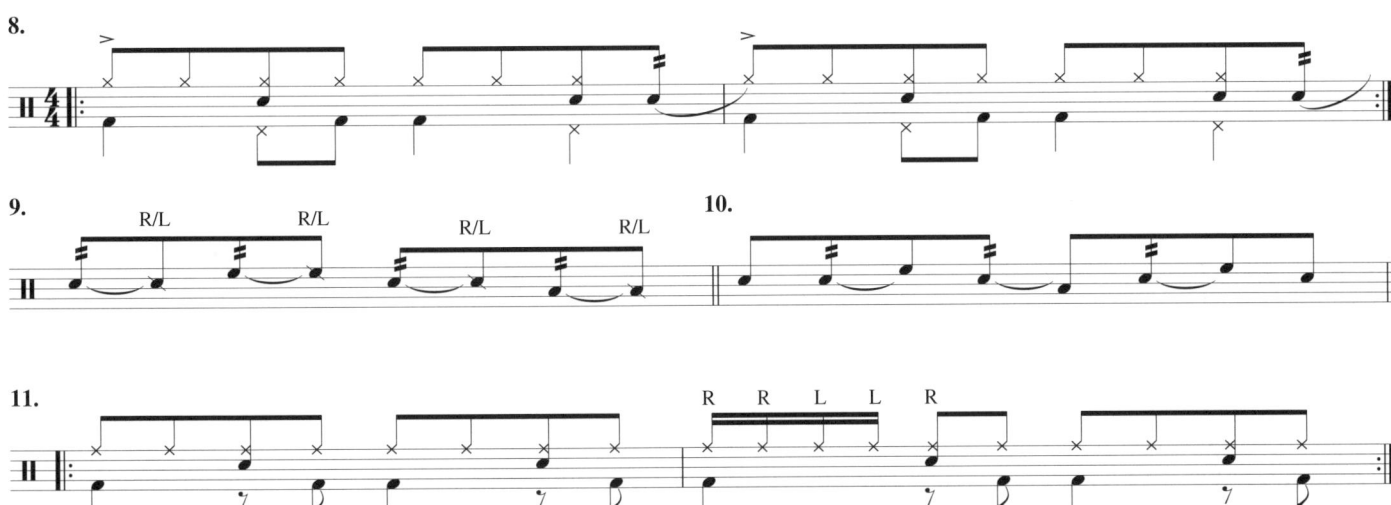

Swiss Army triplets can be orchestrated around the drumset as triplets fills (Example 12) or "inverted" to create upbeat accented flam fills (Example 13).

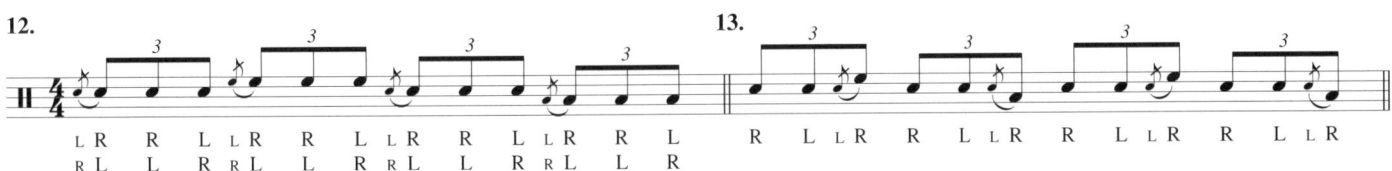

39

Lesson 20

Basic Double Kick (Double Bass Drum)

Double bass drumming, sometimes also known as playing *double kick*, is a technique that can be used in many different styles of music. The famous jazz drummer Louie Bellson used a double bass drumset as far back as the 1940s. Metal and rock drummers frequently use two bass drums or a *double bass pedal*, which allows a player to play one bass drum, but sound as though they're using two bass drums.

Exercises 1–12 are warm-up and coordination builders that will help you become more comfortable alternating between your hands and two bass drums. Playing double kick also means that your left foot will be more active, so you will need to build some stamina and coordination. Practice these exercises slowly at first (45–75 beats per minute) until you can play them comfortably at a steady tempo (always use a metronome) before attempting to play them at the speed you hear on recordings.

TRACK 42

Here are some grooves that begin to integrate double kick with snare backbeats. You may play the ride pattern on either the ride cymbal or closed hi-hat.

TRACK 43

Lesson 21

Intermediate Double Kick (Double Bass Drum)

The intermediate-level triplet double kick exercises in this lesson are excellent for developing technique and will be used later for triplet-based grooves. Be sure to use a metronome when you practice and always keep the triplets very even.

TRACK 44

Here are some triplet-based double kick grooves. You may play the ride pattern on either the ride cymbal or closed hi-hat.

TRACK 45

Lesson 22

Advanced Double Kick (Double Bass Drum)

After mastering 16th-note and triplet double kick patterns, the next level of complexity with double kick drumming is the use of 16th-note triplets and 32nd notes. Practice the warm-up exercises (Exercises 1–12) slowly at first (50–100 beats per minute), and then move on to the groove exercises.

TRACK 46

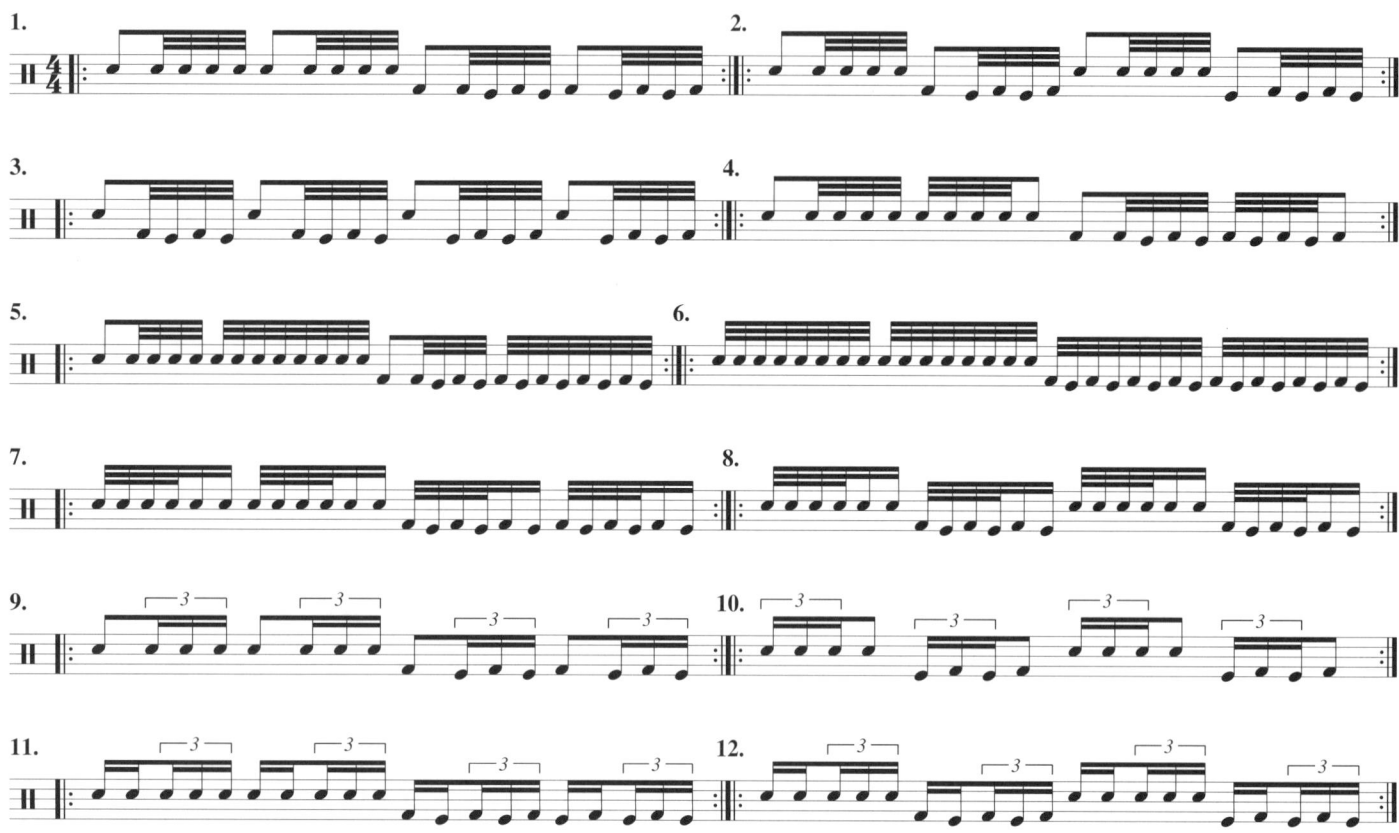

Here are some grooves that incorporate 32nd notes and 16th-note triplets. You may play the ride pattern on either the ride cymbal or closed hi-hat.

TRACK 47

44

Lesson 23

Basic Blast Beats

Blast beats are the fast alternating snare drum/bass drum grooves developed by drummers in the 1980s and '90s to accompany the metal movement that was emerging in Europe, which eventually spread around the world. The music is very aggressive and requires a tremendous amount of endurance and technique, due to the tempos at which it's played (often above 200 beats per minute). Blast beats can be written two ways—either as 16th notes or 32nd notes. We'll write them here as 16th notes for simplicity's sake. Most blast beats are played with two bass drums (double kick), so you can decide which bass drum combinations (either right or left foot) you use on each groove. The ride pattern may be played either on a ride cymbal or closed hi-hat. Practice these examples slowly at first to develop your accuracy and then work up the tempo until they can be played with your favorite songs.

TRACK 48

TRACK 49

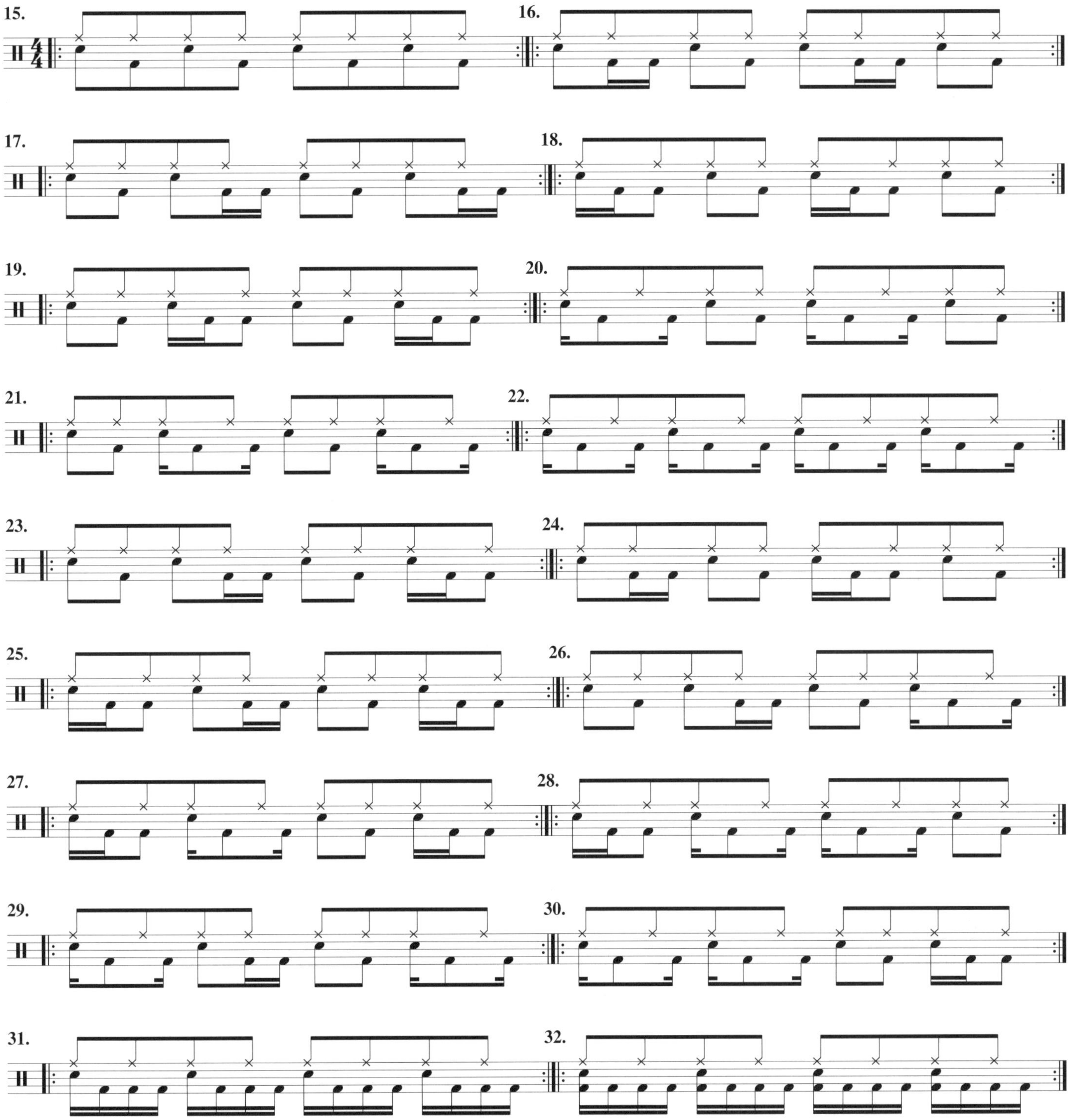

Lesson 24

Basic Metal/Hard Rock Fills

In this lesson, we'll look at some basic metal/hard rock fills. They're written for a drumset with three toms, but if you have more than three toms, you can experiment with moving some of the notes onto your other toms. To practice using the fills the same way you will use them in a song, play three measures of any metal groove you like and then make the fourth bar one of the exercise bars:

You can also play a crash cymbal on the first beat of each four-bar exercise if you wish. Try to play the hi-hat on beats 2 and 4 (or on all four beats) during the fills, as this will help you keep the fills from speeding up or slowing down. Make the unaccented notes much softer than the accented notes and try different stickings to create new ways of moving around the drums. On the audio for the next exercise, there are three bars of rock groove followed by the notated one-bar fills each time through.

TRACK 50

The next fills incorporate crashes and can be used to play accents along with the rhythm guitar player or the rest of the band. As before, each fill will be preceded by a three-bar rock groove on the audio.

TRACK 51

Here are some useful hand/foot combination fills using a single bass drum:

If you have two kick drums or a double pedal, Exercises 31–42 will show you how to incorporate them into some fills. If you don't play double kick, you can still play them on one bass drum.

TRACK 52

Lesson 25

Intermediate Blast Beats

Exercises 1–16 are blast beats based on the triplet subdivision and may begin with either a snare/kick sequence or kick/snare sequence.

TRACK 53

1.

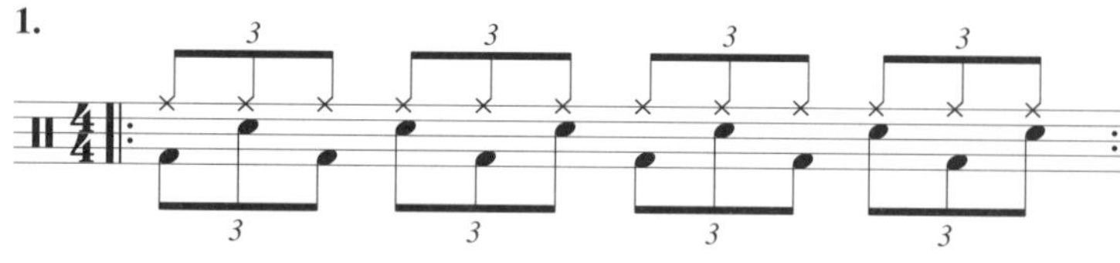

2.

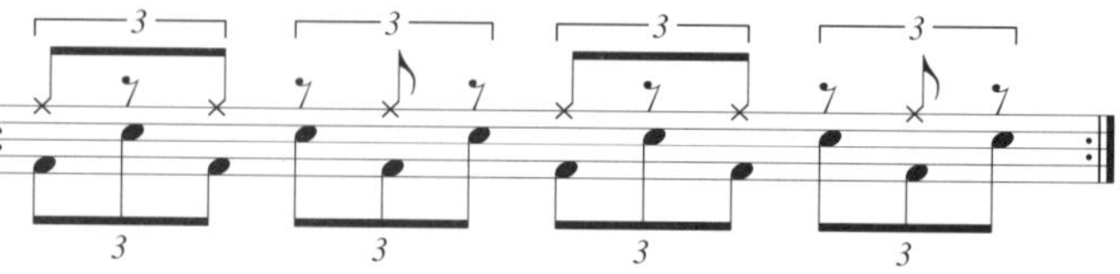

3.

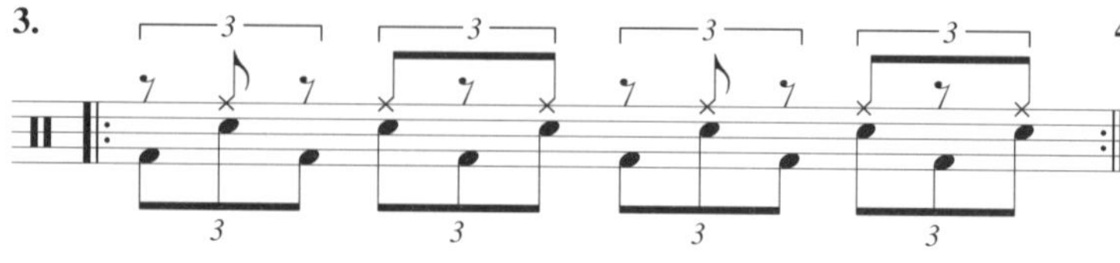

4.

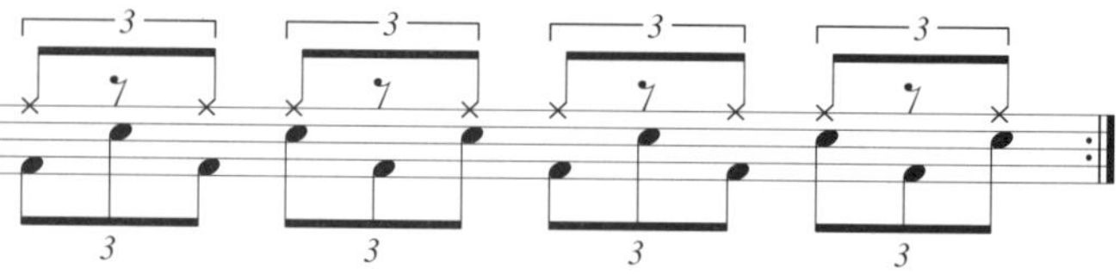

5.

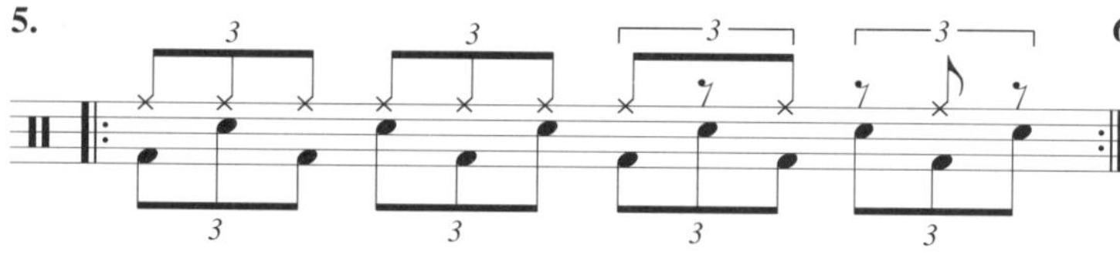

6.

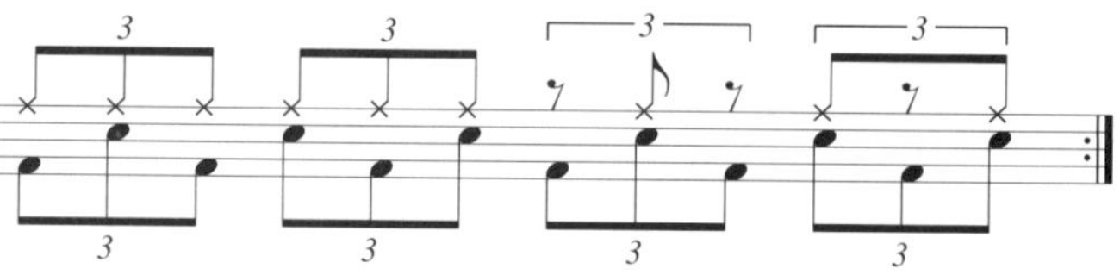

7.

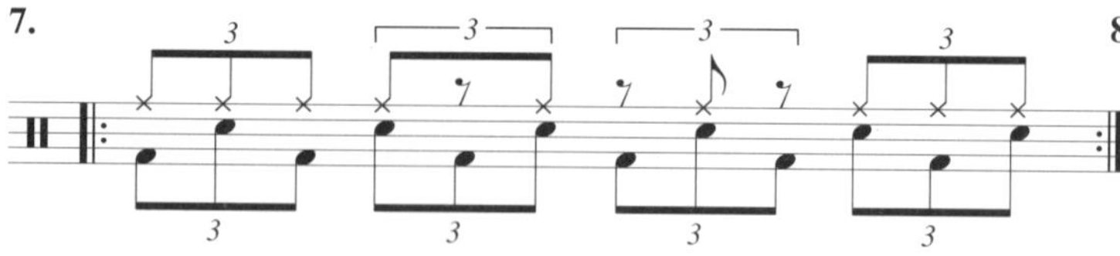

8.

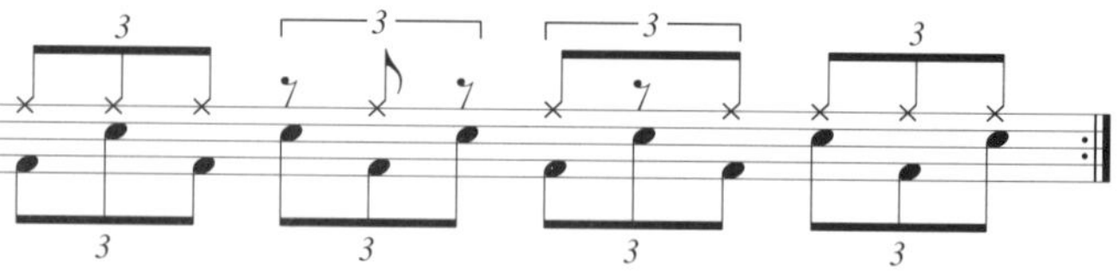

9.

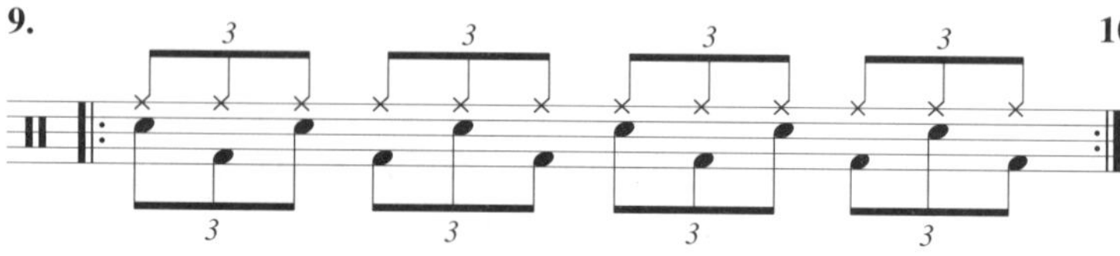

10.

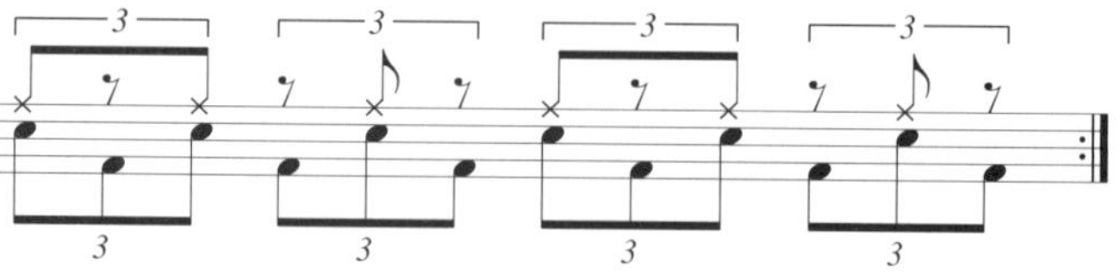

11.

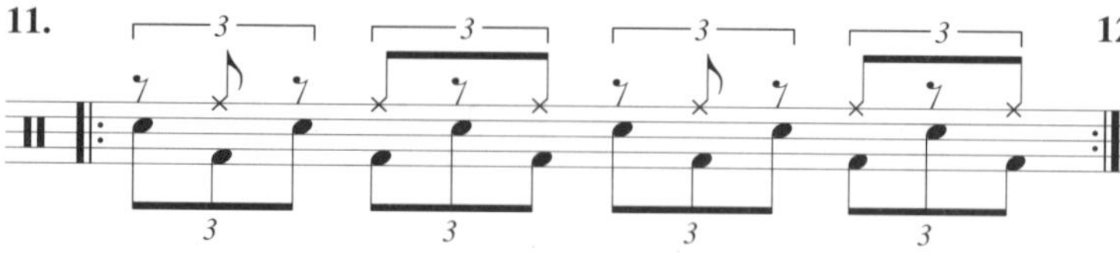

12.

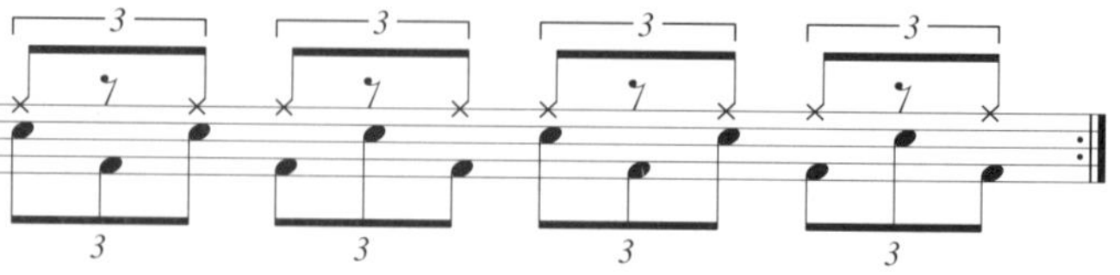

13.

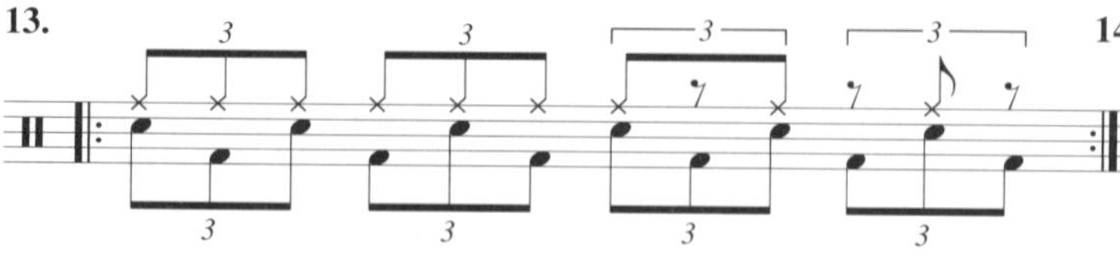

14.

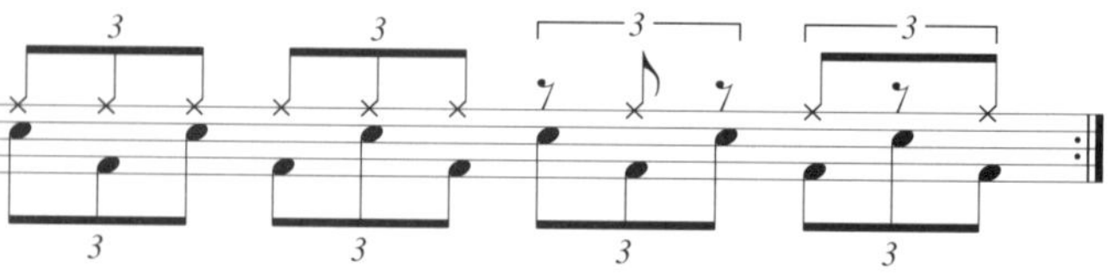

15.

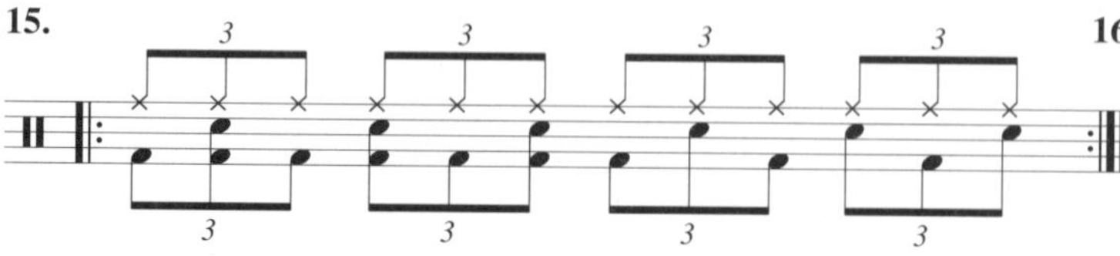

16.

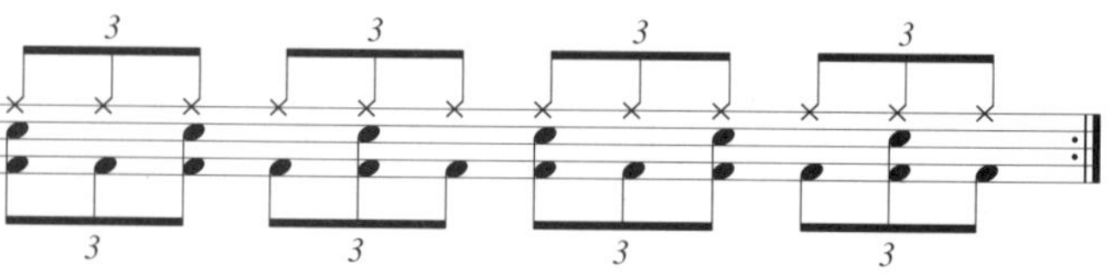

Exercises 17–32 are blast-beat variations that feature the thunderous sound of the double kick in shuffle grooves.

TRACK 54

Lesson 26

Advanced Blast Beats

The advanced blast beats in this lesson utilize 16th- and 32nd-note double kick combinations. Mastering these patterns will allow you to play many of the most extreme blast beats. The ride pattern may be played on either a ride cymbal or closed hi-hat.

TRACK 55

1.

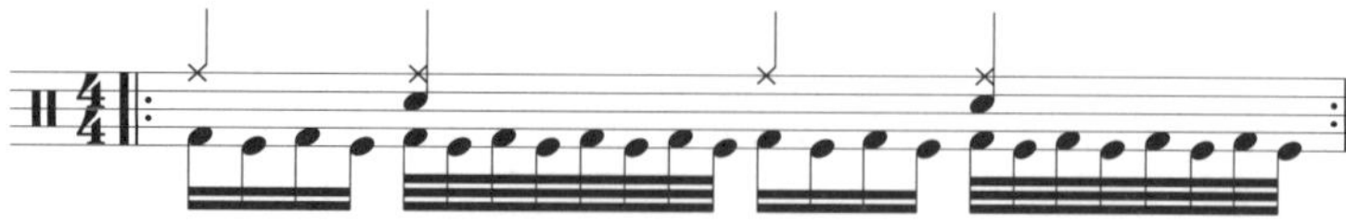

2.

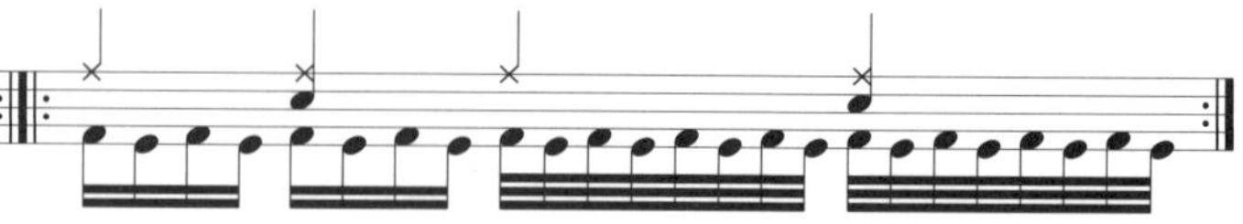

3.

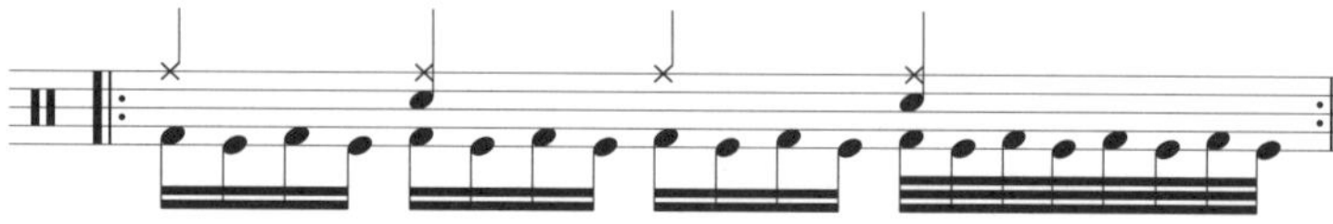

4.

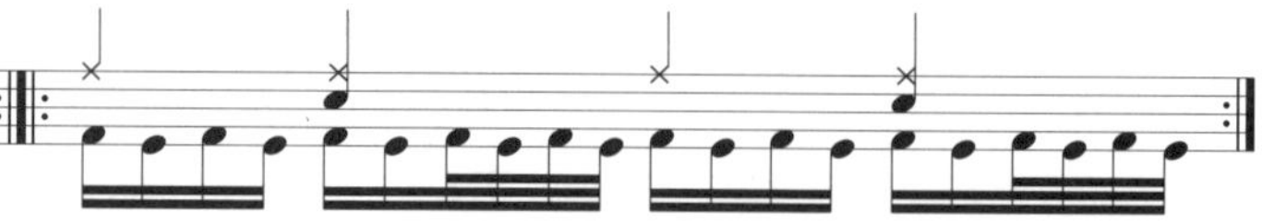

5.

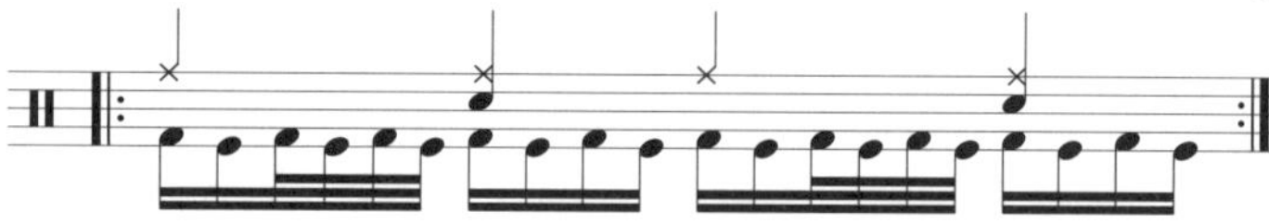

6.

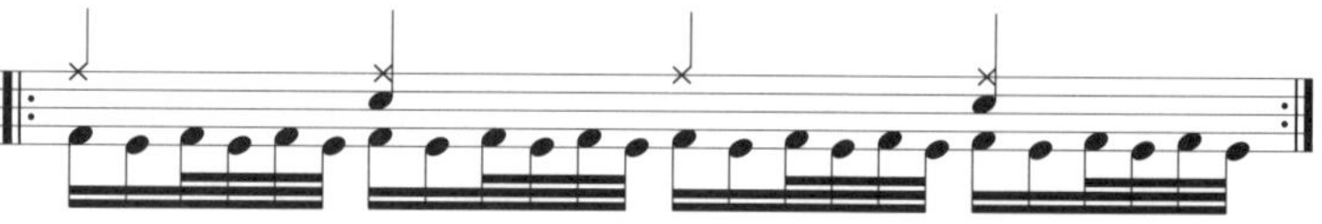

7.

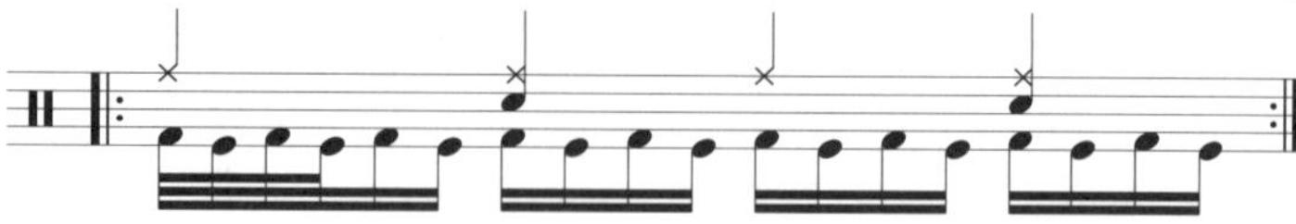

8.

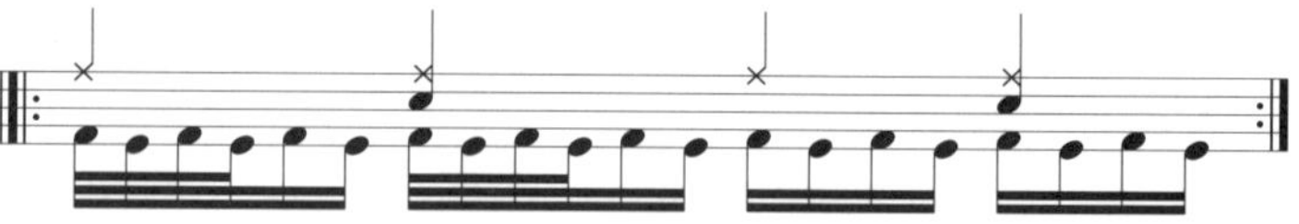

9.

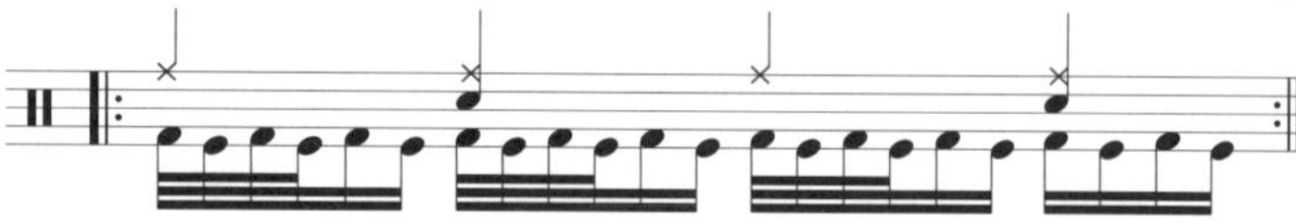

10.

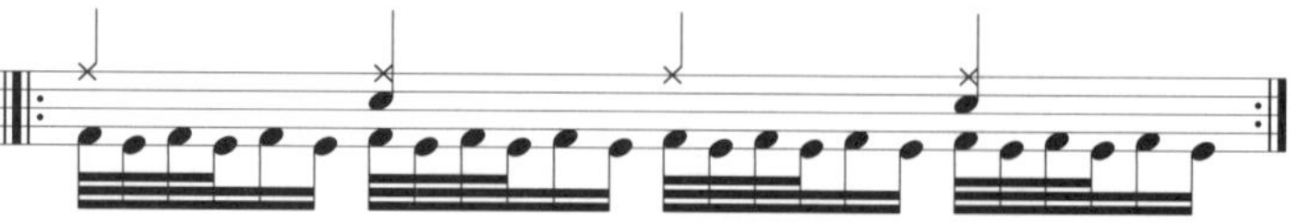

11.

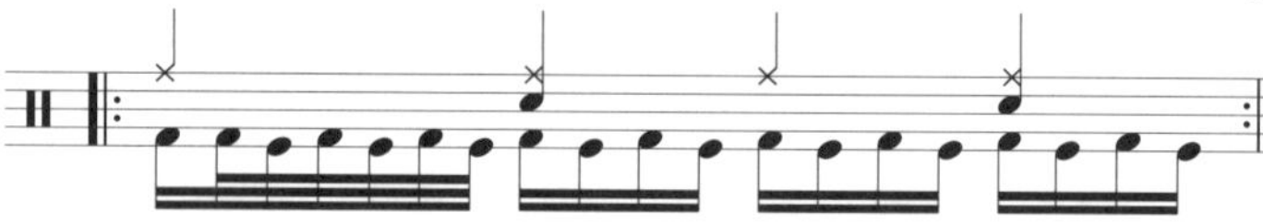

12.

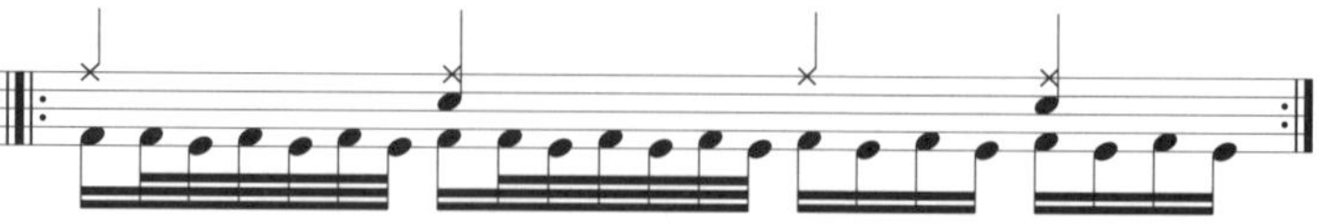

13.

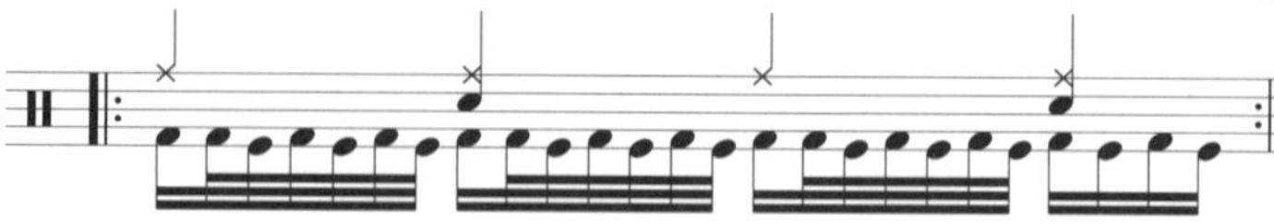

14.

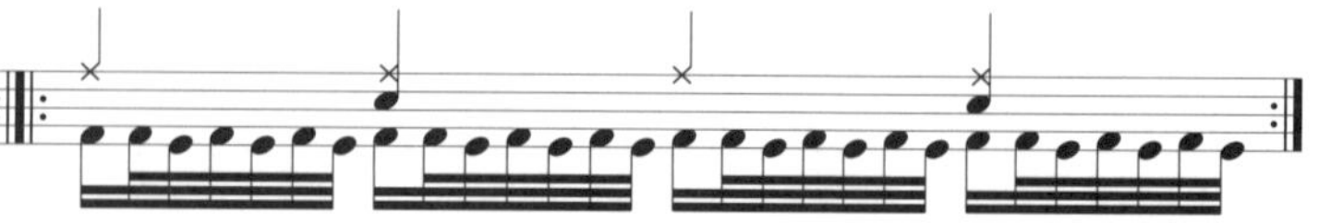

15.

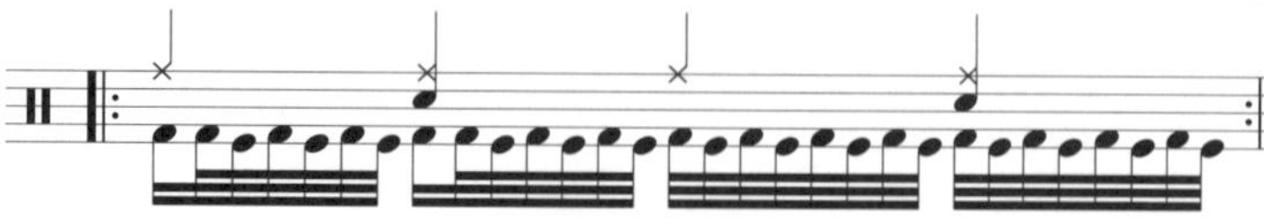

16.

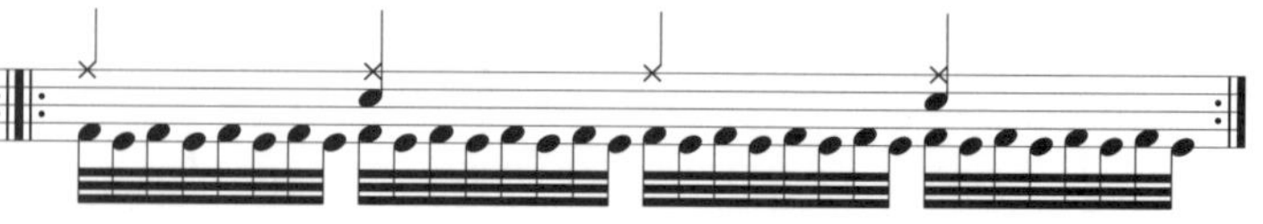

Exercises 17–30 are advanced blast beats that utilize 16th-note triplets and sextuplet (six notes per beat) double kick combinations. The ride pattern may be played on a ride cymbal or closed hi-hat.

TRACK 56

17.

18.

19.

20.

21.

22.

23.

24.

25.

26.

27.

28.

29.

30.

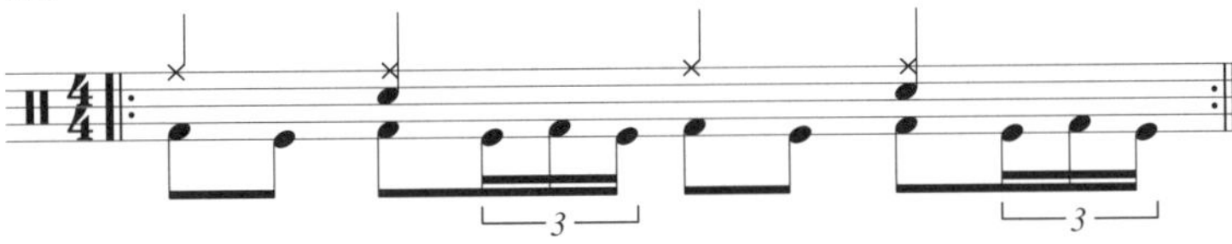

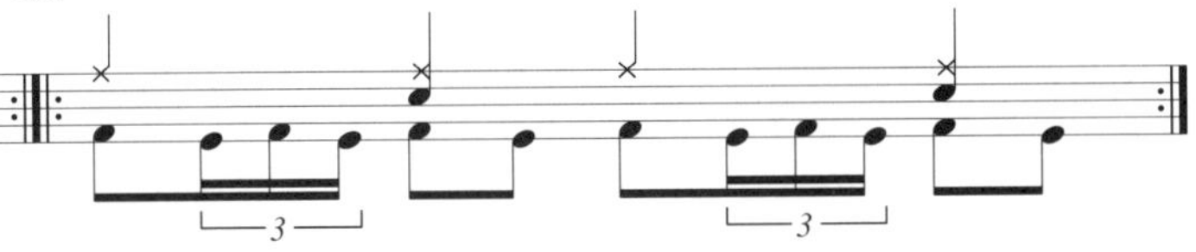

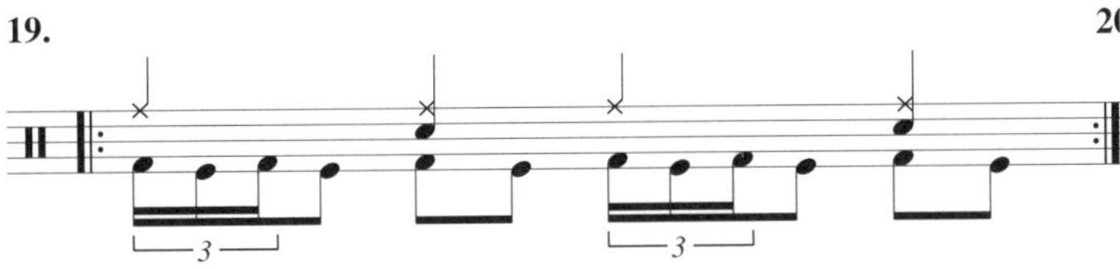

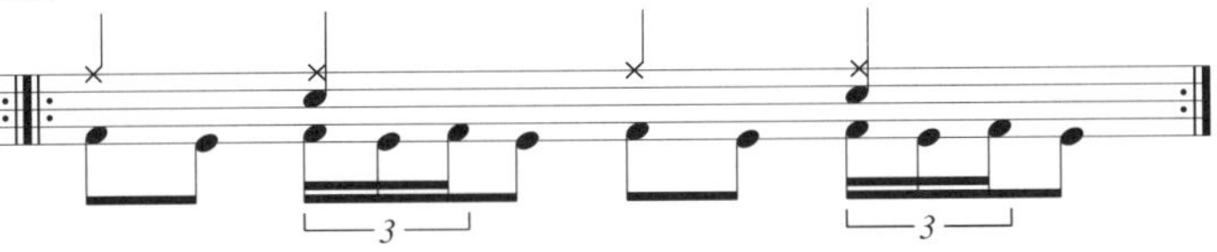

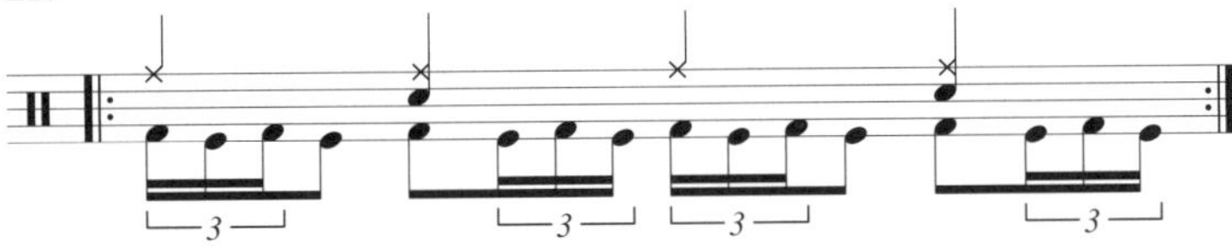

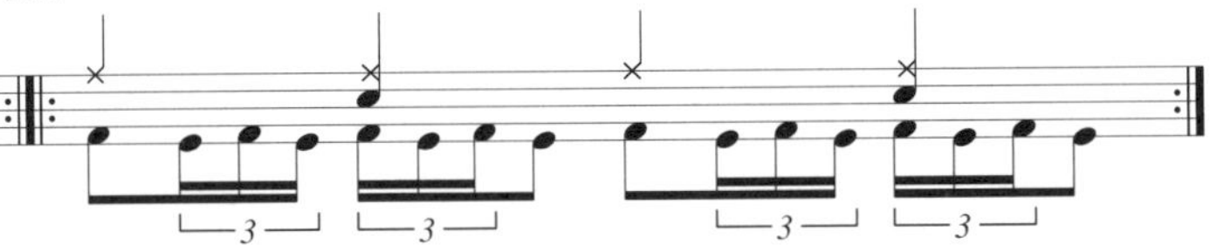

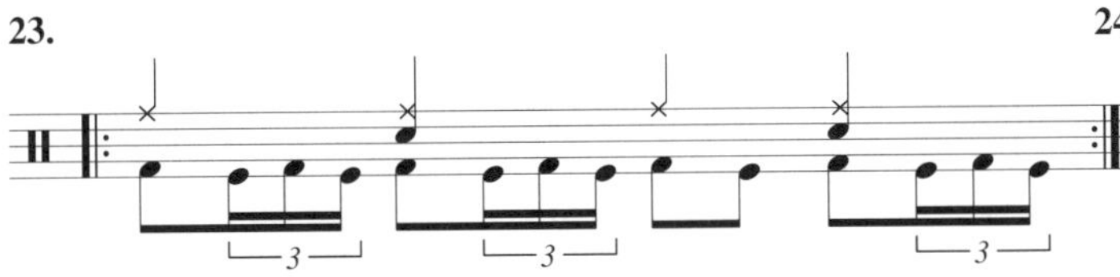

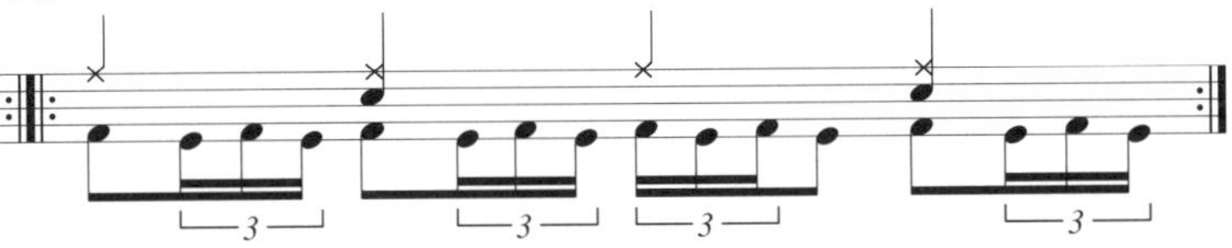

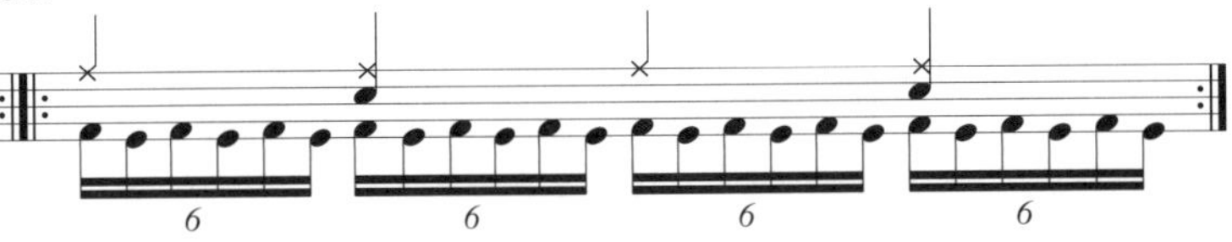

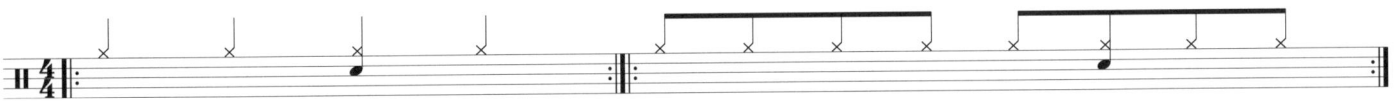

These double-kick combinations may also be played using this snare/ride drum pattern on either a ride cymbal or closed hi-hats.

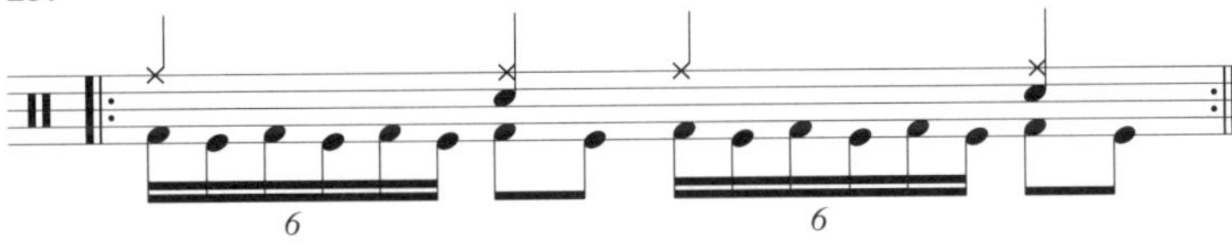

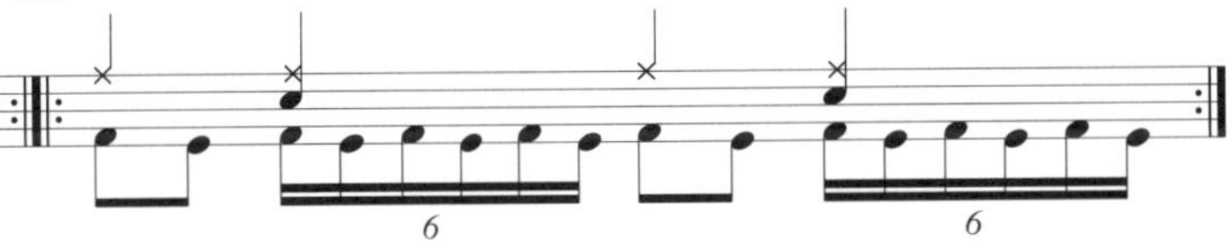

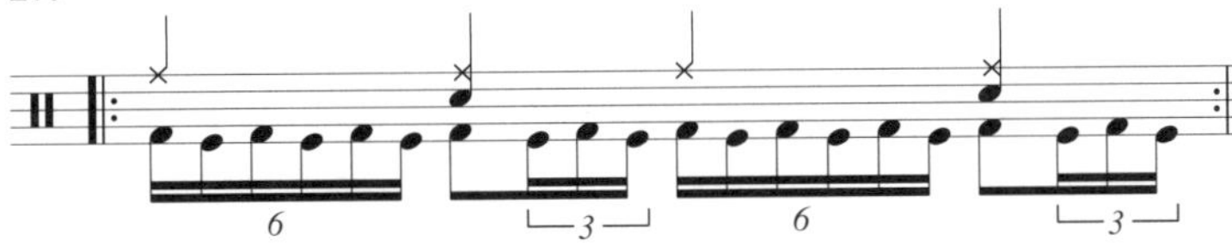

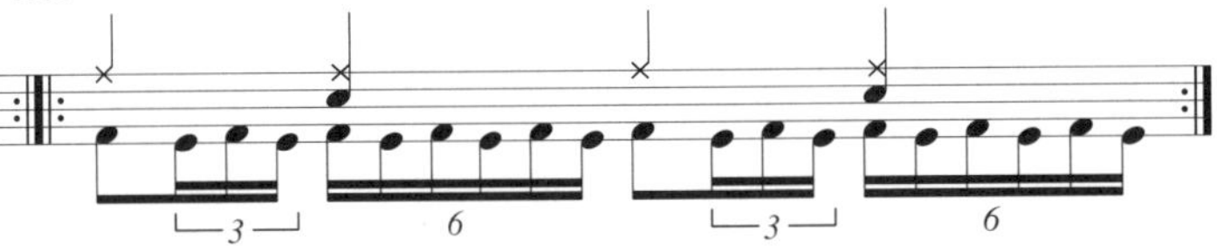

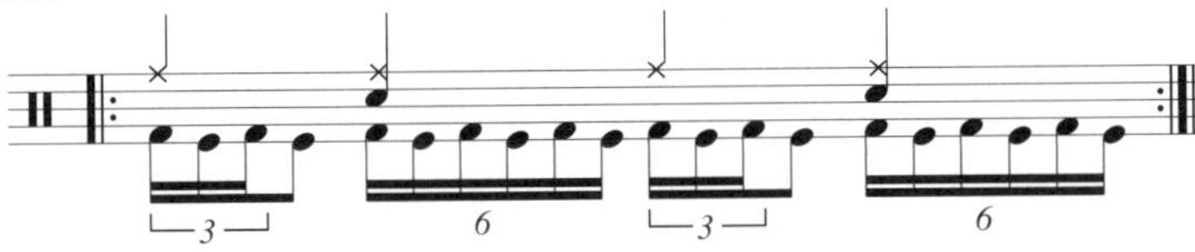

Lesson 27

Prog Metal

Prog (progressive) metal is a musical style that began in the U.K. in the 1970s. A combination of progressive rock and heavy metal, it's a diverse style that often utilizes musical concepts from other genres (classical music, jazz fusion, etc.) and combines it with aggressive drumming, lightning-fast riffs (melodic phrases), and a guitar-driven sound. In addition to the traditional drumming patterns in 4/4 time, prog metal is often performed in odd meters (5/8, 7/8, 5/4, 7/4, etc.) or with mixed meters (combinations of different meters).

Exercises 1–6 are four-measure examples of prog metal-style grooves and fills in various odd meters.

TRACK 57

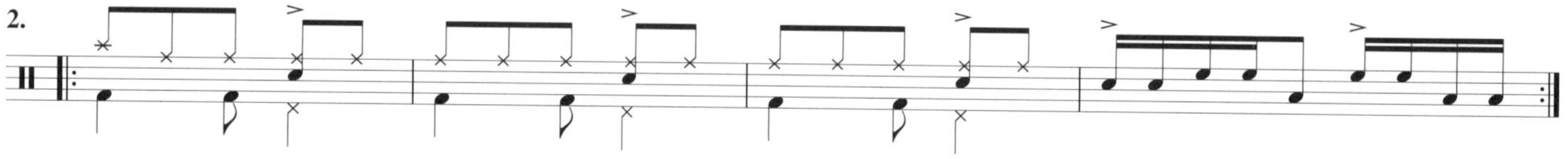

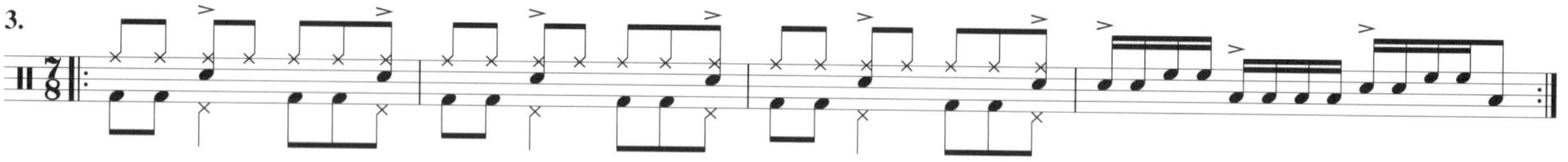

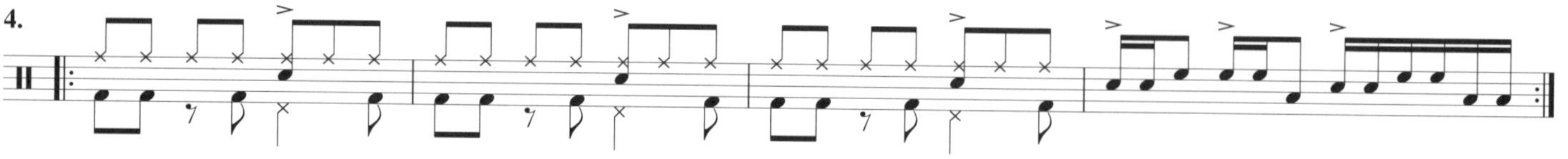

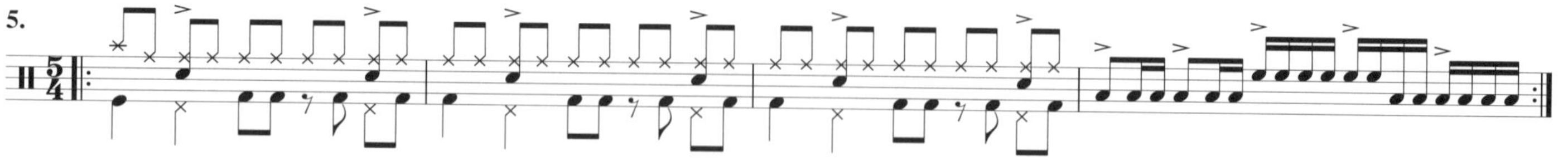

Prog metal also frequently includes combinations of different meters in one song. Any two meters may be used when mixing meters (4/4 and 7/8, 5/4 and 3/8, 7/4 and 5/8), but the most common use of mixed meters in prog metal involves alternating 4/4 time and odd meters with an eighth pulse (5/8, 7/8, or 9/8). When mixing meters, the speed of the eighth note normally stays the same. Notice that eighth note odd meters may be phrased in different ways, which changes where the snare drum backbeat is played (see Exercises 7 and 8, etc.).

TRACK 58

7.

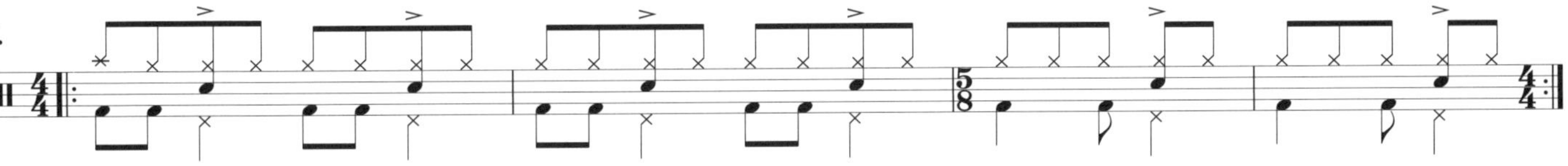

8.

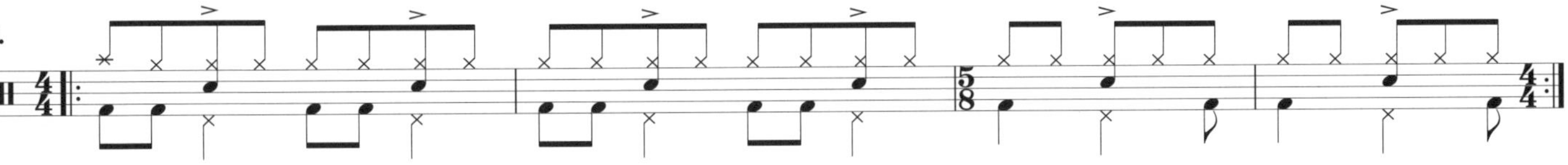

9.

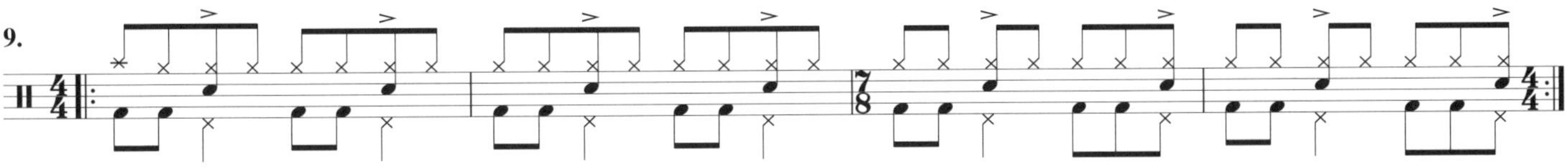

10.

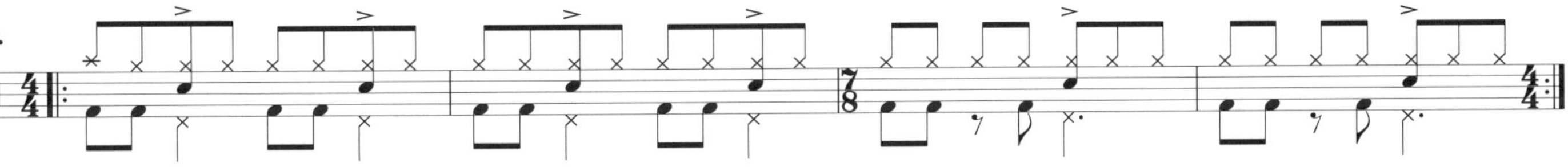

11.

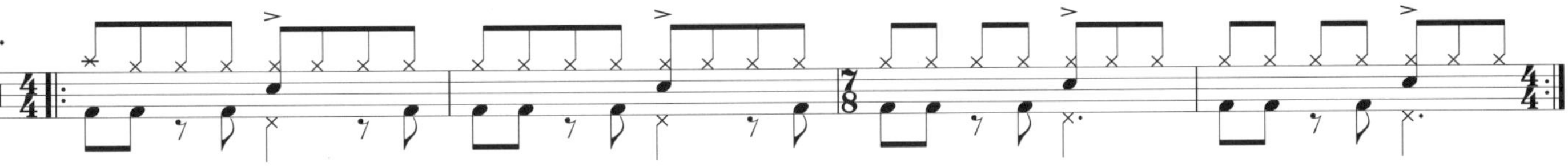

12.

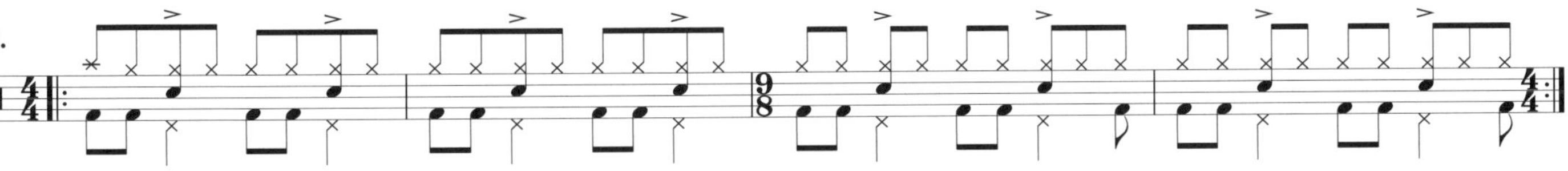

13.

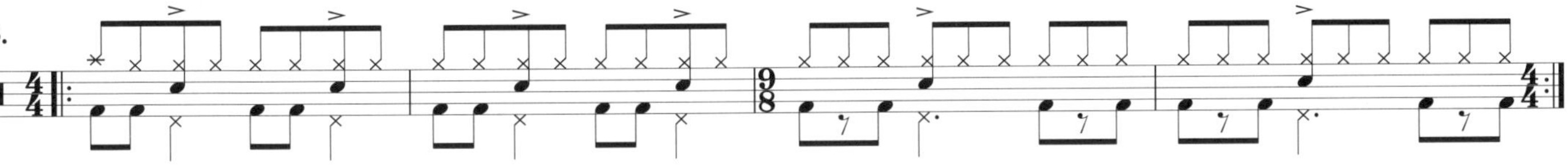

14.

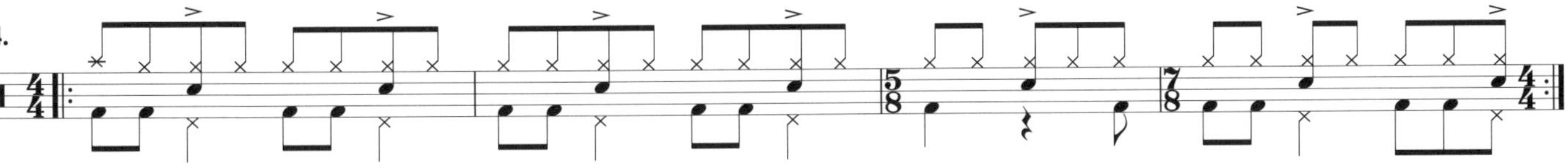

Lesson 28

Hand/Foot Solo Patterns #1

Many drummers begin playing fills and solos using only their hands and forget that their feet can also be incorporated. The hand/foot combinations in this lesson demonstrate some of the various permutations (variations) that can be created using three-note hand/foot patterns. The three-note patterns are bracketed in the first example (and once in each subsequent exercise) so that you can see the pattern and how it fits into a four- or eight-bar phrase. As with any unusual note grouping, it's not possible to fit three-note groupings evenly into a four-bar phrase, so to complete the four-bar phrase, a few additional notes are required to be added at the end. These notes are referred to as a "remainder"—just like the amounts that are left over when you do long division.

Practice these exercises as written on the snare drum (beginning with either a right or left stick) and then move the snare notes to various toms. Add some flams or double stops (two drums simultaneously or a drum/cymbal combination) for more variety.

TRACK 59

Three-note hand/foot patterns may also be played in triplet subdivisions, which would work well in jazz settings or any other music using a triplet-based beat subdivision (blues, some African music, etc.). Practice these exercises in eight-bar phrases—four bars of a groove (using whatever groove you wish) and then four bars of the exercise measure.

TRACK 60

Three-note patterns may also be used as 16th-note one-bar fills and solo patterns (Exercises 13–18). As with the previous exercises, there will be a remainder at the end of the bar that is not a complete three-note grouping.

TRACK 61

Lesson 29

Hand/Foot Solo Patterns #2

The hand/foot solo and fill patterns in this lesson use eighth-note groupings of five and seven to create solo figures that are very different than traditional two- or four-beat phrase patterns. As with most odd grouping phrase exercises, there will be an incomplete grouping at the end of the phrase (known as a *remainder*) that is necessary to complete the four-bar phrase and return to beat one of the next phrase. Practice each exercise with four bars of a groove (your choice) followed by the written exercise (A). Part B, C, and/or D of each exercise demonstrates how the phrase could be orchestrated around the drums. There are additional ways to orchestrate the patterns, so you should experiment with your own orchestration ideas based on these concepts and employ other stickings if you wish.

TRACK 62

8th-Note Groupings of 5

[Musical notation exercises 1A, 1B, 1C, 2A, 2B, 2C, 2D]

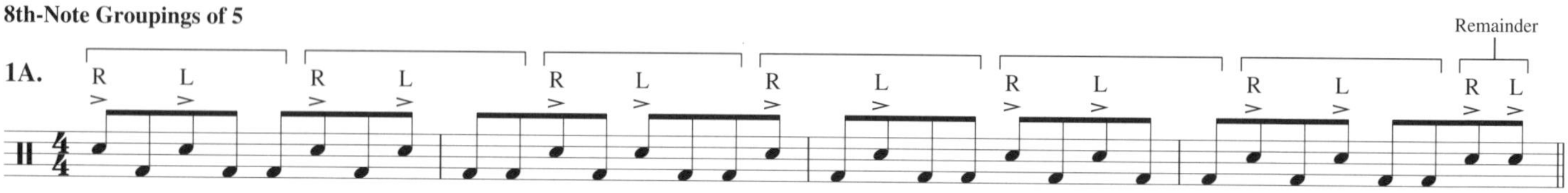

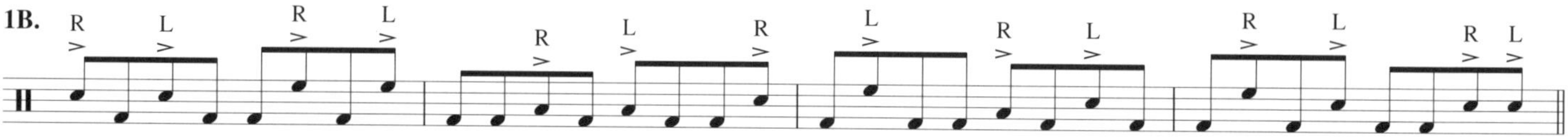

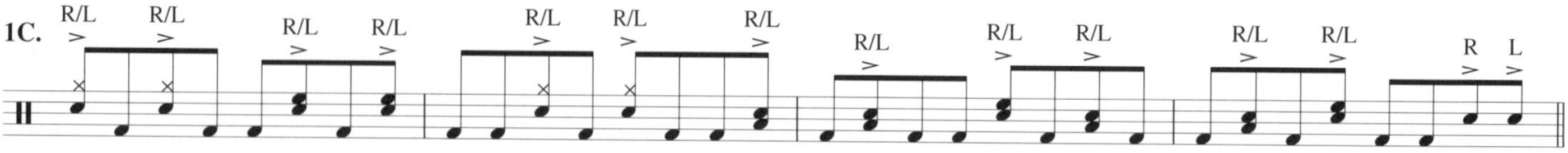

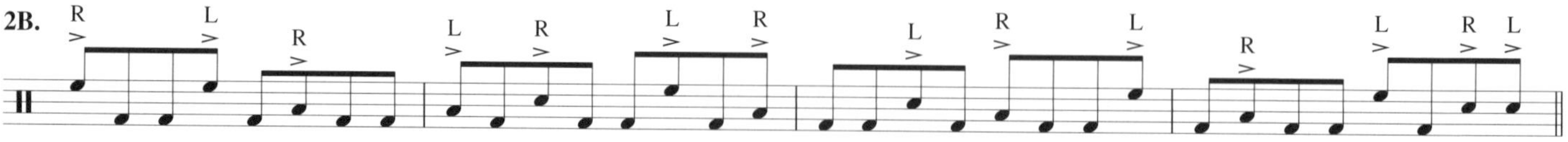

8th-Note Groupings of 7

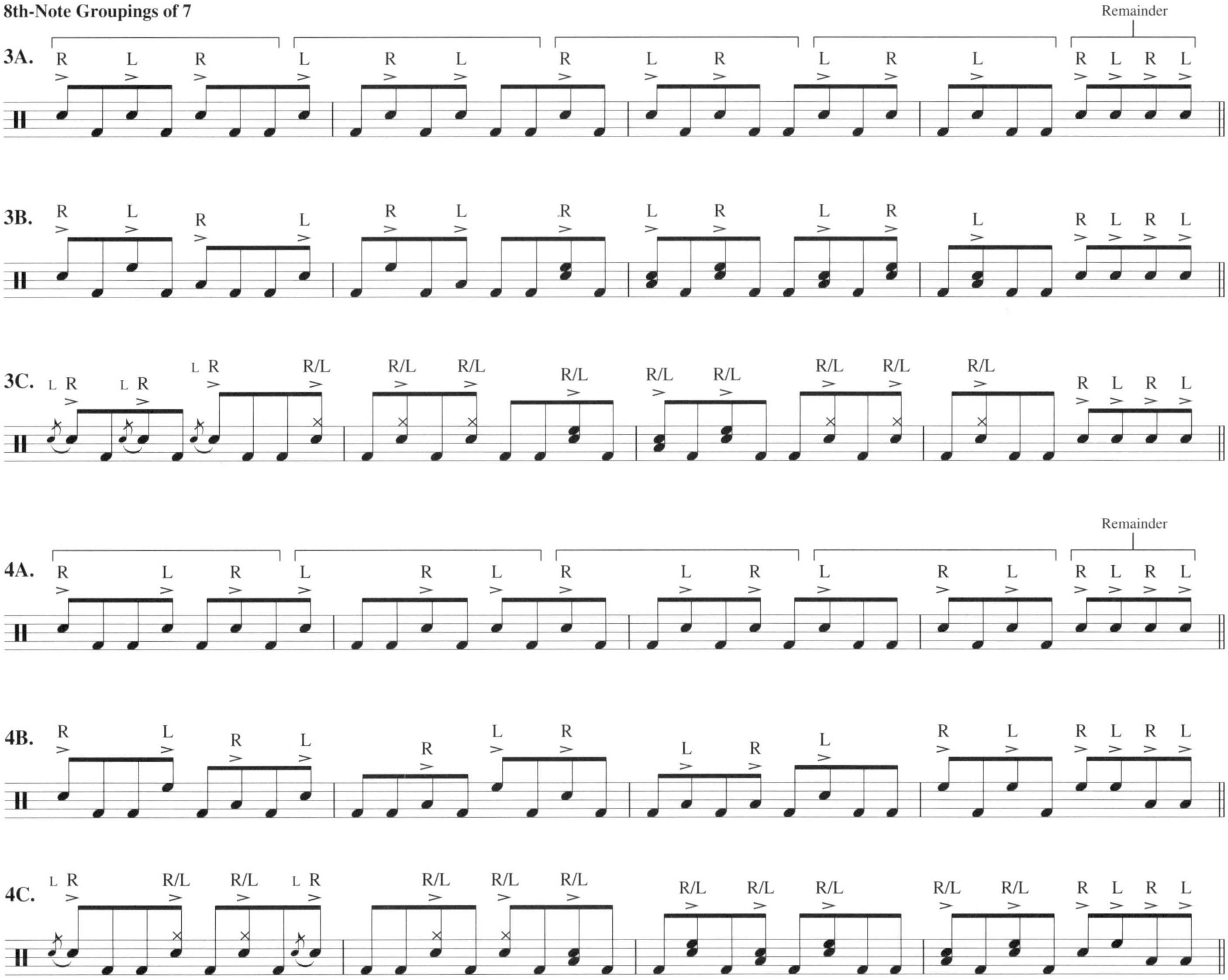

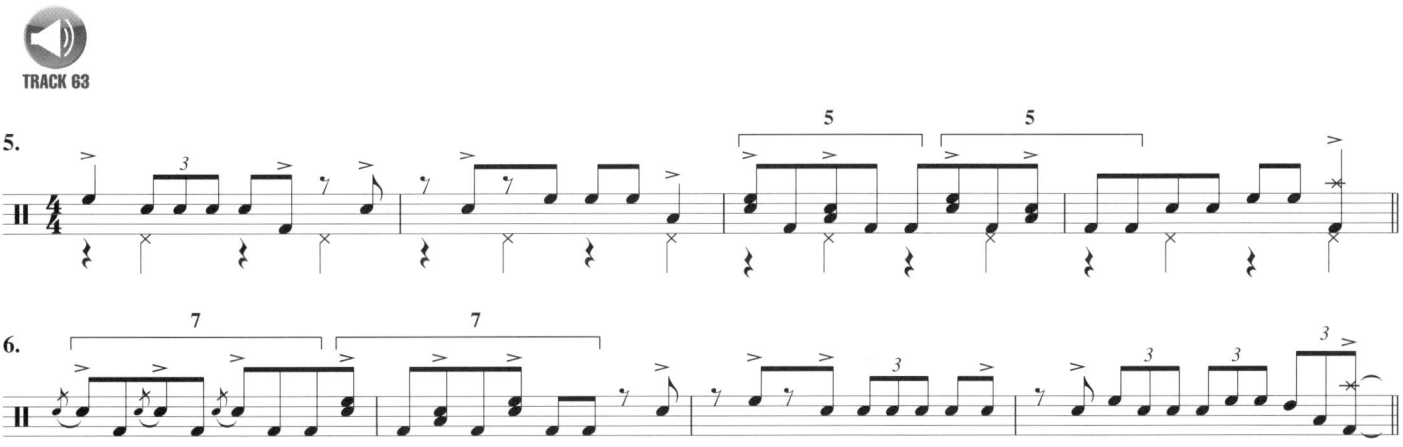

Keep in mind that mastering these exercises is the beginning of the process of integrating hand/foot patterns into your solo vocabulary. You probably wouldn't play four bars using only odd groupings in a real musical situation (although you could). These exercises are designed to be "idea builders" and are normally integrated into solo phrases as part of a solo to add some variety to the phrasing. Here is an example of how to integrate groupings of five and seven into a four-bar solo:

TRACK 63

Basic Swing Comping Patterns

Jazz music, also commonly referred to as *swing* music due to its relaxed triplet-based feel, started in the early 1900s and evolved into a variety of styles such as bebop, hard bop, cool, and post-bop. Most of the jazz/swing music heard today is based on principles developed during the bebop period of the 1940s. Bebop drumming patterns are based on using a repetitive ride cymbal pattern and hi-hat, which are the primary instruments responsible for providing the time feel. The ride cymbal rhythm and hi-hat pattern seen here is often referred to as "the jazz ride cymbal pattern." Accent the beats of 2 and 4 on the ride cymbal to provide the proper feel for this groove.

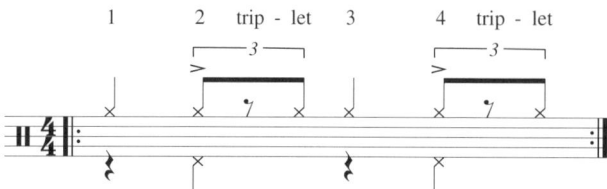

In jazz, the snare drum and bass drum are often required to improvise accompaniment patterns while other musicians are soloing. This process is known as "comping," and the snare and bass drum rhythms are collectively known as "comping rhythms" or "comping patterns." The bass drum and snare drum improvise rhythms while the ride cymbal pattern and hi-hat parts stay consistent.

The following exercises will help you develop the ability to improvise snare drum comping patterns while maintaining the repetitive ride cymbal and hi-hat patterns. Since most comping patterns are based on some combination of triplet rhythms, almost any conceivable comping pattern can be created by adapting or combining these exercises (adding different accents, combining different parts of different measures, etc.).

TRACK 64

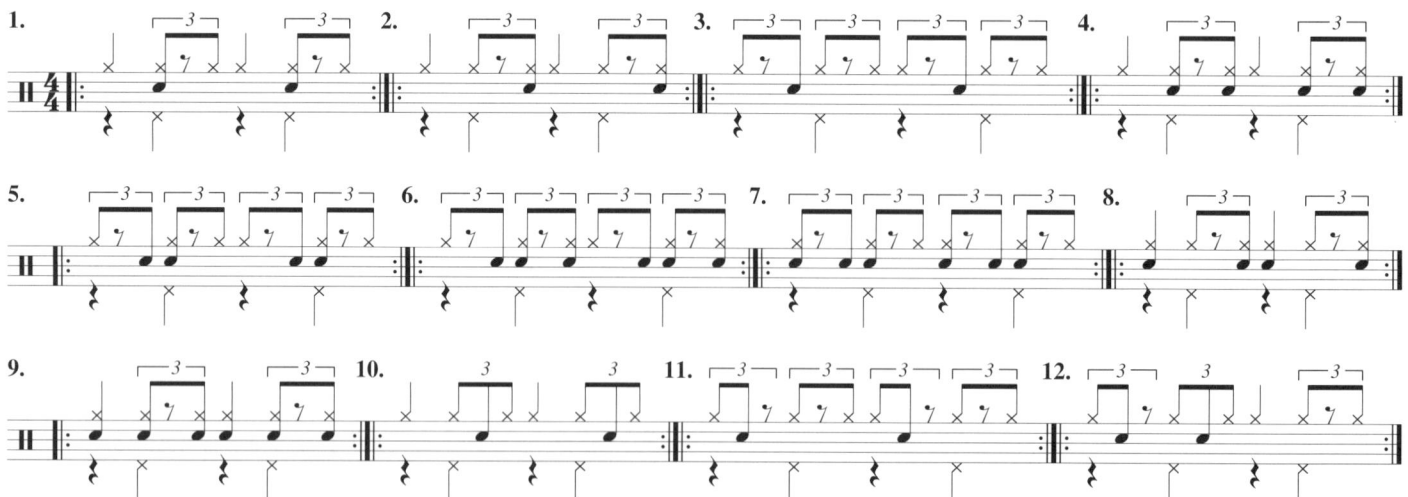

TRACK 65

After playing these exercises, play along with some jazz recordings and improvise some snare drum comping patterns. Also try transcribing some comping patterns you hear on records to expand your comping pattern repertoire. Drummers Max Roach, Art Blakey, Roy Haynes, Art Taylor, Jimmy Cobb, and others can clearly be heard comping on jazz recordings from the 1940s, '50s, and '60s. Bill Stewart, Eric Harland, Jeff Hamilton, Joe LaBarbera, and Lewis Nash are all excellent drummers and can be heard comping on many recent jazz recordings.

Lesson 31

Basic Swing Fills

In swing music, as in rock music, drummers often add fills at the end of phrases to add interest and excitement to the music. Fills also signal the end of the phrase and possibly a transition to the next musical phrase or section.

Since swing music is based on the triplet rhythmic subdivision, most swing fills use triplets for fills instead of straight eighth or 16th notes. Fills may be any number of beats—two, three, or even four—but are normally not longer than one bar. In swing music, fills are not always followed by a crash cymbal on beat one of the next bar (although you could do that if you choose). Fills often end by simply returning to the ride cymbal pattern. When practicing the following exercises, try these suggestions:

- Improvise snare drum and bass drum comping rhythms in the first three bars of each exercise (you'll hear some of this on the audio).
- Try different stickings, keeping in mind that you might need a double sticking (e.g., RR, LL) to get back to the ride cymbal after the fill.
- Once you're comfortable with the rhythms, try moving them around the toms for variety.

TRACK 66

TRACK 67

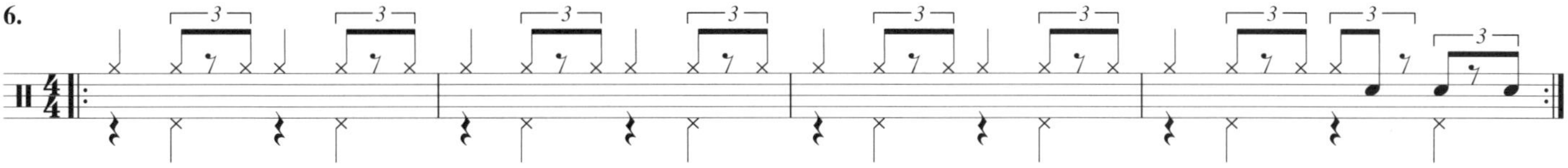

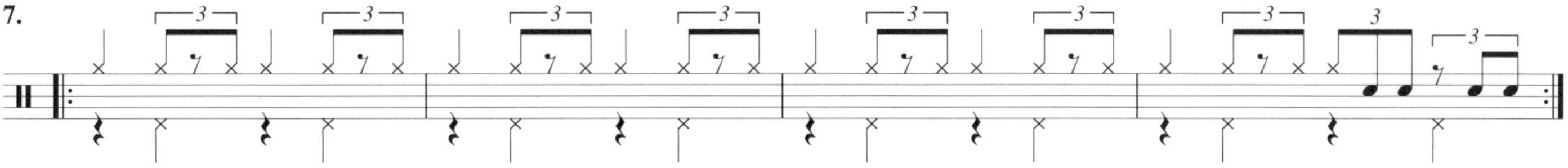

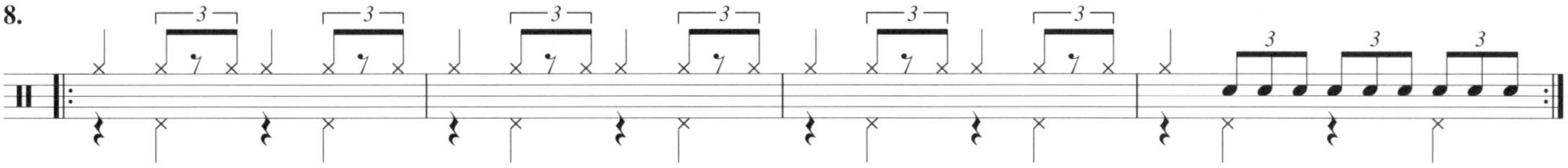

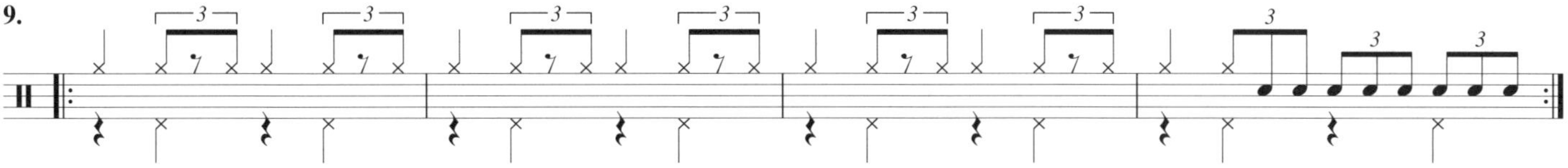

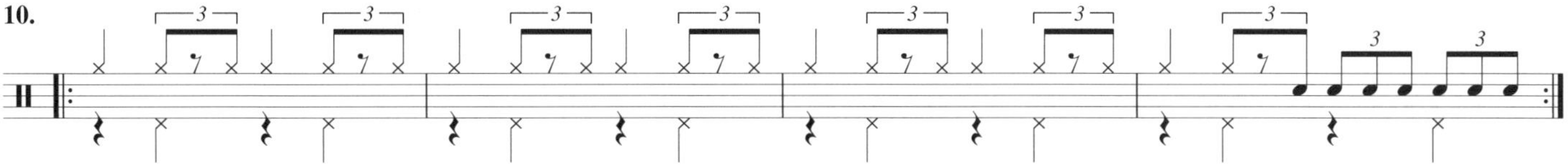

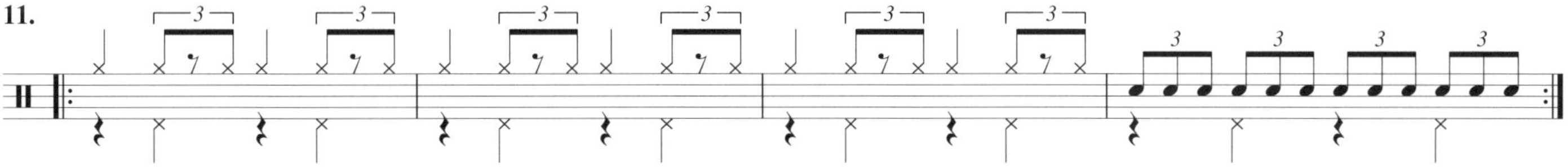

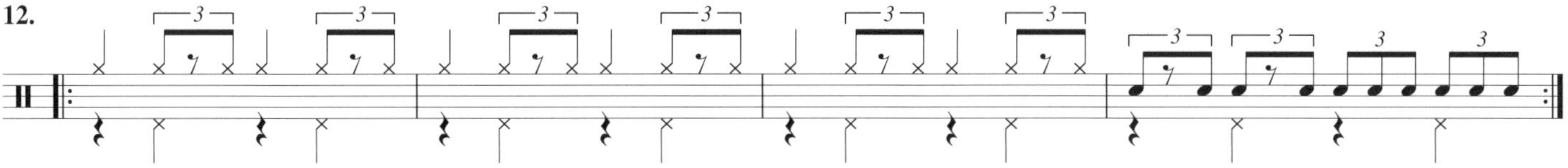

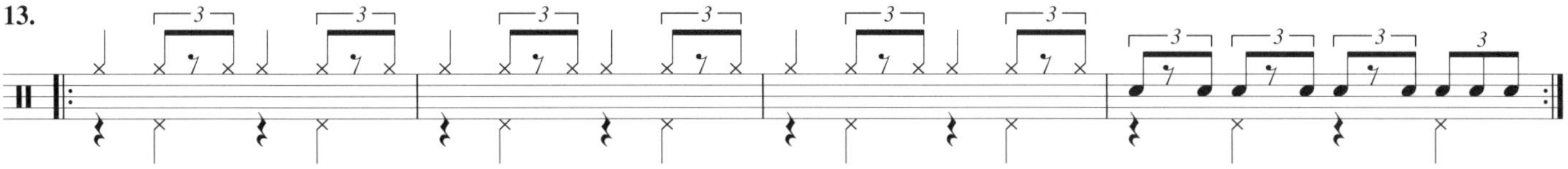

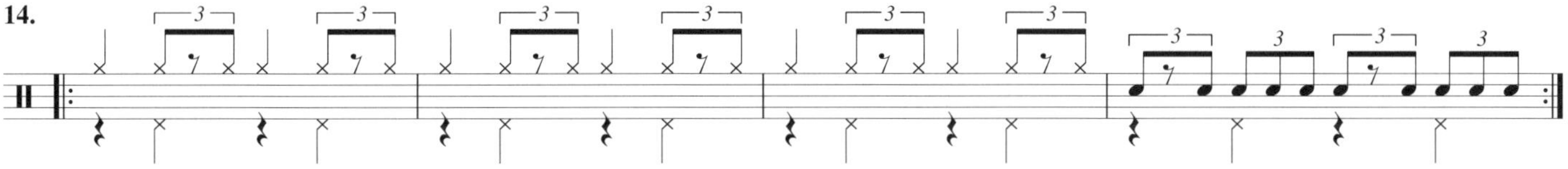

Lesson 32

Intermediate Swing Comping Patterns

After learning some basic swing patterns ("comping" with the snare drum while playing the swing ride cymbal pattern), the next step in swing playing is to develop the ability to freely improvise bass and snare drum rhythms while playing the ride cymbal. The ability to maintain a repetitive rhythm in one limb while playing a completely different rhythm in other limbs is often called *drumset independence*. Countless books have been written to address the issue of independence, which is required of a drummer playing any style. This concept might also be expanded to include the concept of drumset *interdependence*, meaning that the rhythms played by a drummer's four limbs are related to and reliant upon one another to create a total drumset groove.

The following one-bar exercises are examples of drumset independence in a swing style. They demonstrate how jazz drummers realistically comp during tunes. Comping is always improvised, and these exercises can (and should) be altered in different ways to create variety when comping. If you listen to a swing tune, you'll notice that drummers don't always comp in every measure; often they let a few beats or a few measures go by without any bass drum and snare drum notes (but they continue the ride cymbal and hi-hat throughout the tune). Jazz drummers often add comping rhythms when the soloist finishes a phrase or does not play any notes for a few beats.

In order to replicate more accurately how you will use these comping rhythms and independence exercises, try the following suggestions:

- Play the one-bar exercises and leave a few measures "blank" (with only the ride cymbal and hi-hat continuing to play their normal pattern) for a more realistic comping experience.

- Occasionally move a snare drum note to a tom.

- Add accents to various notes in an exercise to imply different phrasing.

TRACK 68

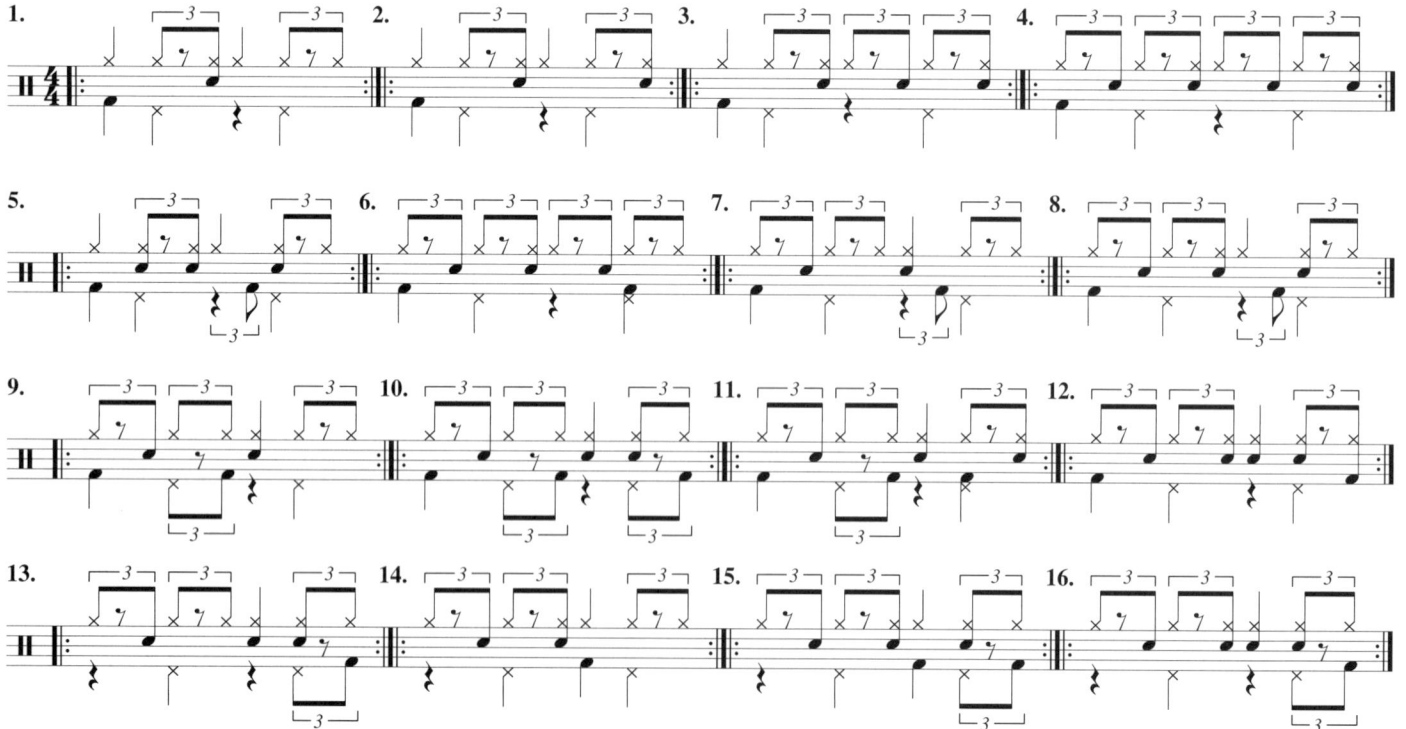

TRACK 69

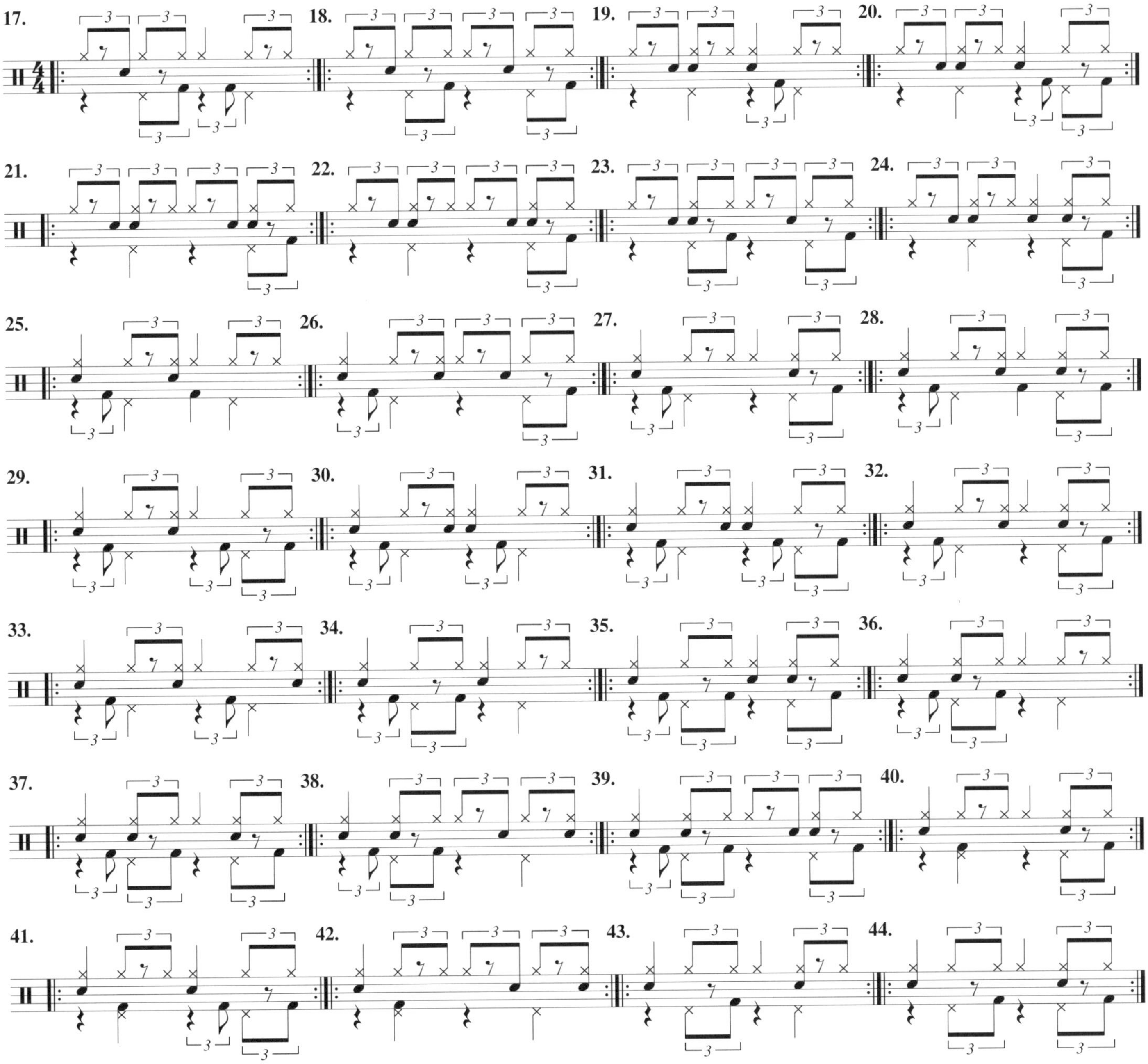

Find a recording of a medium tempo jazz tune (or drummer-less play-along track) and improvise some of your own snare drum/bass drum comping patterns with the recording.

Lesson 33

Intermediate Swing Fills

In swing (jazz) music, drummers often add a short fill at the end of the phrase to add some excitement to the music and to help define phrases. One big difference between rock and jazz, however, is where the fill normally ends. Rock fills normally conclude with a crash on beat 1 of the next bar, while swing fills often end on the "and" of beat 4 of the fill bar.

One important element of swing is its use of *syncopation*—or "weak beat accenting." To fully understand the difference between swing and rock, it's important to understand some musical history. Much of today's music is based on the *march*—music and drumming that was used by armies to keep soldiers in step with one another as they marched. Beats 1 and 3 in 4/4 "march time" were considered strong beats, probably because they were the beats on which people's feet landed when marching. Beats 2 and 4 were considered weak beats because they were not where people's feet landed when marching. If you take it one step further, the eighth note immediately before beat 1 would also be a weak beat and is referred to as an *upbeat*. It is this tendency to start swing phrases on the upbeat that gives swing its sense of momentum; it's one of its strongest rhythmic characteristics. This means that the fills in this lesson will end with a cymbal crash on the third partial of the triplet (the "let" of the beat) of beat 4 instead of beat 1 (as it would happen in most rock tunes). The *tie* symbol (curved line attached to the cymbal note) on the crash cymbal means that the crash is connected to the first beat of the next bar. Do not play the cymbal note on beat 1 when repeating the exercises; let the crash on the "let" of beat 4 ring through. Begin the ride cymbal part in the measure following the fill on beat 2.

Another important distinction between jazz and rock is how drummers play a cymbal crash. Jazz started out being played at a soft volume, and often jazz drummers used the ride cymbal for crashes as well as for riding. Jazz drummers often play a "shoulder crash"—a crash using the shoulder of the stick on the edge of the ride cymbal. This is a softer crash and creates a different sound than the regular ride cymbal "ping" sound. Of course, jazz drummers also use a separate crash cymbal for loud crashes, but the softer shoulder crash is often used in medium to low volume musical settings. Try playing these exercises using both a full crash on a separate crash cymbal and a shoulder crash on the ride cymbal.

When practicing the following exercises, try these suggestions:

- Improvise snare drum and bass drum comping rhythms in the first three bars (you'll hear some of this on the audio).

- Start with the suggested stickings, but try other stickings to vary your phrasing and technique.

- Use either the shoulder crash or a separate crash cymbal to play the cymbal crashes at the end of the fill bar.

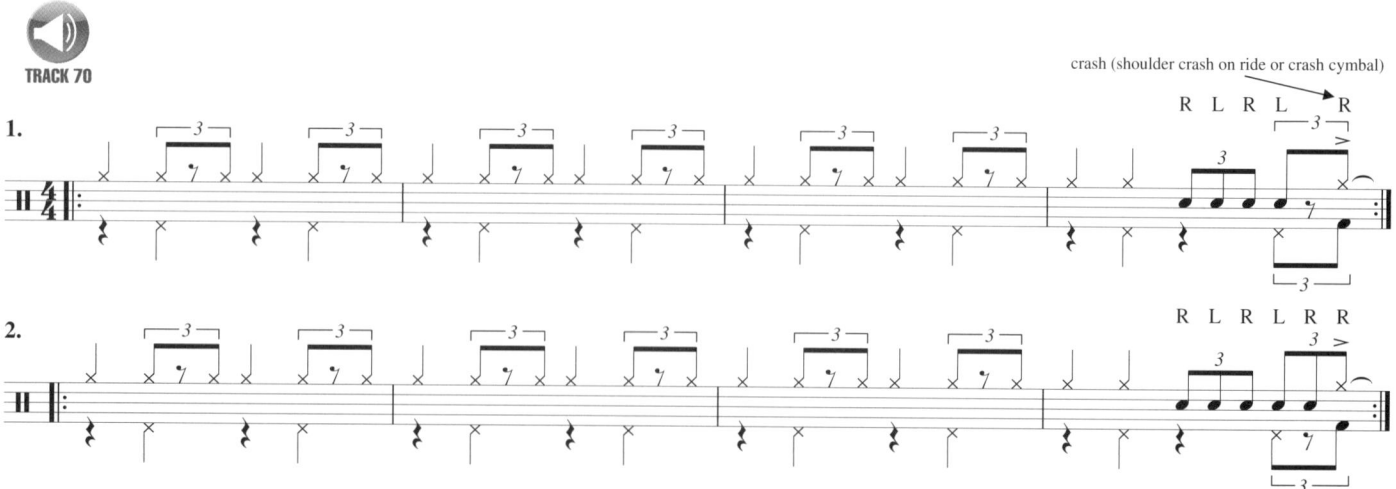

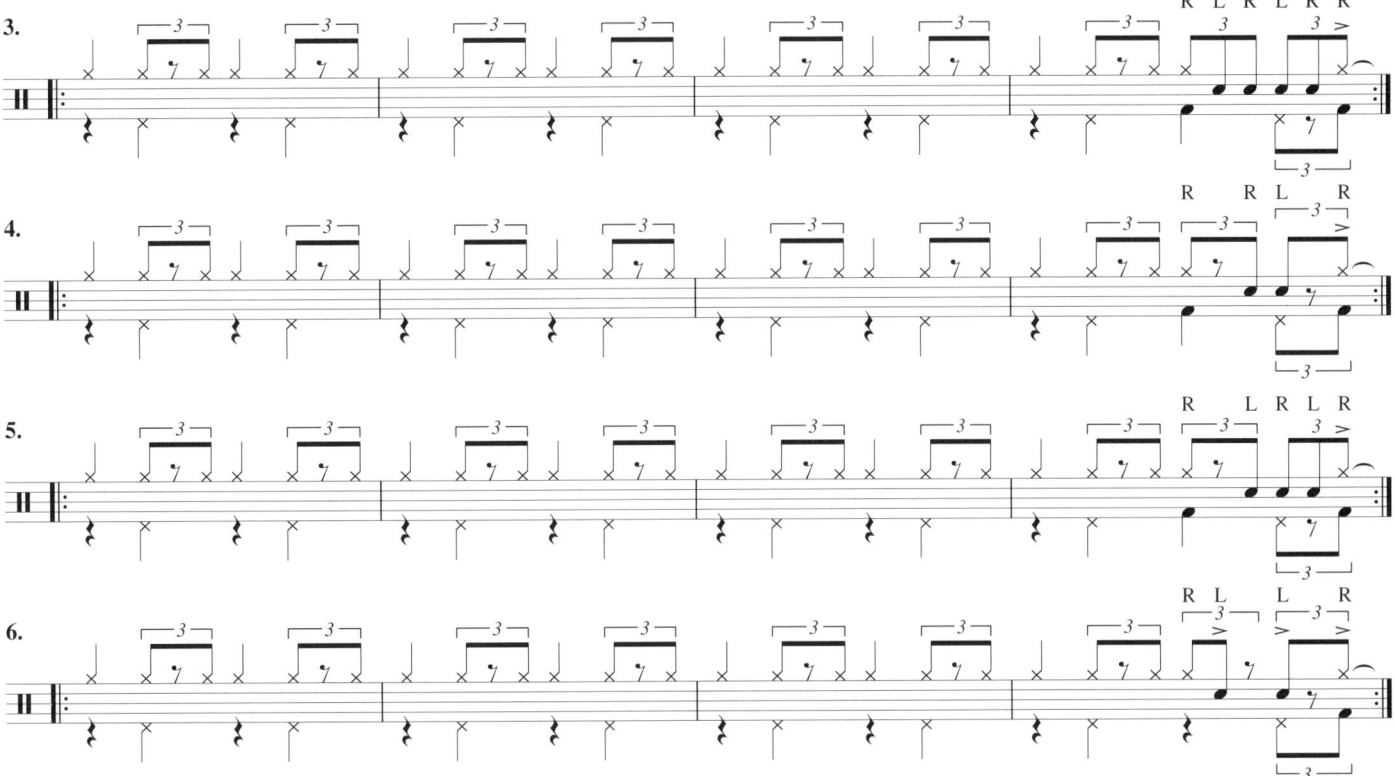

Here are some fills that end with a crash on the second partial of the triplet: the "trip."

TRACK 71

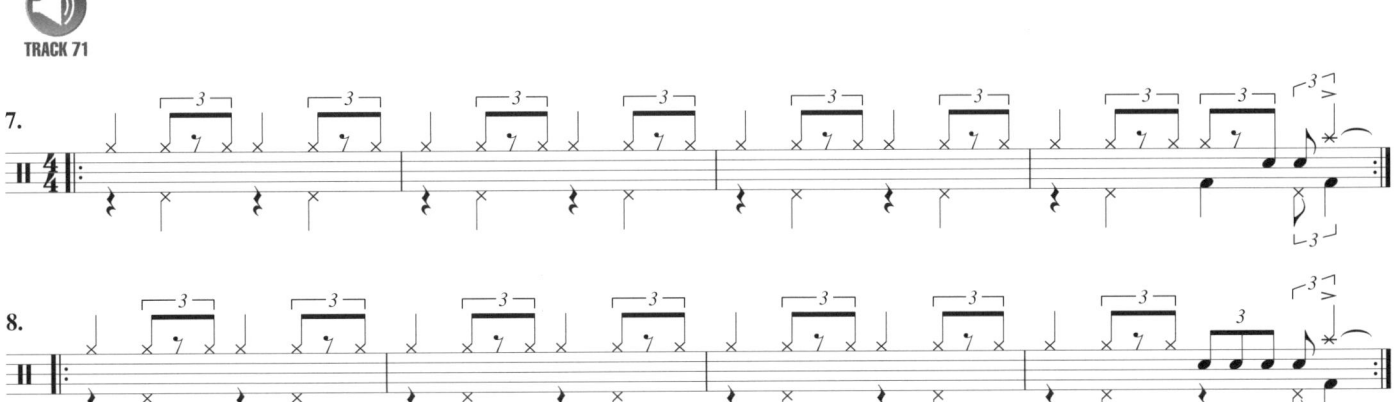

Once mastered, try substituting various tom notes for the snare drum rhythms to create a variety of different fills.

Lesson 34

Advanced Swing Comping Patterns

Advanced swing comping patterns involve integrating different triplet "partials," or parts of the triplet subdivision, into the comping vocabulary. These are more difficult than quarter-note and eighth-note comping rhythms and will be more useful at medium or slow tempos, due to their rhythmic density. These exercises will be written only on the snare drum line. (You may wish to write the ride cymbal part above the exercises at first in order to learn them, but strive to ultimately play the exercises without the ride cymbal part written in.)

Practice these first examples to prepare for the exercises on the following page. The top line shows the snare drum part alone; the middle line shows how the ride cymbal will line up with the partial if playing the snare drum; and the bottom line shows how the ride cymbal will line up with the partial if playing the bass drum.

TRACK 72

Practice the two-bar exercises as four-bar phrases at first by playing two bars of just ride cymbal and hi-hat followed by the written exercise. These two "empty bars" will allow you to relax momentarily and "catch up" so that you can be prepared to execute the exercise properly. It will also help you develop a sense of pacing, because no jazz drummer plays comping figures in every measure. (You can verify this by listening to some recordings!)

Always use a metronome with these exercises. Try setting the metronome at a medium tempo (e.g., 60 beats per minute) and play the exercises so that the metronome sounds on beats 2 and 4 (exactly with the hi-hat). This will promote a better sense of swing and immediately indicate if you have dropped or skipped a beat (known as "flipping the time") because the hi-hat should always be playing exactly with the metronome.

Try to use a practice strategy known as "continuous practicing," which means to keep playing the ride cymbal and hi-hat even if you make a mistake. This accomplishes several things:

- Your ride cymbal will soon become automatic, and you won't have to think about it, allowing you to concentrate on other things (reading, listening to the other parts to see if you're playing them correctly, etc.).

- You'll develop your ability to recover from mistakes and keep going (which all drummers need to be able to do).

- You will build stamina.

- You'll develop the concentration to be able to hold a tempo for a long period of time.

Play the following exercises using the jazz ride cymbal pattern in the right hand and the hi-hat on beats 2 and 4 in the left foot. Read and play these rhythms first on just the snare drum, then just the bass drum, then alternating between the snare and bass, and finally, mix and match different combinations of snare drum and bass drum using the rhythms provided.

TRACK 73

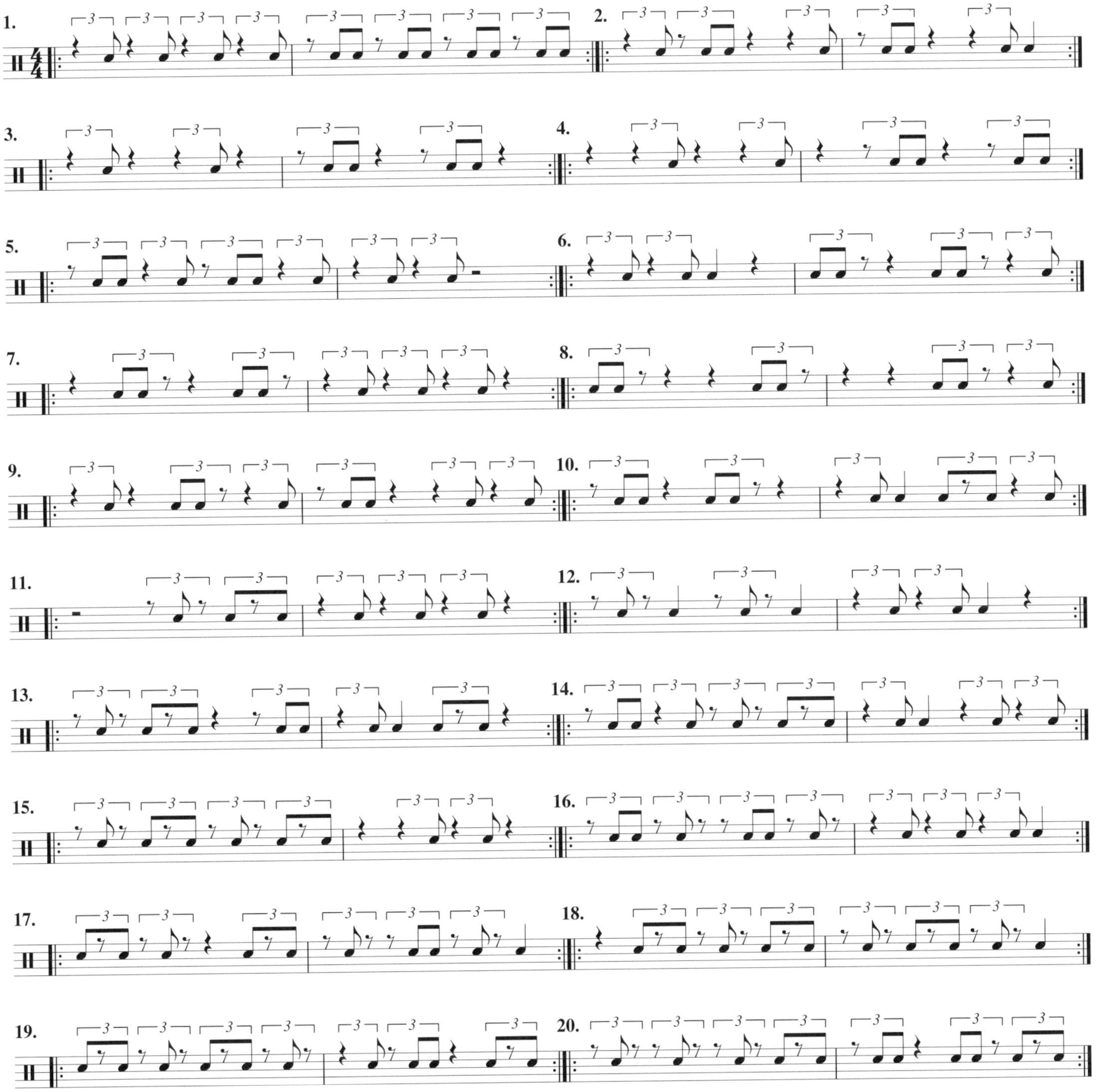

These exercises represent only the tip of the iceberg in terms of comping ideas. Take some of these rhythms and create your own comping sequences. Listen to how drummers such as Max Roach, "Philly" Joe Jones, Art Taylor, Art Blakey, Elvin Jones, Roy Haynes, Jimmy Cobb, Adam Nussbaum, Jeff Hamilton, Bill Stewart, John Riley, and others use these (or similar) patterns in their playing.

Lesson 35

Advanced Swing Fills

The advanced swing fills in this lesson incorporate accented upbeat crashes (on the "ands" of the beat), which can be played either on a crash cymbal or on the edge of the ride cymbal, depending on the volume required. The fills may be moved to any other toms to create even more variety.

TRACK 74

1.

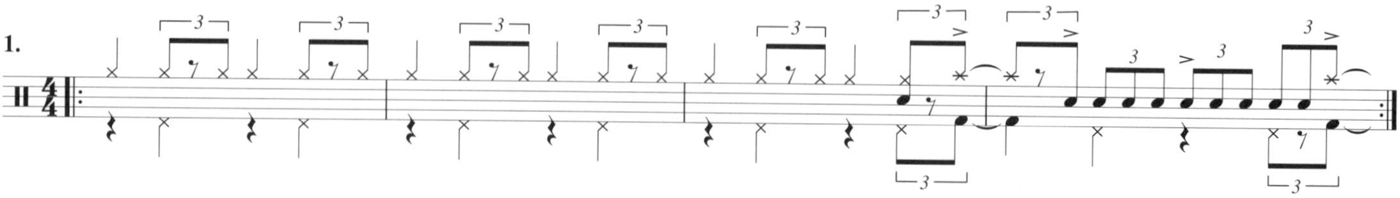

2.

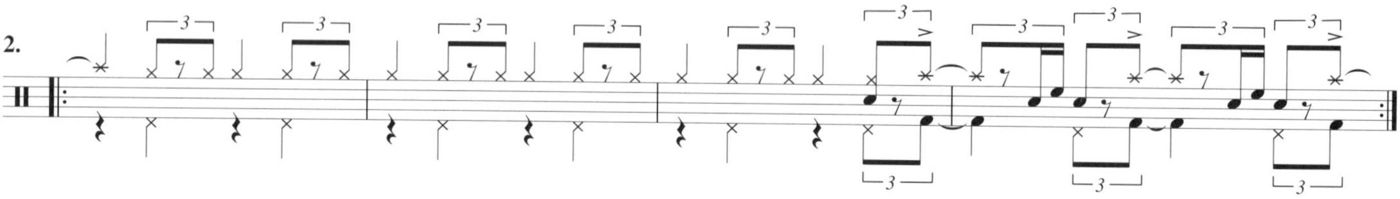

3.

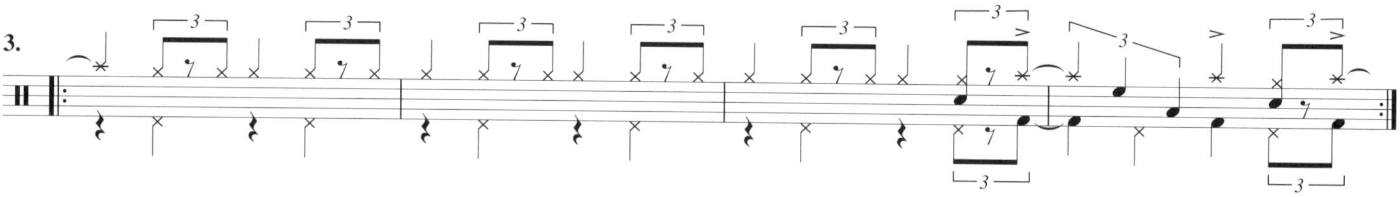

4.

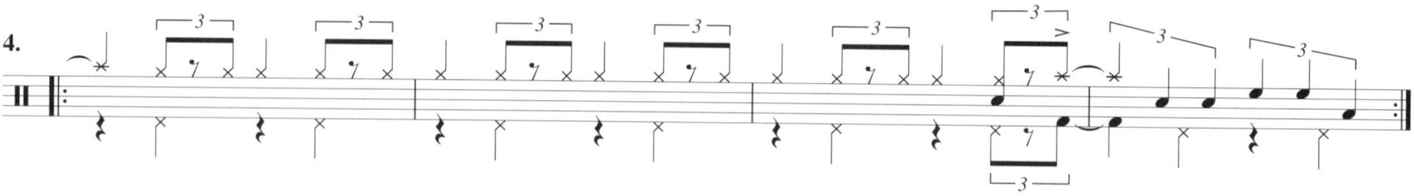

5.

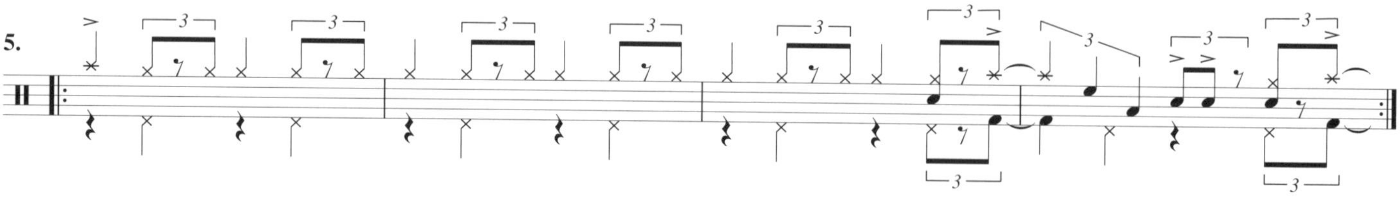

6.

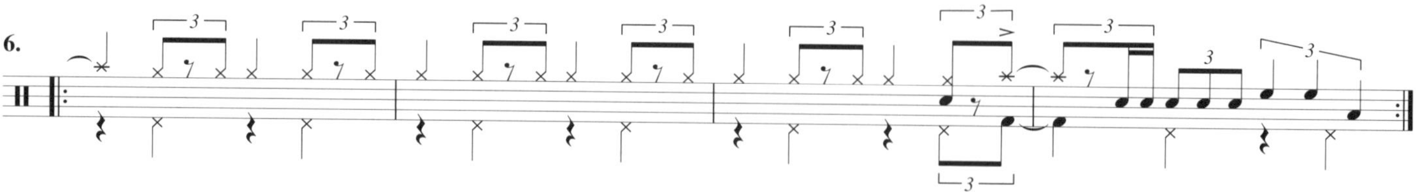

7.

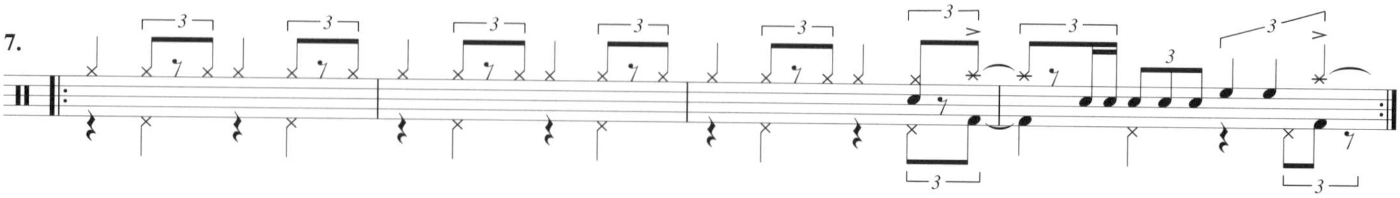

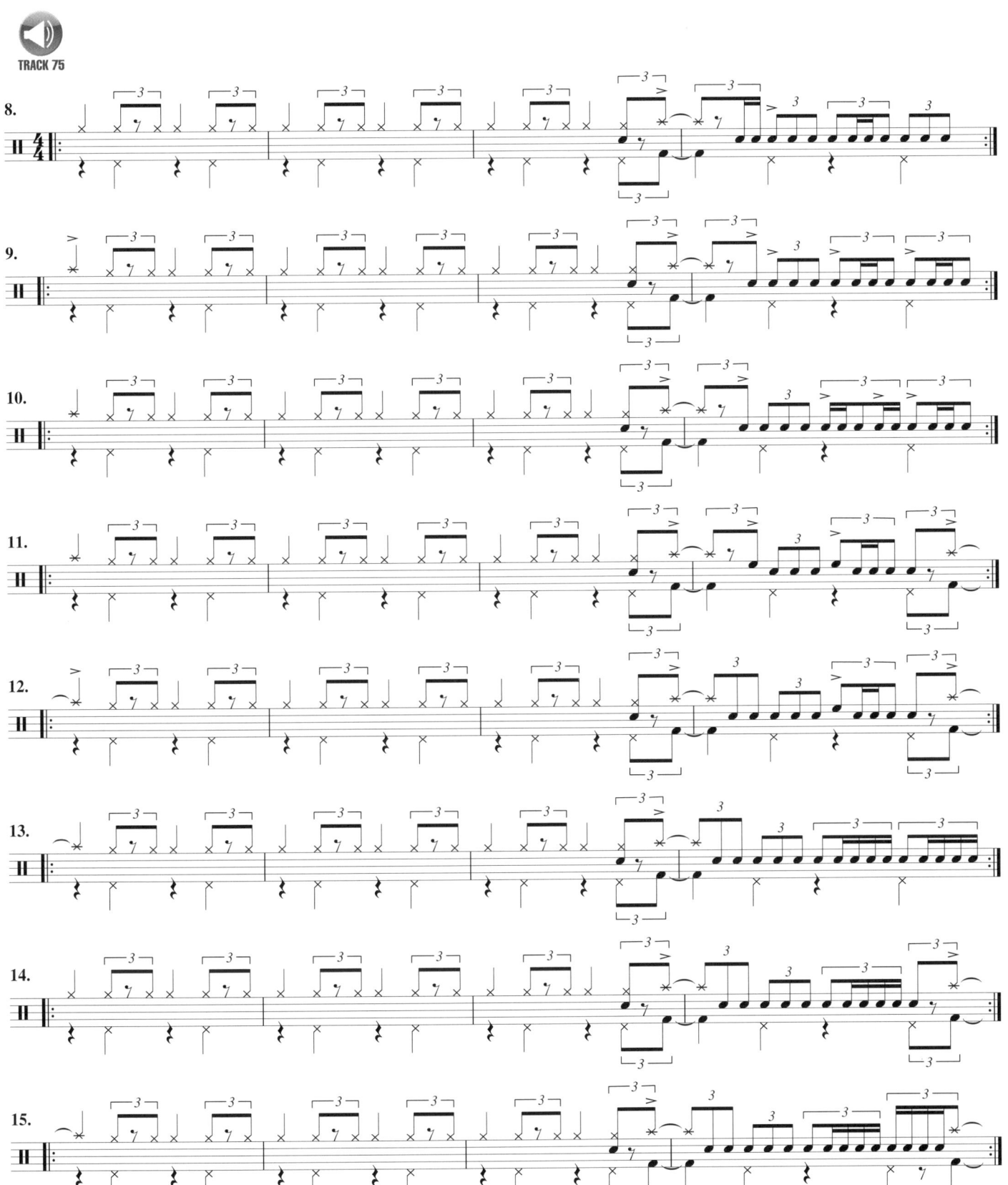

Lesson 36

Advanced Hi-Hat Comping Patterns

Before 1960, most jazz drummers played the hi-hat only on beats 2 and 4. In modern jazz, however, the hi-hat is used as an independent comping instrument. Exercises 1–10 demonstrate some other hi-hat comping rhythm options. In order to be able to smoothly transition between traditional hi-hat patterns and these more advanced ones, practice the following exercises in four-bar phrases starting with two bars of traditional swing time with hi-hat on 2 and 4, followed by the two-bar advanced hi-hat exercises:

TRACK 76

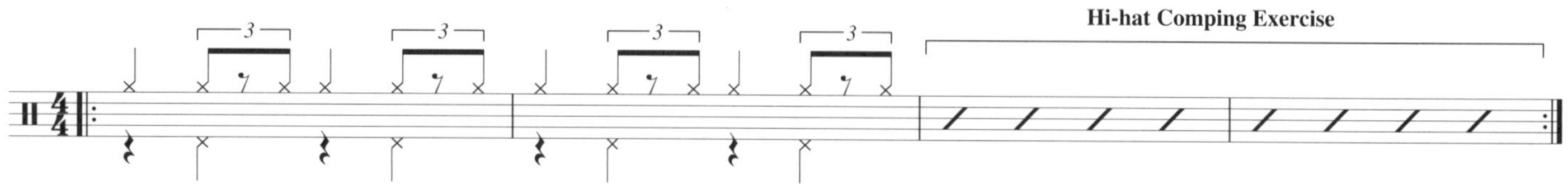

Two-Bar Exercises

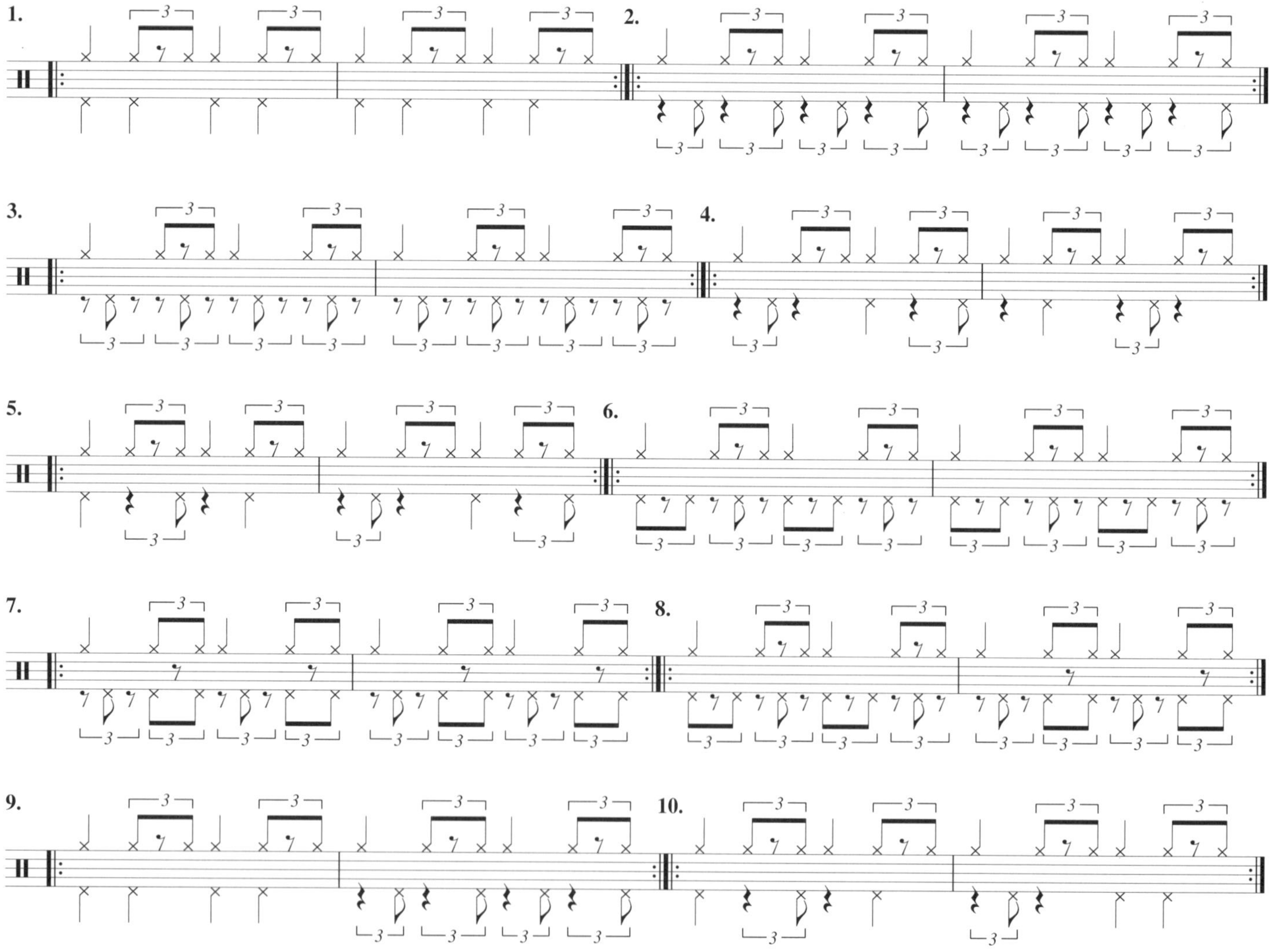

These snare drum/bass drum/hi-hat combinations reflect a more advanced, modern approach to jazz timekeeping using the hi-hat as an independent voice. All of these exercises will not be feasible at the same tempo, due to their rhythmic density, but will be feasible in a certain tempo range (e.g., 90–130 BPM). While practicing these exercises, try different tempos to determine which are most suitable for each exercise.

TRACK 77

Lesson 37

Drumset Accent Study #1

Accents help make music more interesting and expressive, and every drummer needs to develop their control of accents. The following exercises will develop your accuracy with accents, may serve as warm-up exercises, and will also lead to better, more musical soloing. One of the most important aspects of accent control is the ability to keep the unaccented strokes very soft and close to the head (approximately a half inch above). The accented strokes should be approximately eight inches off the head. As you begin practicing, watch your hands often to ensure that you are using smooth, consistent hand motions to make each stroke. Strive to match each accented note's dynamic level with every other accented note and each unaccented note's dynamic level with every other unaccented note. You may also add the bass drum on every beat if that's helpful. Playing the hi-hat on beats 2 and 4 will help you maintain the 16th-note subdivision and a steady tempo. Always practice with a metronome, keep a journal of your practice tempos in order to gauge your progress, and try to increase your speed each week.

Play all of the exercises on the snare drum using the following routine:

- Play each measure eight times starting with a right stick and alternate all strokes.
- Play each measure eight times starting with a left stick and alternate all strokes.
- Play each measure once and read the exercise from beginning to end.
- Play each measure once, read the exercise from beginning to end, and move each accent to a tom of your choice (always leaving the unaccented notes on the snare).

TRACK 78

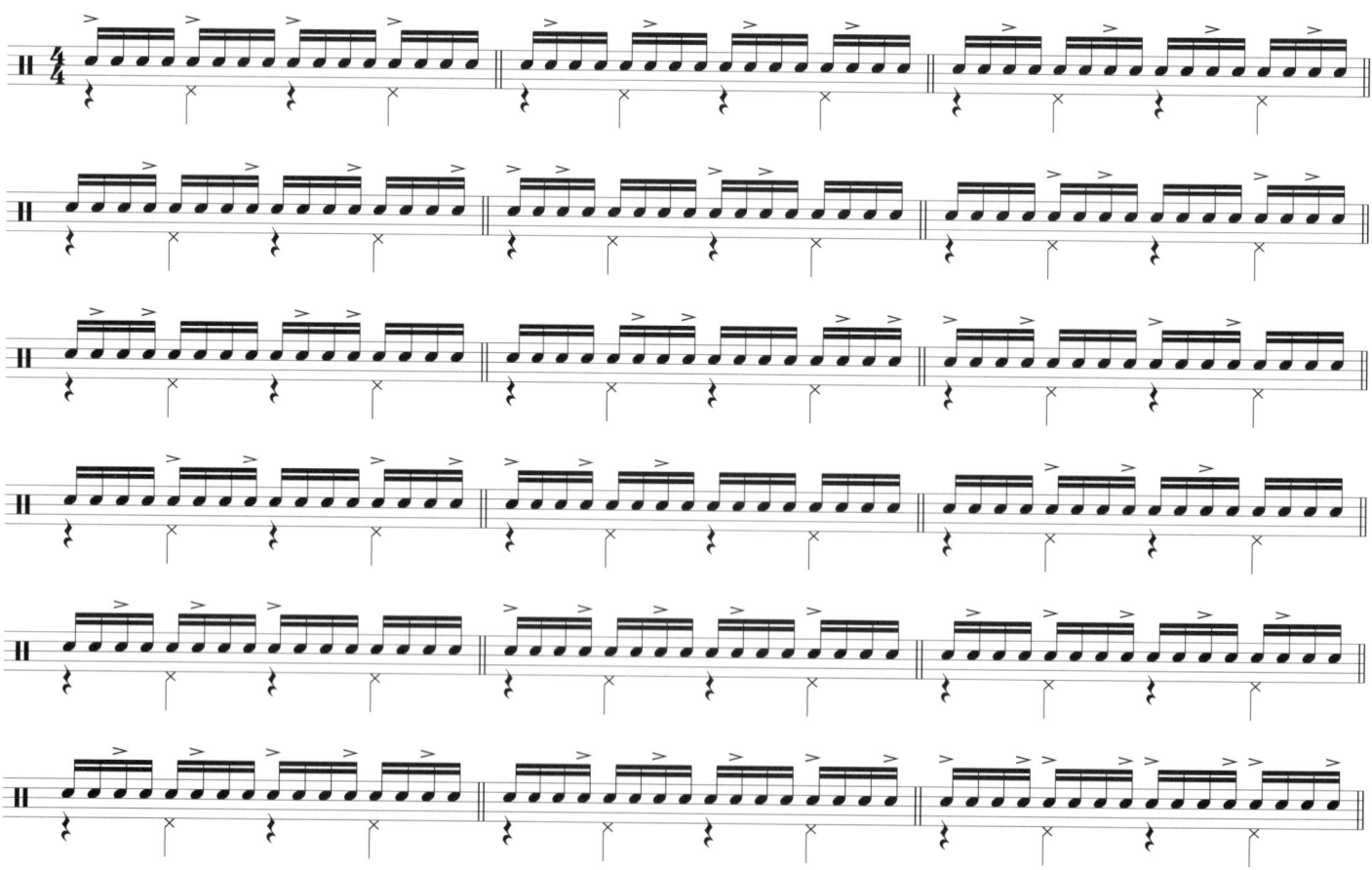

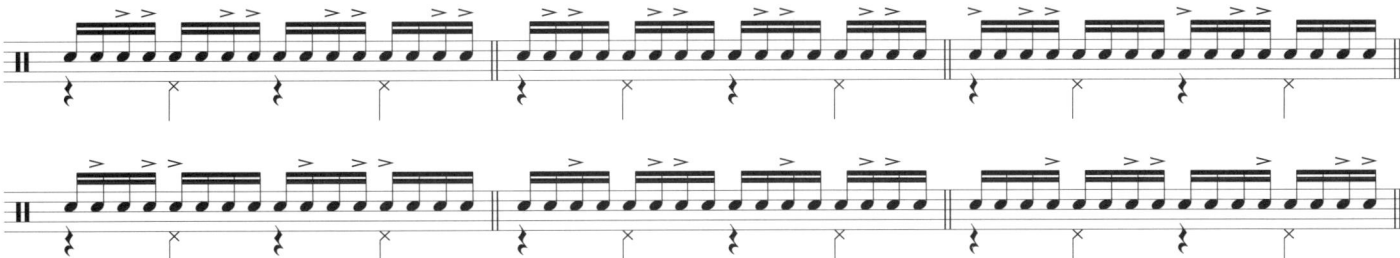

Another way to play these exercises involves an approach to sticking sometimes known as *right hand lead*. Right hand lead means that you play the strongest notes (in this case the accents) with your strongest hand (which is your right, if you're right-handed). Play the accents with only the right hand and the unaccented notes with the left hand. In cases where there are three unaccented notes in a row, you will need to alternate the strokes to return to the correct hand or play two left strokes. (Using this system, some accent patterns will have to begin with a left hand or will only have one sticking that will allow for right hand lead.) Here are some examples of right hand lead stickings:

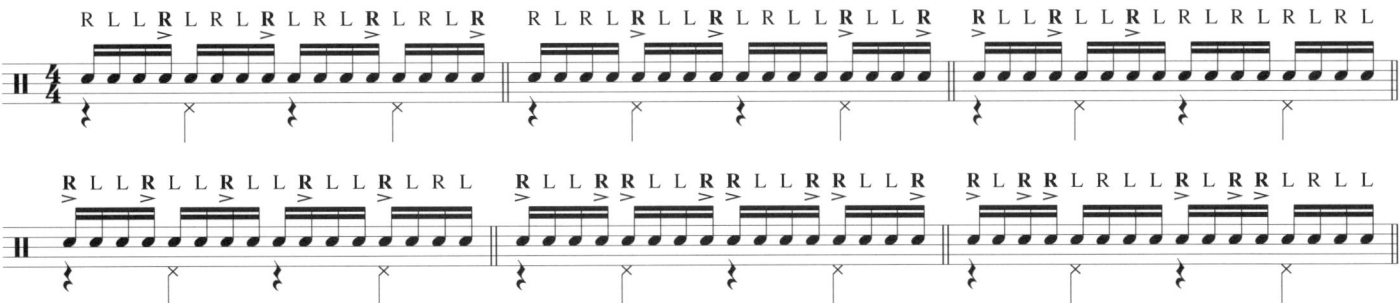

Once you have developed some ability using the right hand lead approach, move the accents onto the toms (leaving the unaccented notes always on the snare).

TRACK 79

Experiment and have fun with these exercises (develop your own sticking formulas!) and you will discover new ways to move around the drumset.

Lesson 38

Drumset Accent Study #2

The exercises in this lesson will help develop your ability to play triplet accents around the drums. They can also serve as warm-up exercises and can lead to creative soloing ideas. Remember that it's important to keep the unaccented strokes very soft and close to the head (approximately a half inch) and the accented strokes approximately eight inches off the head. As you begin practicing, look at your hands often to ensure that you are using smooth, consistent hand motions to make each stroke. All accented strokes should match one another dynamically, and all unaccented strokes should match one another dynamically. You can also add the bass drum on every beat if that's helpful. Always play the hi-hat on beats 2 and 4 (at least at first), as this will help you maintain the triplet subdivision and a steady tempo. Always practice with a metronome, keep a journal of your practice tempos in order to gauge your progress, and try to increase your speed each week.

Play all of the exercises on the snare drum using the following routine:

- Play each measure eight times starting with a right stick and alternate all strokes.
- Play each measure eight times starting with a left stick and alternate all strokes.
- Play each measure once and read the exercise from beginning to end.
- Play each measure once, read the exercise from beginning to end, and move each accent to a tom of your choice (always leaving the unaccented notes on the snare).

TRACK 80

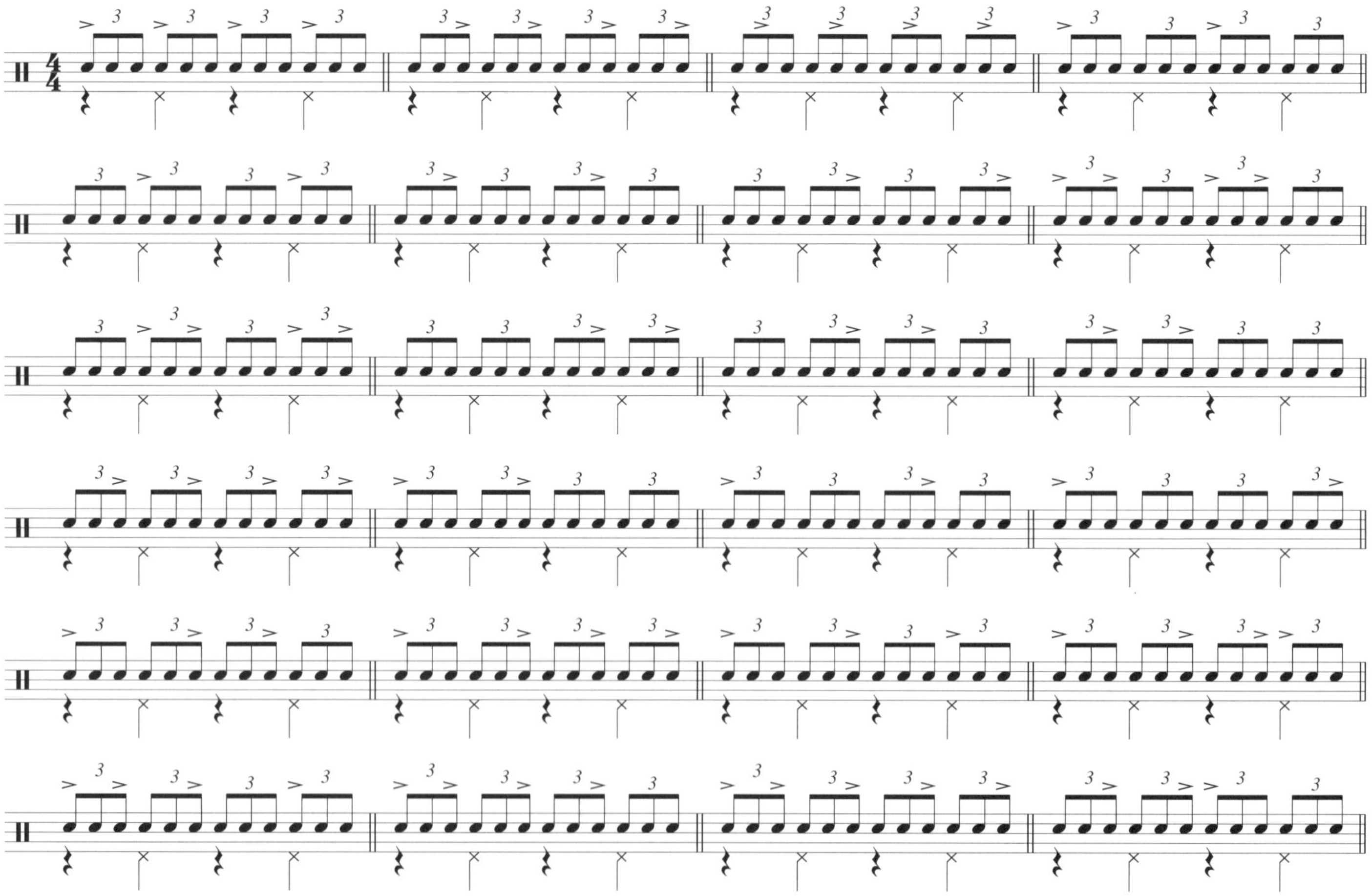

Another way to play these exercises involves an approach to sticking sometimes known as *right hand lead*. Right hand lead means that you play the strongest notes (in this case the accents) with your strongest hand (which is your right, if you're right-handed). Play the accents using only the right hand and the unaccented notes using only the left hand. In cases where there are three unaccented notes in a row, alternate the strokes to return to the correct hand or play two left strokes. Using this system, some accent patterns will have to begin with a left hand, or there will only be one sticking that creates a right hand lead outcome. Here are some examples of right hand lead sticking applications:

TRACK 81

Once you've developed some ability using the right hand lead approach, move the accents onto the toms to create new fills and solo ideas.

Lesson 39

Drumset Accent Study #3

These advanced accent studies involve accents and rudimental sticking patterns—specifically, the paradiddle and double paradiddle. Exercises 1–32 are based on the paradiddle, and are excellent warm-up exercises and technique builders, but may also be used as solo material when orchestrated around the drums. Start practicing these exercises slowly (using a metronome), repeating each exercise at least eight times before moving on. Keep the unaccented notes consistently soft to bring out the accents. Once the accents have been mastered, move the accented notes and/or the unaccented notes around to the toms for solo purposes.

TRACK 82

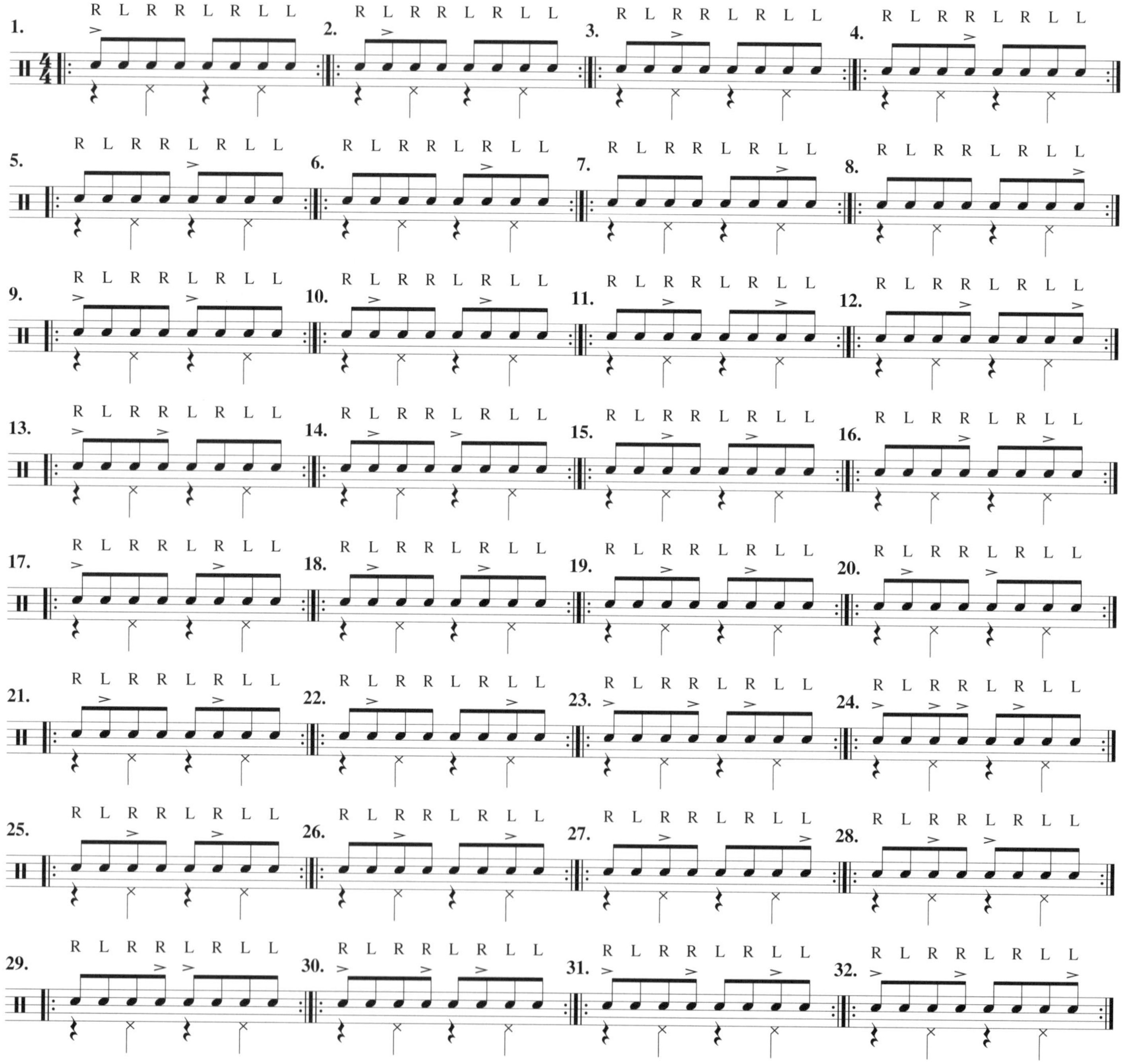

Exercises 33–48 are based on the double paradiddle. After mastering the accent patterns, move the accented and/or unaccented notes around the drums (both cymbals and toms) for more fill and solo possibilities.

TRACK 83

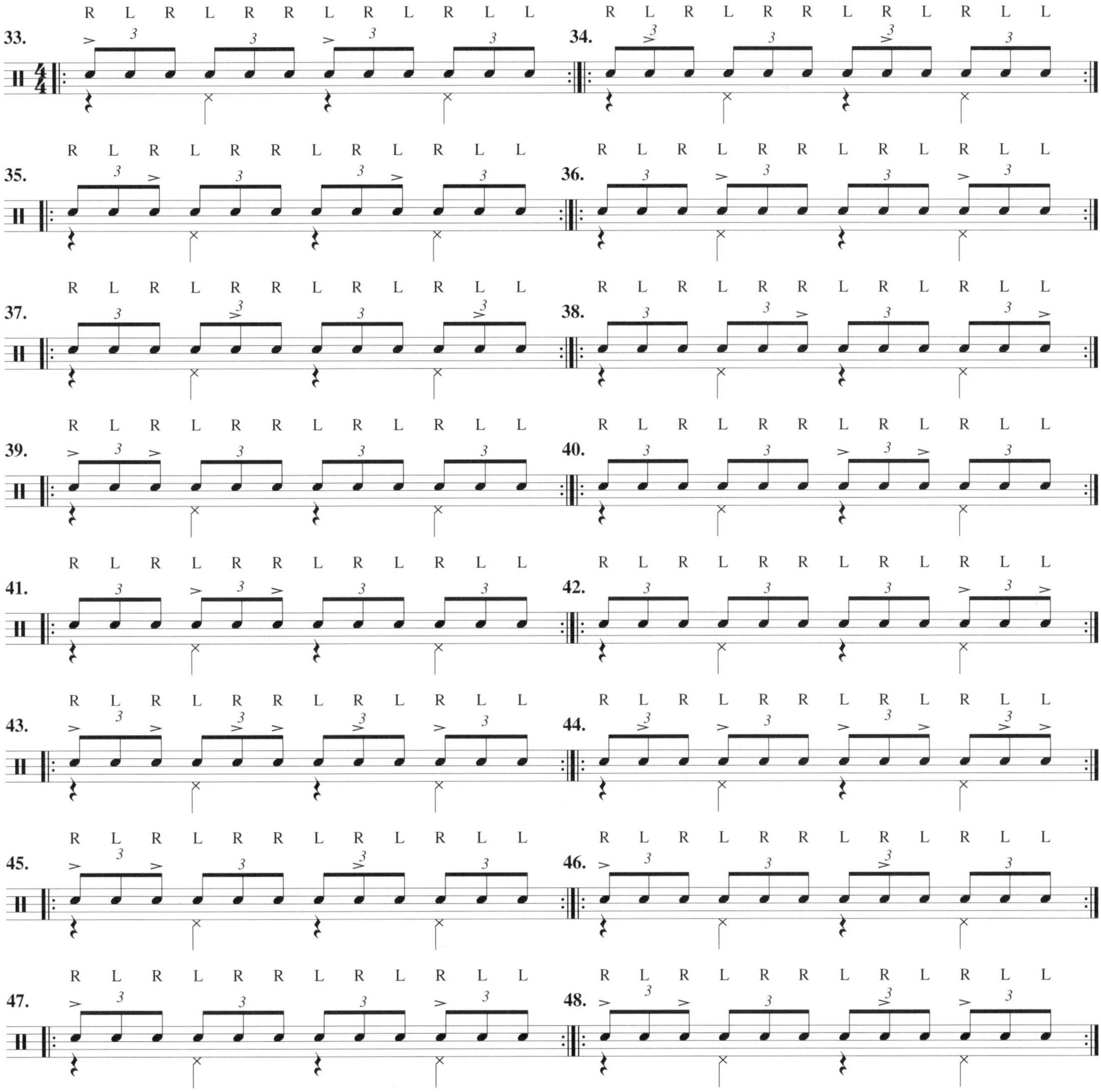

Lesson 40

Jazz "Two" Feel

In traditional jazz, there are two basic swing "feels"—known respectively as a "two" feel and a "four" feel—that drummers need to be aware of and use appropriately. Which feel to use in a given musical situation depends on several factors, including the arrangements of the song (if there is one) and/or what the bass player is playing. When the bass player is playing four even quarter notes per bar, that's a four feel (meaning four bass pulses/notes per bar), and you can play the regular jazz ride cymbal pattern:

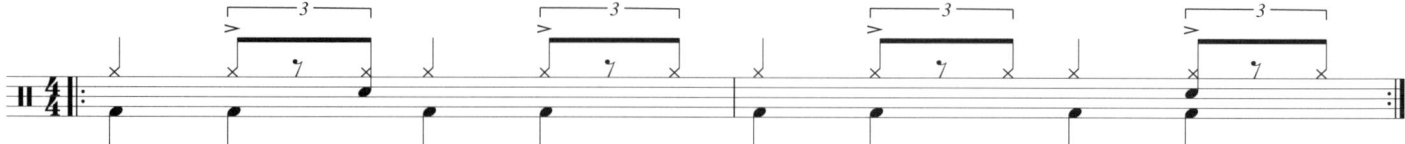

If the bass player is playing only two half notes per bar, then a two feel is more appropriate (two pulse/notes per bar, thus the name "two" feel). The traditional two feel is played on the hi-hat, using an open (or more accurately, half-open) sound on beats 1 and 3 and tightly closed hi-hat on beats 2 and 4. When creating a two feel on the hi-hat, slightly release the pressure on the hi-hat footboard just enough to allow the two cymbals to sizzle together slightly; you shouldn't actually hear the open "ping" sound of the cymbals while doing this. A two feel on hi-hat can be written several ways (see A, B, C, or D), but it basically all means the same thing.

TRACK 84

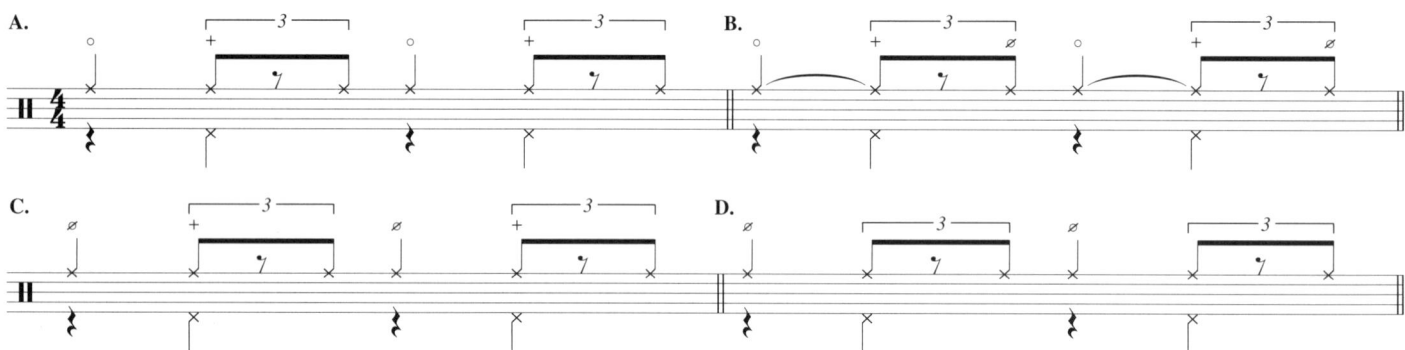

In a two feel, the bass drum is often played very softly on beats 1 and 3 (which is a technique called *feathering*). Another way to play a two feel is to play it on a completely closed hi-hat, like this…

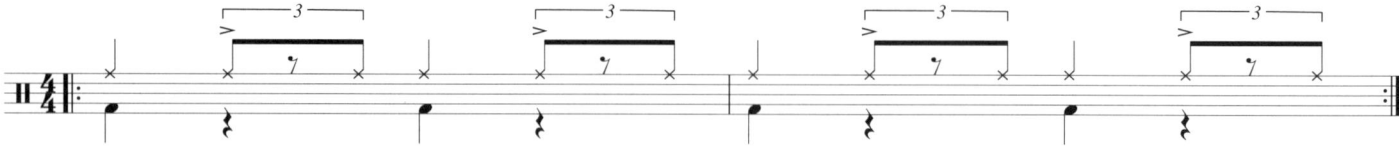

…or on the ride cymbal, like this:

A very common approach for traditional jazz tunes is to change from a two feel to a four feel as the tune progresses. The decision to change from two to four may be pre-arranged or may be made spontaneously on the bandstand. The change of feels never occurs in the middle of a phrase, so a good time to anticipate a change from two to four is at the beginning of a chorus, at the B section of a song (if there is one), when a soloist indicates it through their solo intensity, or when a new soloist begins. For example, in the standard 32-bar AABA jazz form (shown here), the melody is often played using this format: the first two A sections in a two feel, the B section (the bridge) in a four feel, and the last A section in a two feel again.

TRACK 85

In the older, more traditional style of swing, the bass player almost always plays half notes during a two feel. Starting in the 1960s, however, bass players started adding additional notes to create more rhythmic energy while still emphasizing beats 1 and 3. In reaction to this "new" way of playing a two feel, drummers started to change the way they played a two feel by constantly varying the ride pattern (while still trying to emphasize beats 1 and 3). The non-repetitive way of playing the ride cymbal became known as "breaking up the time," "breaking up the ride pattern," or "playing a broken feel." Here is an example of one way to play a "broken two feel."

TRACK 86

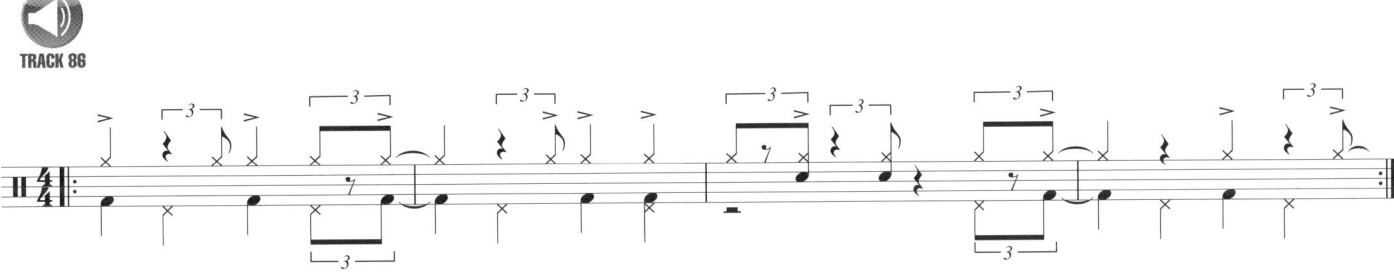

This is one way to play a two feel using brushes. In this example, the right hand plays beat 1, the "and" of beat 2, 3, and the "and" of beat 4, while the left hand provides the "swish" sound by making a circle with an accent on beats 2 and 4.

TRACK 87

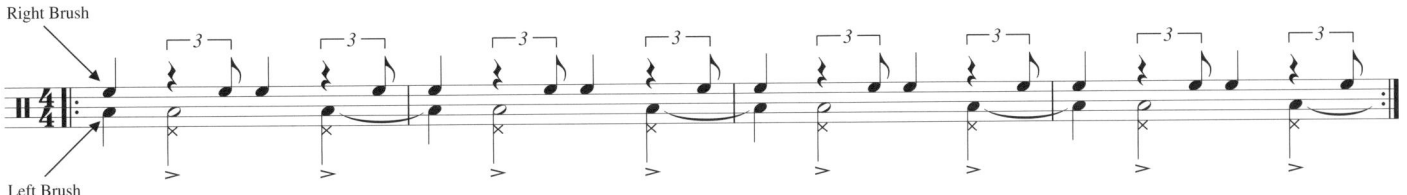

Often the bass player will signal their intention to change from two to four by playing quarter notes a few bars before an important point in the tune (the beginning of a chorus, the bridge, soloist change, change of energy in a solo, etc.). You also have the choice to change feels. Ways to signal your intent to change feels include playing a very obvious fill, playing the new feel a few measures before you want to change, or by visually cueing the bass player with a head nod.

Lesson 41

Basic Brush Patterns

Brushes are an important part of any drummer's "tool box," and you should know at least a few basic brush techniques. (You never know when they're going to come in handy.) Brushes were first used in jazz, so the oldest and most common brush patterns apply to it. But brushes are also common in softer, modern acoustic settings and can make playing quietly much easier. Brushes can always be substituted for sticks in low volume situations, and sometimes a fat brush backbeat is just the right sound when accompanying a singer or for a slow song.

First, let's look at a few basic brush concepts. Traditionally, the characteristic brush sound is created by the sound of the brush being swept across the drumhead, so *lateral strokes* (left to right, right to left) are the best way to achieve this sound. Matched grip can be used for brushes, but many players use traditional grip. Brushes are generally shorter than sticks, so in order to achieve the correct balance with the brush, hold the left brush as far back as possible. Hold the right brush held between the thumb and index finger with your thumb on top of the brush and the end of the brush (the ring) resting in the palm of your hand. This will enable the brush to move easily from side to side (left to right) and to achieve some rebound (bounce).

The most common use for brushes is during slow songs, or ballads. For a ballad groove, pretend the drumhead is like the face of a clock with 5:00 and 11:00 as two imaginary points. Beginning with the right hand, start at the 11:00 point, make a small counterclockwise circle with your brush (about the size of a small grapefruit) and arrive back at 11:00 on each quarter note (1, 2, 3, 4). With the left hand, start at the 5:00 point, make a small clockwise sweeping motion with your brush, and arrive back at 5:00 on each quarter note (1, 2, 3, 4). It is important to apply a little pressure and sweep the brush a little faster as you approach each "point"—this will create a slight accent and give the circle a pulse. (If you don't do this, it will all just sound like static on a radio!) Be sure to cross your right hand over your left hand to avoid collision and to keep the groove very connected and smooth. When the brush motion is comfortable, add the hi-hat on beats 2 and 4 to complete the ballad groove.

TRACK 88

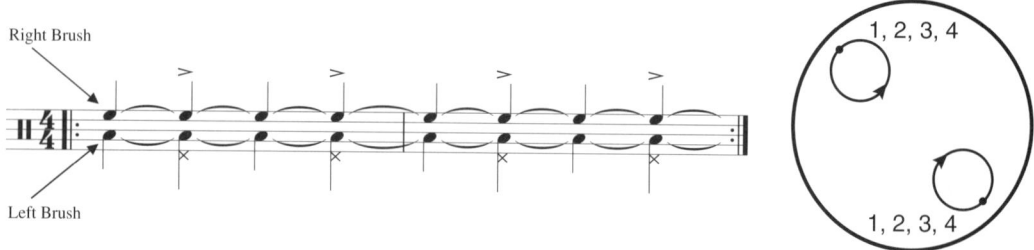

For a basic slow-to-medium tempo swing brush pattern, the left hand will make the same sweeping motion as in the ballad (above), but instead of making a circle on every beat, it now makes a circle that arrives at 5:00 only on beats 2 and 4. The right hand will play the traditional jazz ride pattern, crossing over the left hand on beats 2 and 4. In order to prevent the brushes from becoming intertwined, the right hand will play each one of the notes of the ride pattern at three different places on the head (see the diagram below). Beat 1 is at 2:00, beat 2 is at 11:00, and the "and" of 2 is at 12:00. This serves two purposes: it helps the right brush stay out of the way of the left brush, and, if done properly, it will allow you to get a slight bounce from the brush, making it easier to play.

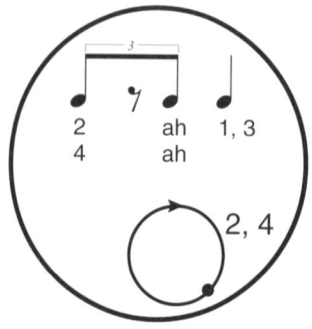

TRACK 89

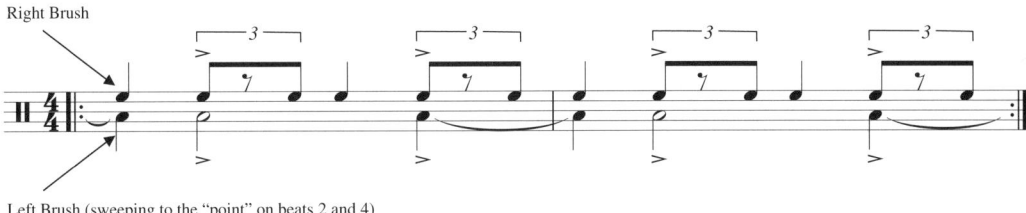

Brushes are also useful when playing a Brazilian bossa nova groove. Use a brush in the right hand and play it on the snare head while playing a cross-stick in the left hand.

TRACK 90

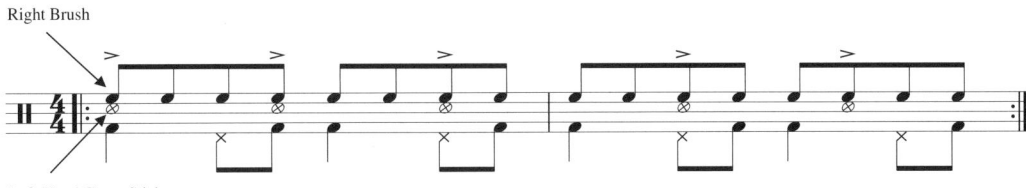

If a smoother, more legato sound is required, the right brush can be swept back and forth to create the eighth notes.

TRACK 91

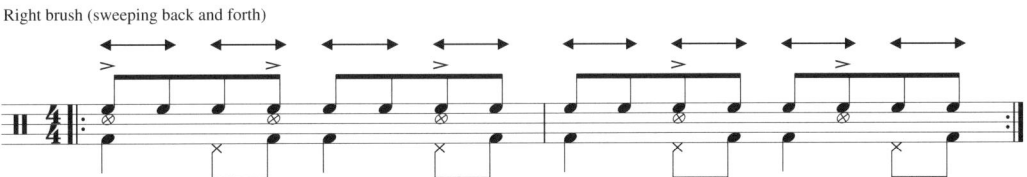

Lesson 42

Basic Brush Comping Patterns

Once you're able to play a standard swing brush pattern on the snare drum, the next step is to add some additional improvised rhythms that help support another jazz musician's solo. These rhythms are known as *comping rhythms* (an abbreviation for "accompanying" or "complementing"). When playing with sticks, comping rhythms are played on the snare drum or bass drum against the jazz ride cymbal pattern and hi-hat. When playing with brushes, basic comping rhythms are first incorporated into the basic brush timekeeping pattern. This means that the right hand will continue to play the traditional jazz ride cymbal rhythm on the snare head, while the left hand will add some comping rhythms as well as the "sweep" sound.

When playing brushes, it's helpful to imagine the surface of the snare drum as a face of a clock with the 12 numbers spaced around the circumference. The right hand will begin at the 2:00 position and play a stroke (beat one). It will then cross over the left hand and play beat 2 at the 10:00 position, followed by the "and" of 2 at the 12:00 position before playing beat 3 again at the 2:00 position. The second half of the measure repeats this sequence of motions. In example 1A/1B, the left hand adds an accent on the "and" of beat 3 as a comping rhythm. To execute this rhythm, the left hand starts at the 10:00 position, makes a clockwise circle that arrives at the 5:00 position (on beat 2), and continues the circle back around to the 10:00 position (for beat 3). It then lifts momentarily to prepare for the accent on the "and" of beat 3 before continuing to sweep across the head to the 5:00 point (for beat 4). The left brush continues the clockwise sweeping motion back to the 10:00 position to prepare for the next measure.

Examples 1A and 1B are exactly the same exercise. Example 1A illustrates each hand motion, while Example 1B illustrates a composite version of how it might be notated.

TRACK 92

Examples 2A and 2B illustrate how to add two 16th-note triplet comping notes into the time feel.

TRACK 93

Examples 3A and 3B illustrate how to integrate a four-stroke comping figure (starting on the "and" of beat 3) into the basic swing brush pattern.

TRACK 94

Another comping approach is to use accents. In order to accent any beat or any offbeat (the "and" of any beat), you can momentarily switch to this brush pattern. In this pattern, the right hand starts at the 10:00 position and sweeps in quarter notes on the beat. The left hand starts at 5:00 and sweeps quarter notes on the "ands" of the beat. Also, this time the eighth notes are written straight, but a swing indication is included at the top of the exercise, telling you to swing all the notated eighth notes—a commonly used notation device.

TRACK 95

Once you've mastered Example 4, you can now execute any combination of comping accent patterns either on the beat (using the right brush) or off the beat (the "ands" using the left brush). Example 5 illustrates one possible pattern. Beat 1 is a right brush accent, and the "and" of beat 2 is a left brush accent. Use this brush pattern and accent concept to create your own comping patterns.

TRACK 96

Lesson 43

Jazz Waltz

A jazz waltz is in 3/4 time but is different than a traditional waltz. For a jazz waltz, drummers normally play the first three beats of the traditional jazz ride cymbal as the basic beat and the hi-hat on beat 2. (Playing the hi-hat on beats 2 and 3 often sounds too much like an old-fashioned waltz.)

In a jazz waltz, drummers normally improvise snare drum and bass drum rhythms—a technique known as *comping*—while the ride cymbal and hi-hat parts stay constant. In performances, drummers normally mix and match rhythmic comping patterns similar to Exercises 1–20. Practice each one of the following exercises as a two-bar phrase—one bar with just ride cymbal and hi-hat followed by the exercise bar in order to develop a sense of space between each comping idea and the overall time flow.

TRACK 97

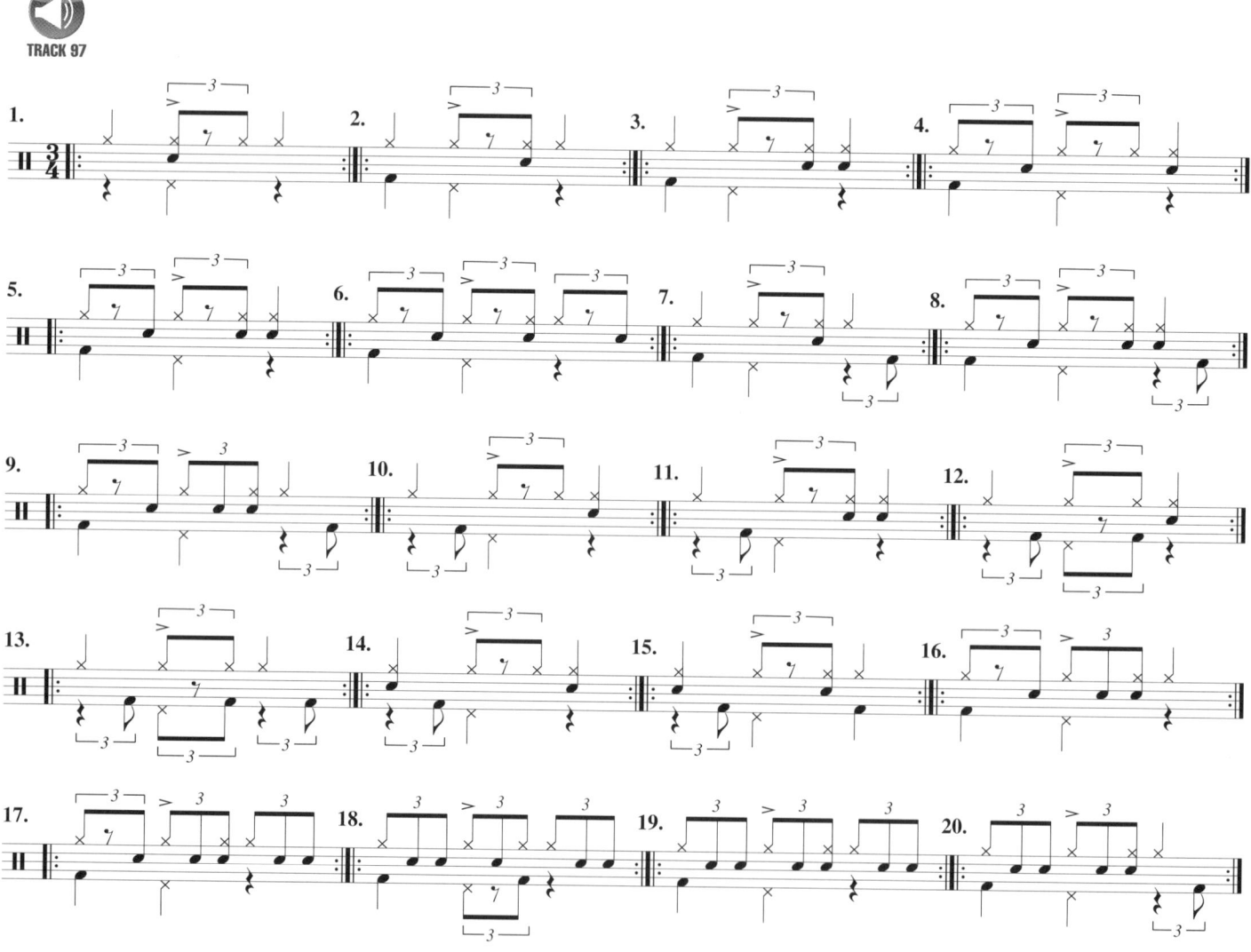

Exercises 1–20 are the patterns you may use when the bass player plays a strong accent on beat 1 (and possibly a few other notes later in the bar). This is known as "playing in a one feel." In many jazz tunes, however, the bass player will eventually change the feel by playing three quarter notes in each bar—known as a "walking bass line," or, in this case, "playing in a three feel." When the bass player walks a bass line, the ride cymbal may be changed to three even quarter notes on the ride cymbal with comping figures on the snare drum and bass drum. Exercise 21 is an example of this approach.

TRACK 98

21.

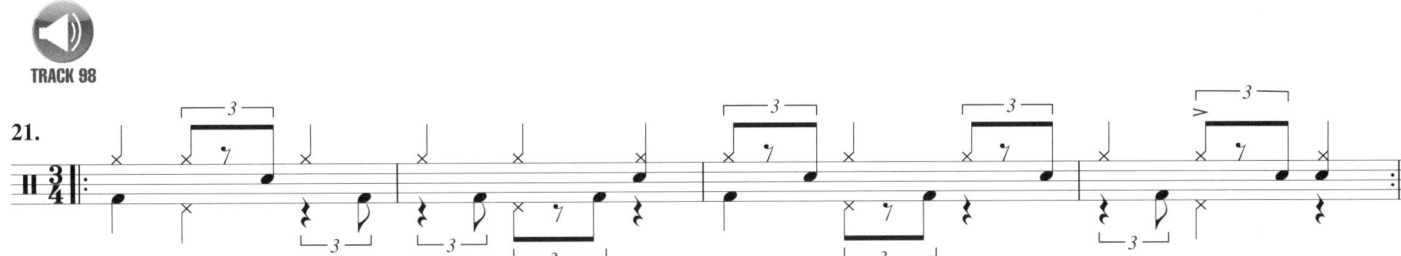

Exercises 22–26 are examples of some common fill-like groove variations between the ride cymbal and bass drum that help break up the monotony of endlessly repeating the same ride cymbal pattern. The snare drum rhythms may also be played on the toms (occasionally) for more variety.

TRACK 99

22.

23.

24.

25.

26.

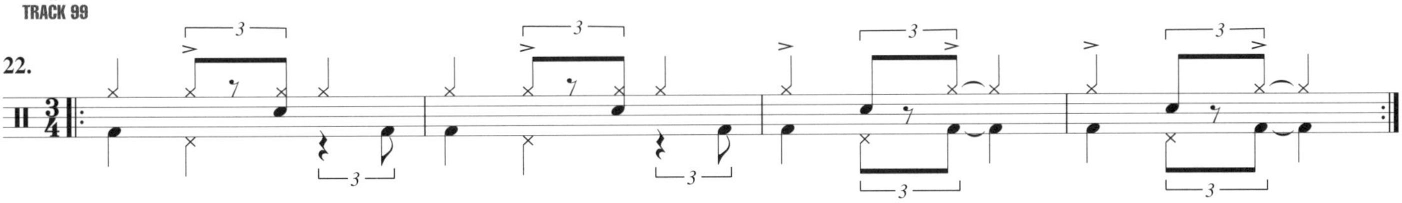

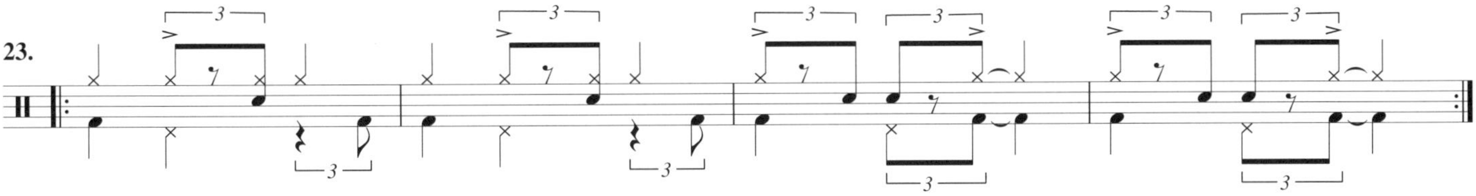

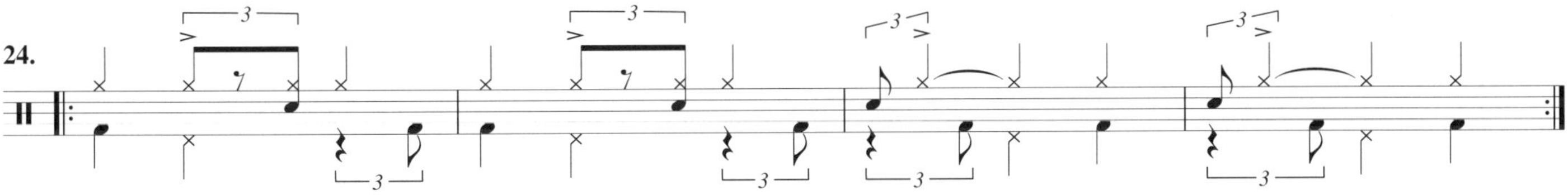

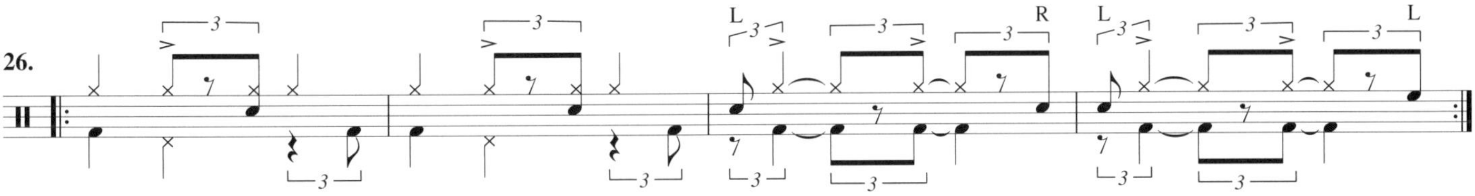

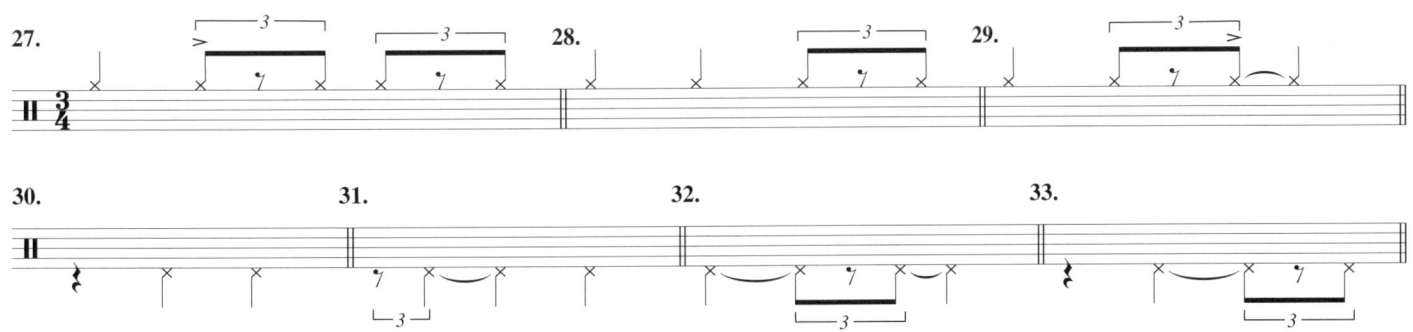

More variations and technically challenging exercises may be created by playing the previous exercises (1–26) with different combinations of ride cymbal patterns and/or hi-hat patterns found here:

27.

28.

29.

30.

31.

32.

33.

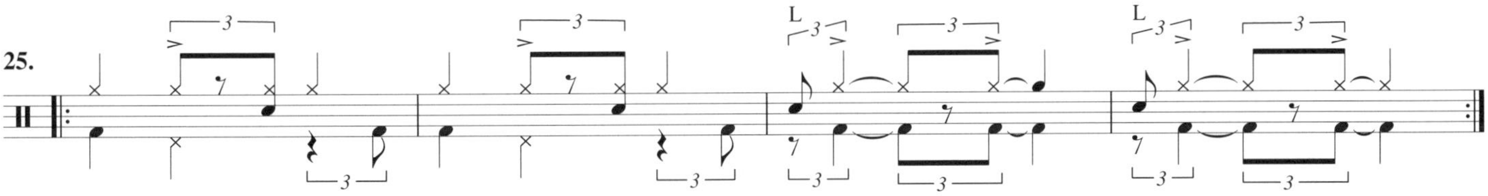

Lesson 44

Jazz Waltz Fills

After mastering some of the basics of playing a jazz waltz, the next step is to learn to integrate some fills into the musical phrases. Jazz waltzes normally use triplet-based beat subdivisions, so most of the fills will involve triplets.

These exercises are written in four-bar phrases to simulate how you will use the fills in real musical settings. Practice with a metronome on all three beats in each bar. When you become comfortable playing in 3/4 time, set the metronome to sound only on beat 1 of each bar, starting somewhere in the 40–60 beats per minute (BPM) range.

When practicing the following exercises, try these suggestions:

- The first three bars of each exercise only show the ride cymbal and hi-hat part. Practice as written and then practice comping on the snare drum and bass drum during first three bars of each exercise.

- Substitute a crash cymbal on beat 1 of each four-bar exercise (the beginning of each line).

- Try different stickings in each exercise to decide what works best for you or to create new phrasing ideas.

- Move the fills around the drums (which may require using a new or different sticking).

- Practice the exercises at various tempos, from slow to fast, in order to be ready for any musical situation.

TRACK 100

Listen to jazz drummers such as Max Roach, "Philly Joe" Jones, Elvin Jones, Art Taylor, Art Blakey, Jimmy Cobb, Paul Motian, Tony Williams, Jack DeJohnette, Adam Nussbaum, Bill Stewart, and others for more ideas about jazz waltz fills.

Lesson 45

Advanced Jazz Waltz Concepts

Once the basics of playing a jazz waltz have been mastered, more challenging concepts can be explored. The following advanced exercises will develop a deeper sense of independence and better reading skills when playing jazz waltzes.

To apply these exercises, select a ride cymbal pattern from the examples below (Examples 1–8), and then pair it with a hi-hat pattern (Examples 9–16) and a bass drum pattern (Examples 17–28). Then read the exercise on the next page for the snare drum. The reading exercise may also be played on the bass drum or by alternating the rhythms between the snare drum and bass drum.

TRACK 102

Reading Exercise (♫ = ♩♪)

Lesson 46

3/4 Brushes

Playing brushes in 3/4 time is similar to playing with sticks in 3/4 time—simply start by thinking of it as "4/4 time minus one beat." Example 1 is a basic 3/4 brush groove that will work in many situations because it stresses the quarter-note pulse and relies on the use of the hi-hat and accents to identify the meter as 3/4 time. With this groove, you have several options with the hi-hat and the accent pattern. You could play the hi-hat on either beat 2 or beats 2 and 3. The accent may be played on all three beats evenly or just beats 2 and 3, depending upon the situation.

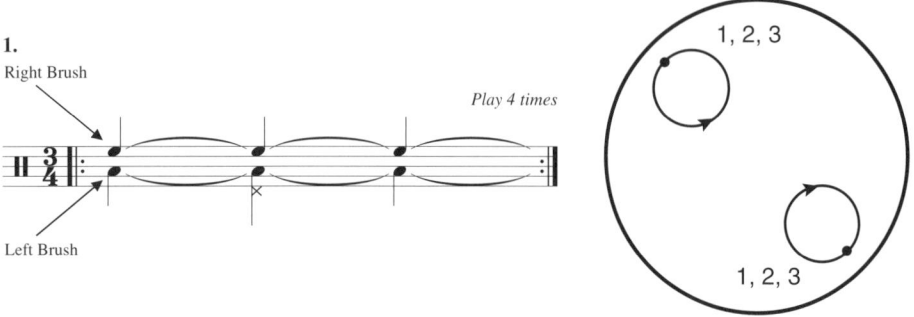

When working with brushes, it's helpful to think of the drum head as the face of a clock, with the 12 numbers spaced around the edge. For a basic 3/4 swing pattern, play the first three beats of the jazz ride cymbal pattern with the right hand, beginning at the 2:00 position on the drum head on beat 1, beat 2 at 11:00, the "ah" of beat 2 at 12:00, and beat 3 at 2:00. The left hand starts at the 11:00 position, first making a small circle on beat 1 (called the "loop") that returns to the 11:00 point, followed by a bigger circle that sweeps to the 5:00 point on beat 2. The left hand then completes the circle on beat 3 back at 11:00. The brush never leaves the surface of the head nor does it stop moving throughout the whole groove; it simply arrives at these different points (11:00 and 5:00) in tempo.

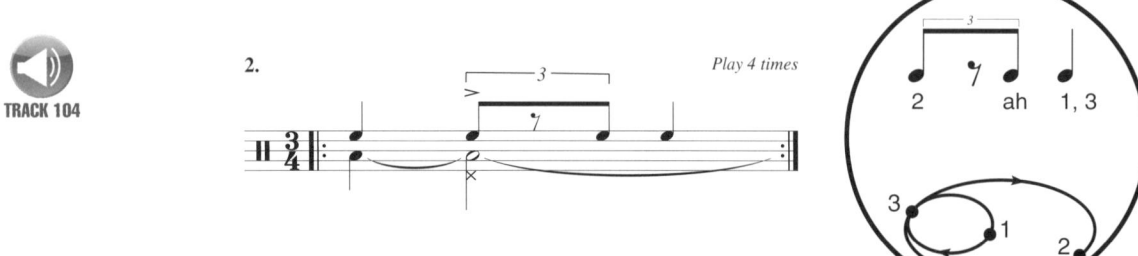

For fast 3/4 swing tempos, try "splitting" the ride pattern between the two hands. In this case, the right hand will play only three notes: beat 1, the "and" of beat 2, and beat 3 (starting the pattern on beat 1 each time at the 2:00 position on the drum head). The right hand will cross over the left hand momentarily to play the "and" of beat 2 and beat 3, then return to the 2:00 point to begin the next measure. Starting at 11:00, the left hand will play one large circle that accents only beat 2 (but keeps sweeping throughout the entire measure). Beats 1 and 3 are always at the 2:00 position, while the "and" of beat 2 is at the 11:00 position (crossed over the left hand).

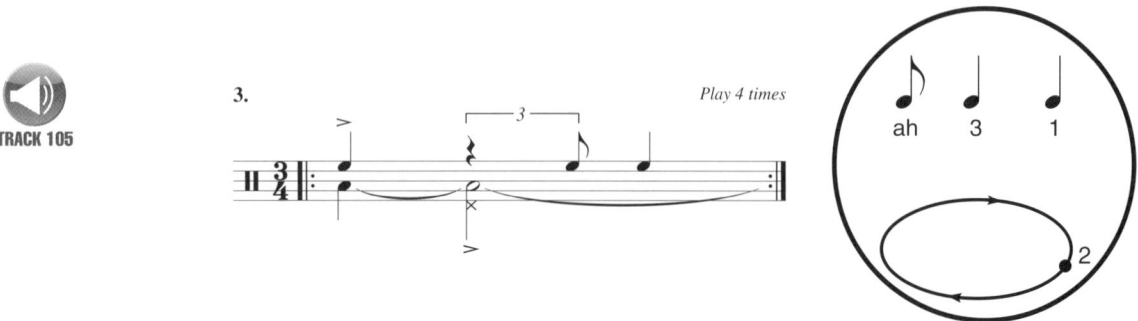

Example 4 is a 3/4 pattern that makes use of eighth notes to create a "busy" 3/4 brush pattern. Both hands play eighth notes using small circles; the right hand makes counterclockwise circles on the beat (starting at 11:00), while the left hand makes clockwise circles off the beat (on the "ands," starting at 5:00). They play simultaneously to create a constant eighth-note pulse that can be used as a groove (Example 4) or as fill material by varying the accents (Examples 5–7).

TRACK 106

Lesson 47

Basic Soloing Concepts

In order to play a good drum solo, it helps to know about what *makes* a good solo. A good solo should be musical, somewhat organized, interesting for the audience, and should fulfill a function. When you first began soloing, your solos probably sounded disorganized and random. Good drummers know how to put together a solo that makes musical sense by organizing it, having the solo develop (often from simple to complex), having several ideas that relate to one another, etc. Here are some basic soloing concepts and ways to apply them.

One of the best ways to organize a solo is to use the same melodic material/idea several times, which is known as *repetition*. Repetition is used in all musical styles (to create melodies as well as solos) and helps an audience recognize a musical idea.

Using repetition during a solo is important, but merely repeating the same unchanged idea several times might become boring and predictable. (Think of a person saying the same sentence over and over again!) So it's often necessary to have some other ways to develop your musical ideas.

One way to organize a solo using repetition is to start with a one-bar idea on the snare drum and repeat it on some other drums. This example shows a one-bar idea (the first bar) that moves to the rack tom, back to the snare, and finally to the floor tom:

TRACK 107

The fact that you are repeating the same rhythm of the first measure in each of the following measures instantly makes the solo seem more organized. You may also re-use the rhythm of the idea but vary the pitches (which drums) you play, like this:

TRACK 108

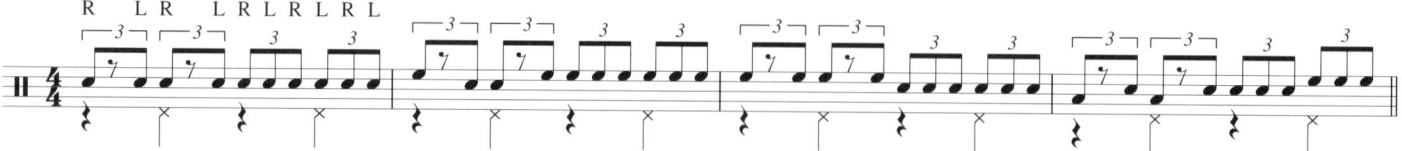

Another way to organize a solo is to take a piece of your first idea, or a *fragment*, and repeat that fragment later in your solo. This is known as *fragmentation*. It is important to select a fragment that stands out as somehow unique or different from other parts of the solo idea, like this:

TRACK 109

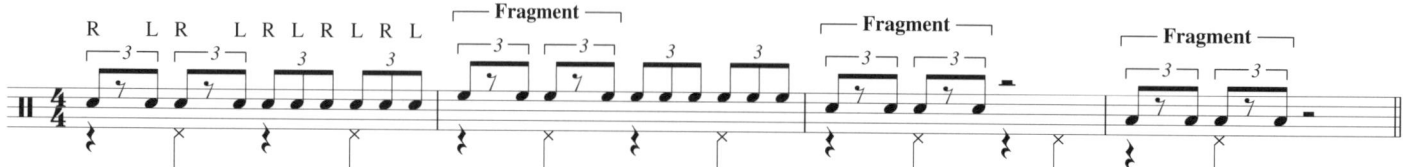

Playing an idea and then playing it backwards—a concept known as *retrograde*—is another soloing approach. (Not every idea can be used in this way, so it takes some practice and thought about how to play an idea forward and how it will work to play it backward.) In this example, the solo idea moves from the snare to the rack tom and ends on the floor tom (twice). Then it moves backwards from the floor tom to the rack tom and the snare.

TRACK 110

Another common solo concept is to repeat the idea starting on a different beat in a subsequent bar—a concept known as *rhythmic displacement*. This works well most of the time, but in some cases, the last part of the solo idea will often need to be shortened in order to fit into the phrase. Notice that the last time the idea is played, it only contains three beats in order to fit into the four-bar phrase.

TRACK 111

These concepts may be applied to any style of music—rock, funk, jazz, Afro-Cuban, hip-hop, or others. In order to practice these concepts in an organized context, practice them in the context of trading fours—four bars of any groove followed by four bars of a solo. Use this play-along track to practice using your own ideas.

PLAY-ALONG
TRACK 112

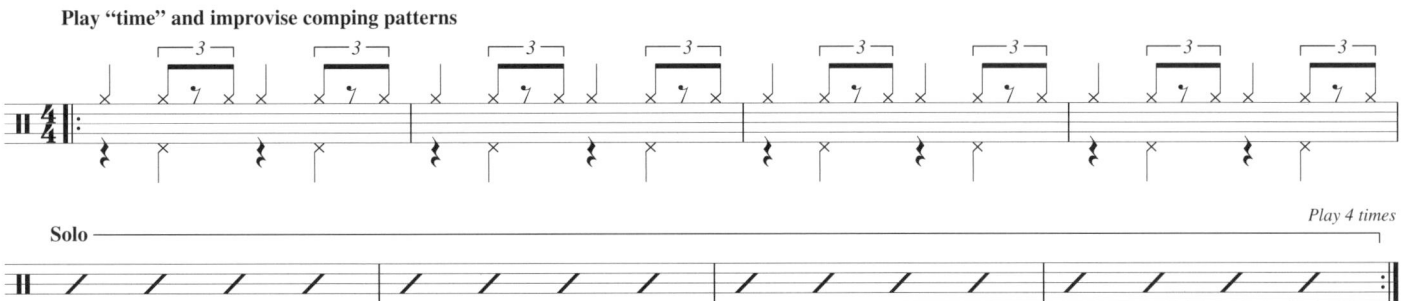

Keep in mind that not every one of these soloing concepts will work with every solo idea, so it's important to work with each of your solo ideas to know how they can be changed or developed during a solo. Mastering and combining these four concepts with different solo material will produce an infinite number of solo ideas and more organized-sounding solos.

Lesson 48

Basic Trading Fours

The term "trading fours" refers to the alternating four-bar solo sections that take place between a drummer and another instrumentalist in jazz tunes. This practice developed in 1940s bebop jazz as a way for the drummer to have some solo opportunities.

To understand trading fours, it's necessary to know about the form of the tune the band is playing. The most common song form used in jazz is the 32-bar AABA form. This means that there are 32 bars divided into four eight-bar phrases. The phrases are referred to as A-A-B-A because the first, second, and fourth (the A sections) are usually the same or similar (melodically or harmonically) to one another, whereas the B section (sometimes referred to as the *bridge*) is somehow different. The band uses this 32-bar form as the basis for their performance and will repeat it many times to create a song. This is how an AABA form would be organized into four eight-bar phrases:

If you listen to a traditional jazz tune from the '40s, '50s, or '60s, it will probably follow this format:

- Melody (or "head")
- Solos (e.g., sax, piano, bass)
- Possibly trading fours between a soloist (or soloists) and drummer
- Melody

If trading fours takes place, it's customary for an instrumentalist to play the first four bars of the phrase and let the drummer solo on the second half. If you were playing a typical 32-bar jazz tune, this is how trading fours would fit into the 32-bar format:

In many cases, the idea to trade fours between the drummer and a soloist is decided spontaneously on the bandstand. Often an instrumentalist (say, a pianist) will play four bars and then stop; this is the drummer's indication that trading fours is now taking place. The decision may also be made during rehearsals (if there is time to rehearse), and in this case, the drummer should be prepared for trading fours to take place.

The ability to keep track of how many bars you've played during your solo is important, and the ability to count four bars while soloing is critical to successfully trading fours. If you lose track of how long you've been soloing, you may stop your solo too soon or too late. When you're beginning to practice trading fours, you should also practice counting the four bars of "time" (the jazz ride cymbal pattern) followed by your four-bar solo. Count the four-bar phrases by saying the number of the bar you're playing instead of "1" every time—e.g., **1**-2-3-4, **2**-2-3-4, **3**-2-3-4, **4**-2-3-4.

When starting out, you'll need some basic raw material that you can mix and match in a variety of settings. The following examples are simple, triplet-based ideas for trading fours. Play them as written first, but then begin moving these rhythms around the drums (toms and cymbals) to create some variety. Continue to play the hi-hat during your solo to help keep a steady tempo.

TRACK 113

Now that you have some experience trading fours, here's a play-along track that you can use to practice in a realistic setting (i.e., with a band):

PLAY-ALONG
TRACK 114

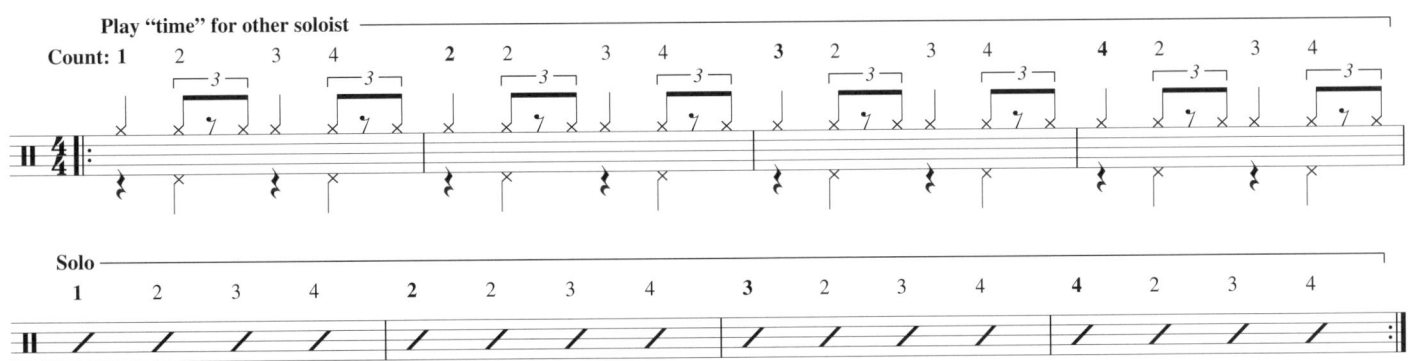

Listen to recordings of Max Roach, Art Blakey, and "Philly Joe" Jones for more solo ideas.

Lesson 49

Trading Eights

Like trading fours, trading eights is a term used to describe an approach to soloing on a jazz tune that involves alternating eight-bar solo phrases back and forth between an instrumentalist and a drummer.

Learning to trade fours, eights, or any other sized phrase is a gradual, long-term project. You should become proficient at trading fours before moving on to trading eights because the concepts you learn and the abilities you develop while trading fours (e.g., being able to count the number of bars you're playing while soloing) will help you when you start trading eights.

When trading eights, it's important to understand a few things about the form of the tune you are playing. In a standard 32-bar jazz tune with an AABA form, a soloist (typically a sax, piano, bass, or other melodic instrument) would solo during the first A section, drums would solo in the second A section, another instrumentalist would solo in the B section (often referred to as the *bridge* of a tune), and the drums would solo in the last A section, like this:

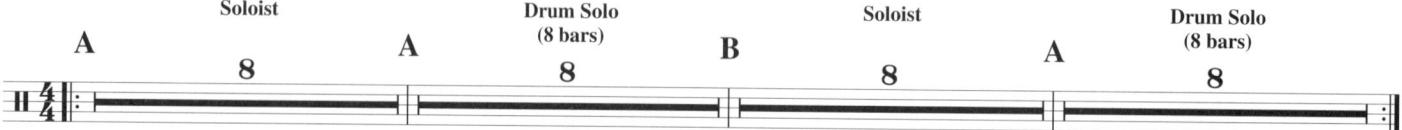

This trading back and forth may continue several times through the form of the tune, with each time through the form referred to as a "chorus." There can be an unlimited number of trading eight choruses in any one tune, time permitting. When first starting to trade eights, you might discover that eight bars seems like a long time to solo. (You're right!) Instead of thinking about soloing for eight bars, trying thinking of the eight bars as two four-bar solos joined together (in other words, two sets of trading fours). This should make it easier.

Another important concept to learn about swing music and trading eights is the interpretation of eighth notes. Transcribed examples of jazz solos use a special kind of notation interpretation when writing swing music. Groups of two eighth notes are not played as two evenly spaced notes (as they would be in rock music) but are played as the first and third parts of a triplet.

In a swing setting, for example, a measure written like this:

…would be interpreted (played) like this:

Eighth-note swing passages written with an eighth rest on the beat, like this…

…will be interpreted like this; the eighth note on the "and" of the beat will be the played on the third part of the triplet:

In the future, whenever eighth notes are written in a swing-style tune, interpret them as the first and third parts of a triplet. This interpretation concept is often referred to as *swing eighth notes* or *swung eighth notes*. This is usually not written anywhere on the music; it is assumed that a jazz drummer (or other instrumentalist) should know how to properly interpret rhythms in a jazz setting.

This example of trading eights shows how a solo can be constructed using two four-bar phrases (with swung eighth notes):

TRACK 115

Try these suggestions when trading eights:

- Count the number of bars you've played (**1**-2-3-4, **2**-2-3-4, etc.) to keep track of where you are in the form.

- Always play the eight bars of "time" when practicing trading eights—even if you're alone. This will eventually help you intuitively "feel" how long eight bars of time last.

- Try to play the hi-hat on beats 2 and 4 throughout the solo; it helps to keep the tempo steady and lets the band know what beat you are on.

- Use a metronome (with the click on beats 2 and 4, where the hi-hat plays) as a reference when practicing by yourself.

- Don't limit yourself to just drums during your trading eights. Use cymbals to create a sense of variety, for a change in sound, and as a way to play sustained notes.

Use this play-along exercise to practice trading eights:

PLAY-ALONG
TRACK 116

99

Soloing on a 12-Bar Blues

Another common song form found in jazz is the blues. The term "blues" can have many meanings (depending on the context), but in a traditional jazz setting, it usually refers to a 12-bar form that is repeated over and over again.

Blues tunes often contain lyrics and instrumental solos and generally follow this format:

- Melody (with or without lyrics)
- Many instrumental solos
- Melody (with or without lyrics)

The standard blues is a 12-bar chord progression (or pattern) that is made up of three four-bar phrases. You've probably heard a 12-bar blues already without even being aware of it. The blues chord progression uses Roman numerals to represent different chords based on a specific scale and starting note. Here is what a standard blues looks like written out using chord symbols and Roman numerals.

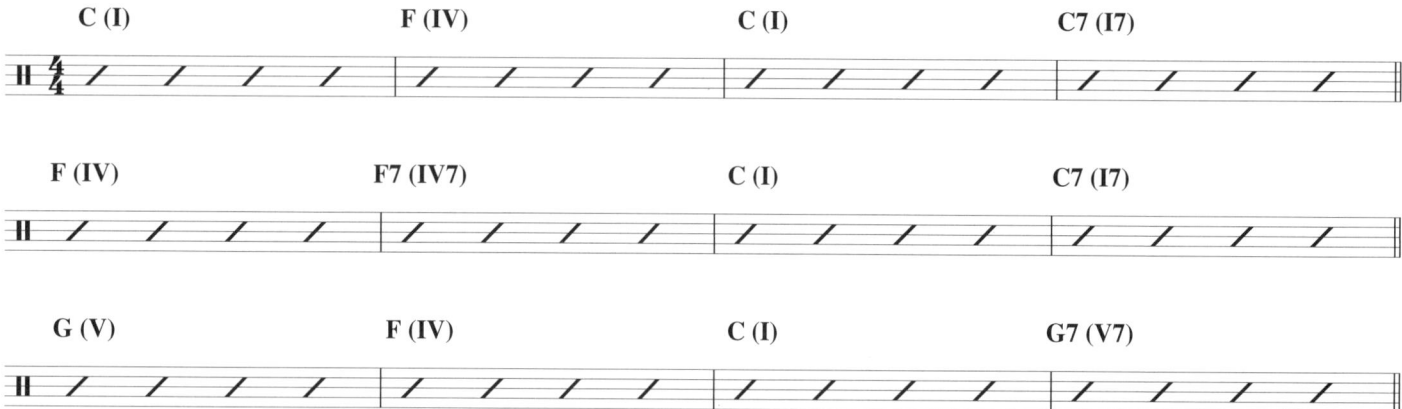

In terms of what to play on the drums during a 12-bar solo, it would be similar to what you might play during trading fours or trading eights, so you can use some of the same "licks" or patterns when soloing on a 12-bar blues. In order to help keep track of how many bars you have played during your solo, begin by thinking of the 12-bar blues form as three four-bar sections. At first, it might be a good idea to "mark off" the four-bar sections with a crash cymbal on the downbeat of each, like this:

TRACK 117

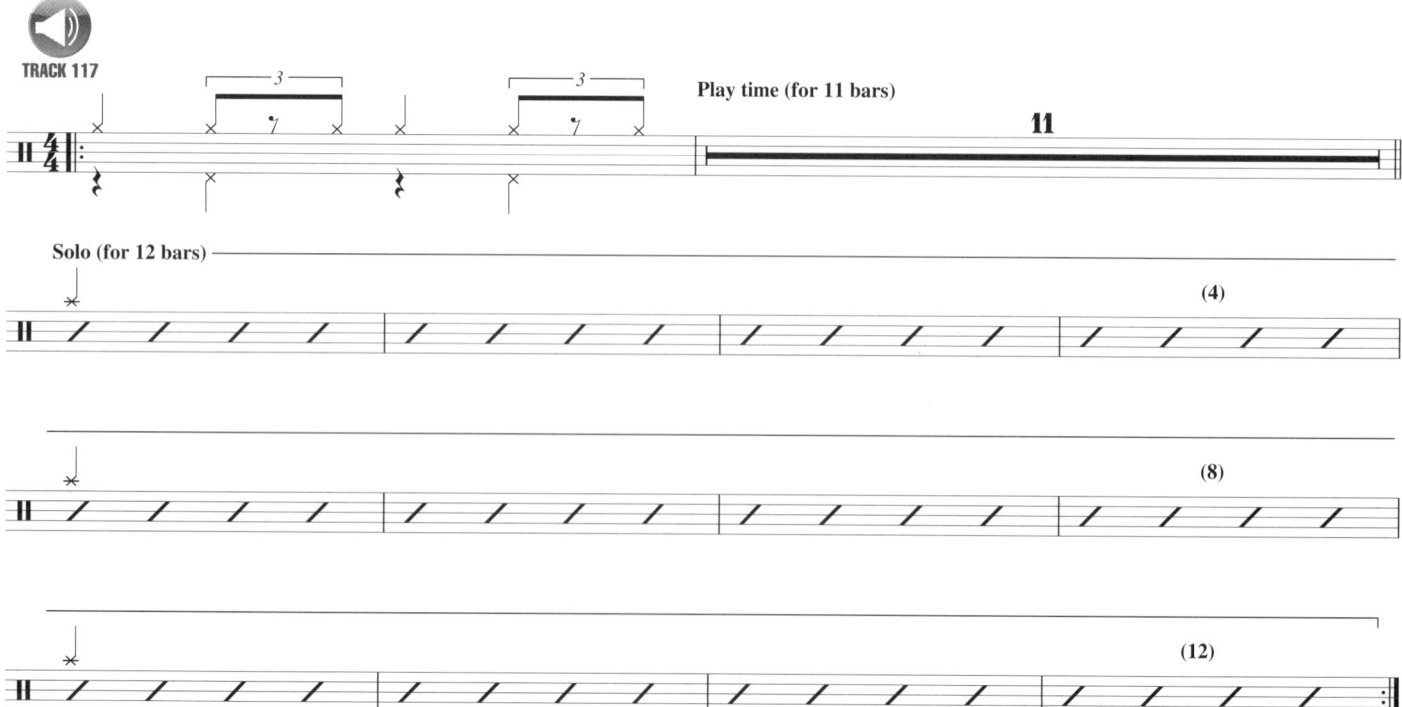

Use this play-along track to practice trading 12-bar choruses with a swing feel:

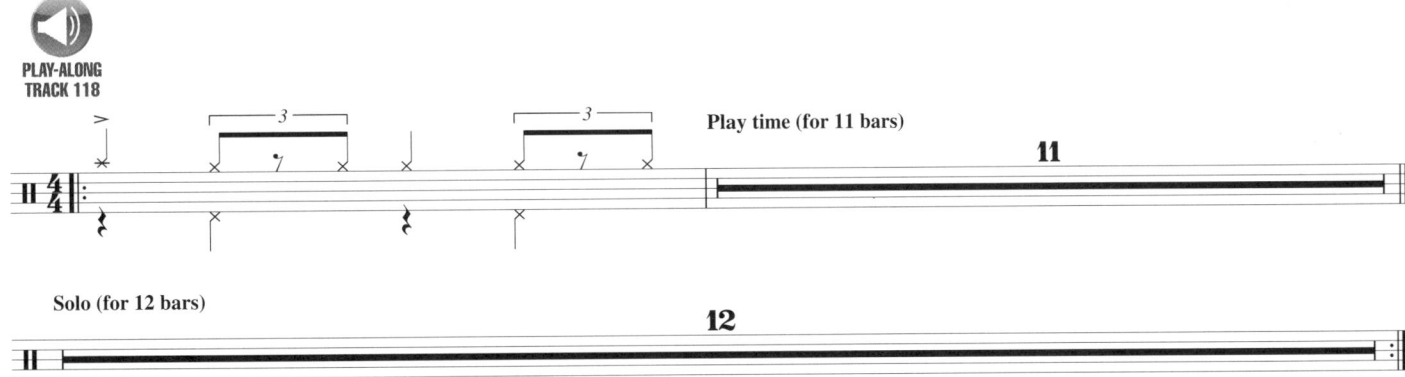

Today, blues can be played with either a swing feel or a straight eighth-note rock feel. Use this play-along track to practice trading 12-bar choruses on a straight eighth-note rock feel:

When soloing over a 12-bar blues, playing one time through the 12-bar form is called a *chorus*. Drummers often solo many times through the form, and this is known as "taking a few choruses."

Use this play-along track to practice soloing for two 12-bar choruses in a row with a swing feel. At first, you'll find it challenging to keep your place and return to the form with the rest of the band; this will take practice and experience. (During this play-along track, the piano and bass will play on the downbeat of every four bars to help you keep your place during your solo.)

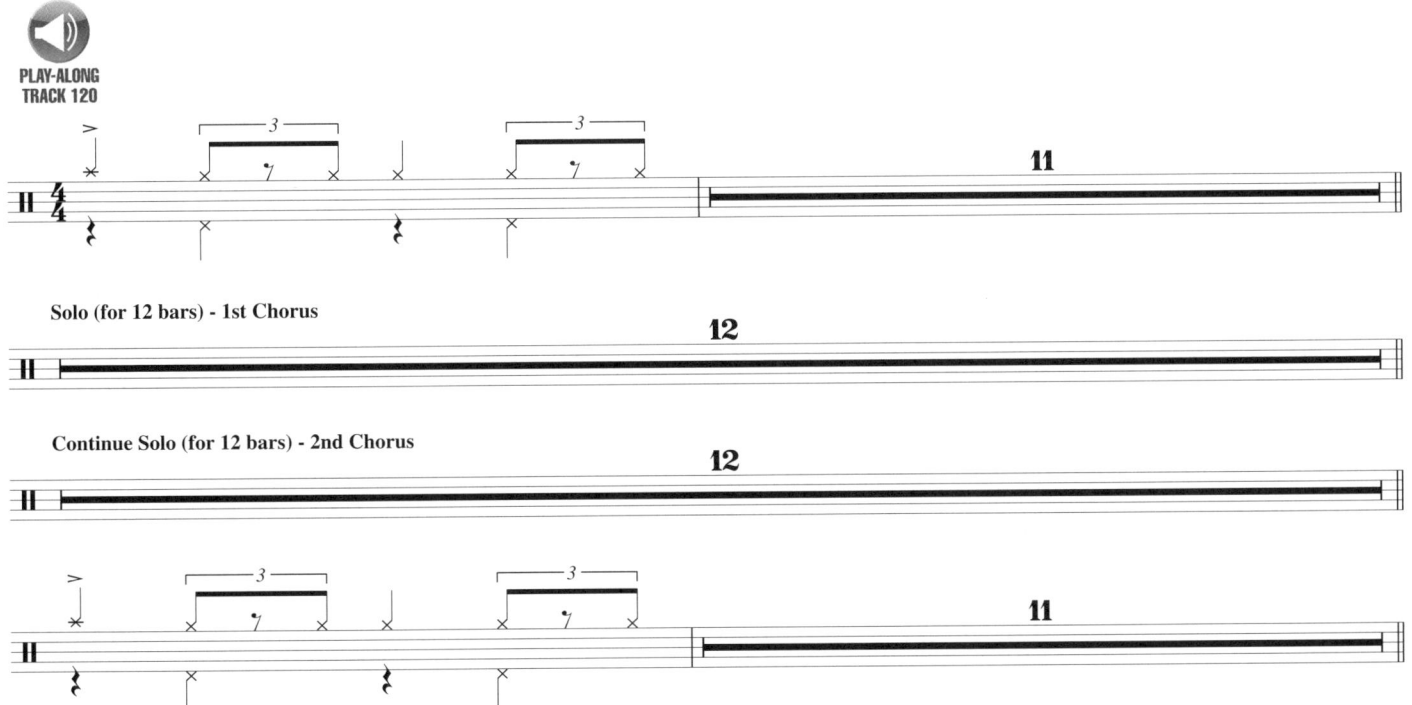

Lesson 51

Soloing on a 32-Bar Jazz Tune

Many standard jazz tunes are written using a 32-bar form (known as one "chorus"), and jazz drummers often are required to "take a solo chorus" during a performance. Soloing on the form of a 32-bar jazz tune is similar to trading fours, trading eights, or soloing over a 12-bar blues form—the solo patterns or "licks" you may use are the same, but the challenge is to be able to solo for an extended period of time.

When soloing on any form, it's important to know about the form (how many bars it contains and how they are arranged) in order to have an organized approach. This is how a 32-bar standard jazz tune with an AABA form is constructed: three sections that are similar (the "A" sections) and one that's different from the A sections, which is known as the "B" section (or bridge):

When soloing for 32 bars, try to think about and apply these concepts and suggestions:

- Thirty-two bars is a long time to solo, and one way to keep track of how many bars you have played is to think of it as four eight-bar phrases.

- Count each eight-bar phrase (**1**-2-3-4, **2**-2-3-4, **3**-2-3-4, etc.) in order to know exactly where you are in the form of the tune.

- Play the hi-hat on beats 2 and 4 throughout the solo to maintain a steady tempo.

- At first, put a crash cymbal on the first beat of each eight-bar section to help you keep track of where you are in the form.

- If you make a mistake, keep playing the hi-hat and counting and try to recover. It will be difficult at first, but you must practice recovering from mistakes in order to play in public.

- Begin your solo gradually. Start with some simple solo ideas and build in complexity. If you start a solo with your best solo ideas or with too much intensity from the outset, you have nothing left to play after only a few bars.

- Try to make each section somehow different from the previous one; this will make each section distinct from each other and reinforce (in your mind) that you have progressed from one section to another section in the tune. For example, the first A section could be played only on the snare drum, the second A section could be played only on the toms, the B section could have a completely different rhythm or main musical idea than the first two sections, and the last A section could include sounds from all around the drumset.

- When soloing, try to take short musical ideas (known as *riffs* or *licks*) and play them several times in a row, slightly altering them each time. Riffs can be altered by playing them on different drums, playing them forward and then backward, re-stating a characteristic part of the idea, inserting some rests in the idea to give it some space, compressing all of the rhythms so that the idea takes up fewer beats, stretching the idea so it takes up more beats, or starting the idea on a different beat each time you repeat it. Being able to alter riffs successfully will mean that you need fewer overall solo ideas, and the listener will hear that you are able to successfully build a solo.

- The end of your solo should be *very solid rhythmically*, so that all of the band members can feel the tempo together. Try to play solo ideas in the last four bars of your solo that are very clear and precisely executed. This will ensure that the band feels the tempo correctly and will rejoin you to finish the tune with confidence.

- It's important to give the band musical cues when you are ending your solo. These may include returning to the main groove of the song during the last four bars of your solo, beginning to play softer as the solo ends, beginning to play rhythmically much simpler, or by having a pre-arranged musical cue that you play only when you are ending your solo.
- Visual cues are also helpful when you are ending your solo. Try to look at the rest of the band during the last four bars of your solo as if to say, "I'm finishing my solo now."
- Be patient; learning to solo for 32 bars takes time (weeks, months, or even years).

Example 1 is a 32-bar solo that outlines the form of the song by making each eight-bar section musically distinct from the previous one. Listen to the various solo ideas, how each is altered, and how this approach makes the solo sound more organized.

TRACK 121

In some tunes, jazz soloists "trade choruses" with a drummer—alternating 32-bar solos with the drummer several times. To prepare for that situation, use Example 2 (Track 122) to practice trading 32-bar choruses with another soloist. Even when practicing, play the 32-bars of ride cymbal "time" (during the other soloist's chorus), as this will help you to internalize the feeling of a 32-bar span of time. In order to assist you in developing your solo ability, there will be a rhythm section chord on beat 1 of every four-bar section, a crash cymbal at the beginning of each eight-bar section, and a hi-hat on beats 2 and 4.

TRACK 122

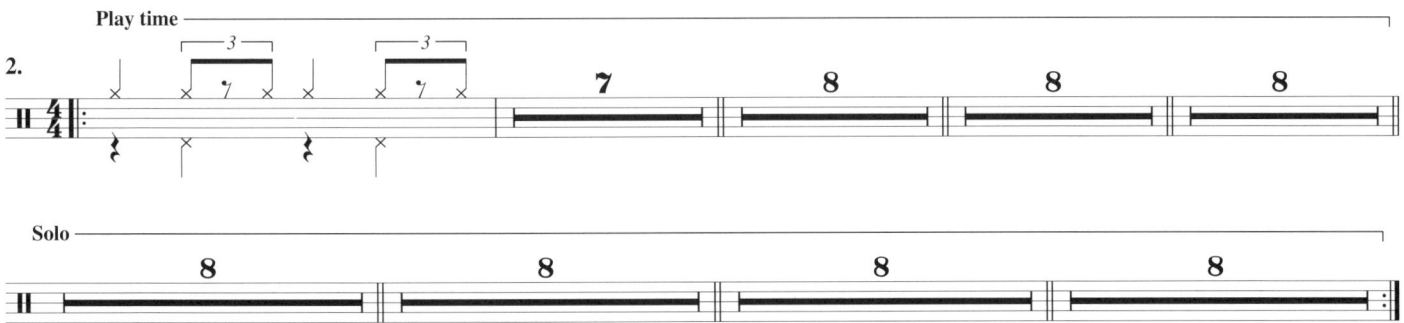

This is just an introduction to soloing on a 32-bar jazz tune. Max Roach, Art Blakey, "Philly Joe" Jones, Art Taylor, and others are the masters of this concept; seek out recordings by these artists in order to become more acquainted with their solo ideas and approaches to soloing.

Lesson 52

Soloing Over a Jazz Ostinato/Vamp

Jazz drummers are often required to solo in a variety of different ways and musical settings. The most common approach is to solo unaccompanied (as in trading fours/eights, etc.), but in some cases, drum solos are accompanied by a repeated rhythmic phrase known formally as an *ostinato* (or more casually as a *vamp*). These rhythmic vamp figures may be simple or complex, pre-determined ahead of time at a rehearsal, indicated in the written music, or they can be spontaneously created by the band.

Vamps may vary in length, but most are either one, two, or four bars in length. Often the person playing a comping instrument (usually the pianist or guitarist) will look at the drummer and begin playing a vamp. It's up to the drummer to recognize that a vamp is taking place and respond accordingly.

In terms of how to solo over a vamp, you can take a number of different approaches. In order to avoid monotony and create some sense of solo development, you might want to try mixing and matching the following approaches:

- Start sparsely with just a few cymbal notes.

- Play the exact rhythm of the vamp using a bass drum/cymbal combination.

- Start to play some rhythms and then "re-quote" the rhythm of the vamp occasionally.

- Play rhythmic ideas that are unrelated to the vamp.

- Play ideas that imply other time signatures (e.g., in 4/4 time, play ideas that sound like they are in 3/4 time), or play long solo ideas that only use the vamp as a metronomic reference (often referred to as "playing through a vamp").

Here are some other concepts and approaches to consider when soloing over a vamp:

- You don't have to play *all the time*—that's the advantage of a vamp. The rest of the band will "keep time" for you, so you are free to take your time and develop your solo slowly.

- Don't be in a hurry. You can afford to play sparsely at the beginning of your solo and then make it more complex later. Don't play your best solo ideas in the first four bars.

- A vamp is an open-ended solo situation, so you must have a way to signal the other musicians that you are done soloing. There are several ways to do this: 1) quit playing anything that sounds even remotely soloistic and return to playing the groove of the tune; 2) rhythmically quote the vamp several times as you look up and visually cue the band that you are ending; or 3) begin to play noticeably softer as your solo winds down. You can often do all three of these things, and this will really alert the band that they should return to the melody of the tune.

On the next page is an example of a one-bar vamp. Notice that the notation for the vamp bars (in all of this lesson's examples) are written as they might appear in a swing chart, with the swing feel implied. This example begins with four bars of time before the vamp occurs. On the audio, listen to how the solo begins sparsely, then the vamp is quoted on the drums, the solo gets more complex, and it ends as the drums get softer and start playing the groove again.

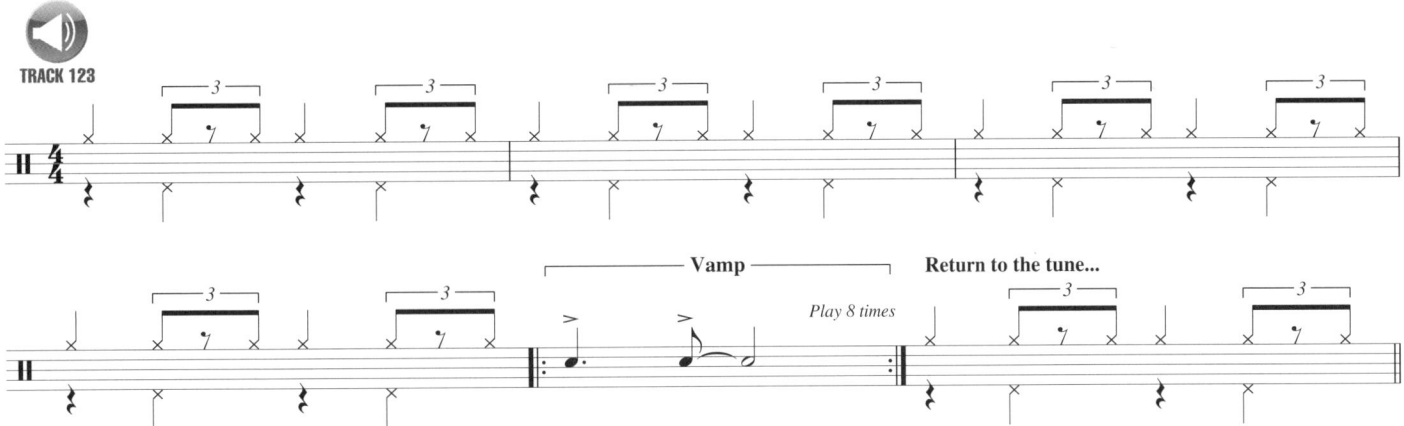

Listen to this example of a solo over a two-bar vamp, and hear the musical cues that lead the band back to the groove at the end. This type of vamp often occurs spontaneously during a performance. On the audio, the first four bars of a swing groove precede the vamp.

Now that you've heard some approaches to soloing over a vamp, use the following play-along tracks to practice soloing over these different vamp figures. Four bars of swing groove precede each vamp.

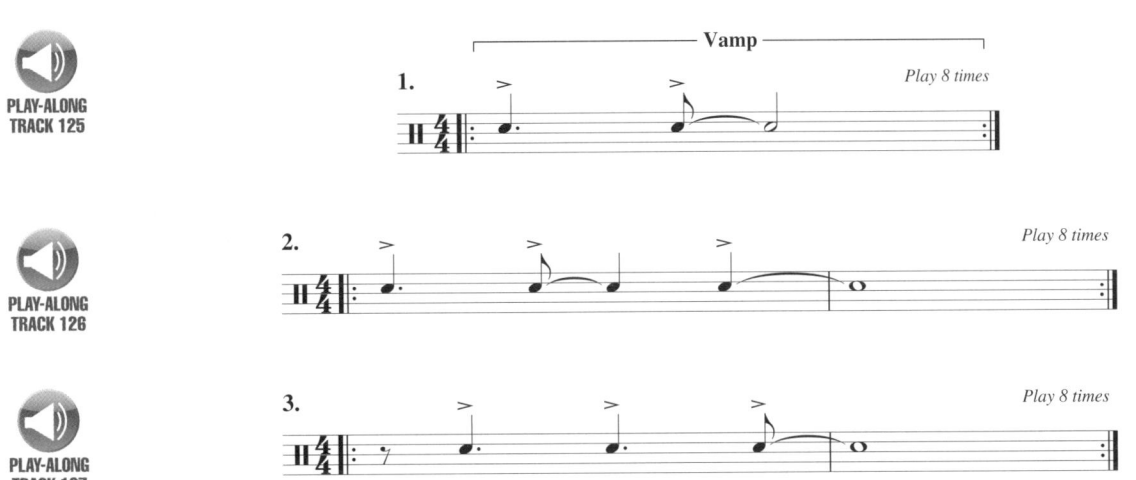

You can use these play-along tracks to practice two common examples of four-bar vamps:

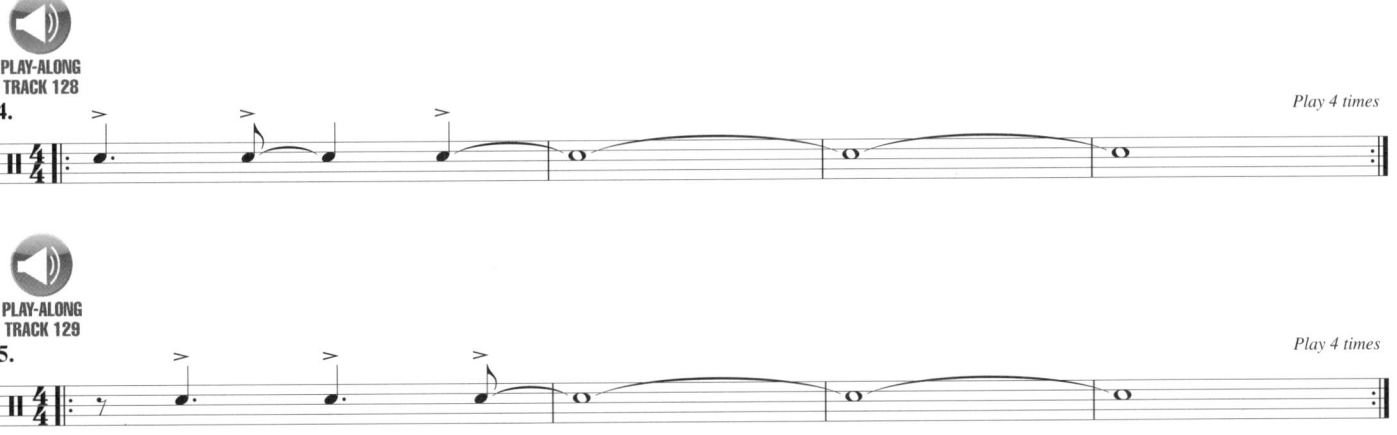

Lesson 53

Basic Swing Chart Interpretation

At some point in your drumming career, you may have to read a "swing drum chart," and being successful requires some knowledge of the notation, understanding of the style, and some experience.

When first encountering a swing chart, one thing that often confuses drummers is the notation of the "swing ride cymbal pattern." It may be notated three different ways: as two eighth notes, as the first and third part of a triplet, or as a dotted eighth/16th note grouping:

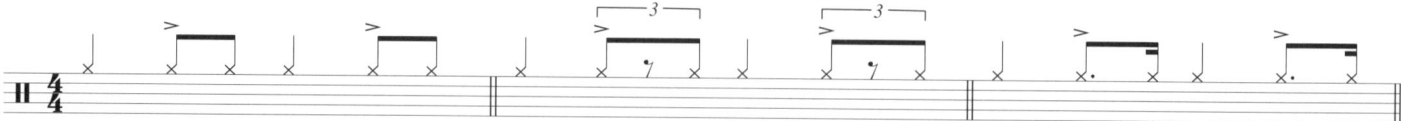

The truth is that there's no difference between the three versions. When it's written as two eighth notes, the composer assumes you (the drummer) know to "swing" the eighth notes. When written as a triplet, the composer more clearly spells out exactly how you should subdivide it. The dotted eighth/16th grouping is some composers' way of trying to approximate the "swing feel." The most important thing to remember is that they are all essentially the same pattern.

Another secret to reading a swing chart is to understand that it's not a specific piece of drum music; it's more like a guide that tells you what the rest of the band is doing. Based on that information, you (the drummer) decide how to interpret the chart (more on this later).

There are two basic types rhythmic figures found in swing charts: *background figures* and *ensemble figures*. Background figures are rhythmic phrases played by different sections of the band that provide "background countermelodies" to accompany instrumental solos (similar to background singers on pop records). Ensemble figures are rhythmic figures that the entire band plays in unison. The difference between the two types of figures determines what you do when you see them in a chart.

Most composers write ensemble figures in the staff and background figures on top of the staff. Then again, some composers don't; there's a lack of standardization for drumset notation, particularly in older charts. To be on the safe side, assume the rhythmic figure is an ensemble figure the first time you play it, but listen as you're playing and take note of it for the second time you play the chart. One possible indicator of whether a figure is an ensemble or background figure is the dynamic. If the dynamic is forte (*f*), it's probably an ensemble figure; if it's mezzo-piano (*mp*), it might be a background figure. (Then again, this rule doesn't always apply either, so you have to listen to the chart as you play it and make some quick decisions about what to do with figures that you encounter later in the chart.)

Ensemble figures require the drummer to take action, normally by "setting up" the figures. "Setting up the figure" is a phrase that means to prepare the rest of the band to play by putting a short fill or snare drum note immediately beforehand. It's like a musical "wake-up call" that gets the band ready to play their parts. A word of advice for all chart-reading: *look ahead*. Since ensemble figures require the drums to play a fill before the rhythmic figure, you have to be one step ahead of the chart.

Exercises 1–4 are examples of the most basic ensemble figures found in swing charts. The top line of each exercise shows what you might see in the chart, whereas the bottom line is what you will actually play. Notice that, when unaccented quarter notes are written in the staff, they are interpreted to mean "play time" during those beats (basically the regular jazz ride pattern and hi-hat). When first starting out, the snare drum is one of the best instruments to play the set-up on because it has a bright sound that everyone in the band can hear. Try to memorize these exercises, as these figures will appear over and over again in many swing charts.

TRACK 130

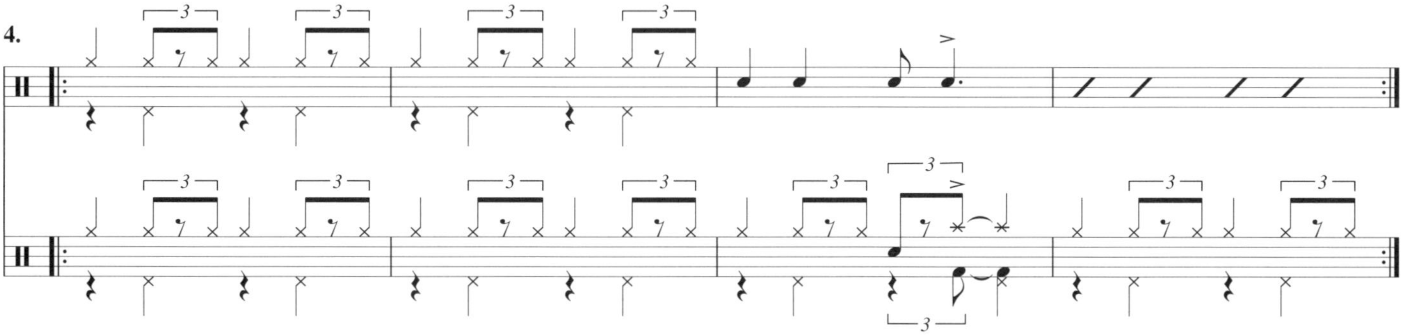

These exercises represent the most basic fills you can use yet still fulfill your role of setting up the band. You can always begin a set-up fill a beat or two before the written examples, but this will become second nature as your familiarity with the concept of setting up increases.

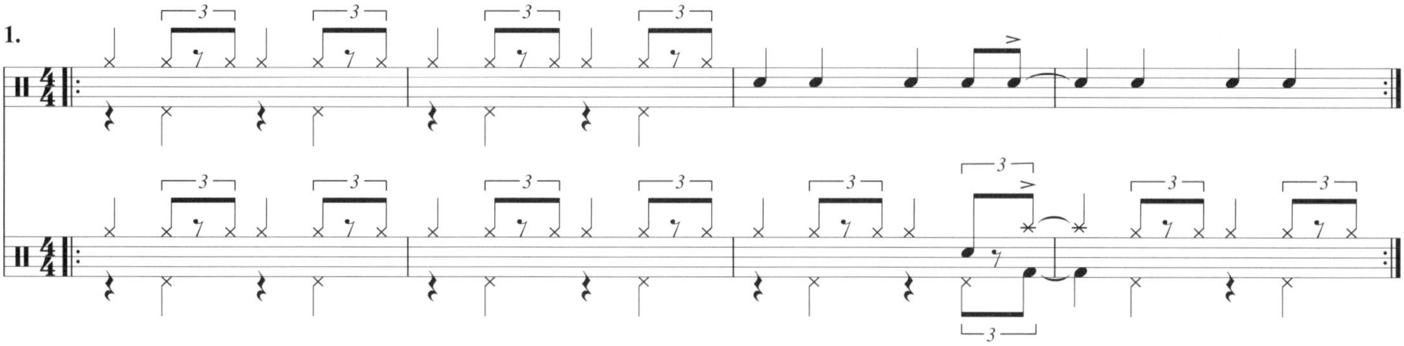

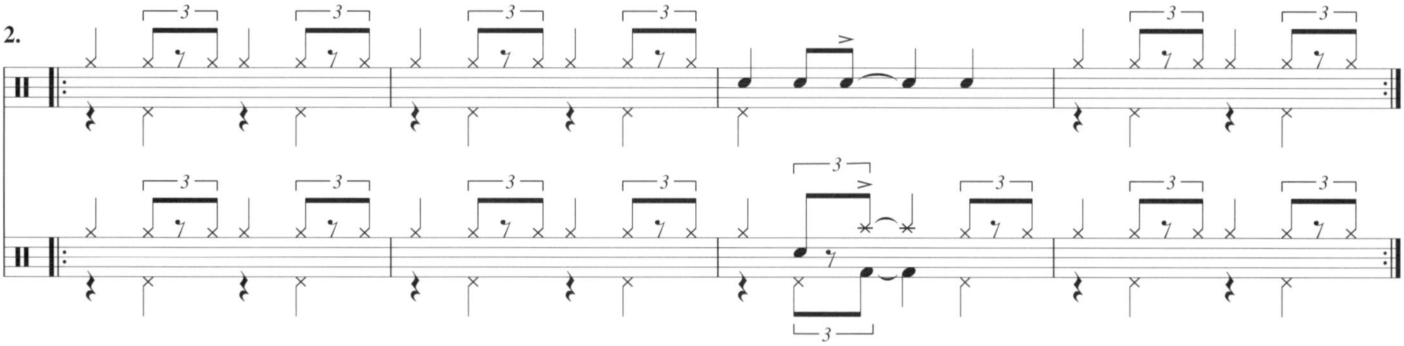

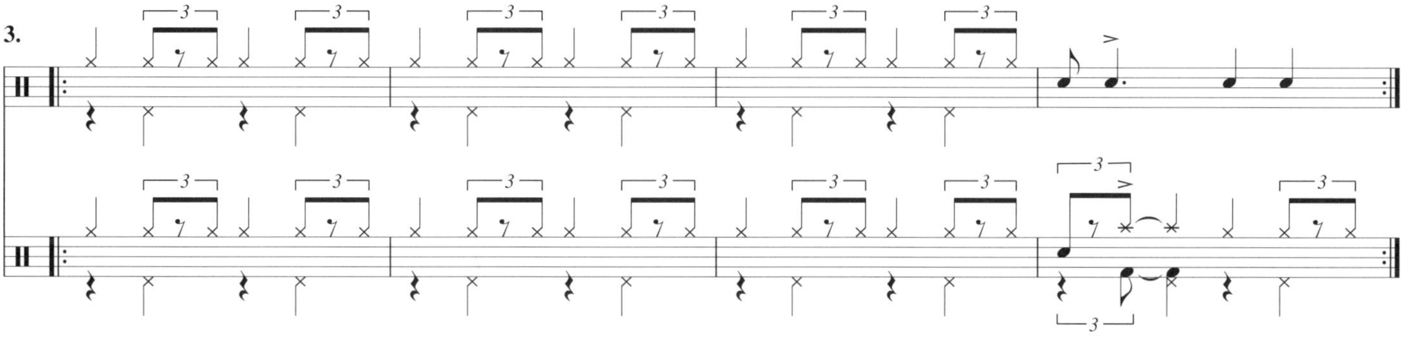

There's no substitute for actually listening to swing/big band music to get a sense of the drummer's role in a swing band. Listen to how the drummer sets up the rest of the band on recordings and start building your own catalogue of fills that you can use when setting up the ensemble figures. Swing/big band drummers to emulate include Buddy Rich, Sonny Greer, Sonny Payne, Rufus "Speedy" Jones, Harold Jones, Jake Hanna, "Papa" Jo Jones (with the Count Basie Band), Jeff Hamilton, John Riley, and Peter Erskine.

Intermediate Swing Chart Interpretation

There are two basic types of rhythmic figures presented in swing charts: *background figures* and *ensemble figures*. Background figures are often written using small notes above the staff, like this:

Background figures are musical phrases that are used to accompany a soloist. Due to a lack a standardized drumset notation, some composer/arrangers write background figures in the staff, so you have to be careful to listen to the arrangement the first time to determine whether the figures you see are background figures (or you may ask your director).

Once you've determined that the figures in a chart are background figures, you need to decide how to interpret them. There are many ways to do so, but the approach described here works in the majority of situations. Exercise 1 demonstrates some examples of background figures that have short durations (eighth notes). These figures may be played either on the snare drum or bass drum (or a combination of both) while still continuing to play the ride cymbal pattern.

To decide which instrument to use, a general rule is: if the background figures are on trumpet, use a snare drum to compliment the high trumpet sound, use the bass drum to compliment the low sound of the trombones, and use a combination of the bass drum or snare for the saxes. (Note: All examples here are illustrated on snare drum; practice substituting the bass drum and different snare/bass combinations for each background rhythm.)

TRACK 131

The following play-along exercises illustrate how to orchestrate background figures with longer notes or with notes that are tied to long notes (for example, eighth notes tied from the "and" of beat 4 to the next measure). Try to memorize the figures and apply them to charts that you see in the future. Notice that some exercises (#1 and #2; #3 and #4) are written differently but identically executed. In these cases, the unwritten rule of chart interpretation is that you need to "set up" the background figures with a snare note before the band enters, even if there is a rest written on the beat. (This is the **only** time you get to "play in the rests" as a drummer!)

PLAY-ALONG TRACK 132

Keep in mind that there are many different ways to interpret a swing chart; the ideas presented here are only to help you get started. You can always begin the set-up fills a few beats earlier, if desired. Listen to as many recordings as you can to understand how ensemble figures are set up by other drummers and what fills work in various musical situations.

Lesson 55

Advanced Swing Chart Interpretation

When interpreting swing/big band/combo charts, there are some essential "unwritten rules" you should understand. The advanced exercises in this lesson will familiarize you with some of these rules and also some common rhythmic figures that appear in swing charts. The top staff of each exercise shows the written chart, and the bottom staff demonstrates how to interpret the figure or figures. Keep in mind that these are general rules of chart interpretation and will work in many situations. There are, of course, many different and more advanced ways to play these same figures, but these guidelines should form a solid foundation on which to build as you gain more experience with chart interpretation.

- Notes written above the staff are background figures and should be played on the snare drum or bass drum while continuing to play the ride pattern either on the ride cymbal or hi-hat (Ex. 3–5).

- Figures written in the staff are ensemble figures and need to be "set up" by playing a fill, or at the very least a single snare note, immediately before the band's entrance.

- Ensemble figures are to be orchestrated using the following format: eighth notes will be played using a snare drum (Ex. 1), offbeat quarter notes (notes that begin on the "ands" of a beat) will be played with a ride cymbal/bass drum combination (Ex. 4), and any note longer than a dotted quarter (including quarter notes tied to an eighth note or half notes) will be played using a crash cymbal/bass drum combination (Ex. 4).

- Any unaccented quarter notes written in the staff will be interpreted as "time playing," which means to continue playing the basic groove of the tune during those beats. Any rests written in the staff should be observed unless it's an eighth rest immediately preceding a rhythmic figure (e.g., the "and" of beat 4); this is where a set-up is normally played (Ex. 3).

- When the band enters playing a note more than 1 1/2 beats long (e.g., a dotted-quarter note length, etc.), it should be set up with a fill immediately prior to their entrance (Ex. 3, 6, and 7).

- Keep playing the hi-hat on beats 2 and 4 through the figures to help keep steady time.

- Following a rhythmic figure, be clear when to restart the ride cymbal pattern (i.e., which beat of the bar). This will help prevent "flipping the beat around" (playing the hi-hat on the wrong beat).

Try to memorize these rules and apply the orchestrations presented in this lesson to other charts. Use the accompanying play-along track to practice Exercises 1–7.

DEMO TRACK 133 PLAY-ALONG TRACK 134

Lesson 56

Soloing Around Rhythmic Figures

Jazz band arrangers will occasionally include a drum solo accompanied by some rhythmic (background) figures. These figures are commonly referred to as "shots" because they're normally very short phrases and may be notated either above the staff or in the staff. Rhythmic figures are never the same in any two songs (so it would be impossible to provide examples for all of the possibilities), but there are some commonly used figures and ways to approach this situation that will make it easier to play when you encounter them in a chart or performance situation. Soloing around figures requires skill, preparation, and some "inside information." Consider these suggestions and approaches when soloing around rhythmic figures:

- It's better to play simple ideas accurately rather than complex ideas with poor execution. One of the most important responsibilities when soloing is to stay with the band and not throw them off. If you don't know what to do the first time through the chart, just continue to play time and add a few fills. Then, set aside some time to practice your soloing ideas before the next rehearsal or concert.

- You don't have to play *every* rhythmic figure, but it is easier for the band if you play the figures the first time through the chart. You can always choose to ignore a particular figure or play something more complex later, after you and the band are comfortable with the chart.

- Try to "set up" some of these figures with a short fill (exactly like "setting up" rhythmic figures in a swing chart) to help the band, particularly when the band is inexperienced, they are sight reading, or if you are playing with the band for the first time.

Exercises 1–9 are four-bar exercises using some of the most common rhythmic figures found in jazz band charts. Practice playing the rhythmic figures on the drumset using only the snare drum for eighth notes, and only a bass drum/ride cymbal combination for notes a quarter note length or longer. Practice preparing the band to play their figures by setting each figure up with a short fill right before the band plays, and then start building your stock of solo licks to use during the rest of the four-bar phrase. Once you have mastered these exercises, the next chart you encounter with soloistic rhythmic figures should be much easier.

DEMO TRACK 135 PLAY-ALONG TRACK 136

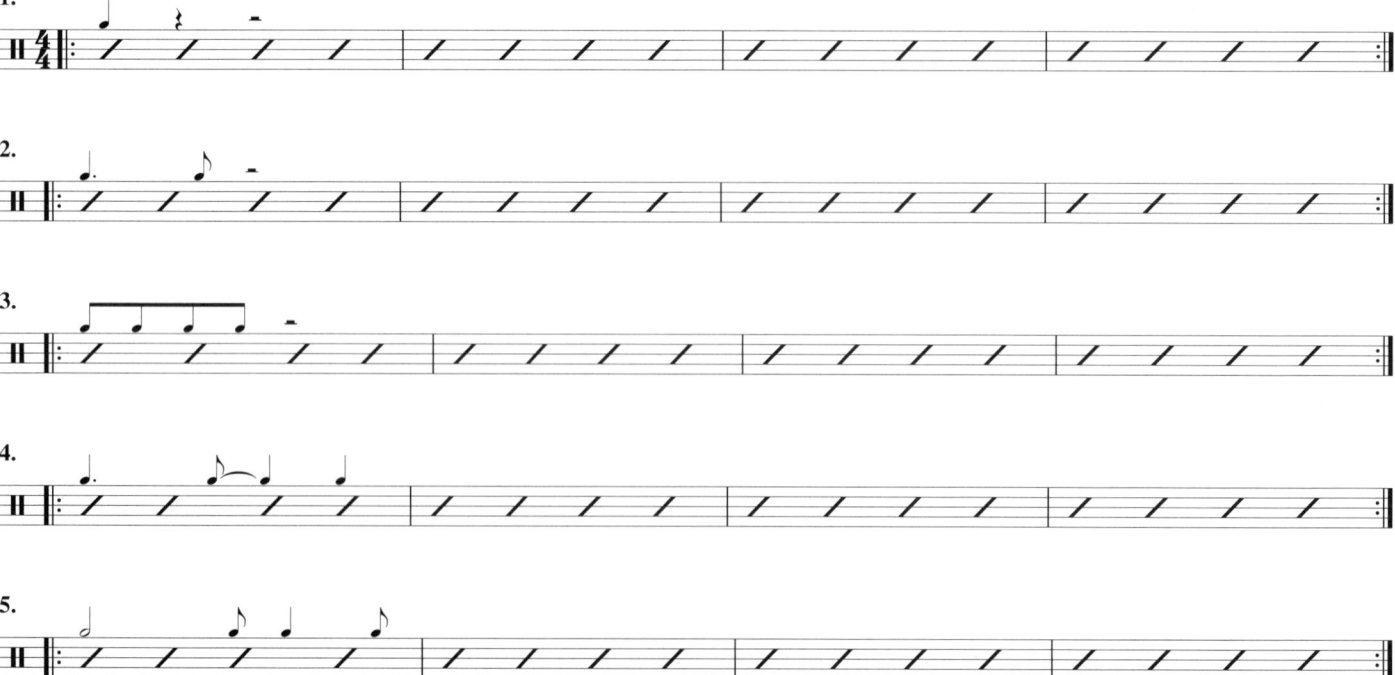

Listen to this sample chart to practice soloing around rhythmic figures.

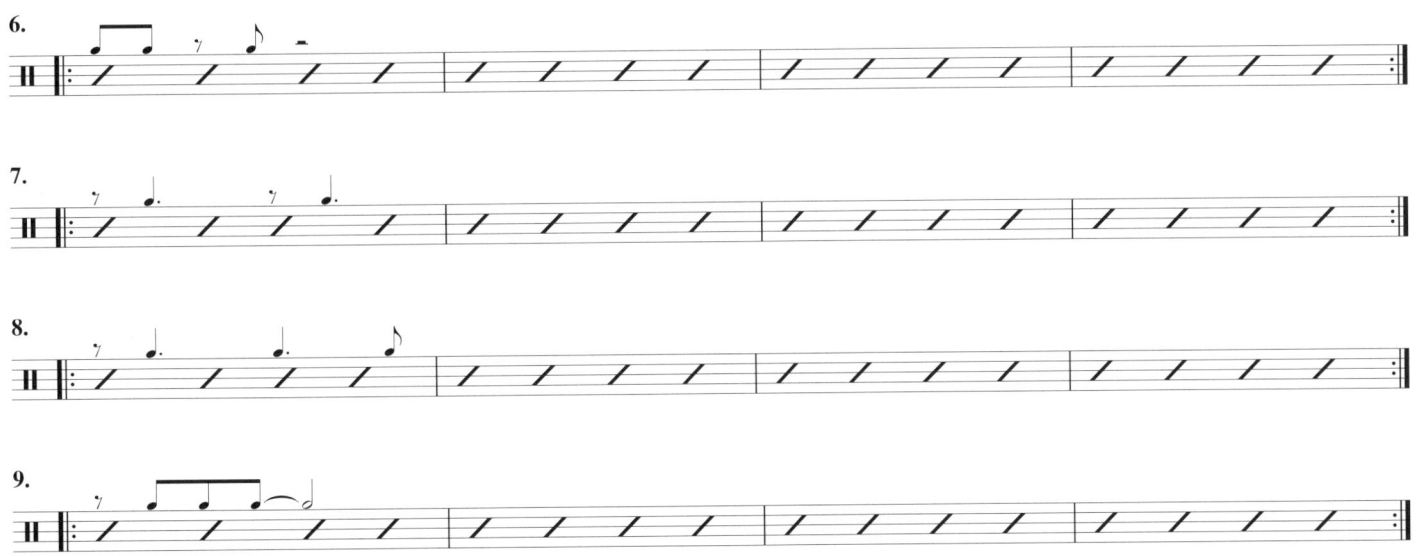

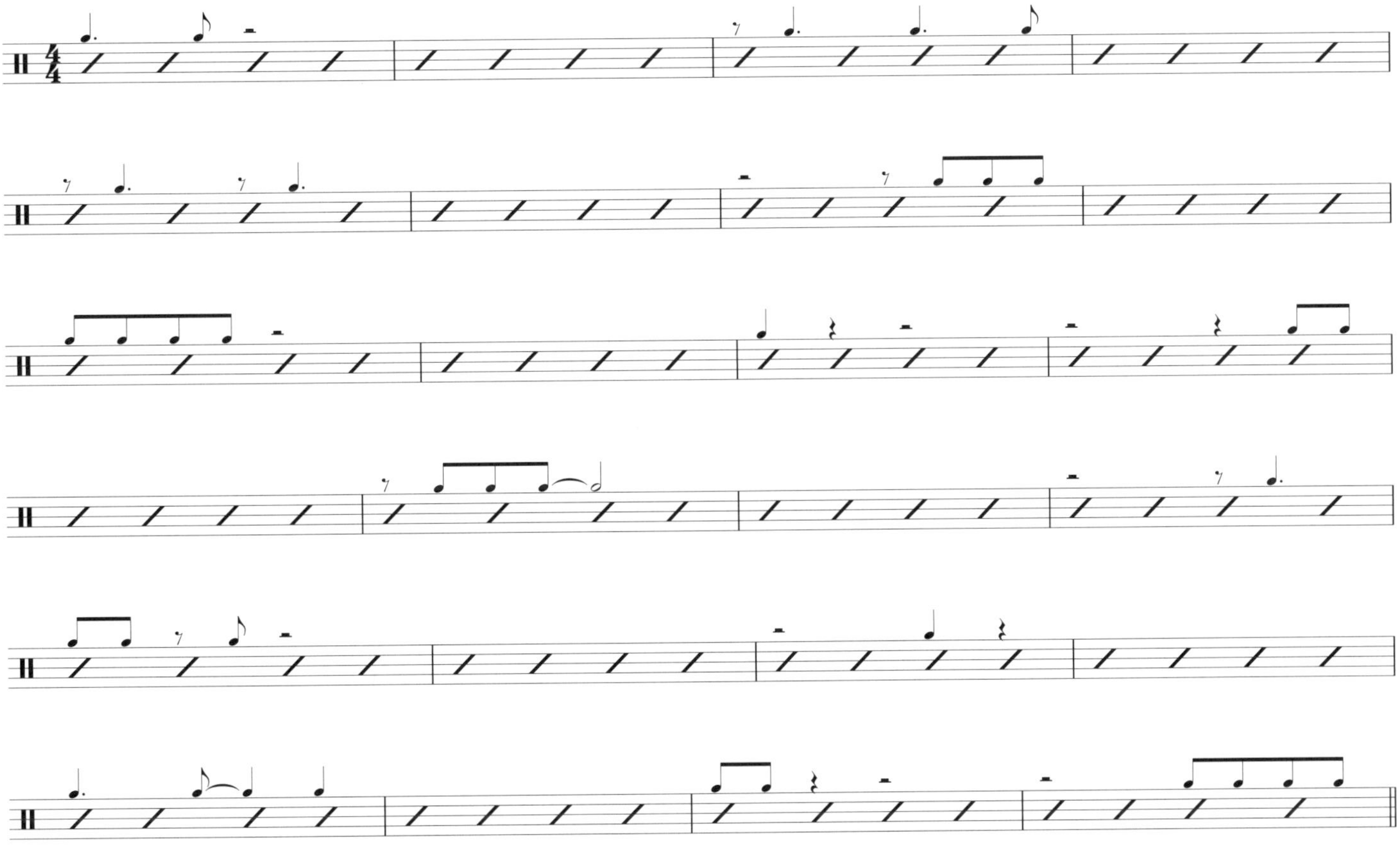

Listen to Louie Bellson, Buddy Rich, Jeff Hamilton, Peter Erskine, John Riley, and others for inspiration and solo ideas in this style.

Lesson 57

Changing Time Feels

In some musical situations, drummers are required to change from one time feel or groove to another during the course of a song. This is necessary to create a different mood in a particular part of a song or to change the energy level of the music. When time feels change, the underlying tempo (speed of the tune) normally does not change—only the drum groove.

One of the most basic time feel changes is from a basic 4/4 rock feel to a "half-time" rock feel. Notice that the backbeat in measures 1–4 of Example 1 (normally played on beats 2 and 4) changes to beat 3 during the half-time section (measures 5–8). Listen as its seems to lower the excitement level starting in measure 5, temporarily giving the listener the impression that the song is being played "half as fast" (which it is not).

TRACK 139

The drums can also inject more energy in a section of a tune by switching from a regular 4/4 rock feel to a "double-time" feel using 16th notes in the ride pattern. Again, the tempo does not change, but the energy level of the song increases with the increased note density of the 16th-note hi-hat ride pattern.

TRACK 140

Another common feel change is from rock to swing (Example 3). One of the secrets to making a transition like this is to play fills that signal the change of subdivision from the straight eighth-note feel of rock to the triplet-based feel of swing (in measure 4). This technique is called *foreshadowing*, and it prepares the band for a change in the music and makes the change of feels less abrupt. The change back from the triplet-based feel of swing to the straight eighth-note feel of rock is accomplished by playing straight eighth-note fills (in measure 8). When you become comfortable with the change from rock to swing, you may also practice comping on the snare drum during the swing section (as heard on the audio).

Exercise 4 demonstrates a change from swing to a bossa nova feel. To change from swing to bossa nova, play a fill with straight eighth-note subdivisions at the end of measure 4 and a triplet-based fill when changing back to swing in measure 8. When practicing these examples, you may also substitute your own fills at the transition points (measures 4 and 8).

The change from a swing feel to an Afro-Cuban mambo is also very common:

The change from swing to an Afro-Cuban 6/8 feel is another common feel change. The quarter-note pulse stays the same, but the 6/8 feel makes the music sound more active.

Lesson 58

Fusion Drumming

Fusion (also known as *jazz-rock fusion*) is a musical style that emerged in the mid-1970s combining the improvisational elements of jazz with the electronic sounds and rhythms of rock, funk, Brazilian, and Afro-Cuban music. There is no "definitive fusion groove," because each fusion group was experimenting with their own blend of styles, which resulted in fusion becoming a true "musical mixture." Over time, however, some musical groups began to assert their individuality by using more Afro-Cuban or Brazilian-inspired rhythms (the Return to Forever band), composing in odd meters (Mahavishnu Orchestra), or drawing more from the funk style (Tony Williams' Lifetime). Other general characteristics of fusion include a great deal of rhythmic interaction between the soloists and the drummer, drummers playing the melody in unison with the other instruments, extended solos (sometimes over vamps), fast tempos, and generally "busy" drum patterns with many ghost notes and frequent fills.

The most influential early fusion drummers included Tony Williams, Jack DeJohnette, Billy Cobham, Airto Moreira, Lenny White, Narada Michael Walden, Alex Acuna, and others. Listen to as many recordings as possible by these drummers and begin to learn some of their signature drum patterns. The patterns found below are similar to patterns found on many fusion recordings.

This quarter-note cross-stick groove, for example, works in many fusion situations.

TRACK 145

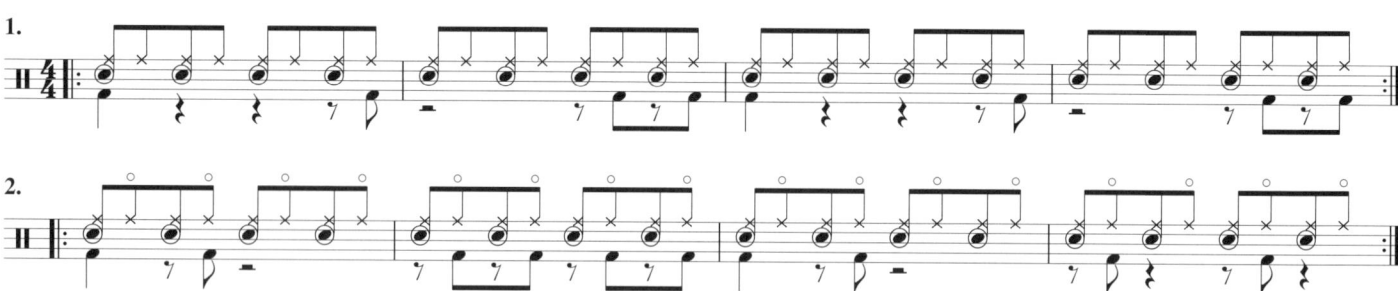

These grooves are more influenced by funk and rhythm and blues, so they have a more pronounced backbeat.

TRACK 146

These fusion grooves were influenced by Brazilian rhythms—primarily samba.

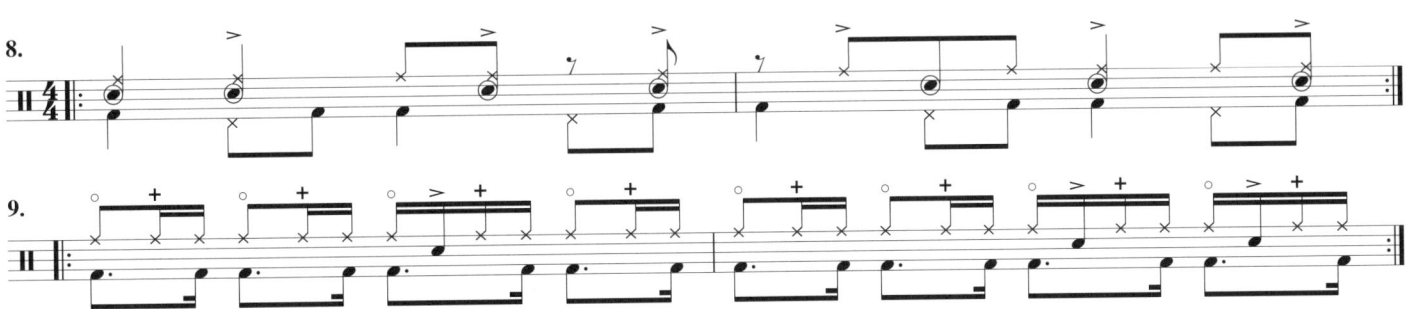

These represent some typical odd-meter fusion grooves.

Lesson 59

Modern Jazz/ECM

Modern jazz (since the mid-1970s) has taken many different directions, and one distinctive style that emerged became known as "ECM" jazz. Beginning in the early 1970s, German record producer Manfred Eicher started ECM Records (Edition of Contemporary Music) and began to record artists such as Pat Metheny, Ralph Towner, Eberhard Weber, Jan Garbarek, John Abercrombie, and others who played improvised music in a non-traditional jazz way. Drummers Jon Christensen, Jack DeJohnette, Joey Baron, Danny Gottlieb, Paul Wertico, Roy Haynes, Paul Motian, and Bob Moses played on many ECM recordings, and their approaches to playing the drums typify the "ECM drumming style."

Much of ECM music is straight eighth-note improvised instrumental music (which differs from the swing feel of traditional jazz). Some of its influences were the rock-oriented recordings of Miles Davis and Herbie Hancock in the late 1960s and early '70s, European classical music, the music of pianist Bill Evans' trio, and modal jazz.

When studying ECM music, the best first approach is to listen to some of the artists mentioned above and try to emulate what the drummers are doing. While there are no "typical" ECM drum grooves (as with bossa nova or rock), there are some concepts that often characterize a great deal of ECM music. Keep in mind that there are always exceptions to these characteristics. That said, you will notice the following:

- Much of the drumming is focused on the cymbals (with less emphasis on a loud bass drum or use of toms)
- It has a subtle presence or implication of a backbeat (but not always)
- It involves playing many different parts of the cymbal (bell, body, edge) with various parts of the stick (tip/shoulder) to create many different cymbal timbres
- The hi-hat is often "splashed" (played with the foot and allowed to ring freely) rather than used to produce a strong "chick" sound that defines the time
- Snare drum buzz strokes are often used
- The use of soft, subtle dynamics and sudden dynamic changes is more prominent than in other styles
- The cymbal part often mimics/accentuates the melody and/or the rhythmic patterns of the soloist
- Each individual "voice" of the drumset (snare, bass, cymbals, hi-hat) creates their own melodic/rhythmic patterns that fit together to achieve an ever-changing rhythmic foundation for the music

This is a transcription of a generic straight eighth-note ECM drum part:

TRACK 149

Listen to this example of an eighth-note ECM tune to get a sense of what the drums do in this style.

TRACK 150

2. **Straight 8th-note ECM feel**

There is also an approach to modern jazz with a swing feel that has been labeled "ECM swing," and the Keith Jarrett Trio (with Gary Peacock and Jack DeJohnette) is probably the best-known ensemble that plays in that style. On the drums, it involves a concept referred to as "implying time" or "breaking up the time," rather than "stating time." This means that all four of a drummer's limbs improvise simultaneously to create a syncopated, swinging "rhythmic jigsaw puzzle" that fits together to provide the rhythmic basis for the music rather than playing the traditional repetitive ride cymbal pattern and hi-hat on beats 2 and 4.

Like traditional jazz, ECM music normally involves improvising over the form of a specific tune and generally follows the traditional jazz format: melody, solos, and restatement of the melody. (Some ECM-style artists, however, also play in a freer manner, without closely adhering to any pre-determined musical form.) In ECM music, the piano and bass frequently play non-repetitive rhythms and take great liberties with their rhythms, so counting and keeping your place in the form of the music is very important.

Listen to this example of an "ECM swing" feel. The first 16 bars are played in an "ECM two feel," and the rest of the tune is played in an "ECM four feel." Notice the non-repetitive drumming style.

татРАCK 151

Here's a transcription of the first four bars of the ECM swing "two feel" you just heard and the first four bars of the "four feel" (starting in measure 17 of the recording).

TRACK 152

When you are ready to begin playing ECM music, use these ECM play-along tracks to practice this challenging style.

PLAY-ALONG TRACKS 153–155

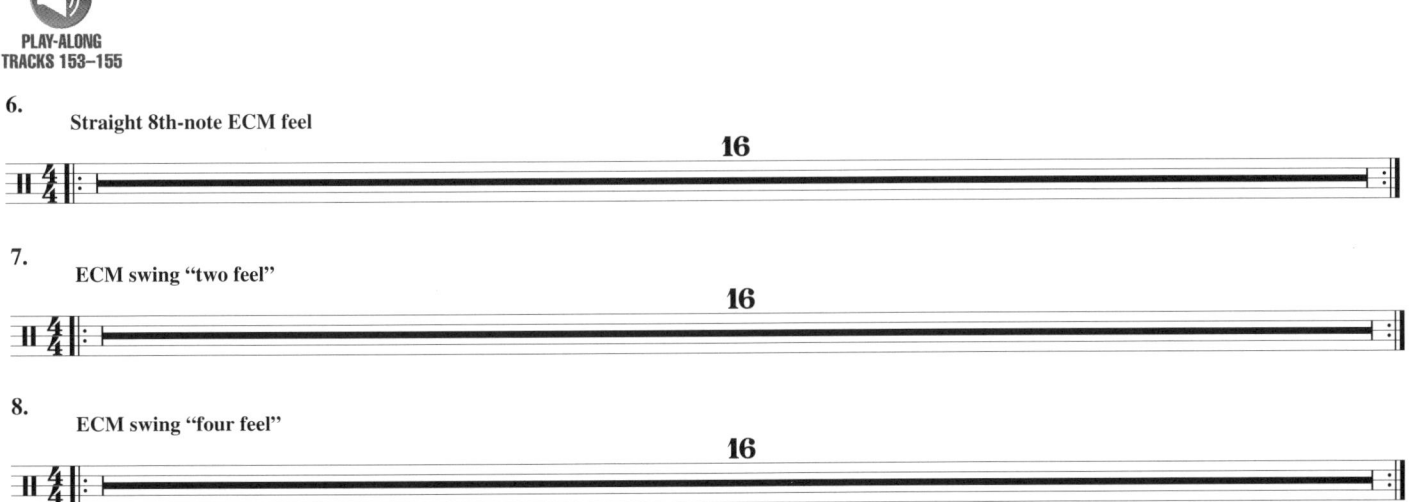

Advanced Swing Ride Patterns

In the 1960s, jazz drummers began to move away from the traditional jazz ride cymbal pattern and began to freely improvise their ride cymbal patterns in a style that become known as "breaking up the time" or "breaking up the ride pattern." This new approach meant that the ride pattern was different in almost every measure and was pioneered by drummers such as Jack DeJohnette, Tony Williams, Roy Haynes, and many others. It's a technically challenging style and should only be attempted after having developed a solid foundation with the traditional ride cymbal pattern. "Breaking up the time" is an advanced approach to jazz timekeeping and is not suitable for all musical situations, but it's one that every modern jazz drummer should understand and use when appropriate.

The concept behind "breaking up the time" is to create a flow of constantly changing rhythms on the ride cymbal, not repeating any of these exact measures per se. In order to accomplish this, however, it's necessary to be able to consistently play any one of these cymbal variations at will. Combine these advanced ride cymbal patterns (Ex. 1–14) with various snare drum/bass drum comping rhythms (Ex. 15–26) and hi-hat patterns (Ex. 27–30) to create challenging jazz accompaniment patterns. Note that the snare drum/bass drum comping rhythms and hi-hat patterns are written as regular eighth notes, but should be swung.

TRACK 156

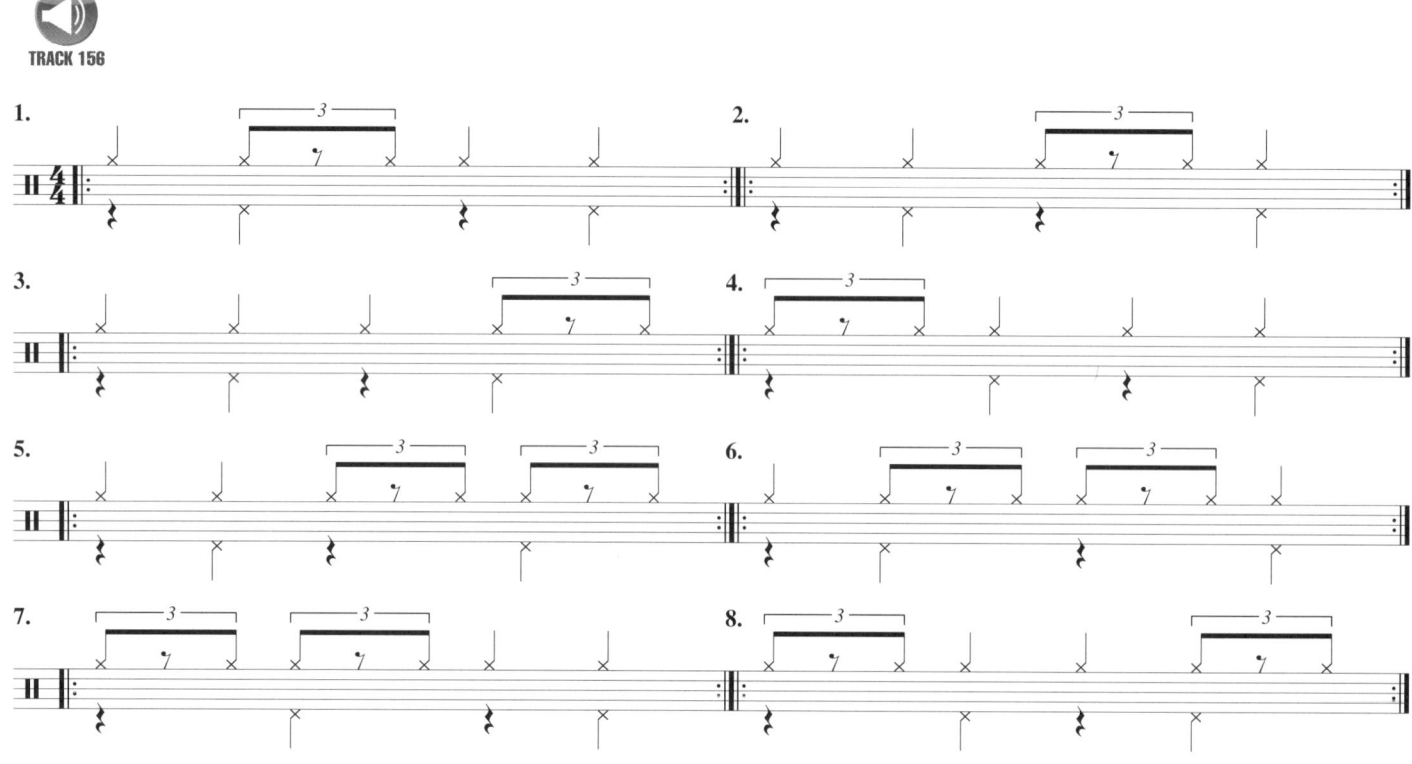

The following two-bar exercises (Ex. 9–14) focus on accented upbeats, which are played on the "and" of the beat. Many of these exercises feature accents immediately preceding beats 1 and 3 (the "strong beats"), which are an important aspect of achieving a good jazz feel and often occur in modern jazz. The tied notes should be played as "edge crashes"—soft crashes with the shoulder of the stick on the edge of the ride cymbal—to achieve the proper sound.

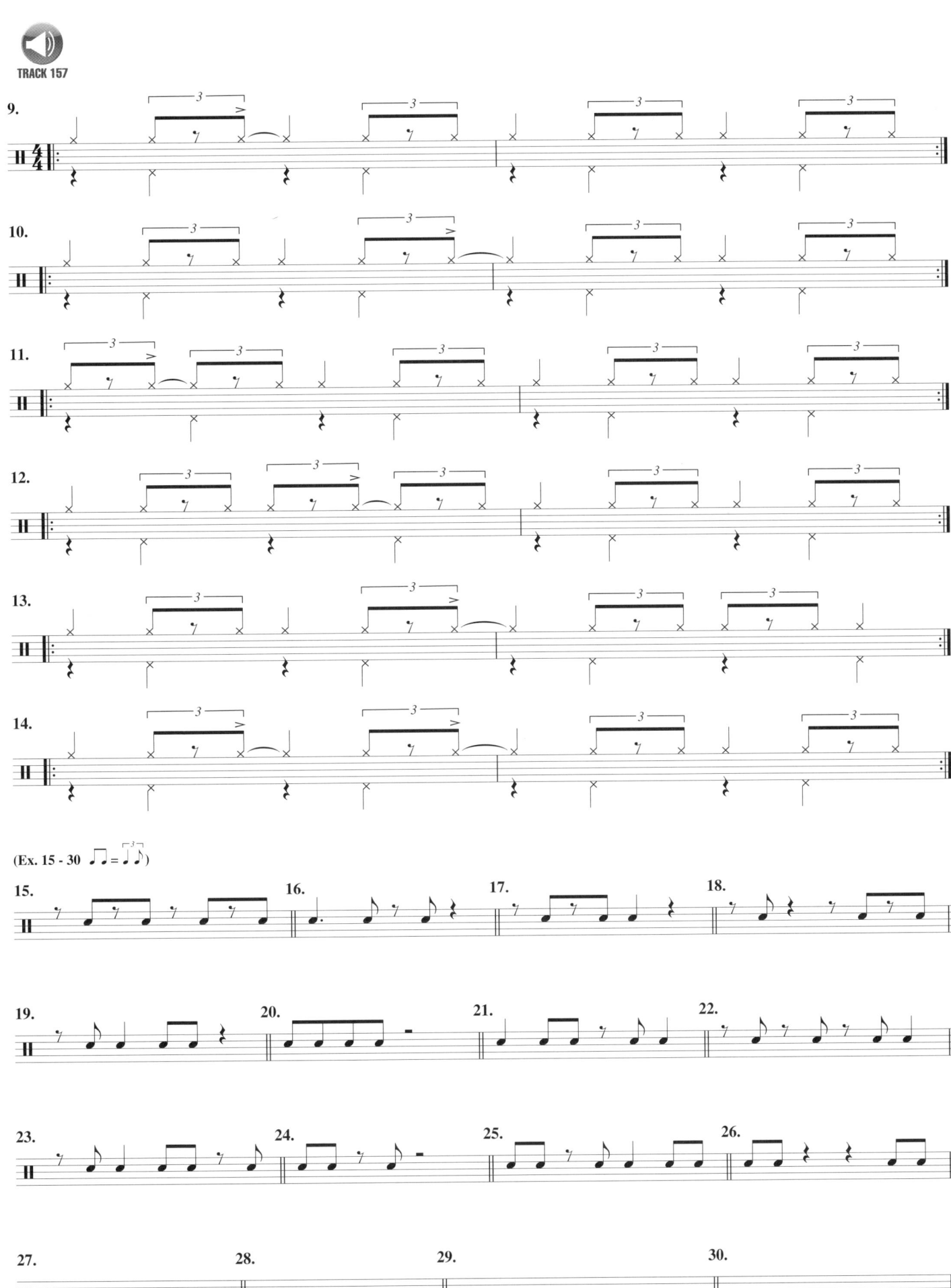

Lesson 61

Odd-Time Rock

"Odd time" or "odd meter" are terms used to describe time signatures that are not divisible by the number 2. (*Meter* is another term for time signature.) The most common meter in rock and pop music is 4/4 (with the exception of a waltz, which is always in 3/4 time). Some styles, such as progressive rock, use odd meters to make their music distinctive.

Three-four (3/4) time is the best odd meter to study first. Practice these basic 3/4 rock exercises first.

TRACK 158

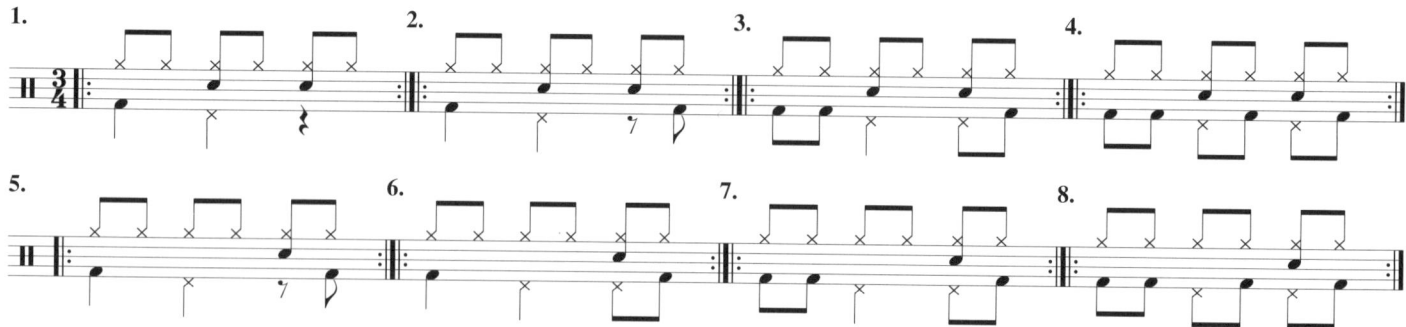

Examples 1–8 may also be played on a closed hi-hat by omitting the left foot hi-hat part.

All odd time signatures can ultimately be broken down into combinations of either 2 or 3 beats for the purpose of phrasing. This process is similar to finding a number's lowest common denominator in math class. There are fundamentally two time signature possibilities (or phrasing subdivisions): *duple* or *triple* meter. Duple means "two" (beats) and triple means "three" (beats). For example, 4/4 is two groups of two (duple meter). Five-four time (5/4), however, is an "asymmetric" meter—divisible completely neither by three or two but a combination of three and two. Therefore, 5/4 time may be divided into only two possible phrasing combinations: 2 + 3 or 3 + 2. Exercises 9–12 are examples of 5/4 time phrased as 3 + 2.

TRACK 159

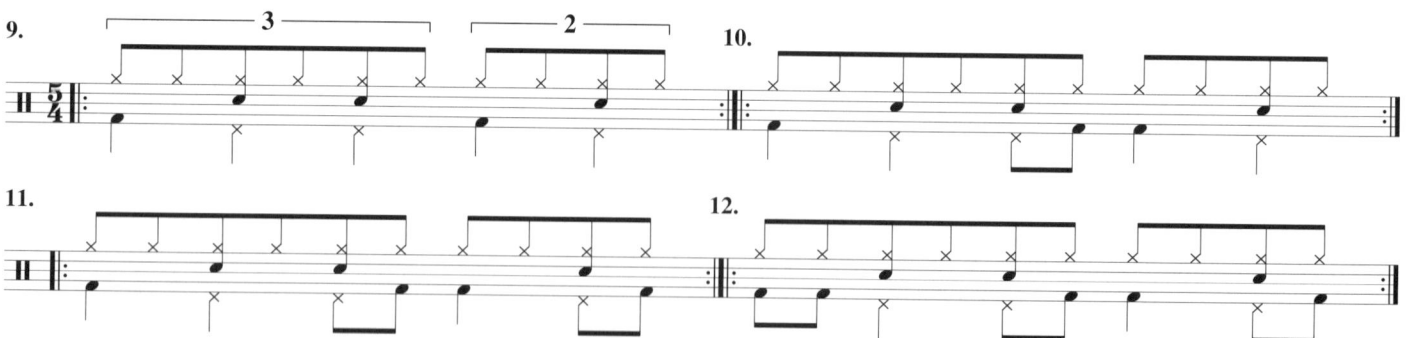

Exercises 13–18 are examples of 5/4 time phrased as 2 + 3.

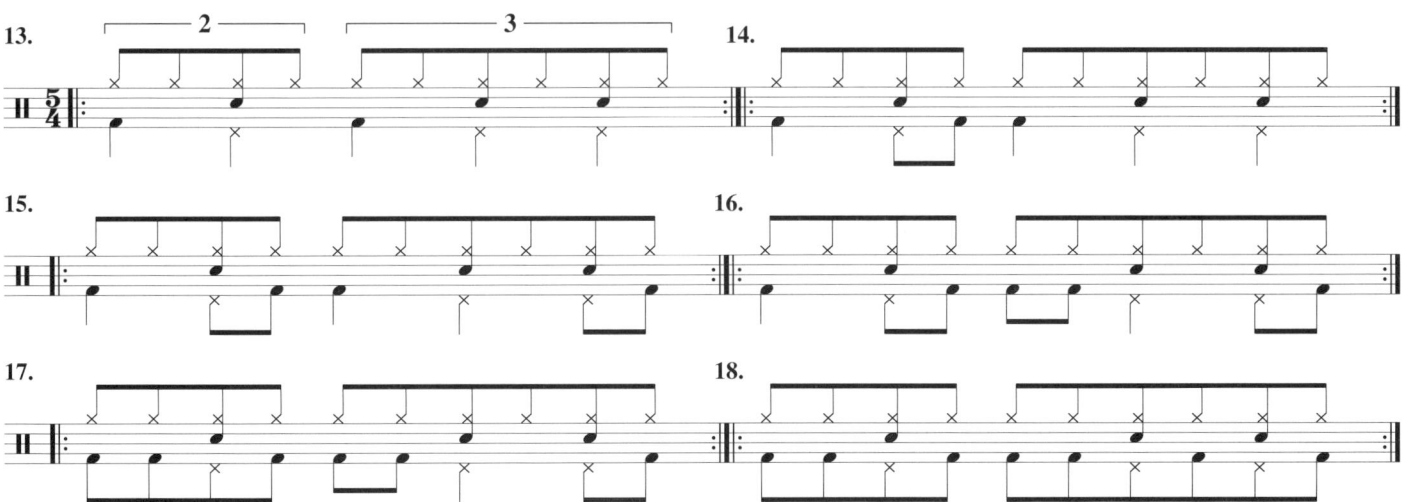

Seven-four time (7/4) is also an asymmetrical meter, and it can be phrased three ways: 2 + 2 + 3, 2 + 3 + 2, or 3 + 2 + 2. Exercises 19–36 are examples of the three ways to phrase 7/4 time.

TRACK 160

Lesson 62

Intermediate Odd-Time Rock

When you first start playing odd meters with other musicians, often exactly what you should play is unclear. If you're using written music, what to play is clearly notated, so there's no confusion. If there is no written music (and the other musicians don't discuss what you should play), it's the drummer's responsibility to determine the correct musical phrasing of a tune and play the appropriate groove that fits the music. Therefore, it's important to understand how the bass line and phrasing of the music influences what to play on the drums. The following examples explain how to determine phrasing in an odd meter. You should realize that it's not uncommon for musicians to disagree on how a song is to be phrased. If, after playing the music a few times, the phrasing is not clear, you should discuss it with your fellow musicians and agree on a phrasing approach. The phrasing can normally be determined by listening to the bass line. For example, in 5/4 time, if the first three beats sound like a complete phrase of 3/4 with two extra beats added (like this pattern), then it's probably 3 + 2:

If the bass part sounds like a "normal 4/4 bar" with an extra beat or space at the end (similar to this pattern), it's probably phrased 2 + 3:

In 7/4 time, for example, if the bass line is similar to this one, the phrasing is 2 + 2 + 3:

If the bass line is similar to this 7/4 bass line, the phrasing is 2 + 3 + 2:

If the bass line is similar to this 7/4 line, the phrasing is 3 + 2 + 2:

Use the following play-along tracks to become comfortable playing rock in odd time with various phrasing patterns. Begin by practicing the written groove in each exercise, but don't forget to push your musical boundaries by experimenting with different drumset patterns (different bass drum rhythms, ghost notes, etc.) that correspond to the phrasing indicated. When comfortable with each exercise, try to add fills at the end of the four-bar phrase.

PLAY-ALONG 5/4 ROCK: 3 + 2

TRACK 166

PLAY-ALONG 5/4 ROCK: 2 + 3

TRACK 167

PLAY-ALONG 7/4 ROCK: 2 + 2 + 3

TRACK 168

PLAY-ALONG 7/4 ROCK: 2 + 3 + 2

TRACK 169

PLAY-ALONG 7/4 ROCK: 3 + 2 + 2

TRACK 170

Lesson 63

Advanced Odd-Time Rock

These exercises demonstrate advanced concepts of odd-time rock playing. For example, some songs are written in 3/4 time but are played in two-bar phrases. This means that the backbeat will actually be on beat 1 of the second 3/4 bar in each phrase, like this:

TRACK 171

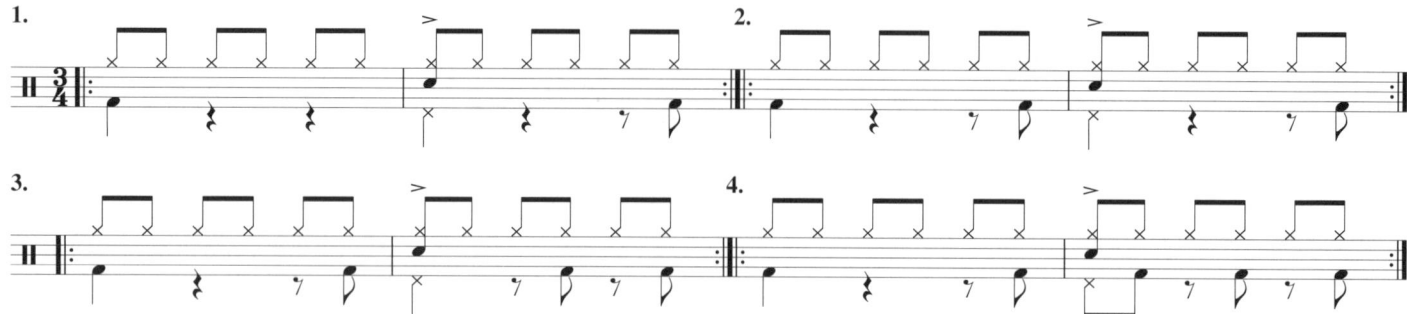

Ghost notes may also be added to these grooves to fill them out. In these exercises, play the snare drum backbeat with a strong accent and unaccented snare drum ghost notes very softly.

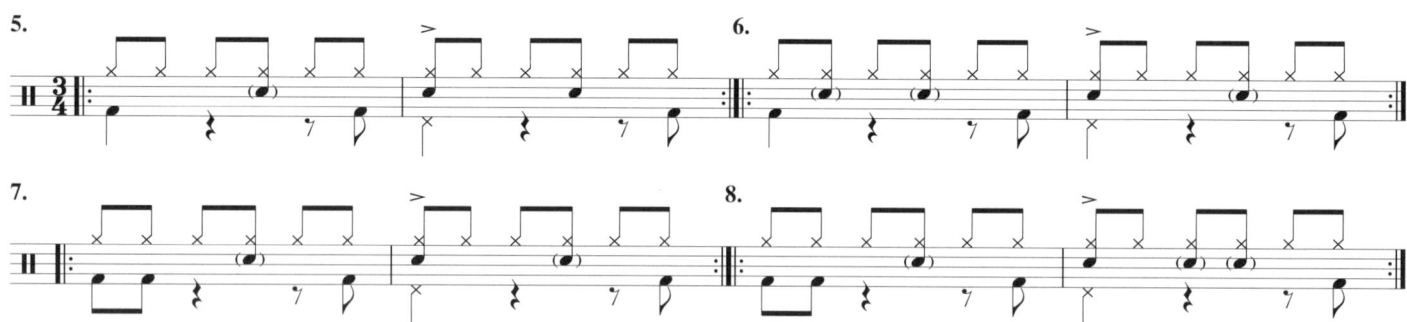

There are many different ways to interpret 5/4 measure phrasing. In many cases, however, when a 5/4 song is phrased 3 + 2, the (snare drum) backbeat is placed on beat 4, as in these examples. Hi-hat may also be played on beats 2, 3, and 5, if desired.

TRACK 172

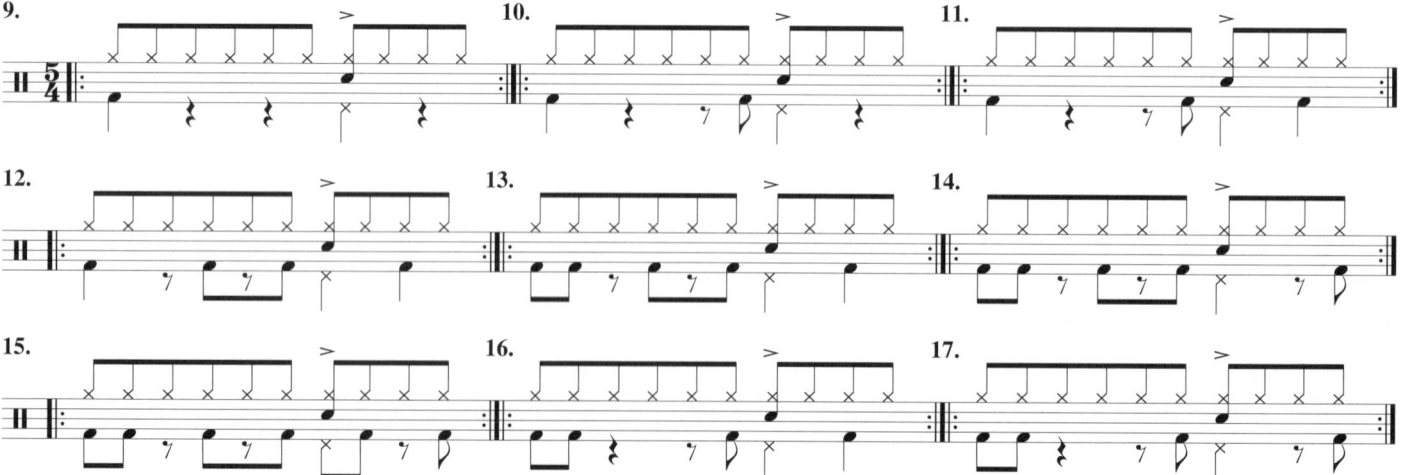

When a 5/4 song is phrased 2 + 3, often the backbeat is placed on beat 3, as in these examples. (Hi-hat may also be played on beats 2, 4, and 5, if desired.)

TRACK 173

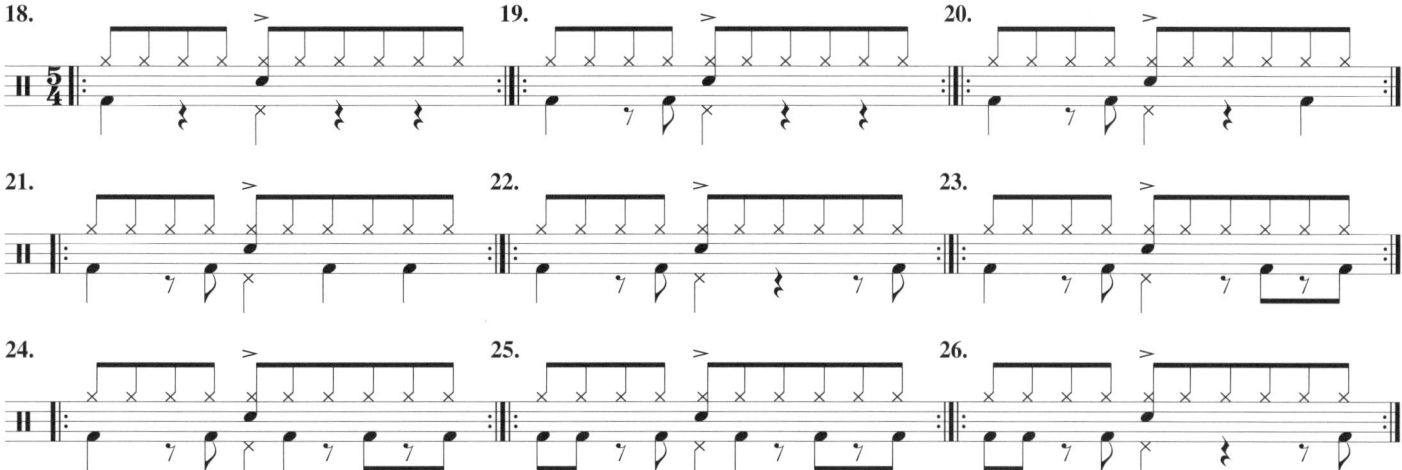

Seven-four time (7/4) may be phrased three different ways, and each way changes where the backbeats are played. Practice these exercises in order to understand where the backbeat occurs in different musical situations.

7/4 PHRASED 2 + 2 + 3
(Hi-hat may also be played on beats 2, 4, 6, and 7, or all beats.)

TRACK 174

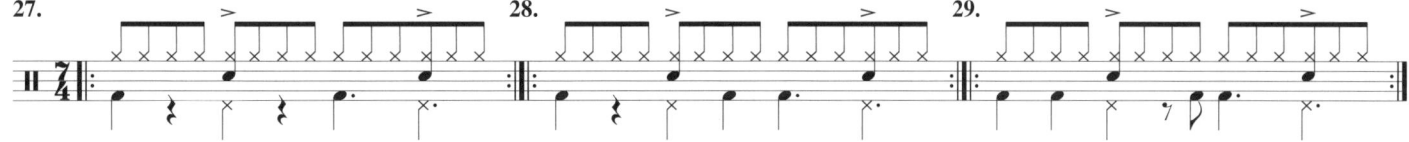

7/4 PHRASED 2 + 3 + 2
(Hi-hat may also be played on beats 2, 4, 5, and 7, or all beats.)

TRACK 175

7/4 PHRASED 3 + 2 + 2
(Hi-hat may also be played on beats 2, 3, 5, and 7, or all beats)

TRACK 176

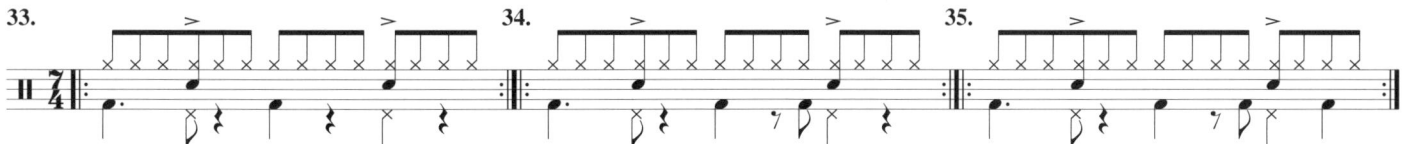

Lesson 64

Odd-Time Jazz

Like rock, jazz (or swing) may also be written and performed in odd meters. The most common example of odd-time jazz is the 3/4 jazz waltz, but tunes written in 5/4, 7/4, or other meters are very common in jazz today. Exercises 1–15 are some basic 3/4 jazz waltz grooves. In most jazz waltzes, the hi-hat plays only on beat 2. Be careful not to play the bass drum on beat 1 too loudly, as the groove needs to have a relaxed, lilting feeling. You may vary the snare drum/bass drum accents to create some different phrasing possibilities.

🔊 **TRACK 177**

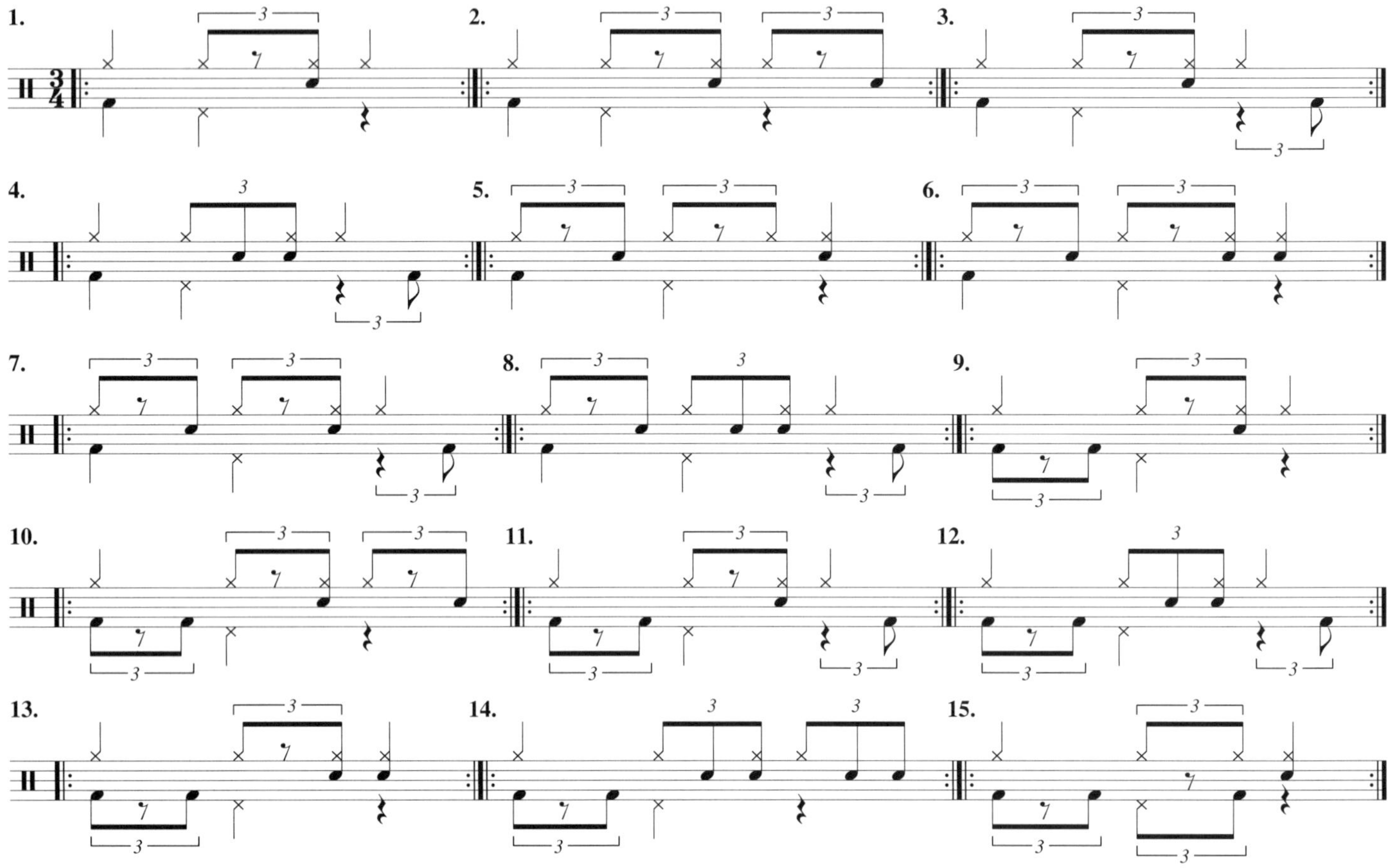

5/4 swing can be phrased in two ways. Beats in Examples 16–21 are phrased as 3 + 2.

🔊 **TRACK 178**

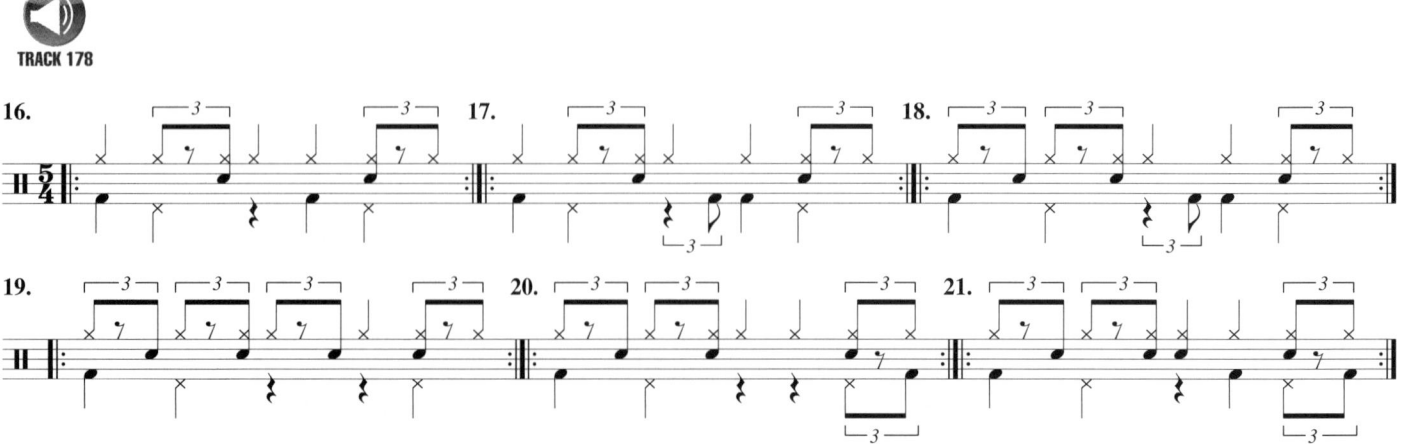

Examples 22–27 are phrased as 2 + 3.

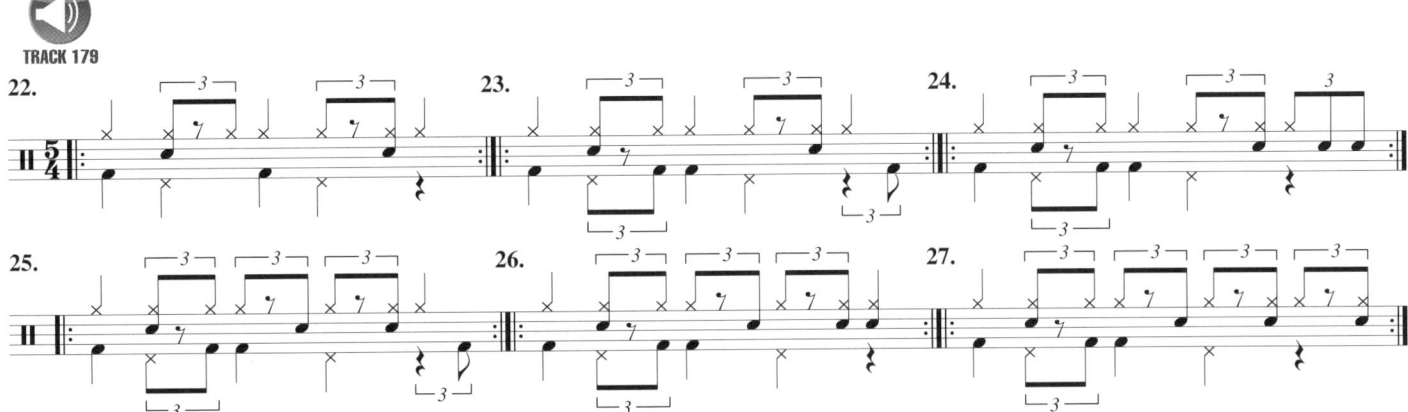

7/4 swing may be phrased three ways: 2 + 2 + 3 (the most common way), 2 + 3 + 2, or 3 + 2 + 2. The ride cymbal pattern reflects that in these exercises.

7/4 PHRASED 2 + 2 + 3

7/4 PHRASED 2 + 3 + 2

7/4 PHRASED 3 + 2 + 2

Lesson 65

Odd-Time Eighth-Note Meters

Songs written in eighth-note odd meters (e.g., 5/8, 7/8, 9/8, 11/8, etc.) are not uncommon and something that every drummer should understand. One of the most important aspects of working in odd meters is knowing how the meter should be counted and where to place the backbeat. Normally 5/8, for example, may be phrased either 3 (eighth notes) + 2 (eighth notes) or 2 + 3. If it's phrased 3 + 2, then the backbeat is normally played on beat 4. If it's phrased 2 + 3, then the backbeat is normally on beat 3. Practice these examples of 5/8 phrased 3 + 2, with the backbeat on beat 4. Count each eighth note of the bar: 1-2-3-4-5.

TRACK 183

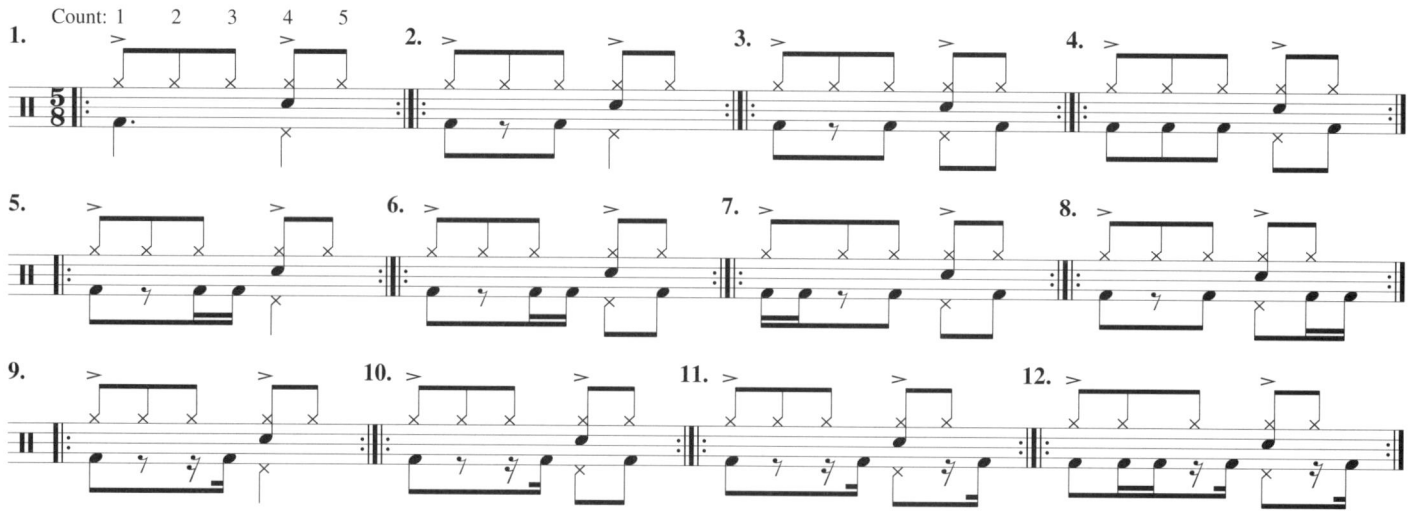

Examples 13–24 are examples of 5/8 phrased as 2 + 3, with the backbeat on beat 3.

TRACK 184

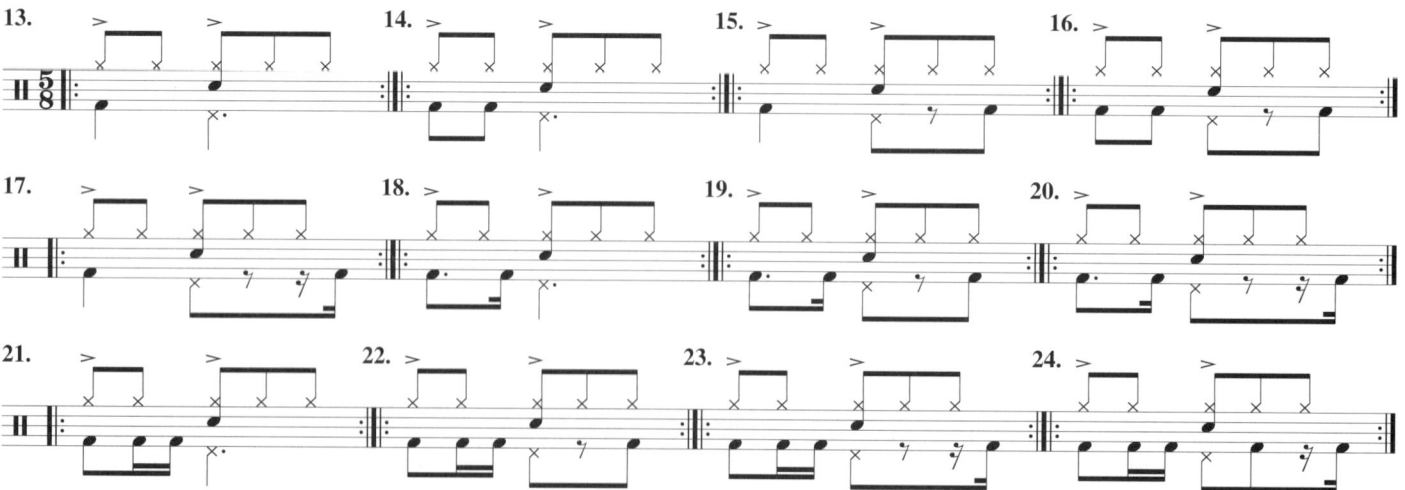

130

Exercises 25–48 demonstrate the phrasing possibilities in 7/8 and how the backbeat changes position depending upon the phrasing.

7/8 PHRASED 2 + 2 + 3 (BACKBEAT ON 5)

7/8 PHRASED 2 + 3 + 2 (BACKBEAT ON 3)

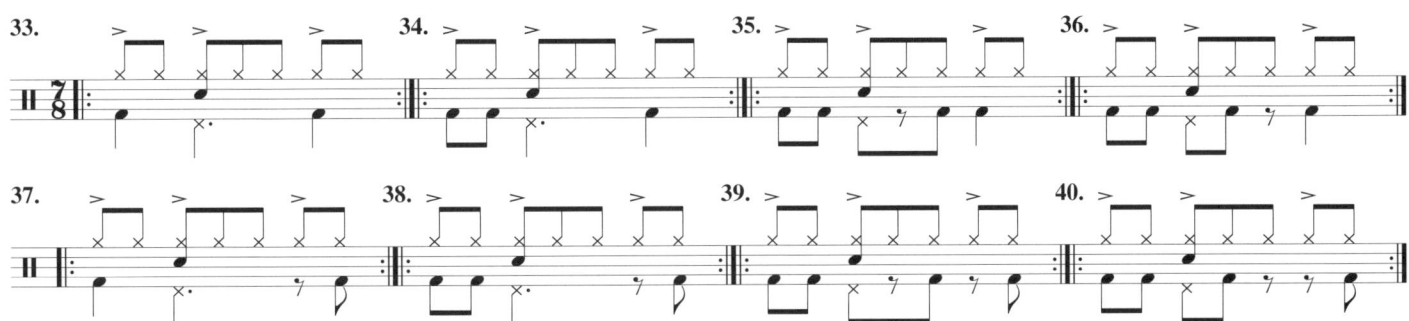

7/8 PHRASED 3 + 2 + 2 (BACKBEAT ON 4)

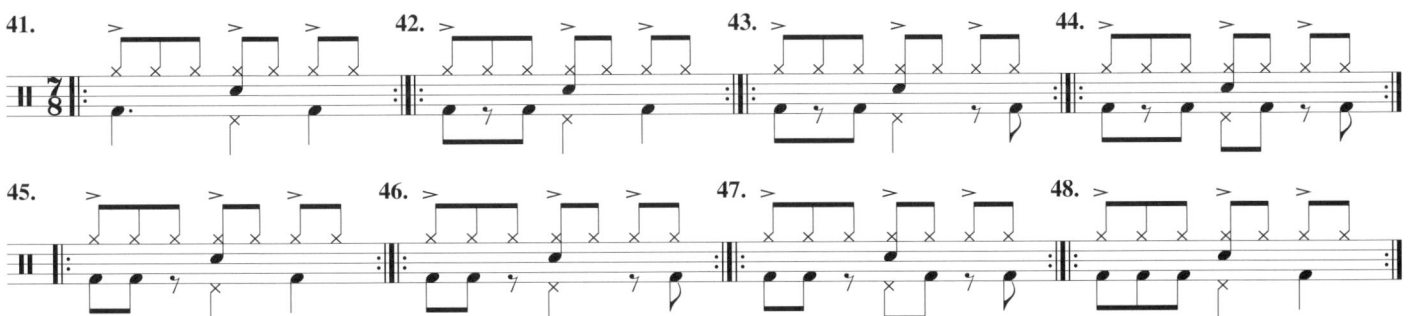

Once you're familiar with several odd meters (5/8, 7/8, etc.), it then becomes very easy to decipher any other, more advanced odd meters. For example, when encountering 9/8 phrased as 2 + 2 + 2 + 3, you could think of it as a 2/4 measure (2 + 2) plus a 5/8 measure (2 + 3). If you had 11/8 phrased as 2 + 2 + 2 + 2 + 3, it could be phrased as a 2/4 bar plus a 7/8 bar (2 + 2 + 2 + 3), or a 4/4 bar plus a 3/8 bar:

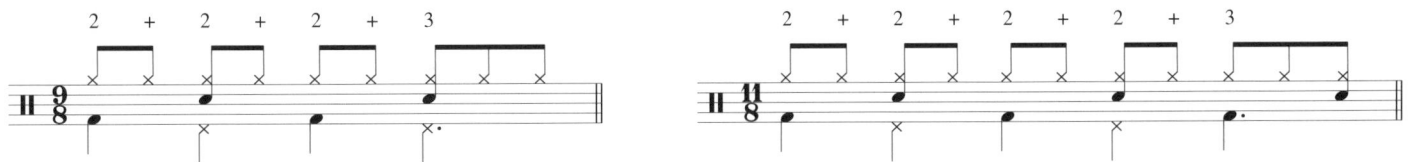

Use this last method to create your own odd meters and decipher any odd meter you encounter.

Lesson 66

Odd-Time Play-Along

Someone once said, "There are no difficult meters—just meters you don't play much (or at all)"—and they were right. No meter, or time signature, is inherently more difficult than any other; it's just that most people listen to (or play) music only in 4/4 time. People outside of North America and Europe grow up listening to their indigenous music in odd meters—6/8, 7/8, 5/8, 9/8, 11/8, etc.—and they think it's perfectly normal (which of course it is!). This means that you have to become accustomed to listening to and playing in odd meters in order to really have a world view of music (and be ready for anything).

Another consideration when playing in odd meters is how the music is written. For example, when someone says, "The meter is 5," does that mean 5/8 or 5/4? It depends. Here are two ways of writing the same music. Notice that the 5/8 example uses eighth notes as the basic subdivision, while 5/4 uses quarter notes as the basic subdivision.

How can you tell just by listening whether music is in 5/8 or 5/4 time? The truth is that you can't. Often, the difference lies in the tempo (speed) of the music; i.e., 5/8 is often used when the tempo is fast, and 5/4 is used when the tempo is slower or the music is more rhythmically dense. It doesn't really matter whether it's written in 5/8 or 5/4 as long as you can feel and play the right phrasing for the music. The only time it is important to know whether or not music is written in 5/8 or 5/4 is when a song "mixes meters"—changes from a meter with a quarter-note pulse (4/4) to one with an eighth-note pulse (5/8), which will be discussed later in this lesson.

Use the following play-along tracks in 5, 7, and 9 to gain experience with the most common odd meters. You can vary the groove as your skill improves, and you may play the ride part on closed hi-hat (by omitting the hi-hat foot part) if you wish. When comfortable, try to add a fill at the end of each phrase and a crash on beat 1 of each phrase.

PLAY-ALONG TRACKS 188–190

(Four clicks to start—representing the downbeat of each bar)

Notice the next play-along exercises have two different ways of phrasing for 11 and 13: 11/8 phrased 2 + 2 + 2 + 2 + 3 or 3 + 3 + 3 + 2, and 13/8 phrased either 2 + 2 + 2 + 2 + 2 + 3 or 3 + 3 + 3 + 4.

PLAY-ALONG TRACKS 191–194

(Click is one bar of 11/8)

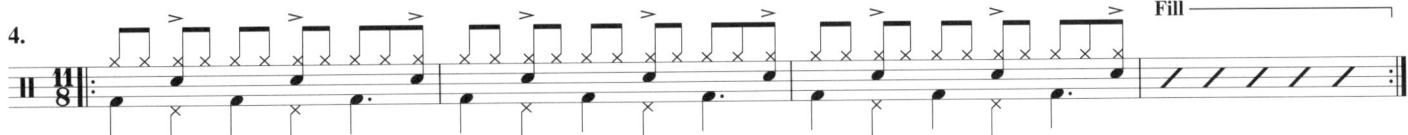

(Click is one bar of 11/8)

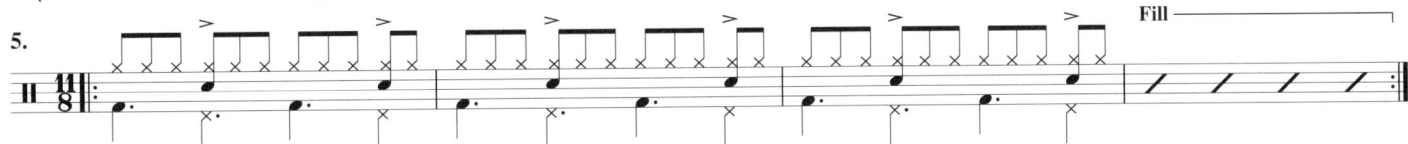

(Click is one bar of 13/8)

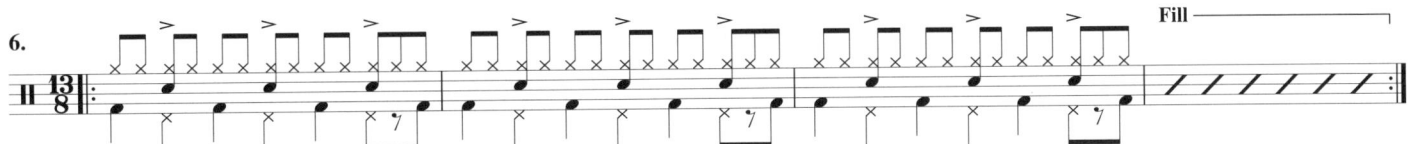

(Click is one bar of 13/8)

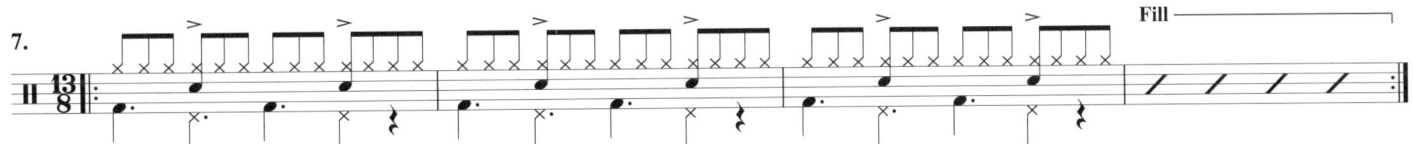

Mixing meters—combining different meters into the same song—can provide an interesting twist to music, particularly if some meters use an eighth-note subdivision and others use a quarter-note one. In the example below, count all of the eighth notes in the 4/4 bars ("1+2+3+4+") and then continue counting eighth notes through the odd meter bar ("1-2-3-4-5") at exactly the same speed in order to keep the correct relationship between the eighth notes in both meters. Listen (and count) this example like this: "1+2+3+4+, 2+2+3+4+, 3+2+3+4+, 1-2-3-4-5," and then repeat for each subsequent time through the form.

TRACK 195

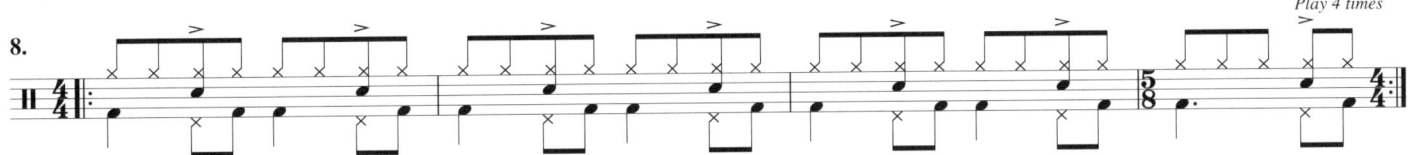

After mastering the previous odd meters (5, 7, 9, 11, and 13), it will be easier to play any new odd meter simply by doing some math. For example, large odd meters can be constructed by combining 2/4, 3/4, or 4/4 bars with an odd meter bar, like this:

METER	PHRASING (IN 8TH NOTES)	CONSTRUCTION
15/8	2 + 2 + 2 + 2 + 2 + 2 + 3	4/4 bar + 7/8 bar
	3 + 3 + 3 + 3 + 3	5 groups of 3 (or 5 groups of triplets)
17/8	2 + 2 + 2 + 2 + 2 + 2 + 2 + 3	4/4 bar + 9/8 (2 + 2 + 2 + 3)

Lesson 67

Odd-Time Soloing Play-Alongs

After learning to play some odd-time grooves alone, it's important to begin working on soloing in odd time as well. Soloing in an odd meter is conceptually no different than soloing in 4/4 time. You may use any of the techniques you've learned in other lessons or while soloing in 4/4 time; you'll simply adapt them to different time signatures. Normally, the most difficult aspect of soloing in odd meters is feeling the downbeat of each bar and knowing how many bars you've spent soloing. To address this issue, begin by playing a crash cymbal on beat 1 of every bar in order to reinforce the downbeat in your mind. When you've become comfortable feeling the downbeat of each bar, try only playing a crash cymbal every two bars; then try to solo in a complete four-bar phrase (without a crash cymbal on the downbeat of every bar).

You may substitute other odd-time grooves for each written example as you become more comfortable; the particular groove you use is less important than synchronizing your part with the track and becoming comfortable with soloing in an odd meter. Use the following play-along tracks to practice trading fours in 3/4, 5/4, and 7/4 rock and swing styles:

PLAY-ALONG
TRACKS 196–201

After becoming comfortable trading fours in odd meters, use the following play-along tracks to practice trading eights in 3/4, 5/4, and 7/4 rock and swing styles. One approach to dealing with this larger amount of solo space is to think of trading eights as two sets of four-bar phrases. Another approach would be to use longer solo ideas or motives. For example, instead of using eight one-bar ideas, try to use four two-bar ideas or two four-bar ideas when trading eights.

PLAY-ALONG TRACKS 202–207

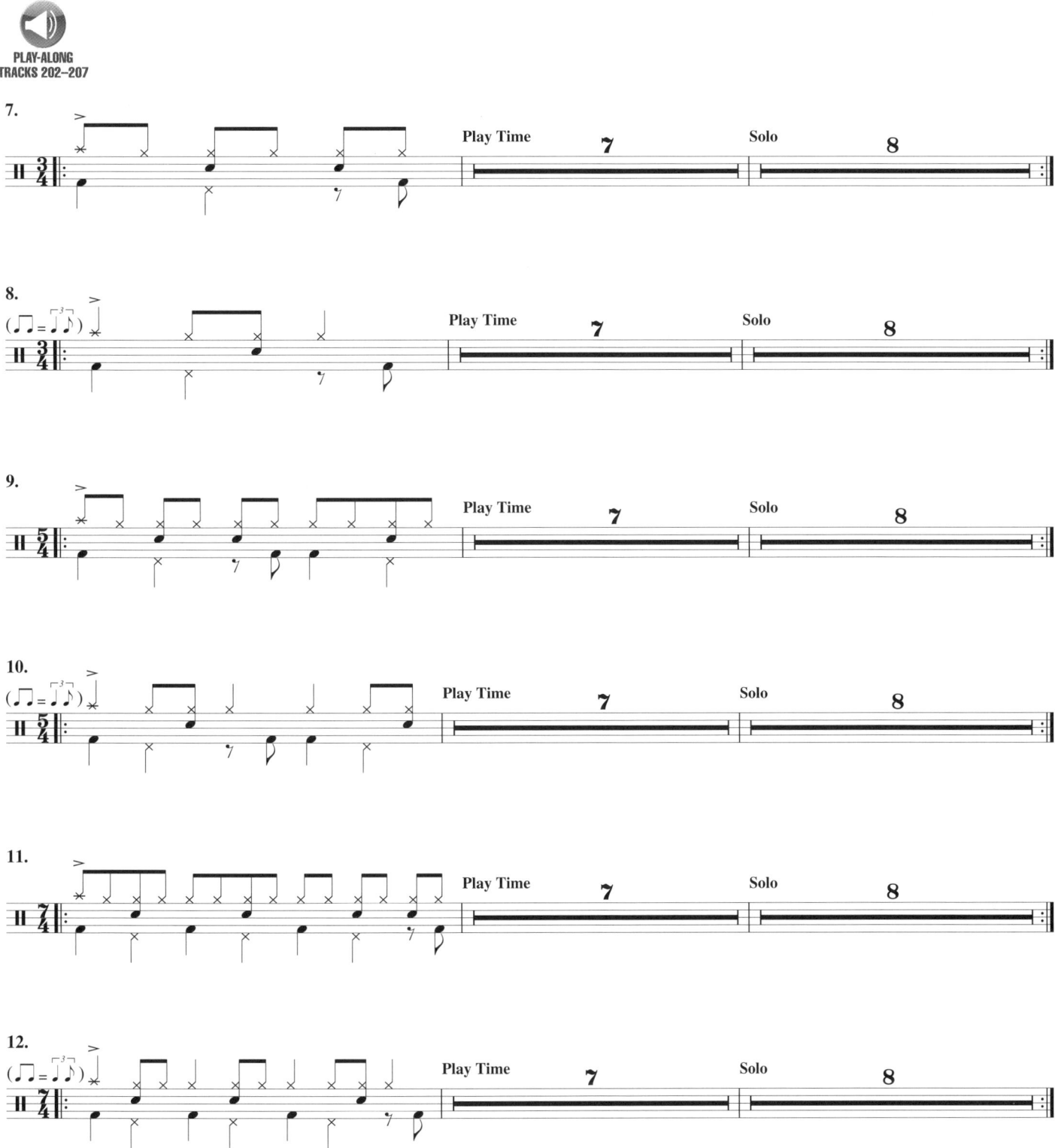

Lesson 68

The 12/8 Groove

The 12/8 groove is one that every drummer should know. It can be played at many different tempos (very slow to fast) and is used in blues, country, pop, and rock. Although it's called the "12/8 groove" (Example A), it is sometimes written in 4/4 time using triplets (Example B). Both versions are the same; they each contain four primary pulses per bar, with each pulse divided into three notes.

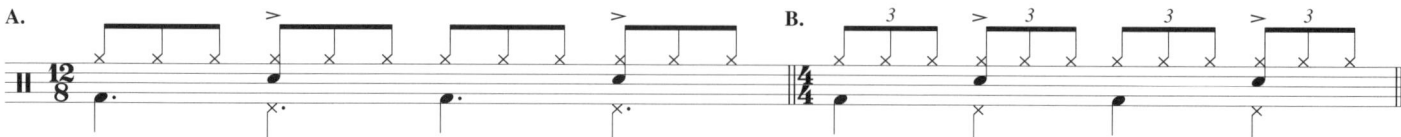

Practice the following grooves as written, and then with these variations:

- Ride pattern (RH) on a closed hi-hat
- Cross-stick on beats 2 and 4
- With brushes in both hands on the snare drum
- With a brush in the right hand playing the ride pattern (on ride, hi-hat, or snare drum) and a cross-stick in the left hand

TRACK 208

These 12/8 grooves have some 16th-note bass drum variations that are frequently used at slower tempos.

TRACK 209

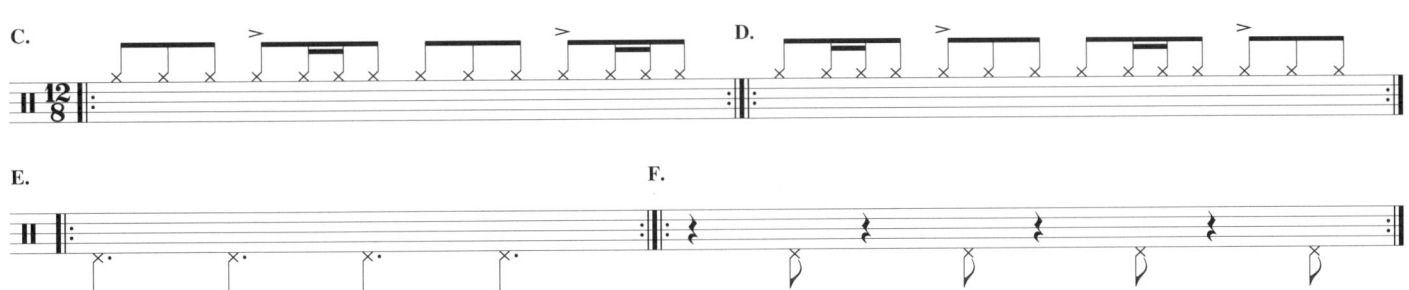

The 12/8 groove may also be enhanced with additional 16th notes in the ride pattern or different hi-hat rhythms. Practice all of the previous exercises with these ride cymbal variations (Examples C and D) and/or hi-hat variations (Examples E and F).

Lesson 69

Blues Drumming

Blues drumming covers a broad range of drumset styles, grooves, and techniques. It involves knowing a variety of different feels—shuffles, swing, straight eighth, and 16th-note patterns—because the blues has evolved and grown since its birth over 100 years ago. To properly play the many different styles of blues, you must be familiar with its evolution and play the style of blues that suits that time period. Early blues grooves (mostly shuffles) were played with two brushes on the snare (1930s); this was followed by the jazz blues in the 1940s and '50s, which used the jazz ride cymbal pattern on the ride.

The blues changed in the 1950s from a triplet-based feel to a straight eighth-note feel, and those patterns helped lead the way for R&B and early rock 'n' roll. Here are some examples of early medium tempo straight eighth-note blues/R&B grooves. Notice that they are very similar to rock patterns played in the 1950s and '60s.

TRACK 210

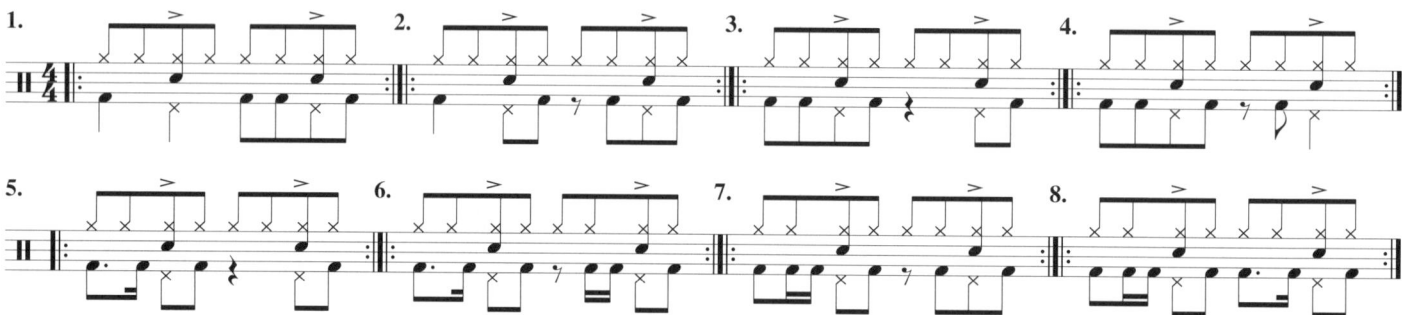

The following 16th-note blues grooves may be played on slower blues tunes from the 1950s and '60s on either a closed hi-hat or ride cymbal.

TRACK 211

These next examples of syncopated blues grooves don't fit into other blues categories, but are still a part of the blues vocabulary.

TRACK 212

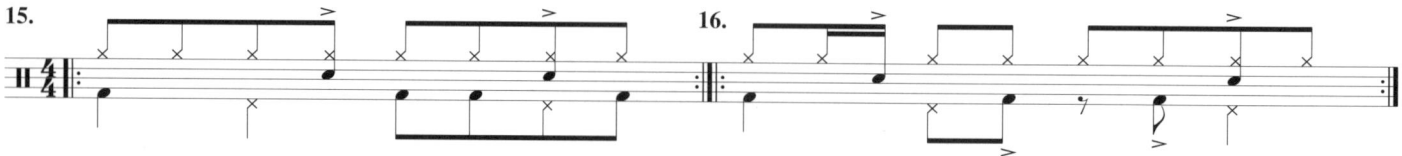

Some slow blues tunes use 12/8 grooves, which may also be played on either a ride cymbal or closed hi-hat.

TRACK 213

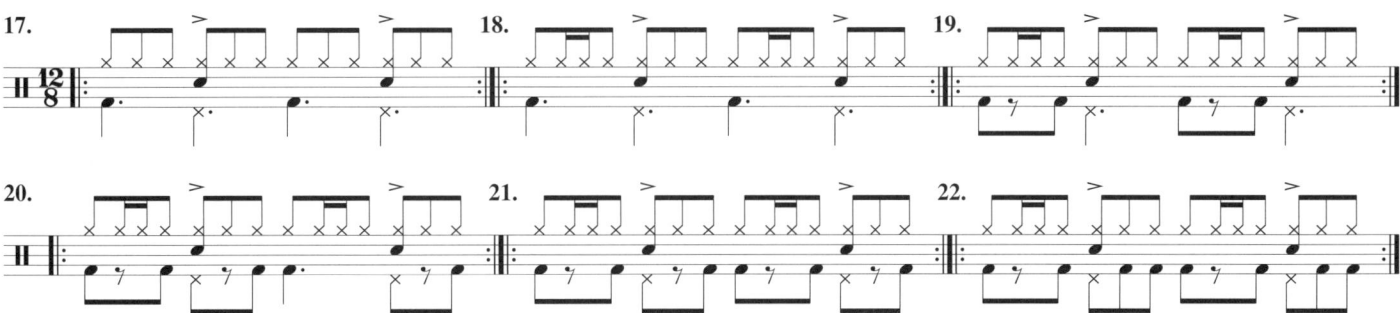

The "Bo Diddley beat" is a drum pattern based on the Cuban 3-2 clave pattern and has been included in blues repertoire since the 1950s. It can be played a number of different ways—entirely on the floor tom or on different parts of the drumset (see below). The eighth notes were originally "swung," but rock players later played this pattern with a straight eighth-note feel.

TRACK 214

Medium-tempo blues tunes may also be written in 6/4 time (or as two 3/4 bars). Singer Janis Joplin frequently sang the blues in 6/4 time during the 1960s.

TRACK 215

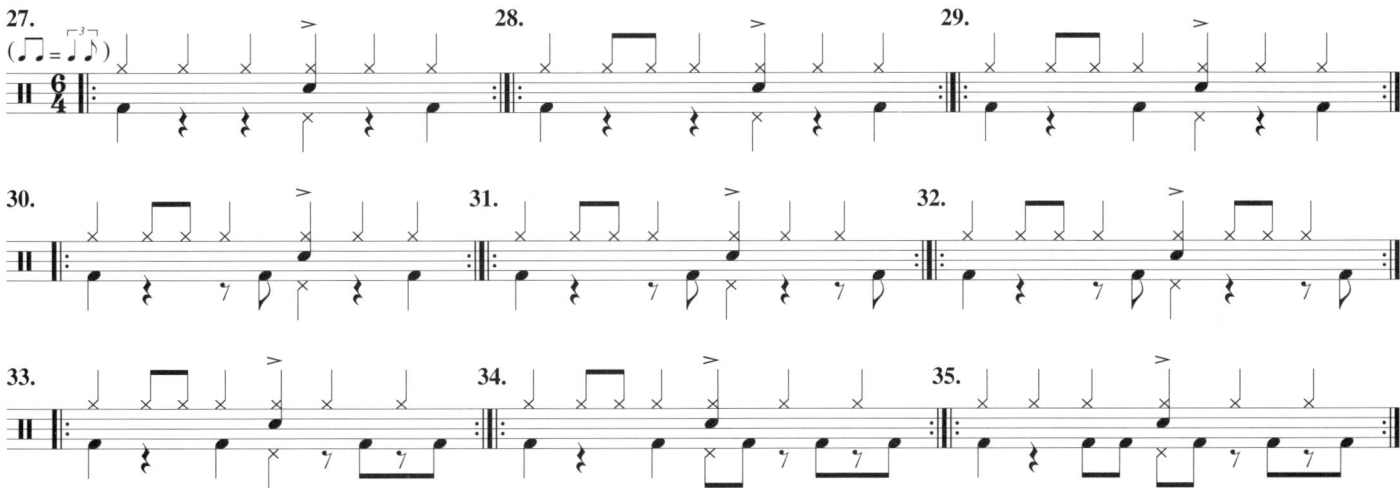

Country Drumming

Country music has evolved over the last 100 years and has historically embraced the influences of other musical styles. Drummers who play country music today must be familiar with a range of styles because country music performances may include a country rock song, a slow waltz, a song requiring a train beat, and/or a song in 12/8 time. A great deal of contemporary country music now uses rock drum patterns, so many rock grooves and fills will work when playing country music. One of the differences between rock and country, however, is the orchestration of a country music drum part (*what* is played and *when*). Listening to the many different styles of country music and noting what the drummer chooses to play in each section of a song is very important when studying country music. One common orchestral trend in country music is to begin a song with the hi-hat alone on beats 2 and 4 and then build into an eighth-note hi-hat groove with a cross-stick on beats 2 and 4 during the verses, followed by a ride cymbal groove with snare drum on beats 2 and 4 during the louder sections of a song (often the chorus).

In addition to being familiar with how to orchestrate a drum part, a drummer must know a number of grooves that are commonly used in country music. One of the most important grooves identified with country music is the *train beat*, which is named for its similarity to the sound of a moving train. The train beat was traditionally played on just the snare drum with brushes, but today can also be played with sticks or brush substitutes. These two examples illustrate how the train beat can be written two different ways but sound the same.

TRACK 216

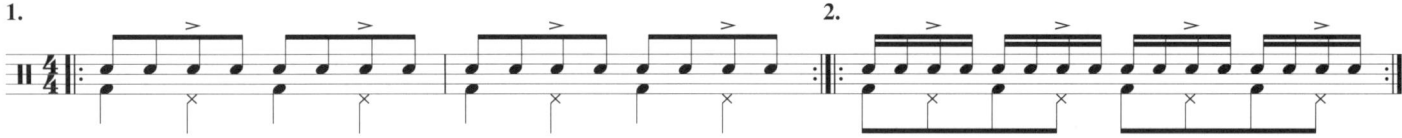

The country waltz is another groove that is an essential part of a country drummer's vocabulary. Here are some common one- and two-bar country waltz variations. The ride pattern may also be played on closed hi-hat.

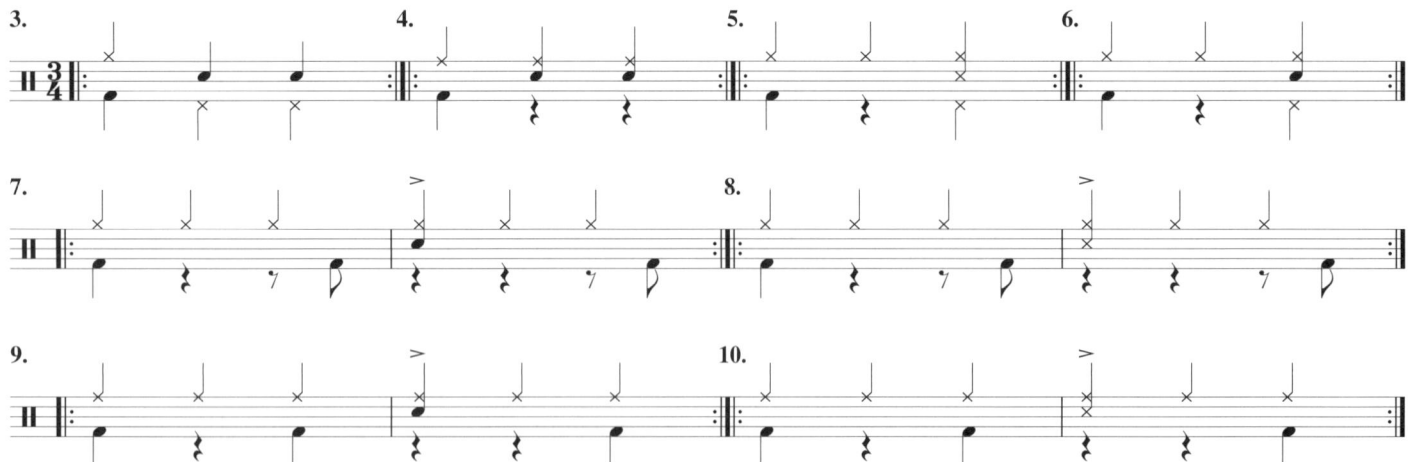

The 12/8 groove became part of country drumming through the blues and swing influence and is often required in country music settings. The ride pattern may also be played on closed hi-hat.

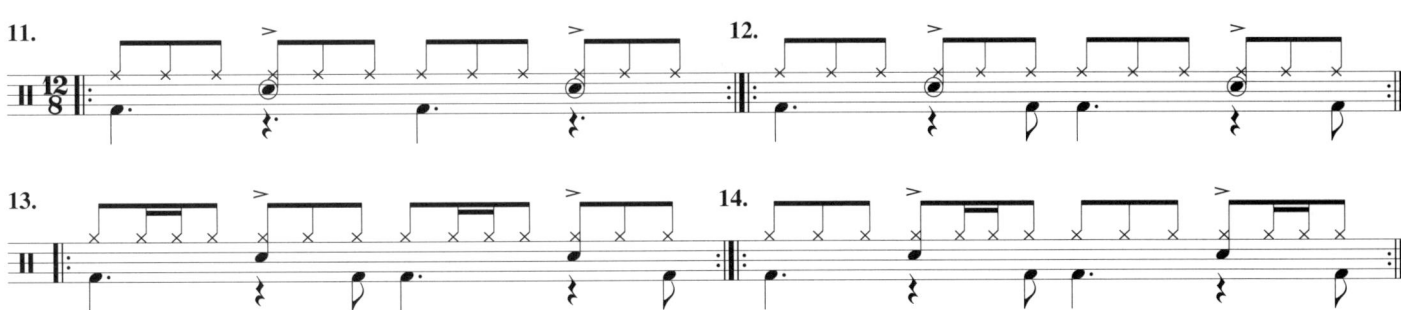

Western swing is part of country music's history, but drums weren't originally used in its early days (the 1930s and '40s). Drums eventually began to be used in the western swing style, borrowing patterns from traditional swing and blues styles. Early drummers often used only brushes. One element that separates traditional swing music from western swing is the backbeat. Western swing *always* has a strong backbeat. It's normally played on the snare drum underneath a ride or hi-hat swing pattern, but may also be played with two brushes (Exercise 19).

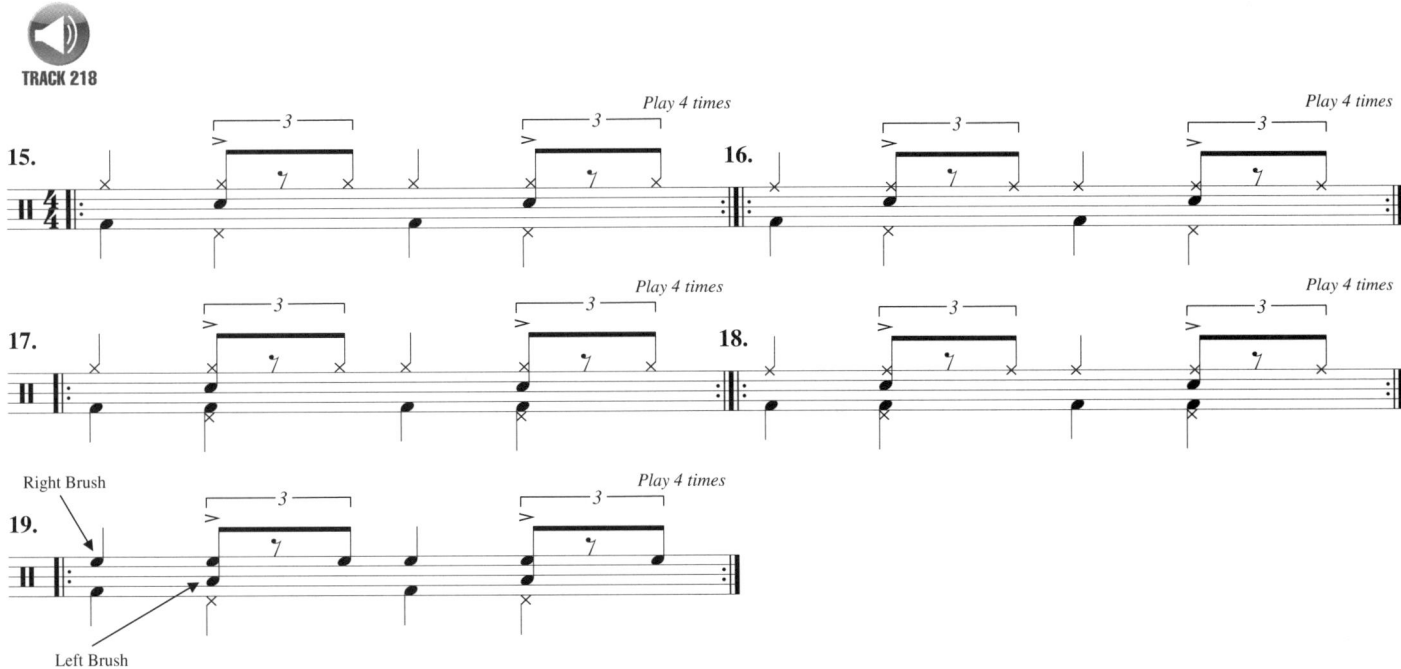

These are some country shuffles—another important groove used by many country drummers.

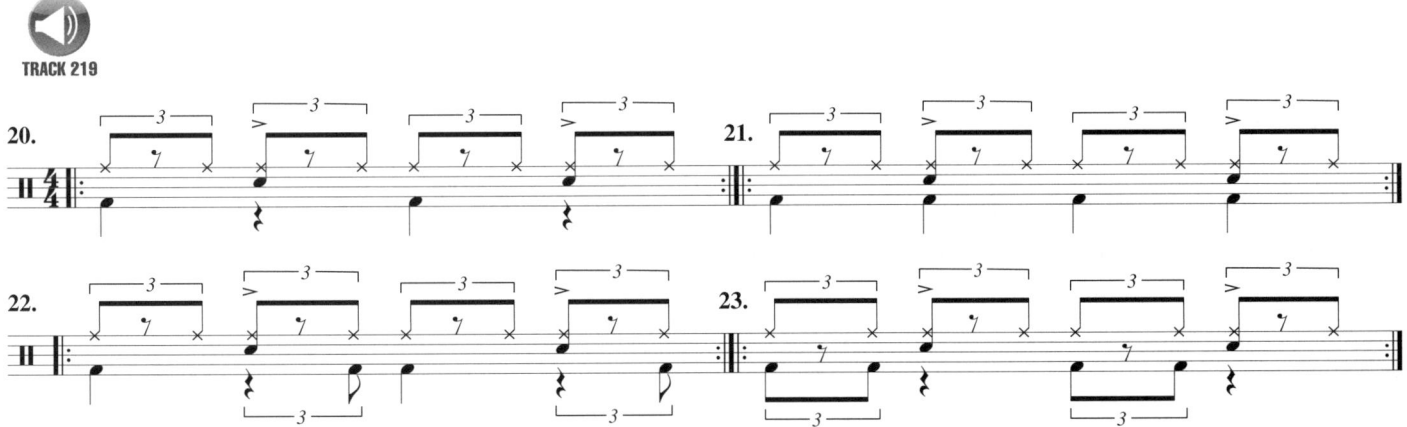

Lesson 71

Shuffle Grooves

A *shuffle* is a triplet-based drumset groove that started in the 1930s and '40s during the swing era. There are many different types of shuffles that have developed over the years in a variety of musical styles—jazz, blues, country, and rock—and the shuffle can be found in most popular musical styles of the 20th century.

Early shuffles were played with two brushes on the snare drum. The right hand played the shuffle rhythm, and the left hand played the backbeat (beats 2 and 4):

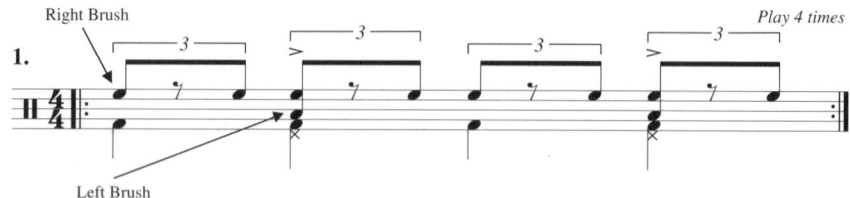

A jazz shuffle, which developed later, can use either the jazz ride cymbal pattern or a triplet ride cymbal pattern that omits the second partial of each triplet. The hands work together to gently stress beats 2 and 4, rather than heavily accent the beat, as is the case in later rock shuffle styles. In this style, the bass drum is "feathered," which means it's played very lightly on all four beats. The bass drum should be felt rather than actually heard and should be soft enough not to obscure the bass player's notes. This can be achieved by playing with the right heel completely resting on the bass drum pedal board (known as *heel down* technique) and playing the bass drum beater from a height of only 2–3 inches from the head.

Jazz shuffles can also include some syncopated bass drum rhythms. Be sure to continue the accents in the snare drum while simultaneously adding the accents in the bass drum part.

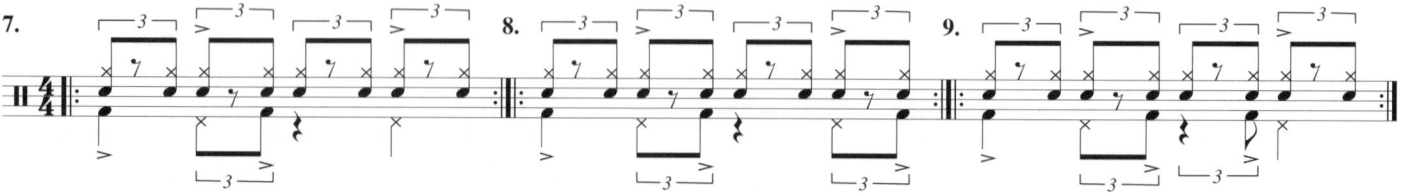

Blues shuffles developed in the 1940s and tend to be a bit heavier and louder than jazz shuffles, with more emphasis on the snare drum and bass drum. Notice that some of these examples are not written any differently than some of the previous jazz shuffles, but the balance between the snare, bass, and ride cymbal is different (the snare and bass are louder). Blues shuffles are often played on a closed or half-open hi-hat.

TRACK 223

If a shuffle is too fast to play with all of the triplets in the ride part, you can substitute this groove, which uses a half-open quarter-note hi-hat part. To create the proper sound for these grooves, release the pressure on the hi-hat footboard slightly (but don't remove your foot completely from the pedal) to allow the two hi-hat cymbals to rub together and create a "sizzle" sound as you strike them. The "slushiness" of the hi-hat, combined with the triplets in the snare drum, creates an overall shuffle feel. The three examples are performed in three different tempos (slower to very fast); master all three and you will have a groove that you can use in almost any musical situation requiring a blues shuffle.

TRACK 224

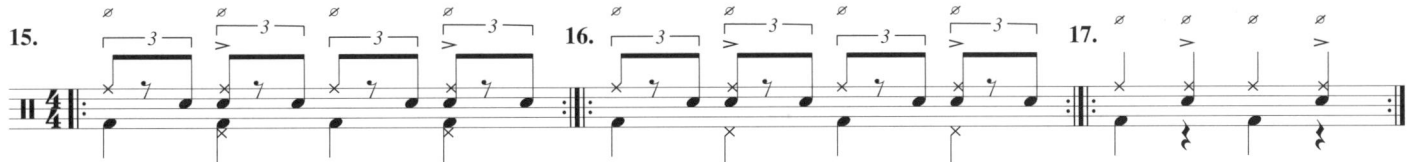

Rock shuffles are normally the heaviest and loudest shuffles and focus more on the "melody" created between the bass drum and snare drum. Often the left hand plays only the backbeat on beats 2 and 4, and the ride cymbal (or closed hi-hat) plays the triplets that give the groove its shuffle identity.

TRACK 225

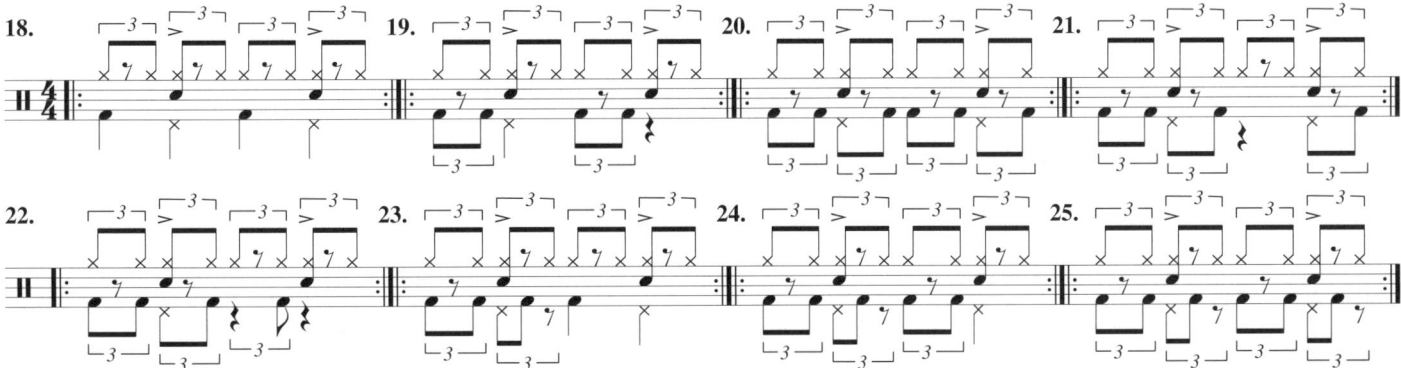

143

Lesson 72

Rockabilly and Surf Drumming

Rockabilly is an early form of rock 'n' roll, and its name is a combination of "rock" and "hillbilly" (country) music. It burst onto the national pop music scene in the mid-1950s. Other influences that helped create rockabilly include R&B, western swing (country) music, honky tonk, and boogie woogie. Many early rock artists, such as Elvis Presley and Eddie Cochran, played in a rockabilly style before it became rock 'n' roll. As a style, it has had several revivals over the years (late 1960s, 1980s) in which a few bands decided to recapture the rockabilly sound for a new generation.

Rockabilly often uses swing drum grooves with a heavy backbeat. Exercises 1–5 are only a few examples of rockabilly grooves. They may also be played with a quarter-note ride pattern on half-open hi-hats for a different sound.

TRACK 226

Surf music, which emerged in the early 1960s, was closely associated with the surfing culture of southern California. Featuring distinctive drum grooves and a twangy guitar sound, it's characterized by the double eighth-note snare backbeats on beat 2. Exercises 6–13 demonstrate some of the famous surf drum grooves found on thousands of recordings that defined an era in pop music.

TRACK 227

One of the world's most famous drum solos can be found in the surf music style. Based on, and similar to, the tom solo played by Gene Krupa on "Sing, Sing, Sing," it substitutes 16th notes for Krupa's swing eighth notes, but the effect is the same. This is a short example that is similar to the solo.

TRACK 228

Lesson 73

Basic Hip-Hop

Hip-hop is a term used to describe music that is part of the hip-hop culture—an urban subculture that emerged in the 1970s. Early hip-hop music involved only DJs, who mixed vinyl recordings and "scratched" turntables (manually manipulating a record back-and-forth to create rhythmic patterns from the sounds on a recording). Hip-hop DJs later began sampling and looping short drum solos (known as *breaks*), found in popular 1970s soul or funk tunes, and rapping over the drum loops. Other artists began creating their own original loops, and the genre evolved into what we hear today. Many hip-hop tunes are created using drum machines or computer programs and are normally characterized by syncopated 16th-note bass drum rhythms, a strong snare drum backbeat (on beats 2 and 4), ghost notes, and sometimes some displaced backbeats (accented snare drum notes on beats other than 2 and 4).

Here are some hip-hop style grooves. Since hip-hop is a descendent of funk and rock, some of the exercises will look and sound like familiar funk/rock grooves. Practice these grooves between 74–108 beats per minute (BPM) and concentrate on a relaxed, consistent time feel.

TRACK 229

Exercises 1–24 may also be played on the ride cymbal and with accents either on or off the beat (on the "ands" of the beat).

In addition to the straight eighth-note feel shown in the previous examples, the *hip-hop shuffle* is an important groove to master. The grooves are normally written with an eighth-note hi-hat/ride pattern (which is played straight), but with 16th-note snare and bass rhythms that are intended to be swung (which means the 16th notes are actually played like 16th-note triplets, as notated in Example B). These exercises also include open hi-hat notes.

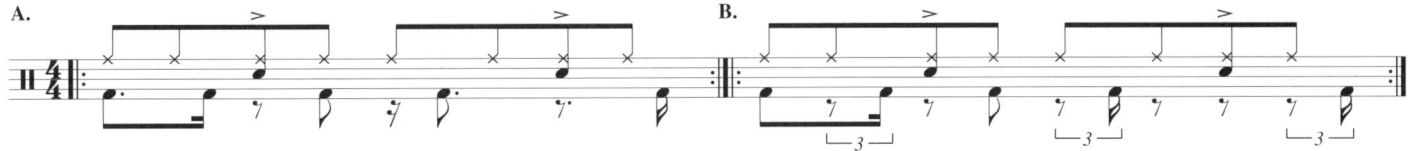

Swing the snare drum/bass drum rhythms while playing straight eighth notes in Exercises 25–52.

Lesson 74

Advanced Hip-Hop

These advanced versions of the hip-hop shuffle are sometimes referred to as a "half-time shuffle" and are also heard in R&B and pop music. The unaccented 16th-note triplet ghost notes are an important part of this feel and should be played very softly, while the backbeat (beats 2 and 4 on the snare drum) should have a solid accent. Use Exercises A and B to prepare for these intricate grooves, and also as warm-ups.

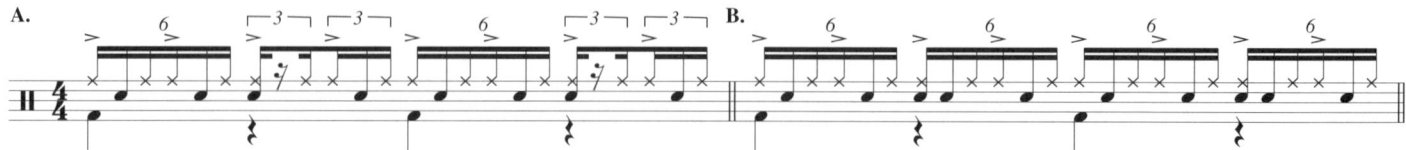

These are examples of the half-time hip-hop shuffle with various bass drum patterns and open hi-hats.

TRACK 231

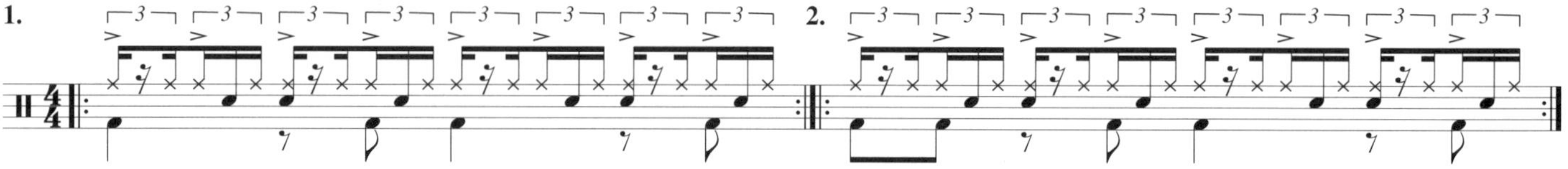

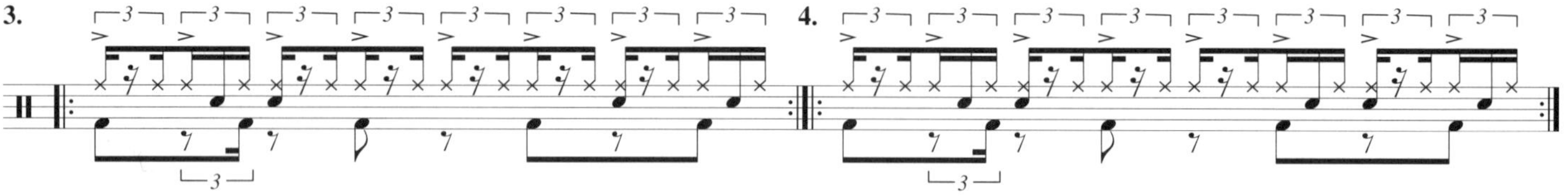

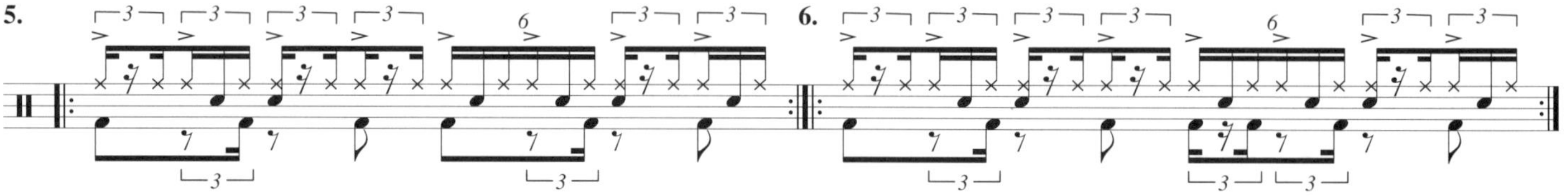

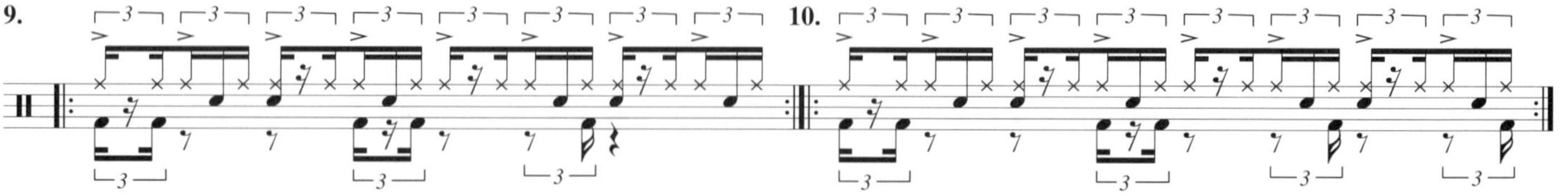

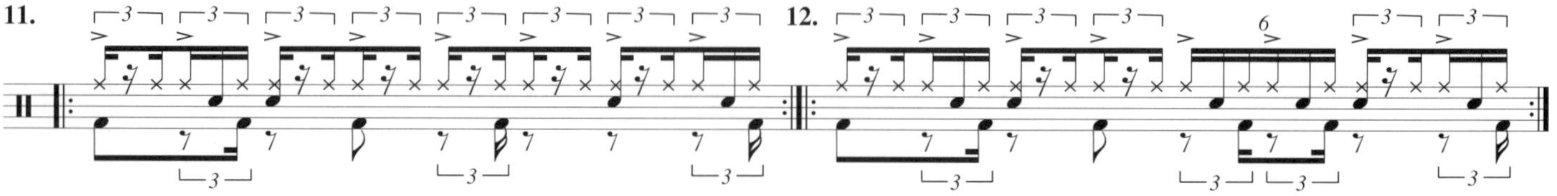

TRACK 232

13.

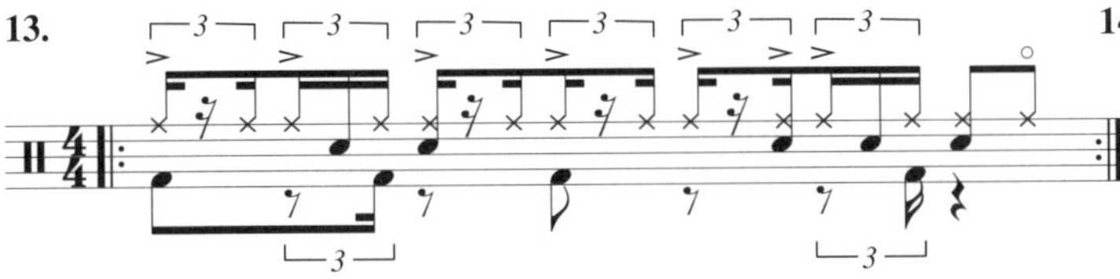

14.

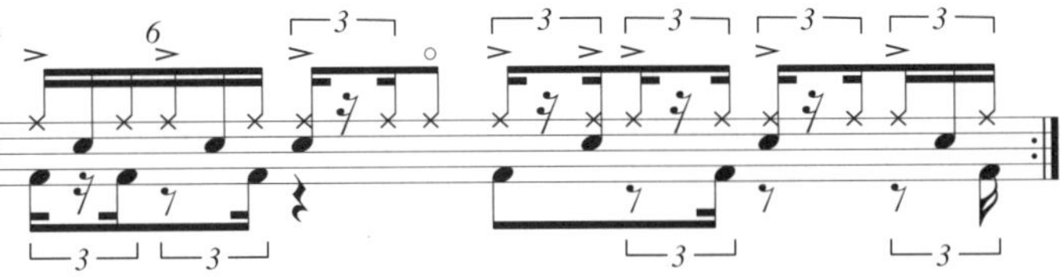

15.

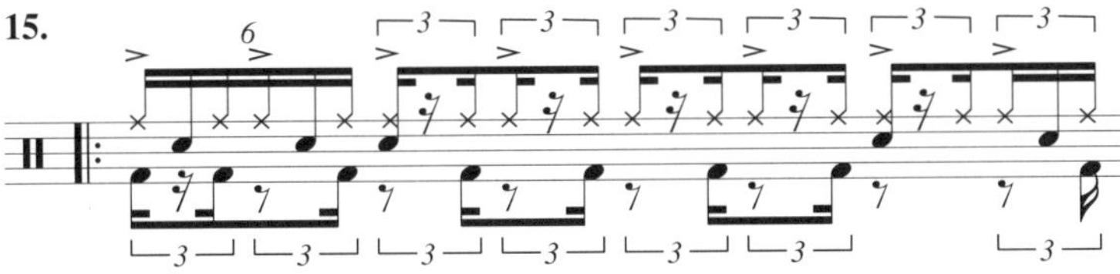

16.

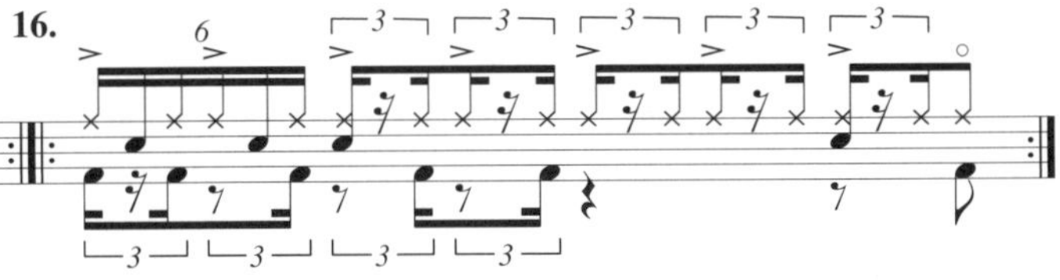

17.

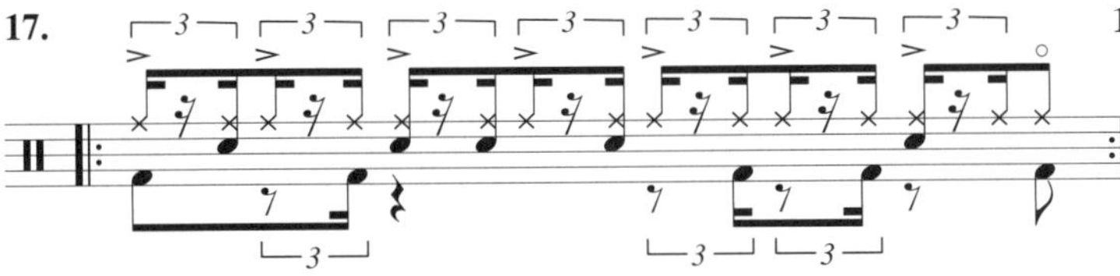

18.

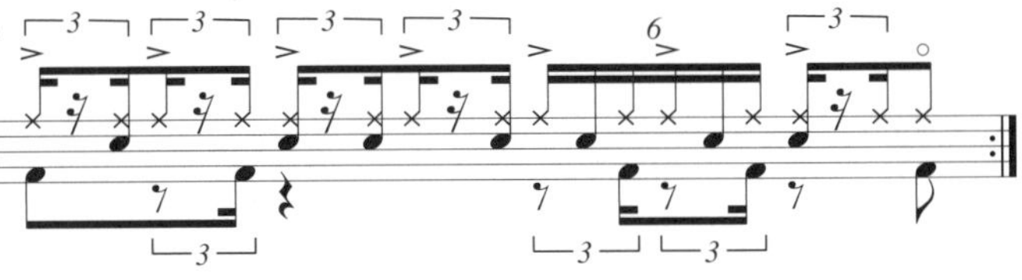

19.

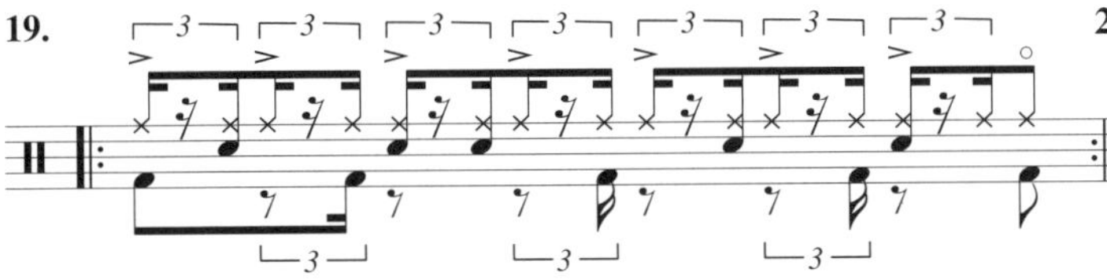

20.

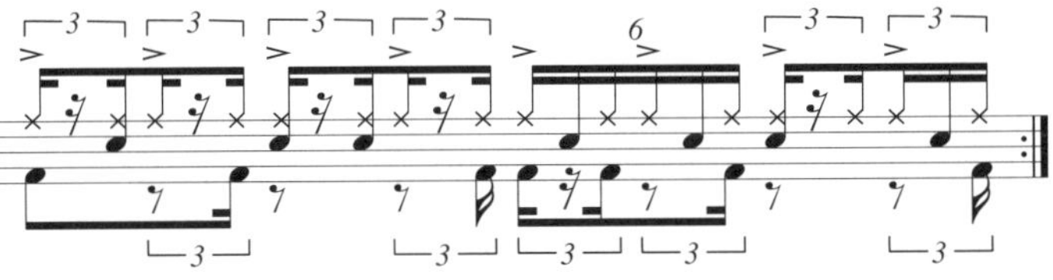

21.

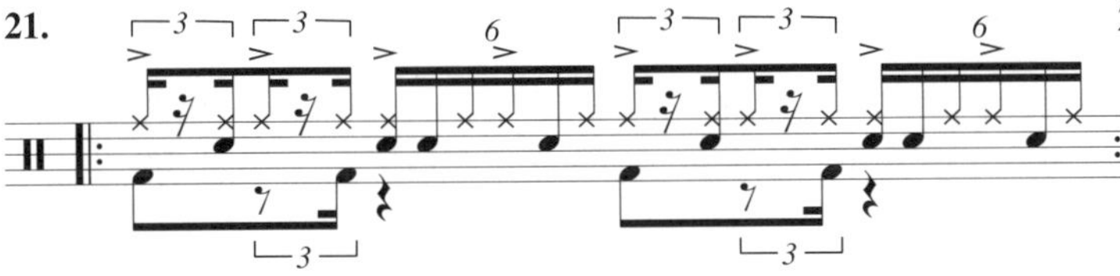

22.

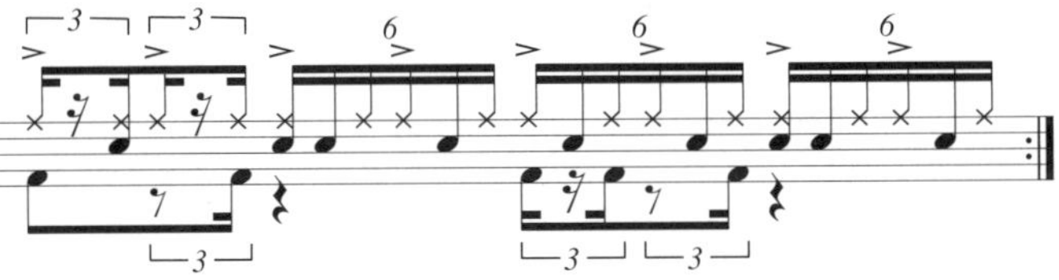

23.

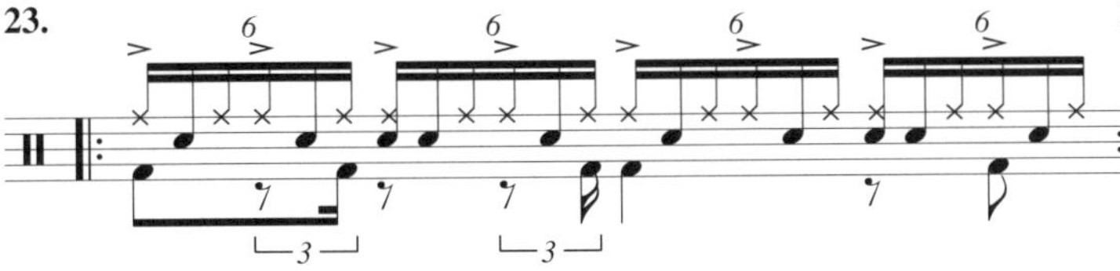

24.

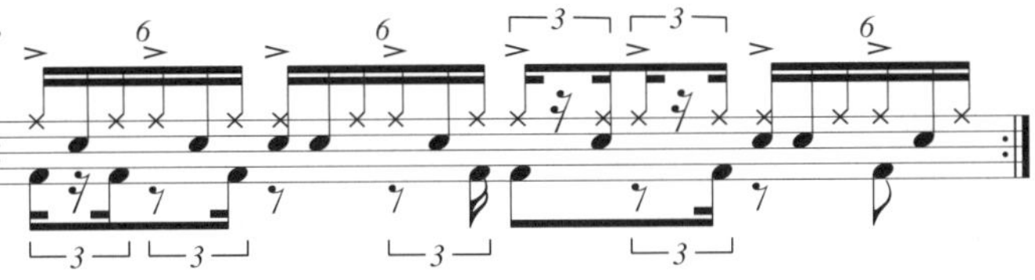

25.

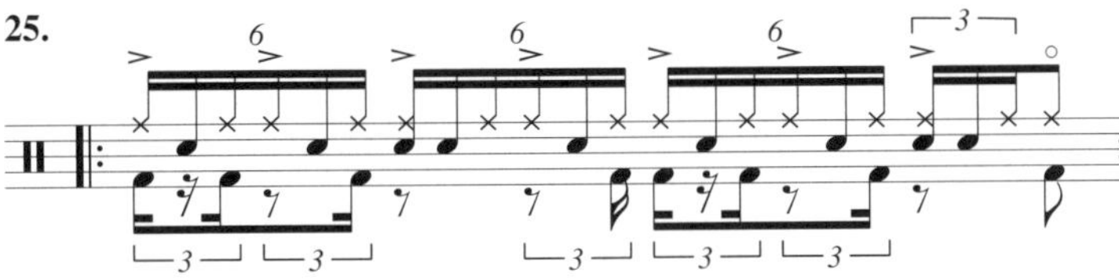

26.

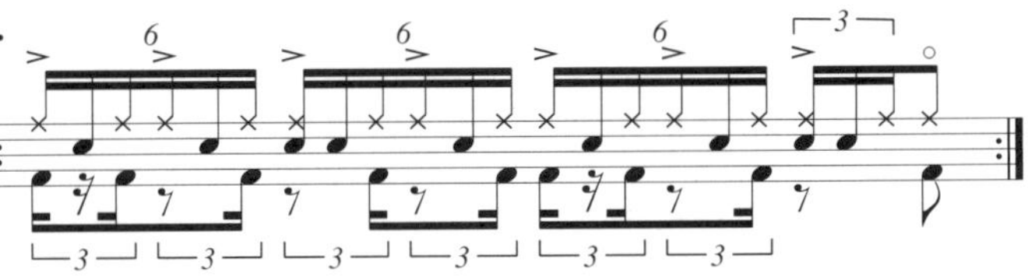

Lesson 75

Drum N' Bass/Break Beats

Drum n' bass is a term used to describe the electronic dance music that developed in the 1990s in Europe. It has a number of related "branches" or subgenres, including jungle, hardcore, techstep, garage, techno, and others. It began when disc jockeys (DJs) sampled short drum solos (called *breaks* or *break beats*) from 1960s and '70s soul, funk, and R&B recordings, looped them, and began rapping over the repeated groove. As a style, drum n' bass now includes a wide variety of music—from completely electronic music, in which the only "performer" is a DJ mixing records, to acoustic jazz-influenced music with live musicians playing drum n' bass-style grooves.

Drum n' bass songs today frequently involve drum grooves created on drum machines or samplers and would be physically impossible for a human to play. Over time, however, drummers have retaken control of the music and learned to create their own drum n' bass-style beats to use in live performances.

Looking back to the roots of drum n' bass, this four-bar drum break from a 1960s soul/R&B recording was sampled by DJs and used as the basis for the vast majority of the first drum n' bass songs. You've heard this beat or its influence in many drum n' bass songs.

TRACK 233

Most drum n' bass grooves are based on this famous break or some variation of it. Some break beats were "borrowed" from funk and R&B, so many break beats may already be part of your vocabulary. Most break beats are rhythmically dense, 16th-note based patterns that can vary in length from one to four bars. Break beats often have shifting accents, displaced backbeats, and often include ghost notes.

Another aspect of drum n' bass performance relates to its interpretation of fills. In many cases, traditional fills are replaced by slight alterations of the groove (e.g., moving a snare drum note, adding some bass drum notes, changing the accent pattern, etc.) instead of playing a fill on the snare and toms that interrupts the groove. The four-bar break-beat phrases below feature this approach.

Exercises 1–7 are examples of drum n' bass style break-beat phrases.

TRACK 234

In some drum n' bass styles and songs, break beats are not organized into repetitive four- or eight-bar phrases or identifiable patterns, but are continuously improvised in an ever-changing "groove flow." Many songs are based on a vamp figure, such as a bass line or keyboard riff, and the drummers will improvise groove variations based on that figure. As you learn to play in the drum n' bass style, practice improvising a continuous 16th-note groove flow that's related to a bass line or keyboard riff in the song. Example 8 uses this approach and is based on this vamp figure:

TRACK 235

Lesson 76

Basic Afro-Cuban Grooves

Cuba is the home to many percussion-based grooves that have influenced and permeated the musical landscape around the world. To understand Cuban music, you must understand the term *clave*, which is one of the most important rhythmic elements and characteristics of Afro-Cuban music. Clave is a two-bar rhythmic pattern, is present in all forms of Afro-Cuban music, and is often played by the instrument known as the *claves* (two pieces of wood that are struck together). There are two versions of clave, each named for the style in which they are played: *son clave* and *rumba clave*:

Clave may be played in one of two directions—either 3-2 or 2-3—depending upon the phrasing of the song. The term "3-2" and "2-3" indicates the number of notes in the two-bar sequence. A "3-2 clave" has three notes in the first bar and two notes in the second; a "2-3 clave" has two notes in the first and three in the second. Any clave sequence may be changed from 3-2 to 2-3 by starting on the opposing bar of the phrase. When listening to music, the clave is often only implied rather than actually heard, but all of the rhythmic parts (even the piano and bass parts) are based on the clave rhythm. An older version of clave, known as the Afro-Cuban 6/8 clave, is also part of the Afro-Cuban tradition and played in 6/8 time. It can be heard in many styles, including the *bembé* (below).

Like other folk music, the rhythmic patterns that define the style were originally played by a group of percussionists, and the drumset rhythms found below are adaptations of those grooves. For example, the popular *mambo* groove presented here adapts the bell pattern (called the *cascara*) from the timbale player's part, the "slap" and "open" sound from the conga player (using the cross-stick sound on the snare for beat 2, and the small tom on beat 4 and the "and" of 4), the low note from the *bombo* player (on the bass drum), and the hi-hat part from the *shekere* (bead-covered gourd) player's part.

TRACK 236

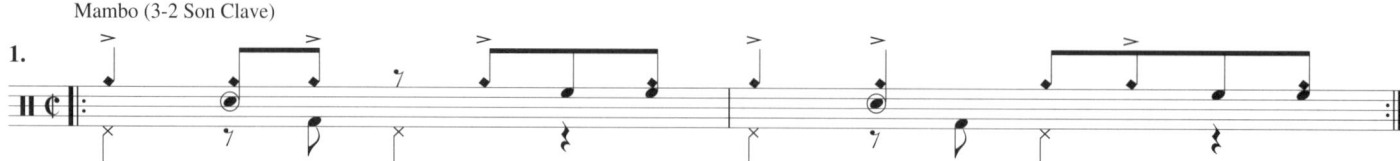

Example 2 is the Afro-Cuban 6/8 groove, or bembé. Example 3 uses the same bell pattern, but puts a snare drum backbeat on the downbeat of the second bar to create a funkier, more modern version.

TRACK 237

Guaguanco (pronounced "wa-wan-ko") is the most popular style of rumba that is played on the drumset and is often used in many Afro-Cuban musical settings.

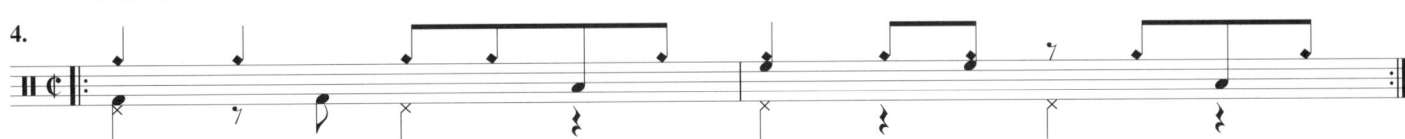

The *mozambique* groove was developed by Cuban artist Pello el Afrokan in the 1960s.

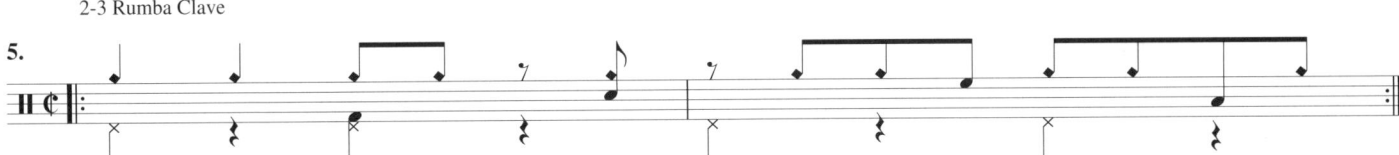

The *cha-cha-cha* is a dance from the 1940s that is derived from the mambo but is rhythmically simpler. Here are two versions:

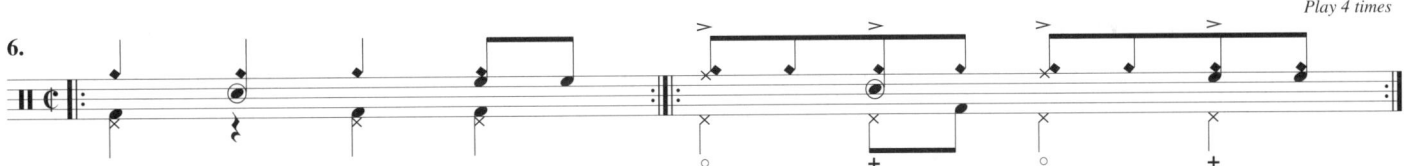

Songo, which is a groove created by José Luis "Changuito" Quintana in the 1970s, is an actual drumset groove. Today the drumset is often used for a style called *timba*, in which the drummer uses a set of timbales to the left of their drumset to play rhythms and fills while adding hi-hat, snare, crashes, bass drum, and fills on the drumset.

Lesson 77

Basic Afro-Cuban/Brazilian/Caribbean Fills

After mastering some basic Afro-Cuban, Brazilian, and Caribbean grooves, the next step is to begin integrating drum fills into the music. The process for integrating fills into any music is exactly the same: listen to the music and imitate what you hear. As you begin listening to various musical styles, start to take notice of the fills you hear. Soon they will become a natural part of what you play, so find some recordings and start your "fill collection."

When listening to Afro-Cuban/Brazilian/Caribbean music, however, it's important to know that some fills are not really *improvised* fills (which is usually the case in rock and jazz), but are actually part of the written musical arrangement. If you were playing a particular arrangement of a song, the fills (sometimes also known as *shots*) would be notated on your drum chart. In situations where you must improvise some fills, you can emulate the rhythmic figures (riffs) played by horn sections (trumpets, trombones, and saxophones) at the end of phrases. These short rhythmic riffs make great fills.

Another important facet of Afro-Cuban/Brazilian/Caribbean-style fills is the distinctive drum sounds that give the music its unique flavor. By integrating some of these characteristic sounds on the drumset, you can make your fills sound more authentic. Characteristic sounds include the slap, open, and muted sound of the congas, the high-pitched slap sound of the bongos, the piercing rim-shot sound of the timbales, and the sound of two or more drums being played in unison (called a *double stop*). Listen to fills and solos by the bongos, timbales, congas, and other instruments to become familiar with the authentic sounds.

The following exercises are some examples of rhythms that may be used for fills. All of the exercises are written in cut time (2/2) because most Afro-Cuban/Brazilian/Caribbean music is written in that meter. For variety, and in order to become more comfortable with playing fills in a number of different styles, you may choose any groove for the first two measures of the exercise (bossa, samba, mambo, songo, merengue, etc.). Then play the written fills. Only the rhythm of the fills is provided here; it's up to you to learn the rhythms and then orchestrate them around the drums. Try orchestrating each fill exercise a number of different ways—first on the snare alone (as written here) and then on different toms. Continue to re-orchestrate them by adding some ruffs, double stops, timbale-like rimshots (played near the edge of the drum to produce a high-pitched, ringy sound), or with a crash cymbal on the last note of each rhythm. The audio example demonstrates five different ways to orchestrate Example 1.

TRACK 242

For more ideas about fills, listen to some recordings by groups such as Irakere, NG LaBanda, Eddie Palmieri, Poncho Sanchez, Tito Puente, Michel Camilo, Danilo Perez, and others.

Lesson 78

Advanced Afro-Cuban/Brazilian/Caribbean Fills

Integrating fills into music from the Afro-Cuban, Brazilian, or Caribbean region requires some understanding about how the music functions and knowledge of the sounds that help give this music its identity. It's also important to realize that many of the rhythmic figures that drummers/percussionists play are actually part of the arrangement and are frequently played by the entire band; i.e., they're not improvised, but actually predetermined or composed. These are often part of what drummers play in these styles. Only a small portion of the fills heard on a recording are completely improvised; normally, it's only the last one or two beats.

The fill rhythms in these exercises are meant to be used in a different way—as original ideas when playing the drums in one of these styles. They may be used when there is a drummer *and* a percussionist in a band. When there are three or more percussionists in a band, the decision to play fills (and what to play) is normally part of the musical arrangement.

For the sake of practicality, these exercises are organized into four-bar phrases. (You may wish to extend the number of groove measures to six or 14, if desired.) Any groove may be used in the first two bars (mambo, samba, songo, guaguanco, mozambique, etc.). Learn these rhythms and then orchestrate them around the drums using rimshots, ruffs, double stops (two drums simultaneously), cowbells, and crash cymbals in order to emulate some of the characteristic sounds found in this music.

The audio example demonstrates five different ways to orchestrate Example 1.

TRACK 243

The audio example here demonstrates three different ways to orchestrate Example 6.

TRACK 244

6.

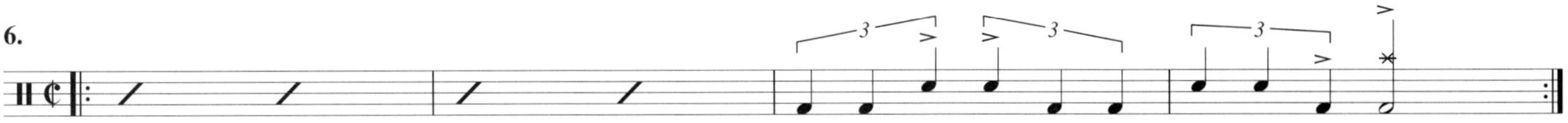

7.

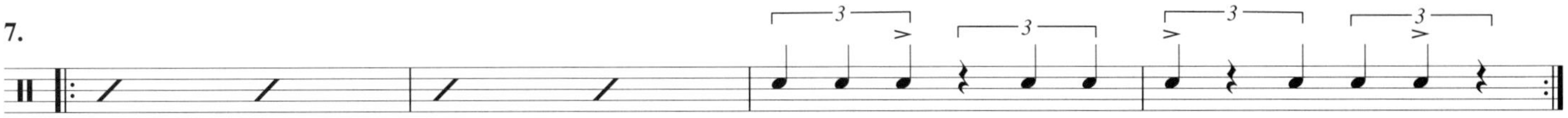

8.

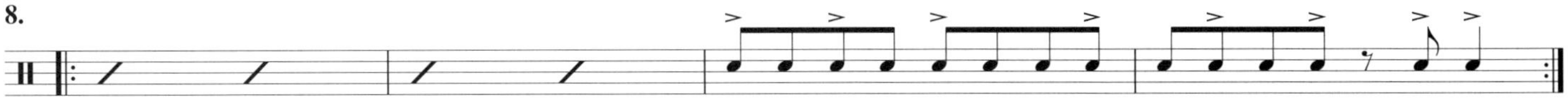

9.

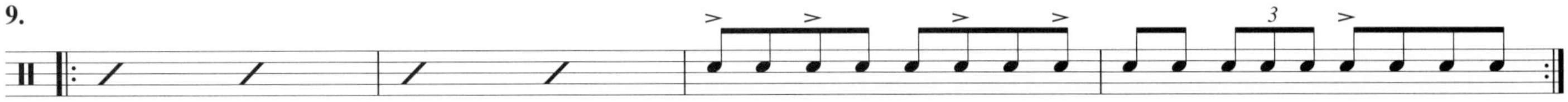

10.

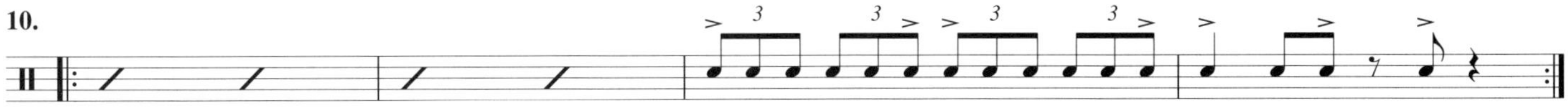

11.

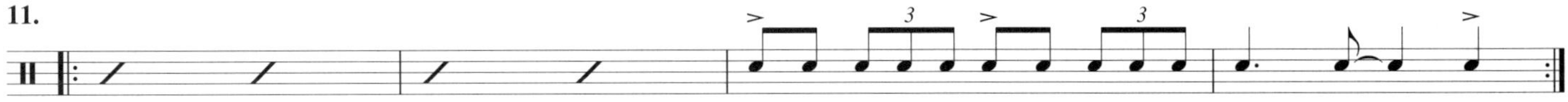

12.

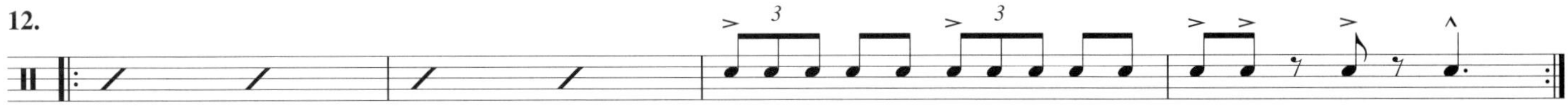

13.

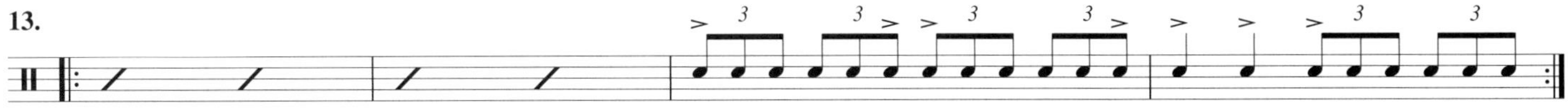

Brazilian Grooves

Brazil is the birthplace of many different musical styles, and most of them involve percussion. The drumset, being a 20th century musical invention, was not part of traditional Brazilian music, but has been integrated through the years to become standard. Brazilian music has greatly evolved and often blends traditional Brazilian styles and instruments with music from other countries. This hybrid style of music in Brazil is known today as *Música Popular Brasileira* (MPB) and is a mixture of many styles, including rock, funk, traditional Brazilian music, and other styles. Important MPB artists include Caetano Veloso, Gilberto Gil, Marisa Monte, Djavan, and Daniela Mercury.

One of the most well-known Brazilian drumset grooves is the *bossa nova*. Started in the late 1950s/early 1960s by Antonio Carlos Jobim, João Gilberto, and others, bossa nova is a blend of Brazilian rhythms and themes, jazz harmonies, and Brazilian musical traditions from the Portuguese and African inhabitants of Brazil. The bossa nova is a two-bar rhythmic drumset pattern with a ride pattern that is played either on the ride cymbal (with the hi-hat closing on beats 2 and 4) or closed hi-hat.

TRACK 245

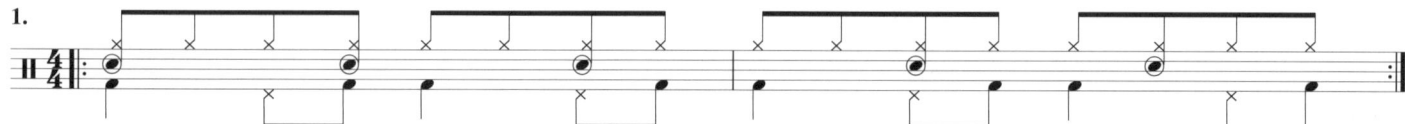

Samba is an older musical style and the predecessor of much of Brazil's music (including bossa nova). Samba began as music to accompany street parades/celebrations and is often very fast and exciting. Playing samba on the drumset involves combining the rhythms of the shakers, tamborim, surdo, and *caixa* (Brazilian snare drum).

TRACK 246

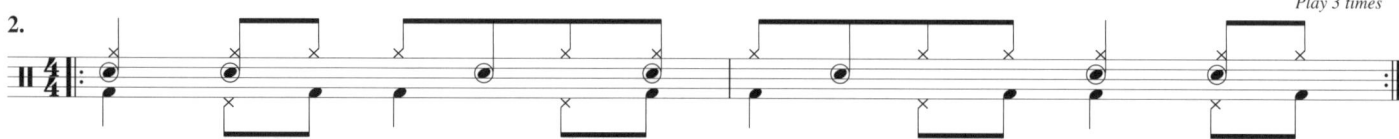

If the tempo of a samba is too fast, some drummers play this variation of it:

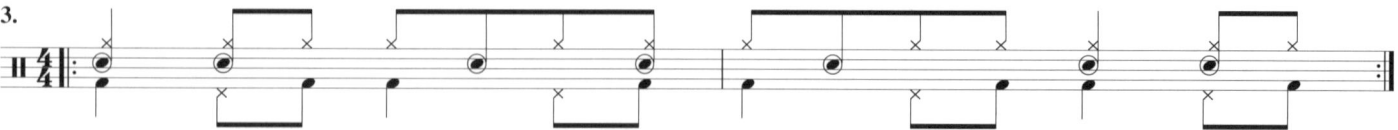

Partido alto is a variation of the samba that is also found in Brazilian music. The following two versions are identical; the first is written in 4/4 time (when it's slow), while the second is written in cut-time (when the tempo is fast). You may encounter either one when reading a drum chart. As a variation, you may also substitute a full snare stroke for the left hand cross-stick part, if desired.

TRACK 247

A lesser-known but equally interesting groove is the *baião* (it's also occasionally spelled *bãion*). It's normally played with a triangle, accordion, *zabumba* (a double-headed drum), *pandeiro* (Brazilian tambourine), and agogo bells (two pitched cowbells), but this is a drumset version. Play the unaccented snare notes on the first three beats very softly.

TRACK 248

The *marcha* style (pronounced "mar-sha") is associated with the Carnaval festival (the Brazilian version of Mardi Gras) and is derived from the military bands. It is similar to a drum cadence used for marching and can be played at either a fast or slow tempo.

TRACK 249

Frevo (pronounced "fray-vo") is also associated with Carnaval festivities and is derived from the marcha. It is usually played very fast. Often the last measure is improvised.

TRACK 250

Lesson 80

Caribbean/South American Grooves

The Caribbean and South America (including Trinidad, Puerto Rico, Columbia, Argentina, and Dominican Republic) are home to many interesting and often used drumset rhythms.

Trinidad is the home to calypso, a musical style that features the steel pan (also known as the steel drum) and is often played during Carnaval time (Mardi Gras) to accompany crowds of people marching in the street. Here are several different versions of a calypso.

TRACK 251

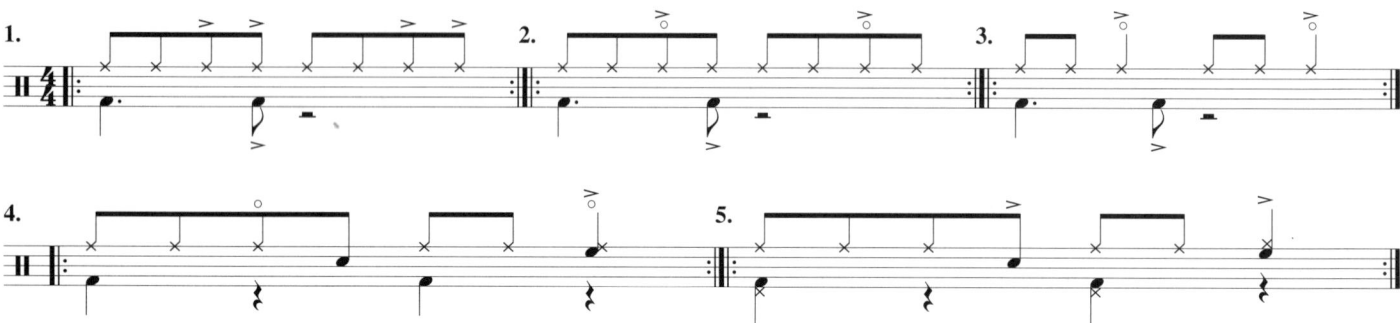

Soca is another style from Trinidad that combines elements of calypso with other dance styles.

TRACK 252

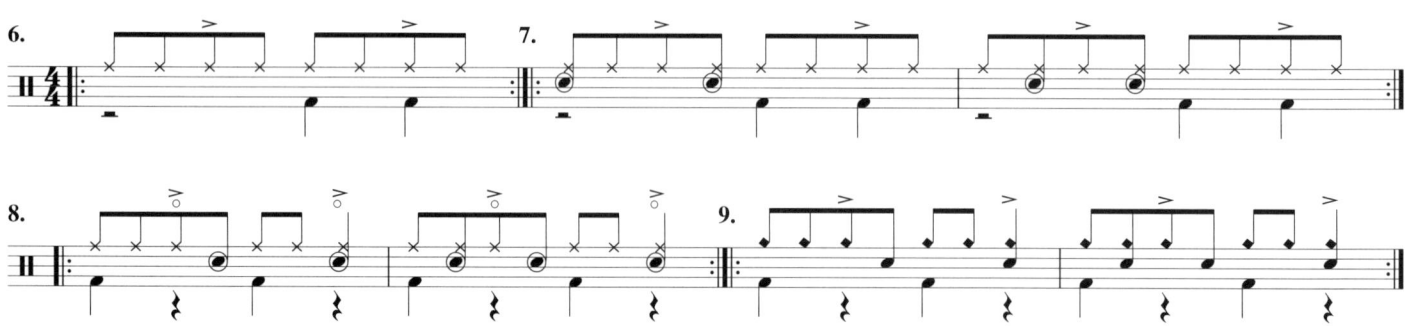

Puerto Rico is home to two prominent rhythms: the *plena* and the *bomba*. Although less well-known in North America, plena and bomba are popular in the Caribbean region. Bomba is normally played with maracas, two conga-like hand drums, and a *cua* (piece of bamboo played with sticks). Plena normally uses small frame drums known as *panderetas* as the main instrument. These are some drumset versions.

TRACK 253

The Dominican Republic's contribution to the world of rhythm is the *merengue*. It's traditionally played with the *guira* (metal guiro) and *tambora* (a double headed drum played with sticks on the shell and on the head).

TRACK 254

Tango is a dance/musical style that originated in Argentina. There are two basic styles: one with a quarter-note feel (Example 14) and one with a dotted quarter-note feel (Example 15). Often the drum part is improvised, and it's important to emulate the accents of the melody where possible. Tango is normally a highly arranged style, and each song has its own characteristic rhythmic figures (particularly at the end of phrases), so it's important to either know the arrangement or read the music that the other musicians are using for a successful performance. The accented rolls on the end of the phrases sometimes change from beat 4 to the "and" of beat 4.

TRACK 255

The *cumbia* is from Columbia. Like other folkloric patterns, it's traditionally played with percussion instruments—several hand drums and maracas.

TRACK 256

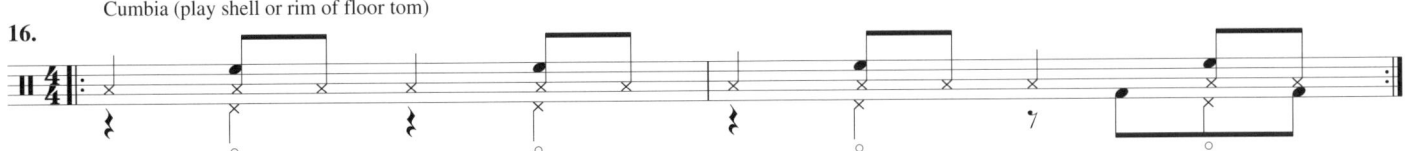

Venezuela is the home of the *joropo*, a rhythm that juxtaposes 3/4 and 6/8 against one another. Maracas are a prominent feature of this music, and often the other instruments (harp, bass, and the four-stringed guitar known as a *cuatro*) create a polyrhythmic feel through their use of contrasting rhythms.

TRACK 257

161

Lesson 81

Reggae

Originating from the island of Jamaica, reggae is now a musical style heard around the world. Bob Marley was the most well-known reggae artist, having brought reggae to the attention of the world in the 1970s, and listening to some of his recordings is a prerequisite in understanding the reggae style.

There are a number of different drum grooves associated with reggae. One of the most common is known as "one-drop," which got its name from the one loud bass drum note on beat 3 of each measure. Notice that some variations use a different accent pattern in the hi-hat part to create a different feel. More variations can also be created by substituting a cross-stick for each snare drum note.

TRACK 258

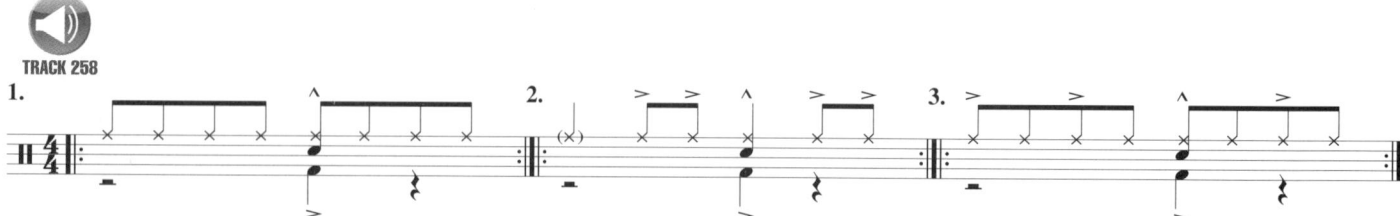

Another important aspect of reggae is its tendency to avoid playing a strong downbeat (beat 1 of each bar), so often the first beat of the drum groove will be omitted, as in this example.

"Four-drop" is another reggae style, and its name is based on the four bass drum notes in each measure.

TRACK 259

"One-drop" and "four-drop" reggae styles may also be played with a shuffle feel on the hi-hat.

TRACK 260

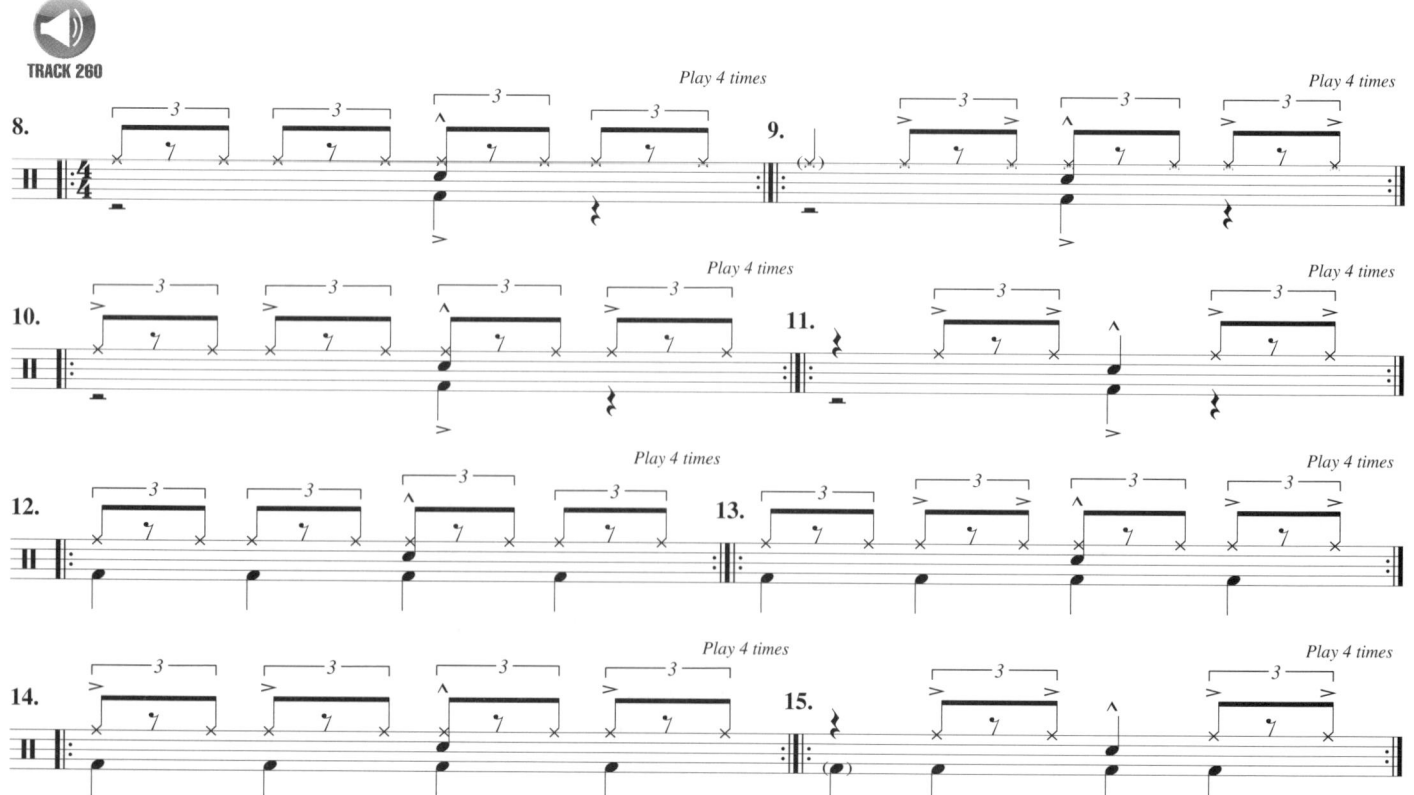

Reggae fills often end differently than fills in other types of music. In reggae, fills often end with a crash cymbal/snare drum unison on beat 4 of the fill measure. Fills often include the use of quarter-note triplets, which provides a momentary sense of rhythmic tension. These fill examples will make your reggae playing sound more authentic. On the audio, each fill is preceded by a one-bar groove.

TRACK 261

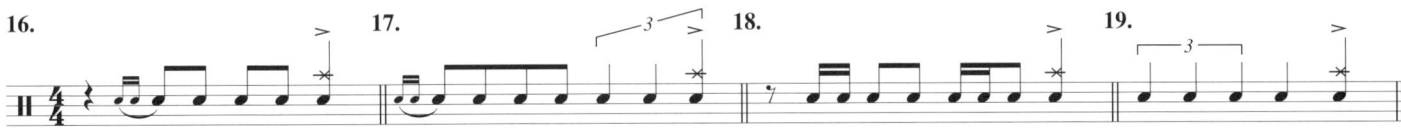

Use these play-along tracks to practice different styles of reggae.

PLAY-ALONG
TRACKS 262–265

One-Drop Straight 8th-Note Reggae
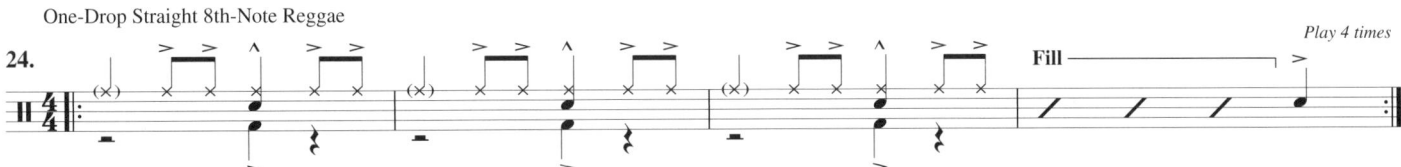

Four-Drop Straight 8th-Note Reggae
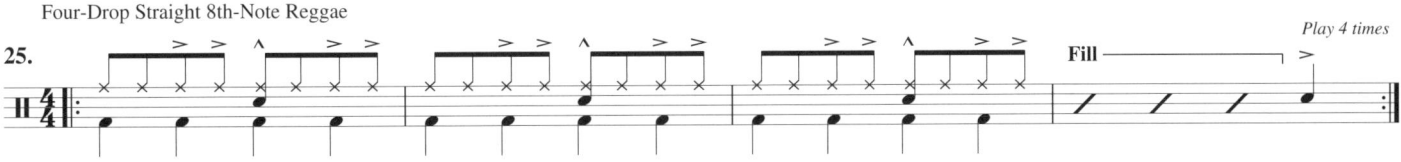

(5 clicks before the track—beat 1 of the play-along is silent)

One-Drop Shuffle Reggae
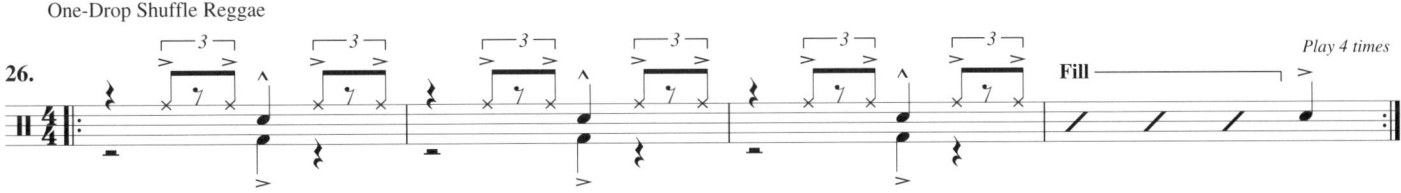

Four-Drop Shuffle Reggae
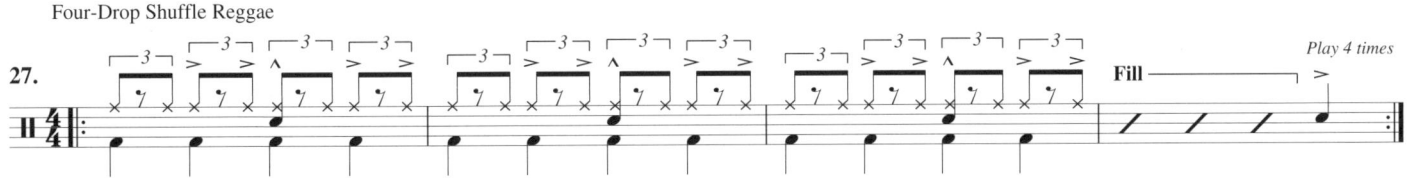

Lesson 82

Basic African Grooves

Africa is a continent with many countries—each with their own rhythmically rich musical traditions. As with other musical cultures, the grooves presented in this lesson are drumset adaptations of complex patterns normally played by numerous percussion instruments (hand drums, cowbells, shakers, etc.) or drumset patterns that are frequently augmented by a battery of percussion instruments. To fully appreciate the music from which these grooves are derived, you will need to explore African percussion more fully through recordings. It is important to remember that all of these styles continue to evolve, so the grooves presented here are the basic patterns, with new variations constantly emerging.

Bikutsi, from Cameroon, is an interesting style that uses a 3:4 (or 3 against 4) cross-rhythm that is typical of African music. Written in 4/4 time, the hi-hat (or ride) is playing triplet subdivisions phrased in groups of four (thus implying a half-note triplet—the "3" in the 3:4 cross-rhythm). This is set against the quarter-note pulse in the bass drum, which is the "4" in the 3:4 cross-rhythm. Notice that only the first three notes of triplet groups in 4 are being played; the fourth note of the phrase is a rest. This gives the groove some space. Listen to artists such as Les Têtes Brûlées, Lady Ponce, and K-Tino for more examples of this music.

TRACK 266

Mangambe (Examples 3 and 4), also from Cameroon, is another triplet-based groove.

TRACK 267

164

From Nigeria, *Afrobeat* is a popular dance groove that was championed by singer/political activist Fela Kuti. In Example 6, the bell part may be played on either a cowbell or bell of the cymbal.

Soukous, originally from the Congo, is a lively dance groove that is rhythmically based on the dotted-eighth/dotted-eighth/eighth rhythm (or the "3" side of the Cuban clave). This rhythm is normally played by a variety of instruments (hi-hat, cross-stick, cowbells, etc.). Listen to Zaiko Langa Langa, Pepe Kalle, and Kanda Bongo Man for examples of soukous.

Mbaqanga is a style from South Africa and was brought to worldwide attention by various pop artists. Miriam Makeba and Mahlathini & the Mahotella Queens are two of the most well-known mbaqanga artists. Notice the syncopated backbeat on the "and" of beat 1 in each bar.

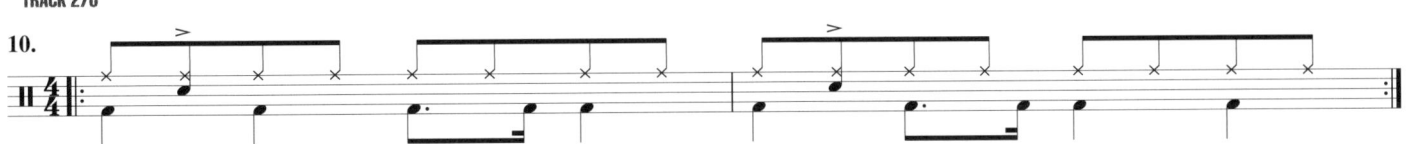

King Sunny Adé is one of the most well-known juju artists. *Juju* is a broad style that encompasses a number of different rhythms, but this is a commonly played groove.

Lesson 83

New Orleans Drumming

New Orleans holds an important place in the history of popular music in North America. Styles and approaches begun in New Orleans can still be heard in the jazz, rockabilly, rock, R&B, soul, funk, and pop music of today. Understanding New Orleans drumming requires knowing its history. Early New Orleans musical groups often included both a snare drummer and a bass drummer (who also frequently played the suspended cymbal).

New Orleans bands would play a variety of different musical styles—marches, ragtime tunes, blues, and popular songs of the day—so the drummers often had to be able to improvise in many different styles. *Ragtime* was a popular style from the late 1890s to the 1920s, and the two drummers would play rhythms similar to this when playing in a ragtime band:

TRACK 272

In the early part of the 20th century, drummers also marched in funeral processions and played a slow drumbeat on the snare drum to accompany the funeral procession to the cemetery, known as a *dirge* (or *durge*).

TRACK 273

After the deceased person was buried, however, the drummers would play a lively, swinging version of a march as the mourners marched/danced back to the *wake* (a gathering following a funeral). The musicians were known as the "second line" in the funeral procession because they were in a group behind the mourners, so the drumming style became known as "second line drumming." Both the snare drum and bass drum part were largely improvised, but it was often loosely based on the 2-3 Cuban clave rhythm.

These are some variations on a second line pattern for snare drum and bass drum. Depending on the situation, the eighth notes may be played straight, swung (like triplets), or "in the cracks." New Orleans musicians use the term "in the cracks" to describe eighth notes played somewhere in between a straight and swung feel. They must be heard to be understood. An open, "splashed" hi-hat sound may be substituted for the suspended cymbal part if played on drumset.

TRACK 274

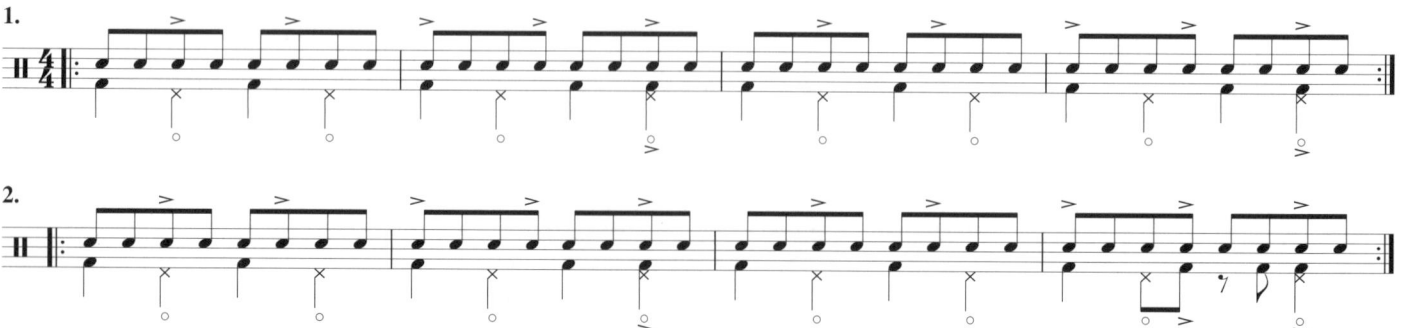

Another important aspect of New Orleans second line drumming is the use of *buzz strokes* (multiple bounce strokes or "buzzes"). Buzz strokes are what you use in a "closed roll" on snare drum. New Orleans drummers often play with their snares loosened to create a very buzzy, continuous sound, so tune accordingly for a more authentic sound. These buzz strokes can substituted for almost any of the eighth notes in a two-bar second-line phrase:

TRACK 275

The fourth beat in the second bar of the two-bar second-line phrase is one of the most important places to accent and is often the loudest note of the phrase. Some jazz drummers today have developed their own interpretations of second line drumming. It has the flavor of second line drumming—with the buzz strokes, general clave accent pattern, accent on beat 4 in the second bar, and syncopated style—but is adapted for the whole drumset. This is an example of a drumset second-line feel used in a jazz context.

TRACK 276

For a more in-depth study, listen to and study the styles of such influential New Orleans drummers as Warren "Baby" Dodds, Zutty Singleton, Vernel Fournier, Ed Blackwell, Earl Palmer, Joseph "Zigaboo" Modeliste, Idris Muhammad, Herlin Riley, Johnny Vidacovich, and Stanton Moore. Experiment and create your own interpretations of second line drumming.

Lesson 84

Famous Drum Grooves

There are some drum grooves that are so famous that even the general public instantly recognizes them. Most people (including musicians) assume that every drummer is familiar with these grooves, so they should be part of every drummer's repertoire.

One of the most famous drum grooves of all time is the solo floor tom pattern popularized by drummer Gene Krupa in the 1930s tune "Sing, Sing, Sing" (Example 1). It was the first well-known "drum feature" in jazz drumming, and many people around the world recognize it. It's basically a lengthy improvised tom solo using eighth notes and different accent patterns. This is an example of what part of the solo sounds like, but you should listen to the original recording for a more complete idea.

TRACK 277

This tom groove/concept has also been used for drum solos/features since the 1960s and as the basis for other pop and rock songs, so it's a good groove to know (Example 2). It may also be played using 16th notes, similar to the famous solo in "Wipeout."

TRACK 278

This groove has been used in many pop/rock songs and the accent pattern is based on the Cuban clave rhythm (Example 3):

TRACK 279

Some drum grooves have been played on so many recordings in a particular musical style that they become synonymous with that style and are soon just called "the disco beat," "the polka beat," or "the reggaeton beat." Here are some basic grooves for disco (Examples 4–7), polka (8–9), and reggaeton (10–11).

TRACK 280

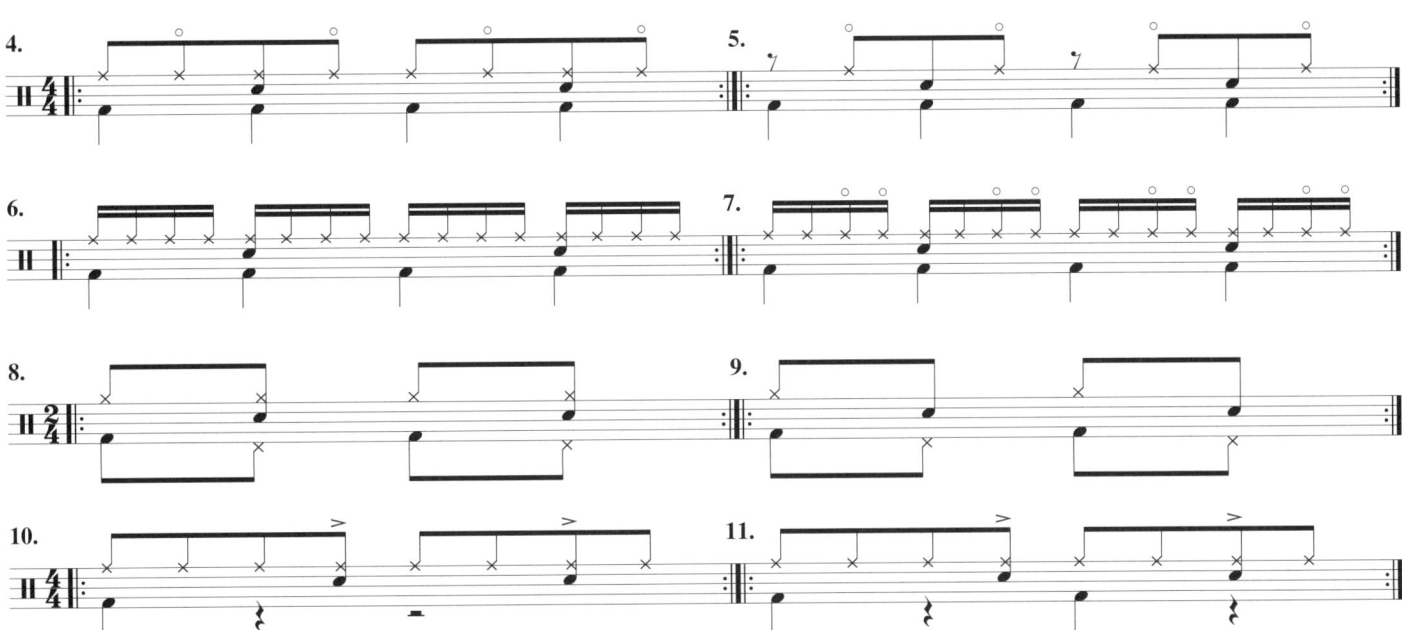

This groove is closely associated with the Motown sound of the 1960s and is often called "the Motown beat." The signature sound is the eighth-note hi-hat part and snare drum on all four beats. The bass drum part can vary, depending upon the song and corresponding bass line (Examples 12–13).

TRACK 281

This groove is sometimes referred to as the "mojo groove" because it came from a song with "mojo" in the title. It's a funky little swing groove that sounds as though it comes from New Orleans (Example 14).

TRACK 282

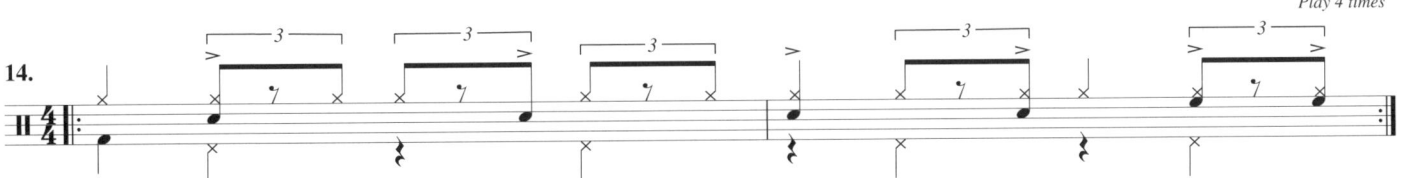

Lesson 85

Odd Groupings

The term *odd groupings* describes musical phrases (usually fills) that are arranged in groups of three, five, seven, nine, or some other odd number of eighth or 16th (or sometimes quarter) notes. This differs from most musical phrases, which are normally constructed using two-, four-, or eight-note groupings. Odd groupings are an advanced way of phrasing and are often used when a player wants to "play over (or across) the barline"—meaning to play phrases that do not resolve within a single measure. The study and use of odd groupings begins by learning to accent the beginning of each odd group in a specific beat subdivision (eighth note, triplet, or 16th note) using a consistent sticking for the accent. Each grouping will begin with a right stick. In groupings of three, for example, each phrase will use a **R**LL sticking. Groups of five will use **R**LRLL, and groups of seven will use **R**LRLRLL (with the accent on the first bold R in each group).

The most common odd grouping is one that you have probably already encountered—groupings of three (Exercises 1 and 2). When working with odd groupings, it's important to understand the math involved. Odd groupings almost never "neatly fit" or "resolve" in a four-bar phrase; there will always be a "remainder" left over at the end of the phrase. In this case, this is how four bars of eighth notes grouped into three works.

Here's the math:
4 (measures) x **8** (eighth notes in each measure) = **32** notes
32 notes divided by **3** (number in each grouping) = **10** groups + *a remainder* of **2**

These exercises use a trading fours format (four bars of "time" followed by four bars of the odd grouping fill) so that you can understand the relationship between the odd groupings and a groove. You may substitute any groove for the first four bars (rock, funk, swing, Afro-Cuban, etc.).

This is how four bars of eighth notes grouped into threes fits into a four-bar phrase:

TRACK 283

4 (measures) x **16** (16th notes in each measure) = **64** notes
64 notes divided by **3** (number in each grouping) = **21** groups + *a remainder* of **1**

This is how four bars of 16th notes grouped into threes fits into a four-bar phrase:

TRACK 284

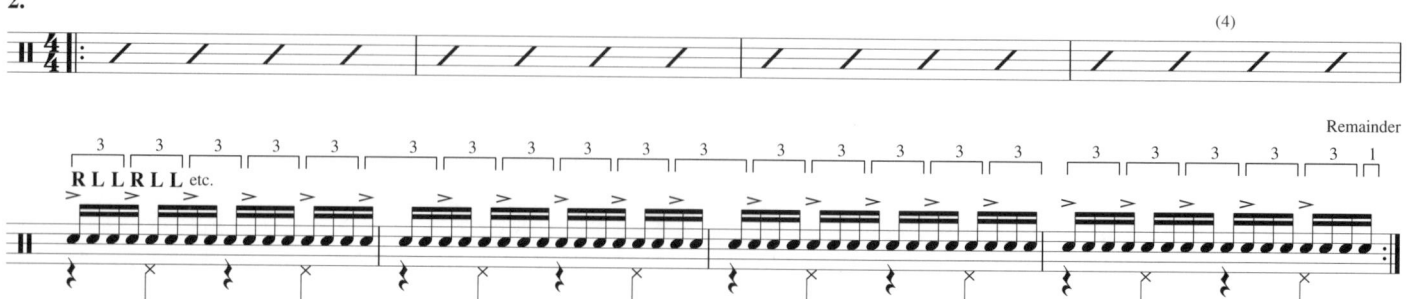

These exercises feature eighth notes, triplets, and 16th notes phrased in odd groupings. Practice Exercises 3–8 in a trading fours format by playing four bars of time followed by the written exercises (as heard on the audio). **Always** practice these with a metronome. Try moving the accents and unaccented notes around the drums to create an infinite number of combinations.

TRACKS 285–290

Eighth notes grouped in 5s (**R** L R L L sticking) — 6 groups with a remainder of 2

Triplets grouped in 5s (**R** L R L L sticking) — 9 groups with a remainder of 3

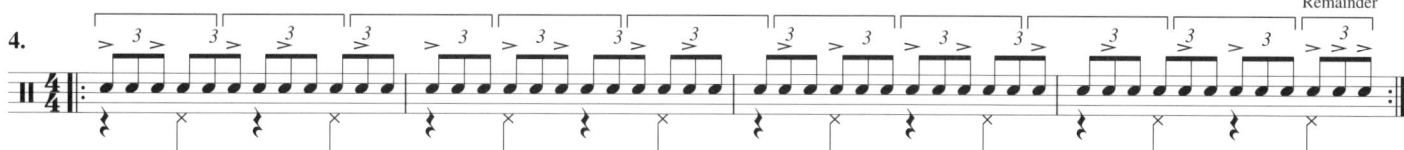

16th notes grouped in 5s (**R** L R L L sticking) — 12 groups with a remainder of 4

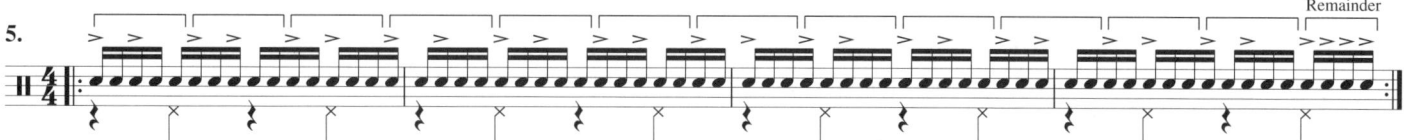

Eighth notes grouped in 7s (**R** L R L R L L sticking) — 4 groups with a remainder of 4

Triplets grouped in 7s (**R** L R L R L L sticking) — 6 groups with a remainder of 6

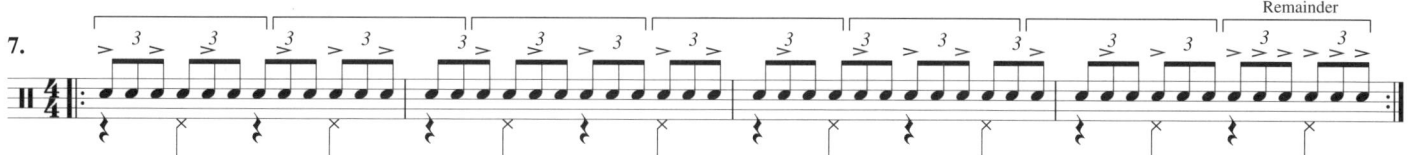

16th notes grouped in 7s (**R** L R L R L L sticking) — 9 groups with a remainder of 1

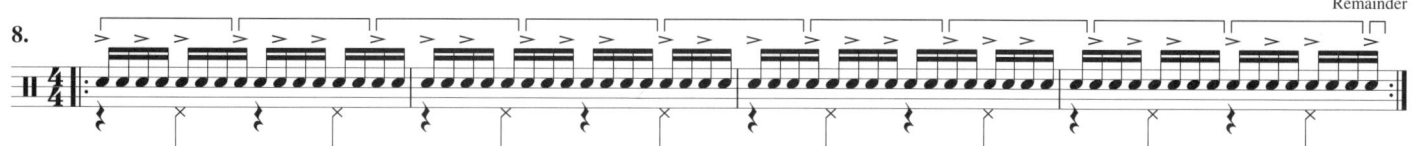

Using odd groupings involves an element of ear training, which means that you must be able to identify an odd grouping by ear as well as instinctively "feel" where the phrase resolves. You don't always have to use a specific number of odd groupings to be effective, but in order to convey to the audience that you are using odd groupings, you should repeat them several times in a row.

Basic Metric Superimposition

Metric superimposition describes playing a rhythmic pattern that creates the auditory illusion that a song is temporarily in a different meter or tempo. This advanced concept has also been referred to as "implied time" or "metric modulation" (although the latter term actually means something different). It is important to keep in mind that the actual tempo never changes during a metric superimposition—only what the drums are playing. In order to successfully use metric superimposition, a good internal sense of time and accurate counting are essential.

The simplest version of metric superimposition is the switch between *half time* and *double time*. Half-time and double-time feels are concepts that occasionally appear in charts and arrangements of tunes, so it's important to understand how to shift to these feels—not to mention (equally important) how to shift back to "normal time." In the case of rock, the backbeat is normally played on beats 2 and 4. To imply a half-time feel, for example, keep playing eighth notes on the hi-hat but move the backbeat to beat 3. This will create the feeling that the time has slowed to half its speed (when in reality it has not). Changing feels often requires or results in a slight change to the bass drum or hi-hat parts, so note how the bass drum part changes in each section.

TRACK 291

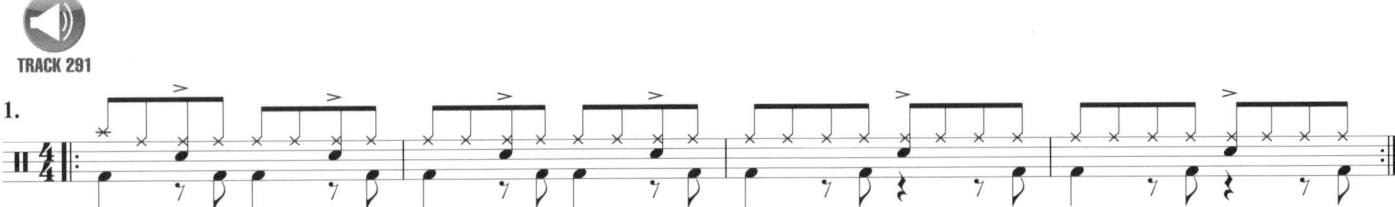

To superimpose a double-time rock feel, change the backbeat to the "and" of each beat. This will create the feeling that the tempo has increased to twice its speed (but again, it has not).

TRACK 292

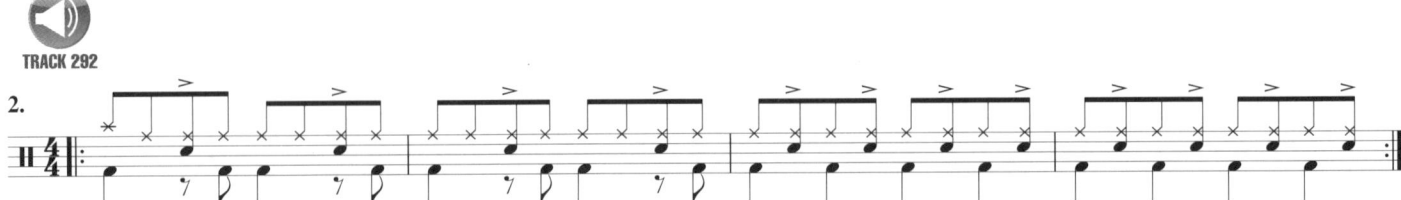

You can use metric superimposition in any style. To imply a half-time feel in a swing feel, move the hi-hat to beat 3 and omit some ride cymbal notes, like this:

TRACK 293

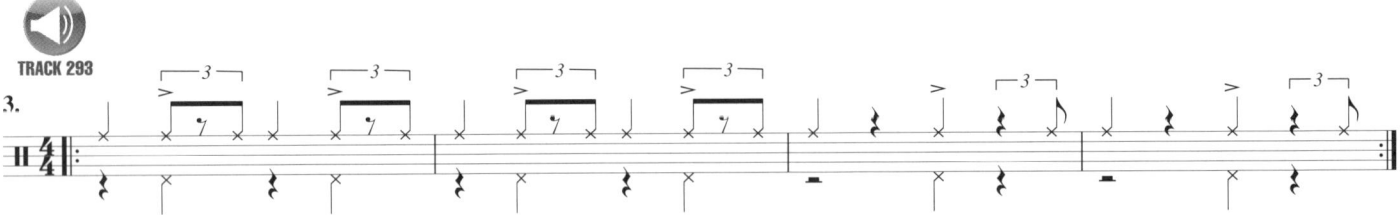

For a double-time swing feel, play the ride cymbal pattern twice as fast and put the hi-hat on the "ands" of the beat.

TRACK 294

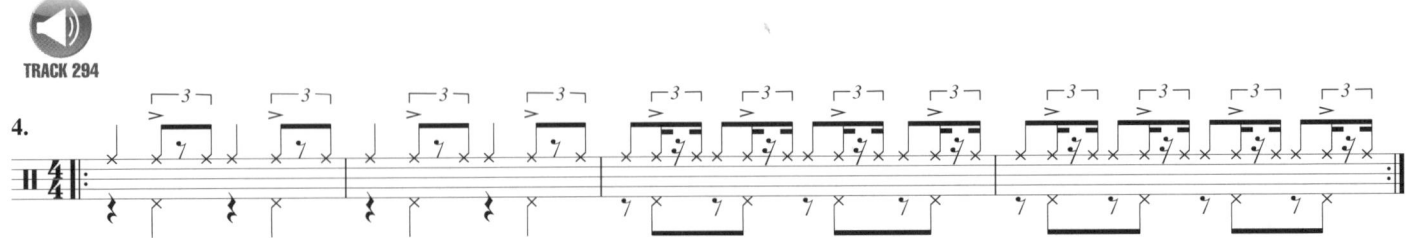

At this point, there is an important distinction to be made between two similar-sounding (but very different) terms: *double time* and *double-time feel*. Double time means the actual tempo changes to twice its existing speed (Ex. 5). For example, at the double bar, the tempo changes from 100 beats per minute (BPM) at the normal tempo to 200 beats per minute for double time:

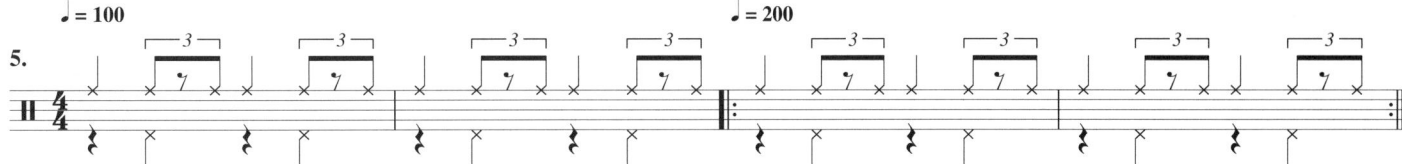

In this example of double-time feel (Ex. 6), the ride cymbal part is played at double the regular speed (at the double bar), but the quarter-note pulse stays at 100 BPM. The difference is in how you count the bars after the feel change. In double time, each bar goes by twice as fast as before, but in a double-time feel, the bars go the same speed, but you play twice as fast in each bar.

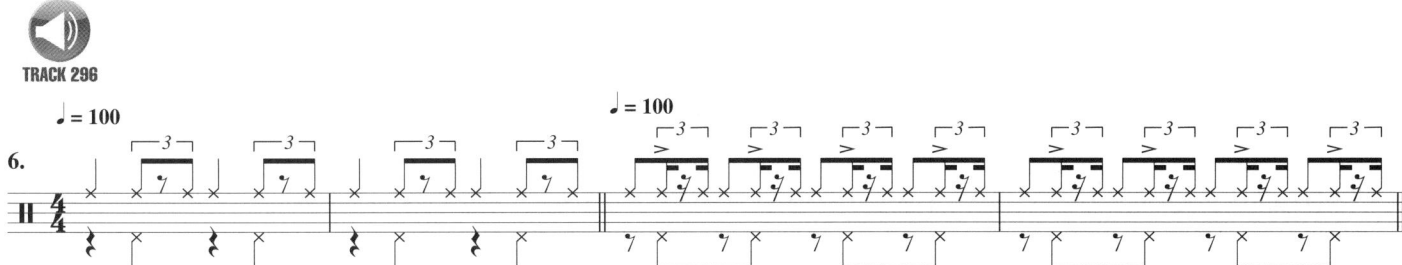

When confronted by either a chart or a musician that asks for either "double time" or "double-time feel," make sure you understand which one they are asking for (because sometimes even professionals confuse these two terms), and proceed carefully until it is clear which concept is being used.

Another form of metric superimposition is created by temporarily changing the phrasing of the drum part. For example, while playing in 4/4 time, if you stop playing the backbeat on beats 2 and 4 and starting playing them on beats 2 and 3 in bar 1 and then beats 1 and 2 in bar 2, you would be "implying" that the meter had momentarily changed to 3/4 time, because that is a backbeat pattern associated with 3/4 time (Ex. 7):

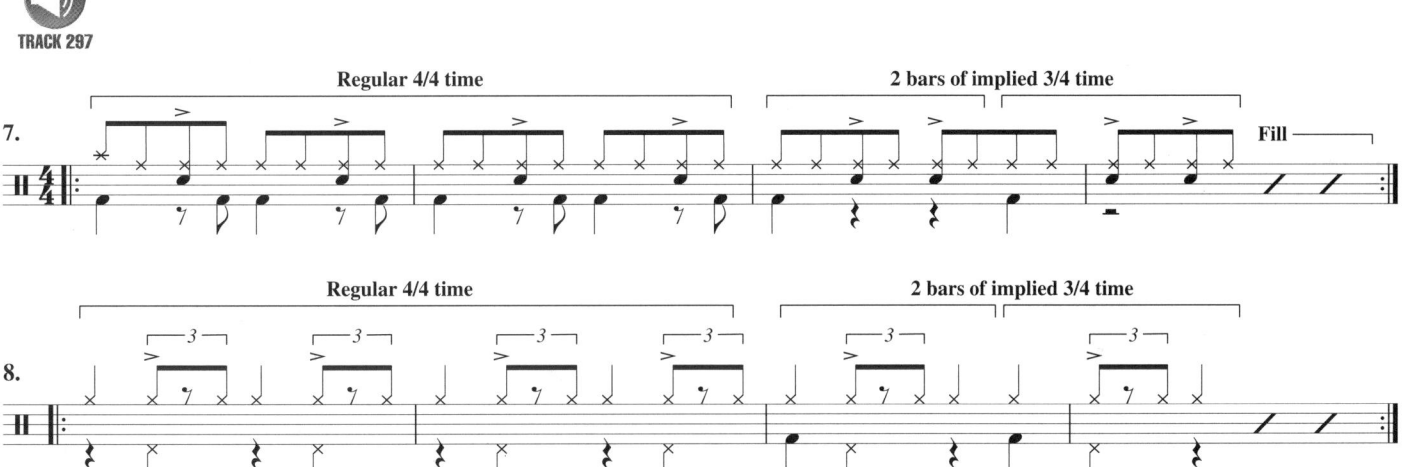

When practicing metric superimposition, use either a metronome that has a different sound on beat 1 of each bar or a regular metronome using the "clicks" on beats 2 and 4. Otherwise, it will be difficult to tell if you have made a mistake when you return to "regular time."

Intermediate Metric Superimposition

Metric superimposition is an advanced concept that means altering the phrasing of a drum pattern to temporarily imply another meter. The concept may not work or be suitable for all musical situations. You should rehearse these techniques with your musical colleagues, discuss it with them before attempting it, and be very certain they understand it before trying it out on the bandstand.

When superimposing meters, the end of the metric superimposition often does not coincide with the end of the phrase. In the following example, after playing one bar of 4/4, followed by two "implied" bars of 5/4, there are still two beats left in a four-bar phrase (similar to a "remainder" when you divide one number by another). During a remainder, you can substitute a fill to mark the end of the phrase. In order for an implied meter to be effective, you should plan to utilize at least two full measures (or "cycles") of the implied meter to ensure that the listener recognizes that a new meter is being implied.

In some cases, you must start the superimposed meter early in a four-bar phrase (and even possibly in the middle of a bar, as is the case here) in order to fit two cycles of implied meter in your phrase.

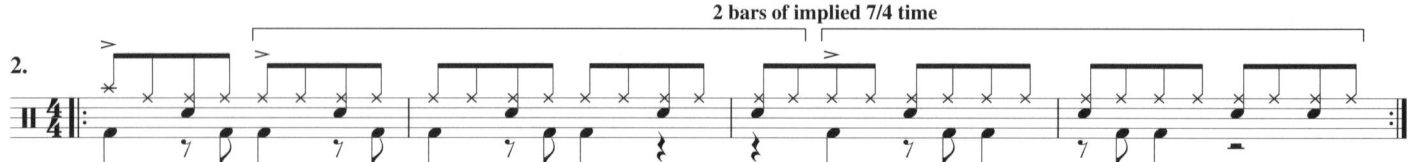

Examples 3–5 demonstrate how to imply eighth-note meters (3/8, 5/8, 7/8) over 4/4 time.

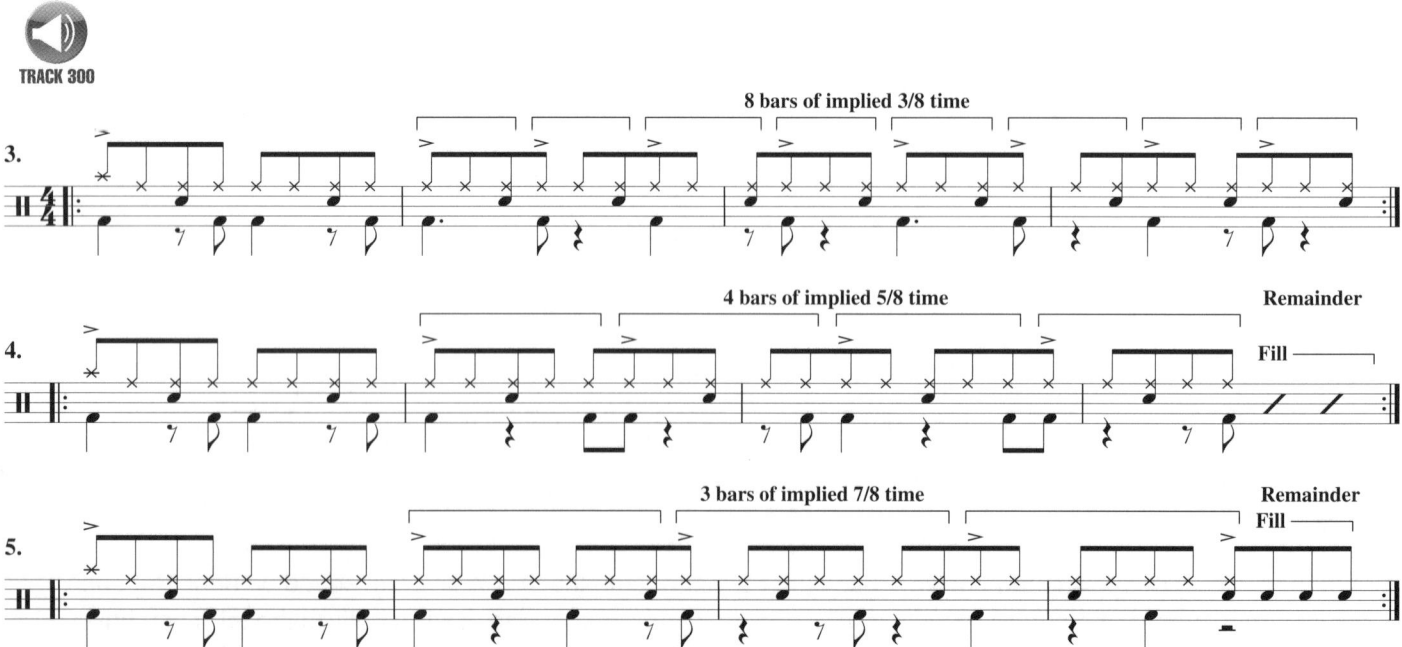

Metric superimposition may also be used in jazz (Examples 6–10). Each example begins with one bar of 4/4 time to illustrate how different the metric superimposition sounds from "regular time." The examples could also be extended over longer periods of time (e.g., eight-bar phrases) if desired. In order to extend the metric superimpositions, notating them completely on manuscript paper is helpful when first attempting this process.

TRACK 301

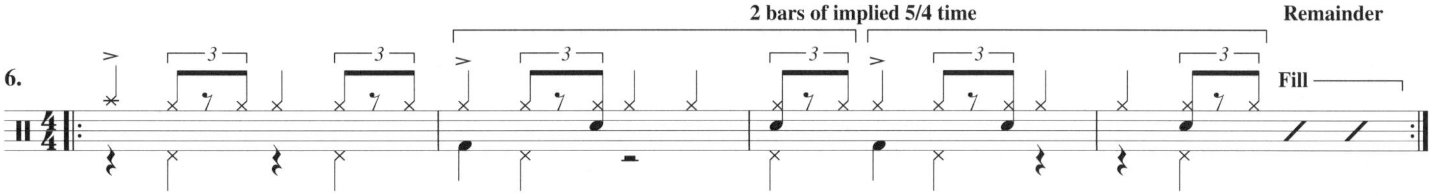

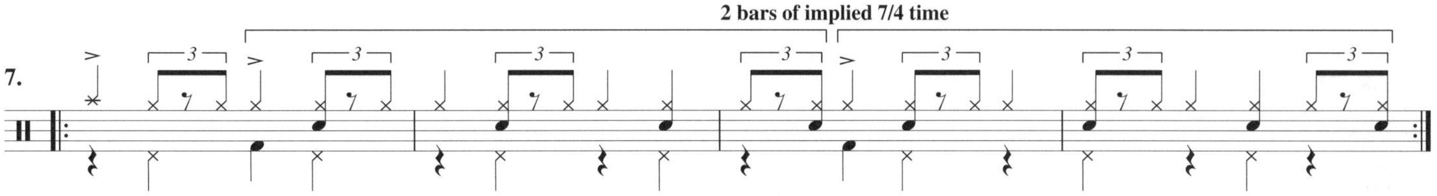

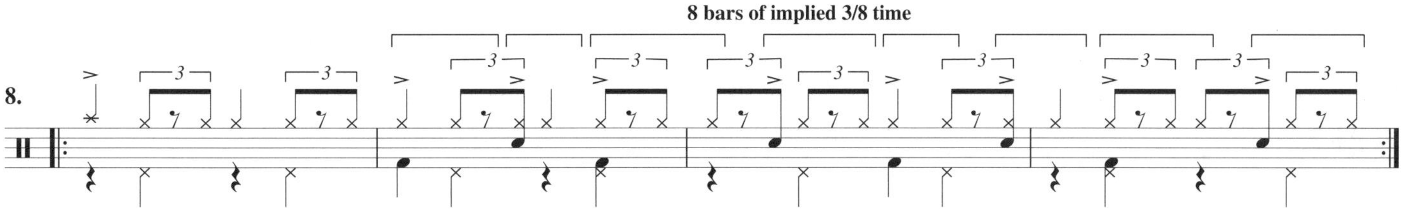

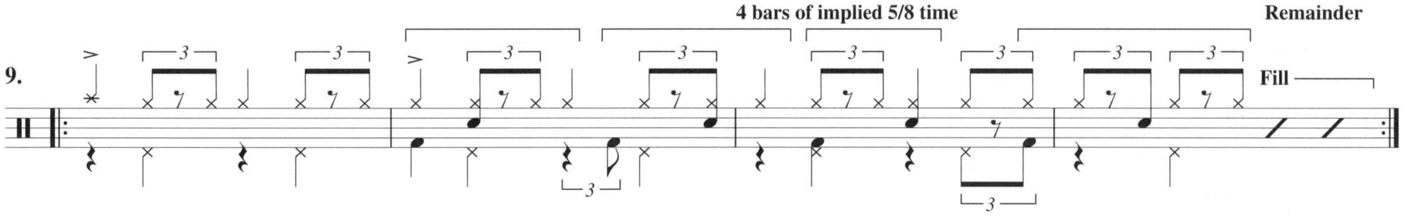

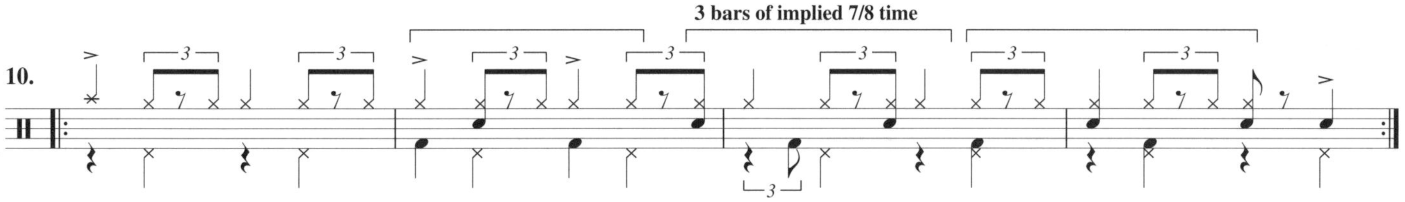

Lesson 88

Advanced Metric Superimposition and Metric Modulation

Metric superimposition began to become commonplace in the jazz world beginning in the 1960s during live performances of the Miles Davis Quintet and the John Coltrane Quartet. It would take place when one member of the band would imply a new meter and the rest of the rhythm section would instantly follow them. For metric superimposition to be successful, you have to develop the ability to hear how one meter fits over or against another meter, so this will require some time and practice. Metric superimposition is an exciting and interesting advanced concept, but you should be careful not to use it too often, with other musicians who are unfamiliar with it, or in musical settings that are not suitable for extreme experimentation.

The following examples demonstrate commonly used jazz metric superimpositions. When metric superimposition is being applied, it is often referred to as "3/4 over 4/4" or "3 against 4" or written using the ratio "3:4." These terms are used interchangeably.

3/4 OVER 4/4 (3 AGAINST 4, OR 3:4)

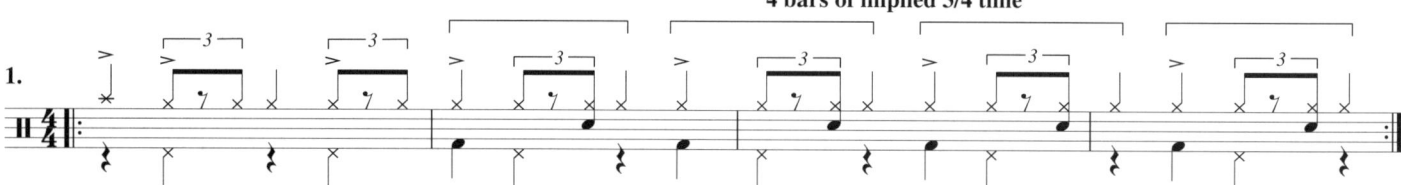

6/4 OVER 4/4

The process of learning to superimpose 6/4 over 4/4 normally requires mastering several steps. First you must develop your ability to hear the speed of the quarter-note triplet, (Example 2) as it relates to the quarter-note pulse, and then be able to instantly play the quarter triplets while also shifting the hi-hat to the second partial of each quarter-note triplet (Example 3). Finally you must create the new jazz ride pattern by adding two eighth notes (Example 4).

Metric superimposition means to temporarily imply that the meter of a song has changed (but the actual tempo does not change). After a few measures of metric superimposition, you return to playing the "normal tempo" and groove of the song. *Metric modulation*, however, means to actually change the tempo based on a metric subdivision, which is a very different concept and a technique that has a very dramatic effect on the music. In Example 5, the tempo of the first three measures is 120 beats per minute (BPM), but the implied quarter-note triplet begins the metric modulation in the second measure. Those quarter-note triplets fully become the new pulse in measure 4. The new tempo is now 1/3 faster (the ratio of 4/4 to 6/4 or 2:3), which means measure 4 (the first measure of the new tempo) would then be played at 180 BPM.

TRACK 304

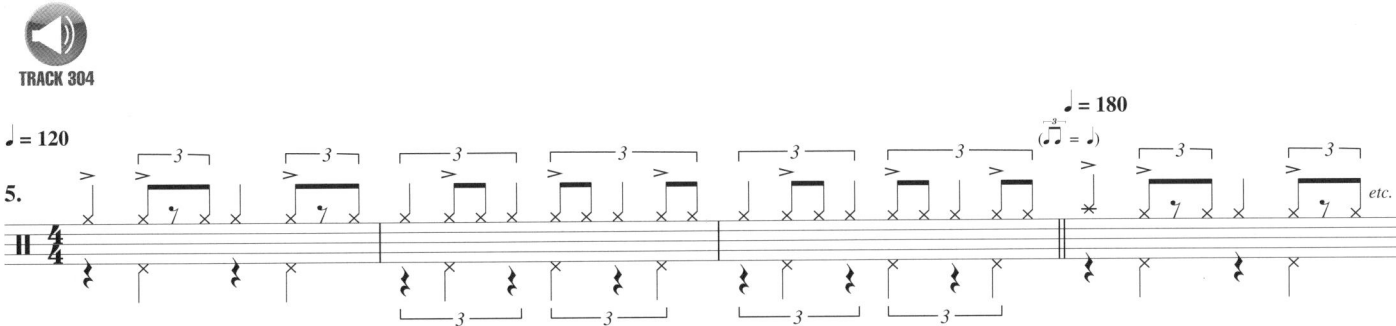

Examples 6 and 8 show how to imply 2:3 and 4:3 and return to the original tempo, while Examples 7 and 9 show metric modulations to new tempos.

TRACK 305

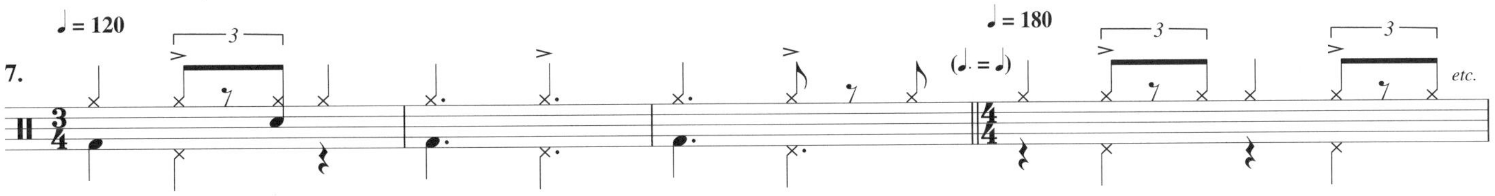

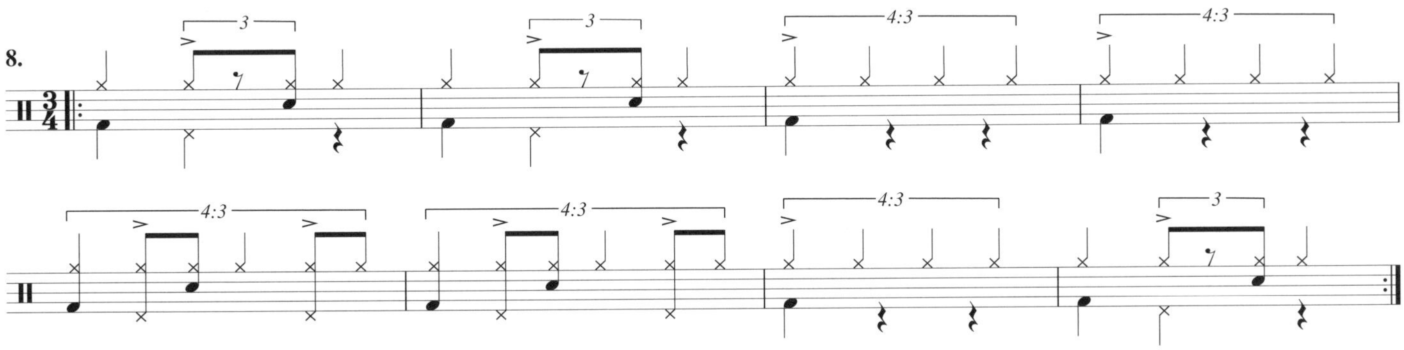

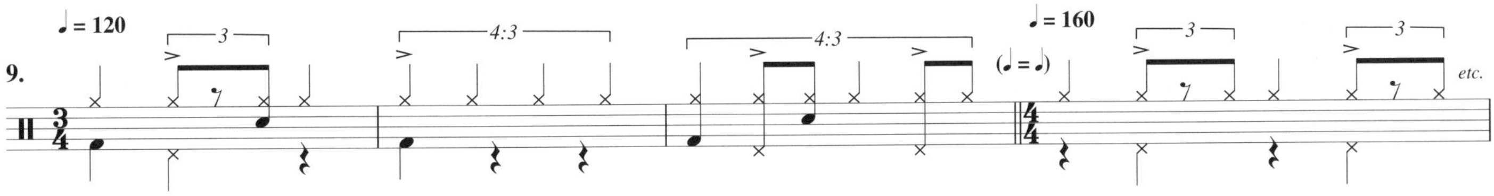

Lesson 89

Beat Placement—Playing Behind, On, or Ahead of the Beat

Beat placement, also known as playing *behind*, *on*, or *ahead* (or *on top*) of the beat, is an advanced concept that is often discussed when musicians really start to hone their craft. Beat placement might also be described as "the relationship between musical sounds in a composition." For example, if a sound (e.g., snare drum) is heard before another sound, it is said to be "ahead of the beat." If it sounds simultaneously with another sound, it is said to be "on the beat." And if it is heard slightly after another sound, it is "behind the beat." This is important because different styles of music require different beat placement approaches. Blues drummers, for example, sometimes play behind the beat to give the music a sense of weight; country drummers often choose to play either on the beat or behind the beat to provide just the "right pocket," whereas rock drummers generally play on or behind the beat as well. Progressive rock and jazz drummers tend to play on or ahead of the beat to provide energy to a song.

One of the first steps to understanding and mastering beat placement is being able to hear someone else's beat placement. Listen to the following examples and notice a change in how the music feels. Each example will demonstrate four bars of playing behind the beat, followed by four bars of on-the-beat placement, and then four bars of ahead-of-the-beat placement.

TRACK 306

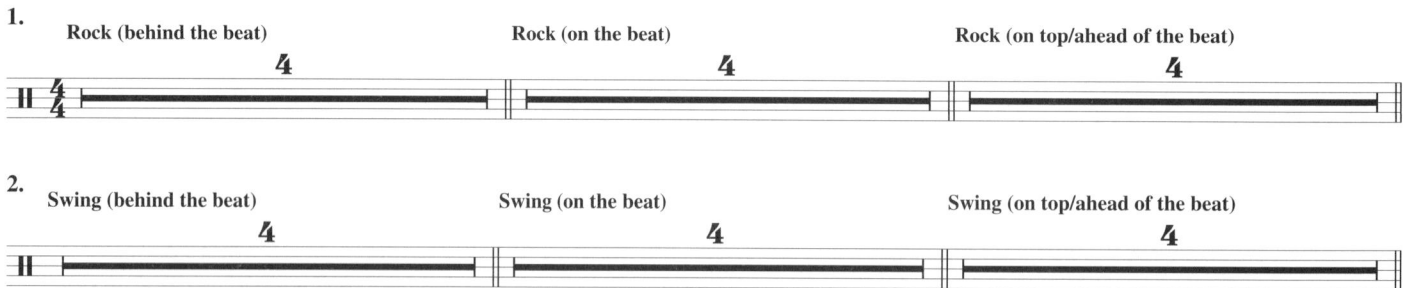

When discussing beat placement, realize that we are referring to subtly changing when a sound is heard by mere *fractions of a second*, but it's enough to dramatically change the music. Before trying to alter your beat placement, you should be very comfortable playing with a metronome (also referred to as the "click"), have a solid sense of time (known as "your internal clock"), and be able to keep a steady beat.

One great challenge when discussing beat placement is answering the question, "Where exactly is the heart of the beat?" That's a good question. Often the bassist is considered the "center of the beat" or the "basic pulse," and the drummer needs to orient themselves to the bassist's notes. (The metronome would be considered the center of the pulse if you were working with one.) Beat placement only works, however, if all of the musicians are able to play steady time and *maintain their relationship to the pulse*. If a drummer is playing ahead of the beat, the bassist tries to "catch up to the drummer," and the drummer reacts by playing more on top of the beat, the result is *rushing* (not a good idea). You should always be very aware of other musicians' beat placement and "guard the groove" as much as possible. In some cases, you might have to abandon your attempts to change your beat placement and default to playing on the beat to keep the band from slowing down or speeding up too much.

Another question about beat placement is "How do you play behind, on, or ahead of the beat?" This requires a combination of factors—both mental and physical. When playing behind the beat, try to relax your limbs as much as possible, anticipate where the click will sound (based on your sense of pulse or "internal clock"), and try to play just a millisecond later. When attempting to play on the beat, try to anticipate the click and adjust your notes so that they eventually sound exactly when the click sounds. Adopting a more aggressive, forward posture on the throne and using a bit more wrist and arm "snap" will help get to the drums a little sooner. When playing ahead of the beat (or on top of the beat), try to anticipate the click and plan to hit the drums a few milliseconds earlier. For this approach, adopt your most aggressive posture and use a great deal of wrist and arm snap to hit the drums much sooner than the click. You will have to experiment and see what technique works for you.

Before trying to manipulate the beat, you must begin by knowing where you place the beat. (Don't try beat placement until you are certain you can maintain a steady tempo.) Record yourself playing with an audible metronome (perhaps plug the metronome into a stereo system or computer with speakers) and listen back to see where you naturally place the beat. Then start working with a play-along track, first trying to play on the beat, then perhaps behind the beat, and finally on top of the beat. Try to remember exactly what you did (both mentally and physically) to achieve each result.

Use the following play-along tracks to practice beat placement. You can use any rhythmic groove you wish to practice—not just the written example. Record yourself while changing beat placements to see if you are successful. Try each example three times—behind, on, and on top of the beat.

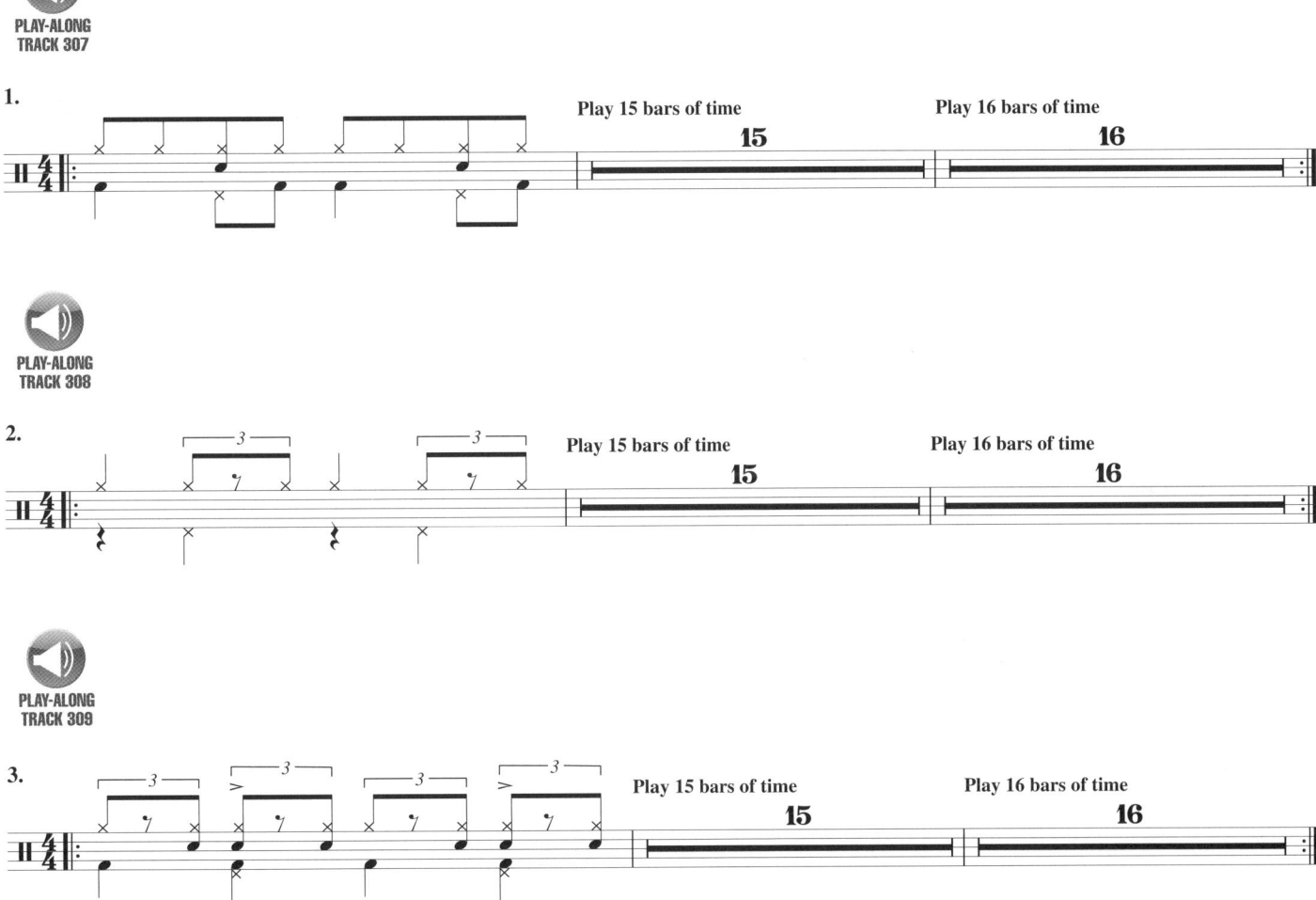

Listen to some of your favorite recordings and make note of the drummers' beat placement approaches. Don't forget to listen to other styles of music that use different beat placement philosophies as well and experiment with beat placement in as many styles as possible.

Productive Practicing Concepts

Drummers are confronted with a particularly interesting problem when they try to practice. The drums are *so much fun to play* that we often just go into the practice room and "mess around" for an hour and call it practicing. *It is not.* To practice means to enter the practice room unable to successfully perform something (an exercise, a groove, a fill, a chart, etc.) and later emerge from the room being able to successfully execute it.

Practicing should involve a number of different facets and approaches. First, you should decide what you want to accomplish by the time you finish your practice session. Develop a practice agenda and stick to it. When you've accomplished your goals in the practice session, then you can "mess around" for as long as you want. Don't underestimate the importance of messing around, which is another way of saying "improvising." Improvisation is an important part of drumming and can often help you discover new ideas, licks, stickings, and concepts.

GOALS

You should develop both long-term and short-term goals and write them down! Goals help you determine what to practice and for how long. Long-term goals can be somewhat vague and involve broad concepts that take an extended time to achieve (learning to read music, play with great time, having better chops, etc.), while short-term goals are usually more defined and specific (the exercises on page 10, mastering a specific groove, being able to use a specific fill in a specific song, etc.). Short-term goals should be ones that can be accomplished in a single practice session or from one to two weeks. Long-terms goals span several months to several years. Successfully meeting your short-term goals will result in accomplishing your long-term goals.

COUNTING

You should be able to count *everything* (in tempo, using the appropriate syllables) that you intend to practice. Counting helps you place the notes and rhythms in time and space correctly. If you can count something correctly, you will be able to play it correctly.

METRONOME

Every drummer should own and practice with a metronome. It is the only objective way to determine if you are maintaining a steady tempo. Think of the metronome not as a mechanical device, but as "the world's greatest bass player" who has an incredible sense of time. The way you use a metronome will depend upon what you are practicing. The most common way to use the metronome is to set it on the quarter-note pulse (beats 1, 2, 3, and 4). This is a great all-purpose approach, but there are also other ways to use it. For example, if you're practicing a rock groove, you could set the metronome so that it sounds on every eighth note in the ride pattern; this would help you determine if all of your ride cymbal notes are being placed properly. Another common way to use the metronome is to set it so that it sounds on beats 2 and 4 for jazz/swing exercises. Having the metronome sound on beats 2 and 4 in a swing exercise (where the hi-hat is played), will instantly indicate if you have dropped or picked up a beat (which is often referred to as "flipping the beat"). When practicing with a metronome, you have to listen very carefully to ensure that you are playing exactly with it. The best way to do this is to record yourself while listening to a metronome running through stereo speakers. Headphones are another option.

TEMPO

Many drummers begin practicing new material at an unrealistically fast tempo. This often leads to frustration (because you can't instantly play this new challenge) and only reinforces playing incorrectly. It's been said that "everyone can play anything at *some tempo*," and that's true. Playing the drums involves muscle memory (just like the ability to develop a consistent, predictable golf swing, tennis serve, baseball swing, basketball jump shot, etc.), and so you have to practice something correctly repeatedly so that your muscles remember what it feels like to play correctly. Begin practicing new material slowly enough to count and execute everything correctly. Only after you can consistently play something correctly (at least ten times in a row) should you even consider playing it at a faster tempo.

PLAY-ALONGS

Practice with play-along tracks if possible. There are literally thousands of great play-along book/audio packages on the market covering almost every conceivable topic, such as the Hal Leonard Drum Play-Along series. These are invaluable. They are the closest way to replicate what you will be doing when you perform with other musicians. Remember: practicing is meant to prepare you to play with other musicians, so why not replicate that scenario as closely as possible by working with play-along tracks?

ACTUAL RECORDINGS

Practice with actual recordings of songs or tunes. There are so many nuances in music, such as feel and note placement, that cannot be notated but are critical to making a tune, groove, or fill feel right. One way to do this is to pretend that "you're the drummer in the band" and listen to a specific tune or song over and over until you can play everything the drummer plays. Then put on some headphones and play along with the recording until you can't hear the drummer on the recording. That will mean that you are successfully placing your notes exactly on top of the drum track. There is a reason that this particular drummer is on a recording; they have the ability to do the right thing for the music. By emulating what great drummers do, when the time comes, you might be the one making the recording.

CONCENTRATION

Part of any performance (or practice session) requires concentration and stamina. You don't want a momentary slip of concentration to ruin the tempo, your fills, or anything else that you are trying to do musically. Developing stamina and concentration should begin early in your drumming career by practicing for extended periods of time without stopping. Strive to be able to play a whole page of exercises without stopping, then two pages, etc. Practice playing a whole song perfectly ten times in a row (just like you might have to do in a recording session). Don't forget to develop the "art of recovery"—when you make a mistake, try to keep playing and recover from your errors (if possible). You will have to develop this recovery ability in order to play in almost any situation.

RECORDING YOURSELF

Recording yourself is truly the only way you can objectively assess how you sound. While you're playing music, you're so involved with the process of making music that you can't really hear the "total musical picture." You can start this process by recording yourself practicing with a metronome. Run an audio cable from the headphone jack of your metronome into your stereo. Turn on the metronome so you can hear it through your speakers, practice an exercise or groove for a few minutes while recording both you and the metronome. Listen back to the recording and assess your accuracy. You should also record your performances with other musicians. A huge part of playing drums is learning to deal with other musicians' sense of time and their performance tendencies. You need to learn how to instantly recognize when another musician is playing too fast or too slow, if the tempo is changing, and how to make adjustments.

THE VISUAL

Use a mirror or, better yet, videotape your practice and performances. This will give you a visual perspective on your posture, playing technique, degree of overall physical relaxation while playing, and many other aspects of your performance. You'll be surprised at what you will discover!

Lesson 91

Transcribing Drum Grooves

At some point, you will probably need to learn how to transcribe (notate on paper) a basic drum groove (or beat) from a recording. This helps you more accurately perform a song and learn new techniques and patterns. If you can learn to transcribe drum parts, then *any* song or pattern you wish to play will be available to you. Transcribing may seem difficult at first, but don't give up; it gets easier with each new transcription. The trick is to start simply and transcribe progressively more difficult material.

Before beginning to transcribe, examine some basic patterns in rock or jazz and try to internalize them (recognize what they look like as well as sound like). It is quite probable that you have played the same pattern before in some drum book. Learn to count the rhythm of each part of the groove (snare, bass, ride, and hi-hat) so that when you hear it on a recording, you will be able to reproduce it on paper. You must be able to play a variety of different patterns before you are able to recognize them on a recording, so you may have to wait until you have enough experience before beginning your transcribing. Most students need a year's worth of lessons before they can begin transcribing.

When you (or your teacher) determine that you're ready to transcribe some drum grooves, these are some suggestions to help you get started:

- **Study some completed transcriptions.** There are many sources for drum groove transcriptions—books, magazines, websites—so find a transcription of a song you know well and compare it to the recording. Look at how songs begin, notice what rhythms are used in the fills, etc. Learn to play some transcriptions before you begin attempting to do them yourself, as this will acquaint you with how transcriptions work.

- **Start with some simple rock patterns.** Try transcribing just one basic groove from a song. Every style of music has some common elements, and knowing that can help you get started. Most pop or rock songs use an eighth-note ride cymbal pattern and snare drum on beats 2 and 4, so write that down first. Then move on to the bass drum and hi-hat parts.

- **Start with the right song.** Your first transcription attempt should be a song that has a beat that you can easily play by ear. Then figure out how to write it. Go one beat at a time if you must. Count the rhythm you are playing so that you can place each note on the right beat in the measure.

- **Write down one part at a time.** Since the ride part is normally played throughout the bar, figure out the rhythm of the ride part first. Write that down. With the ride part notated, you can fill in the other parts as they relate to the ride rhythm. After the ride, determine the snare part, which is normally on beats 2 and 4. Then write the bass drum part, which will probably be the most difficult. Drummers often organize songs into two-bar phrases, which means that the bass drum part won't be identical in each measure, but will be a two-measure repeated loop.

- **Skip a measure.** If you reach a certain point in a song and can't figure it out, leave the measure blank and move on to the next measure. Check with someone who has more experience than you (a teacher or other drummer) and see if they can help you. Eventually, you may be able to work it out.

- **Make an educated guess.** Based on what you have seen or heard other players do, sometimes you can make an educated guess as to what a player is doing. Write down what you think is being played (in pencil); you can always return later and change it if you think it needs fixing.

- **Don't worry about the fills.** You can just write two slash marks and the word "fill" above the measure if you wish. Most fills are improvised, so you can improvise your fills for a song. If you really want to learn every note, then be prepared to spend some time on the fills.

- **Listen for the overall form of the tune.** Drummers often reuse the same drum grooves during identical sections of the tune. As you listen to a song for the first time, create a *macro chart*—one that uses only abbreviations for large musical sections of a song. For example, when the song starts, it normally begins with an introduction (so write an "I" for introduction). If the singer enters and begins to "tell a story," that's normally the verse (write down a "V" for verse). When the main part of the song comes (normally where the title of the song is located), write a "C" for chorus. In most cases, there will be a few more verses and a few more choruses. If there is some music that is neither a verse nor a chorus, then it's probably an interlude (if instrumental) or a bridge (if it contains vocals)—write down a lower case "i" (for interlude) or a "B" for bridge. When the song ends, write down an "E" for ending. In some cases, a song may begin with a chorus, so don't be surprised if a song does not follow a predictable pattern.

Here's an example of a typical macro chart:
I - V - C - V - C - i - C - E

Using this system, you will notice that there are probably only one or two main grooves in a song—normally the verse and chorus. In that case, you would only have to transcribe the grooves from the verse and the chorus to replicate the recording.

- **Check your work.** There are a number of great drum transcriptions available on the market by music publishers such as Hal Leonard, but the best way is to check your work with a qualified instructor.

- **Put it into action.** Now that you have spent so much time transcribing, it's time for the fun part: playing the music. Begin practicing the grooves until you can play them at the recorded speed. Then starting playing along with the recording.

Continue to transcribe new grooves in different styles in order to increase your vocabulary, accuracy, and speed.

Transcribing Drum Solos

Transcribing drum solos (notating the entire solo on paper) is a great way to increase your understanding of *how* to solo, how to learn other players' solo ideas, and how to help build your own solo vocabulary. Finding solos already transcribed is great, but transcribing them yourself is the best way to develop your listening skills, reading abilities, writing abilities, and solo abilities, because by the time you get done transcribing, you'll know the solo by heart. A word of caution: even a published solo might not be entirely correct, so always double check it yourself.

Before attempting to transcribe an entire solo, it's a good idea to practice transcribing something simpler. Transcribing drum grooves (with snare drum, bass drum, hi-hat, and ride cymbal parts) is a great way to begin. Grooves are easier to transcribe because they're repeated, which will help you identify something when you hear it over and over again. In drum grooves, there are also normally some elements that you can assume will be present. For example, in a rock groove, the snare drum is normally on beats 2 ands 4, and there are eight notes in the ride pattern. It's good to focus on the bass drum, because its rhythms are normally the most active. Practice transcribing grooves from your favorite songs and see how proficient you can become committing them to paper.

Once you've gotten reasonably adept at transcribing grooves, then move on to an entire drum solo. Here are some ideas and helpful hints about transcribing drum solos:

- **Listen to as many solos in a particular style as you can.** Listen to a number of solos by the same drummer to become familiar with their signature licks and approaches. Your instructor can probably help direct you to solos that would be appropriate.

- **Learn some previously transcribed solos.** This will help you know what to expect when you start transcribing, will show you how others notate a solo, will build your reading and counting, and develop the concentration necessary to transcribe and play a solo.

- **Don't select a solo that's too difficult.** Your first solo should be one that sounds like you could possibly play it with a bit of work. Transcribing is a long term project and may take several weeks to complete. Try to transcribe in short sections—perhaps just one to eight bars at a time—so that you don't become frustrated.

- **Listen to the "overall" solo.** Try to determine anything you can about it—the number of measures, any repeated passages, important musical ideas or concepts (repeated rhythms, repeated patterns), or the overall shape (simple to complex, complex to simple, etc.). This will help you form an outline of the solo from which you can fill in the blanks as you transcribe each measure.

- **Use a computer program to slow the solo down.** Very few people ever transcribe solos at their recorded speed. It's frustrating and often leads to inaccuracies. There are many software programs available now that will allow you to slow down the speed of a recorded track (some without even changing the pitch). Do some research and find one you can use easily.

- **Listen to the solo enough so that you can sing it almost note for note.** This will help you get a picture of it in your mind. Determining the counting and pitches that correspond to what you are singing will be easier if the rhythms and pitches are already in your ear.

- **Transcribe using staff paper and a pencil.** Section the paper off into four measures per line. Try to jot down the rhythms first and write them above the staff. Don't bother with the noteheads at first, just draw the stems and flags that tell you the value of each note. You can go back and figure out the pitches (which drums they're on) later. Don't spend too much time at first figuring out exactly which tom the note is on; you'll figure that out as you continue transcribing the rest of the solo.

- **Listen to the solo at different speeds.** Transcribing at fifty percent (50%) of the recorded tempo (or exactly half-speed) is a good speed to use. Sometimes changing the speed of the solo while transcribing it—say, at a slightly faster (60%) or slower speed (45%)—will sometimes help you identify rhythms, patterns, or pitches that are not clear at other speeds.

- **"Conduct" your way through the solo.** If you're familiar with what a conductor does, this suggestion will help you. A conductor keeps time by drawing a pattern in the air that indicates (by the position of their baton) each beat in every measure. In 4/4 time, the conductor visually makes (roughly) a "+" sign in the air. Starting at eye level, they swing their baton down to a "point" in front of them to designate beat 1, to their left for beat 2, across their chest to their right for beat 3, and back up to eye level for beat 4 (before repeating it all over again for the next measure), as shown in the adjacent diagram.

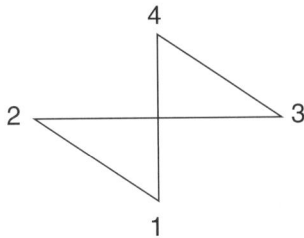

You can use the motions in a conducting pattern to help you transcribe more accurately. As you listen to the solo, try to conduct along with it. For example, if one note sounds each time your hand arrives at a number in the conducting pattern (1, 2, 3, or 4), then the notes you are hearing are quarter notes on beats 1, 2, 3, and 4. If two notes sound between the time you move from one beat to another, then you are hearing eighth notes, and so on. Conducting along with a solo helps you to place the rhythms in a specific place in the bar (e.g., beat 1, or the "and" of beat 2) as well as locate the beginning and end of a phrase, which is very important when transcribing an extended solo. The conducting pattern also marks any rests that exist between phrases.

- **Skip measures if necessary.** Don't get stuck on one bar. Figure out as much as you can, then move on to the next bar. Another transcribing approach is to determine when a specific pattern or rhythm ends and then work backwards from there to figure out what's happening in the previous measure.

- **Most solos are logical and "fit" on the drums.** Most drumming is based on some sort of pattern and/or predictable motion, so apply some logic when transcribing. If a rhythm or pattern seems impossible to execute, it might be. Try a different sticking or other approach to identify what you are hearing.

- **If you can't transcribe an entire solo, that's OK.** No matter how much of a solo you transcribe, you've gotten something out of it. Perhaps you should leave it for now and come back to it later (in a week, a month, or even a year). Sometimes you're not ready to tackle a particular solo. Don't become discouraged—become challenged to finish this solo later when you have more experience.

- **When you've completed as much of the solo as you can, check its accuracy.** Transcription books, drum magazines, and/or a qualified teacher are all great sources to check your work. Compare your solo side by side to another version. Often there is more than one way to notate something. Keep all of your solos for future reference.

- **Now start practicing.** Learning the entire solo is a great experience but not the only benefit from transcribing. One of the most important things to do with a solo is to select parts of the solo you like (one measure, a specific lick, or a broad concept) and try to integrate it into your own solos. Using what you've learned from all of your transcribed solos will help you be able to solo when it's time for you to solo.

- **Transcribe a second solo by the same player.** You might be surprised to see that a second solo by the same artist has some similarities to the first. Every player has their own vocabulary or licks that they count on to play a solo. Your second solo (and third and fourth) will be easier than your first solo because you'll recognize a player's signature licks.

Lesson 93

Creating an Original Drumset Part for a Song

Drummers normally start performing with other musicians by playing previously recorded songs, so they don't have to figure out what to play themselves. They just play what the drummer on the record played. But what happens when it's your turn to record an original song and you have to come up with a whole drum part that fits a song?

The truth is that drummers are often required to make up their own parts to a song written by someone else, and it's important to understand how to do that. Every musical style (rock, pop, funk, country, punk rock, prog rock, metal, jazz, etc.) has its own music "conventions" (common musical practices or ideas) that make it what it is, and knowing those conventions will help you create your own drum part. For example, you wouldn't play a country groove in a metal band, and you wouldn't play a metal groove in a country band, so knowing what conventions make up each musical style is the first step.

When creating your own drumset part, the best approach is to become very familiar with the particular musical style you intend to perform. In this case, you need to study the music you intend to play by listening to as much as you can and by making notes about (or transcribing) what drummers do in that particular style. Write down everything that you can hear—grooves, fills, the form of the tune, what the drummer does during each particular section, how the drummer plays unison rhythmic figures with the rest of the band, etc.

Choosing the right beat or groove for a song is one of the first considerations. The tempo of a song is an important consideration when determining what groove is appropriate for a song. A slow rock song may need a 16th-note hi-hat ride pattern to keep the song moving, while a fast punk rock tune may need only quarter notes on the hi-hat as a ride pattern.

A great deal of popular music (rock, metal, pop, etc.) follows some musical formulas. Try to figure out what some of those formulas are. These formulas will teach you how to orchestrate the drum part. Orchestrating a drum part can mean determining one or more of the following:

- how to start the tune (don't play at all, play just the hi-hat on beats 2 and 4, play a groove but with a cross-stick on beats 2 and 4, play a full-volume groove with snare on beats 2 and 4, etc.)
- what type of groove to play (quarter-note ride, eighth-note ride, 16th-note ride, shuffle rhythm, swing rhythm)
- when to play fills (only at the end of eight-bar phrases, leading into the bridge or chorus section, play many fills, play very few fills, etc.)
- what fills are appropriate (eighth-note fills, 16th-note fills, triplet fills)
- when or if to change the groove (when going from a verse into a chorus, for an instrumental solo, when changing soloists)
- when to move from the hi-hat to the ride cymbal or from one ride cymbal to another (leading into the chorus, when the music gets louder, when changing soloists)
- many other decisions that affect the outcome of the song

One important piece of advice: you should have a good musical reason for everything you do when you play the drums. You must know why you're playing something as much as what you are playing. Don't just play something and not think about it!

By asking yourself the following questions before you play (or even while you are playing), you will be on your way to making informed choices about how to create an original drum part:

- **What is the style and purpose of the song?** Is it an improvised jazz tune, a track for a singer, a metal tune, a punk rock tune? (This will determine how busy you play and how loud you play.)
- **Did the producer/artist give me any instructions about drwhat they want me to play?** If so, it's a good idea to try to follow their instructions if you want to work with them again.
- **How do songs like this normally begin?**

- **Should I play with brushes, sticks, mallets, or some combination?**
- **Should I start simply and softly or forcefully and loudly?**
- **Should I start with a strong backbeat or soft backbeat?**
- **Will there be any change in dynamics?**
- **What is the rhythm of the bass line, and should I try to emulate that on my bass drum?**
- **Should I start on the hi-hat and/or move to the ride cymbal?** If so, when?
- **Where should I put my fills?** Should I play any fills at all?
- **Are there any breaks or stops in the music?**
- **Are there any important rhythms that the whole band will play in unison?**
- **Should the groove get more complex and intense during the song or is it all about the same intensity?**
- **Is there another, unusual groove that would also work in this setting?**
- **Will there be percussion playing along?** If so, should I leave some "musical space" for them by not playing a dense, busy groove or by playing fewer fills?

Here are some very general drumset orchestration characteristics of various styles. Every situation and song is different, of course, but these are some general guidelines.

POP/ROCK/COUNTRY

Most pop, rock, and country tunes have some sort of introduction, followed by a verse-chorus-verse-chorus format. Play the ride pattern on the hi-hat during the verses and ride cymbal on the choruses or during solos. Some slow songs begin with just the hi-hat on beats 2 and 4, followed by a groove with a cross-stick on beats 2 and 4, then a full snare on the louder sections. The bass drum rhythm is frequently the same or similar to the bass player's rhythms. Fills are normally used to transition from one part of the song to another (the verse to the chorus, the chorus to the bridge, etc.). There may be some unison rhythms that the entire band needs to play, so listen for those. Endings often contain repeated phrases (known as *tags*), or a fade to silence, or a slowing down of the tempo (known as a *ritard*).

JAZZ

Many traditional jazz tunes begin with the jazz ride cymbal pattern on the ride, hi-hat on beats 2 and 4, and the snare and bass drum "comping." Tunes may also begin with an open hi-hat ride pattern or with brushes on the snare. Drummers often start a tune with brushes and then switch to sticks for the louder sections or when soloists change. Never change from brushes to sticks or change ride surfaces in the middle of a phrase. In some cases, the groove may need to change from a swing feel to some type of Afro-Cuban or Brazilian feel (bossa nova, mambo, Afro-Cuban 6/8), depending upon the arrangement of the particular tune. Bass solos are often accompanied with just a soft ride pattern on the hi-hat or brushes. There are some standard endings in jazz that have developed over the years, so be familiar with them. Also be prepared for a "tag ending," a vamp ending, a sustained last note, or a short last note (depending upon the tune).

METAL

Each song uses its own specific groove. There are often unison figures that need to be played with the guitar part. Metal often contains many fills, use of double bass drums, drumsets with multiple toms and numerous cymbals, and the volume is generally loud.

FUNK

Grooves are usually eighth-note or 16th-note backbeat grooves, but are often specific to a tune. Busy patterns containing ghost notes are common. Fills are generally used as transitions between sections. Drummers typically make the groove feel relaxed by playing behind the beat. Drum sounds are often very dry and muffled.

Miscellaneous Drumming Concepts

There are a number of factors that can influence your ability to play the drums, and many of them have nothing to do with music, drums, sticks, heads, or cymbals. They include the following…

SET UP

How you set up your drums can have a huge effect on how well you play. The drumset can be adjusted in a million different ways, so make the drums fit you—not the other way around. Try these suggestions when you set up:

- Place the throne at a comfortable height that allows your knees to be parallel to the floor.
- Sit on the *front* of the throne so that your legs can move freely and the blood flow to your legs is not restricted.
- As you sit on the throne, wherever your feet land, *that's* where the pedals should be. Place the bass drum and hi-hat pedals so that they're underneath your feet as you comfortably sit on the throne for maximum relaxation.
- Place the snare drum at a height and angle so that you can play anything on it without hitting your forearms on your thighs.
- Place the toms and ride cymbal within reach so that your arms can hang at your side and you can pivot from the elbow to reach them. This will allow you to move around the drumset easily.
- If you're using a music stand, there are several options for where to place it. You can place it in front of the bass drum, but if you have to turn pages, you'll have to stop playing, stand up, and turn the page (not a great idea). If you place it to your left (or your right, if you're left-handed), then when you turn pages, you can continue to play the ride with your right hand while your left hand turns the page (better idea). With some practice, you can even play both the ride *and* the snare while turning pages—a useful technique to acquire.

TUNING

Tuning drums is a huge and varied topic, but here are some basic rules and tips:

- Mount a new head evenly by putting the head on the drum and tighten the lugs by hand until you can't tighten them any more (this is known as "finger tight").
- Imagine the drum head is the face of a clock. Tension the lugs in an "X" pattern starting with the lug at the 12:00 position, followed by the 6:00 position, 9:00 position, and finally the 3:00 position. Then tighten the other four lugs in the same manner. Turn each of the lugs a half turn until you are close to the desired pitch. Use smaller turning increments to achieve your desired pitch.
- Once you've tuned all of your toms, if you want the pitch to "fall off" or "bend down" as the sound decays, detune one lug on each drum by turning it counterclockwise.
- When tuning the snare, tune the bottom head a little tighter than the top (to start). When you've tuned both heads to your desired sound, engage the snare strainer with the adjustment knob barely holding the snares against the head. Tap the snare drum with a drum stick as you slowly tighten the snare strainer until you achieve the amount of snare sound you like.

FOOT TECHNIQUE

Should you play with the heel-up or heel-down technique? The answer depends on many factors. Many drummers feel that both techniques are valid, but for different musical situations. In quiet, low-volume settings, heel down will probably be the best option, because you have the most control using this technique. When you play with your heel down, you're resting your leg whenever you're not playing, so your leg does not quickly become tired. When the leg becomes tired, most drummers have a tendency to rush the beat because their leg becomes heavier and heavier; naturally, they want to give their leg a rest.

The heel-up technique is excellent for situations where you need a great deal of volume, when the bass drum notes need to be punchy and staccato (in metal, rock, or funk), or when you need to play three or more notes in succession.

Another element of bass drum pedal technique involves the bass drum beater. After you play a bass drum note, if you leave the beater pressed against the head, the next time you want to play you have to make two motions: one to release the beater and one to play the next note. If you don't leave the beater pressed against the head, the next time you want to play a bass drum note, you only have one motion. This will enable you to play more accurately because there is no time delay between when you want to play and when you actually hit the head with the beater.

Keeping the beater pressed against the head also creates more tension in your leg due to the constant pressure being applied by the leg. Pressing the beater against the head dampens the sound, so you will achieve a bigger, fuller sound by allowing the bass drum beater to rebound off the head.

CHANGING FROM STICKS TO BRUSHES

Drummers are occasionally required to change from brushes to sticks in the middle of a song. If there's not a break in the music (say, one or more bars of silence), then you must make the transition smoothly without appearing to stop playing. This can be accomplished over the period of four bars with some sleight of hand. First, you must prepare for this change by having the sticks within reach—either on the floor tom (which is the easiest place to reach) or on top of the bass drum.

This example illustrates how to change from brushes to sticks by bar 3. In the first bar, both brushes are playing—the right brush is playing the ride pattern, and the left brush is creating the "swish" sound. In bar 2, put down the right brush and pick up the stick; the left hand continues the "swish" sound on the snare head. In bar 3, the right stick begins playing on the ride while the left hand stops playing, puts down the brush, and picks up the other stick. In bar 4, the right hand continues to play the ride, and the left hand joins in with some notes on the snare using the other stick. The change is now complete. In order to change from sticks to brushes, reverse the order of events.

TRACK 310

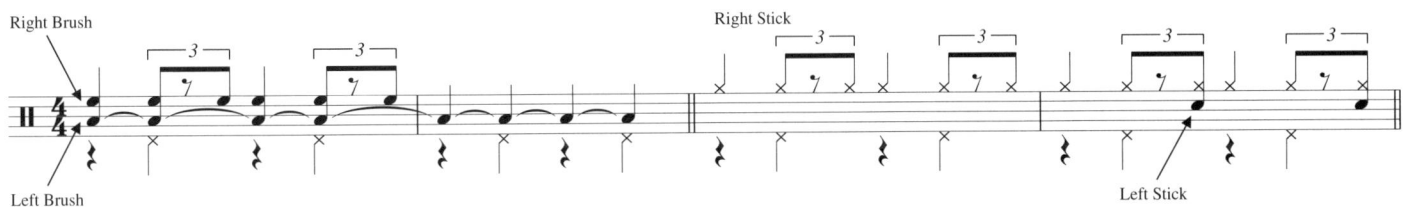

Here are some other miscellaneous pieces of advice that you might find helpful:

- Try playing snare exercises or etudes with brushes. Brushes don't bounce very well, so this will improve your technique, because you must articulate every stroke with brushes.
- When buying a new cymbal, take your own sticks to test it out. After all, those are the sticks you'll be using to play it, and the store may not have your particular stick brand or size. Have someone else play the cymbal (with your sticks) and walk five feet, 10 feet, and even 25 feet away to listen to it—the distance that an audience sits from your drumset. You'll be surprised at how the cymbal sound changes and how the overtones disappear. Take the cymbals you already own and compare them to your potential cymbal. You might find that the cymbal you're considering is either too closely matched to what you already own or it doesn't fit with the other cymbals.

Lesson 95

Polyrhythms

The term "polyrhythm" translates literally as "many rhythms," but it is defined as the simultaneous sounding of two or more conflicting rhythms. Polyrhythms are present in many forms of music, including most pop music. Learning to recognize and play polyrhythms requires several steps, including developing the ability to hear how two rhythms relate to one another, learning how polyrhythms are notated, and learning how to execute them using specific stickings.

One of the first steps in studying polyrhythms is to develop the ability to hear how one rhythm relates to another rhythm. Fortunately, you can use your knowledge of common rhythms to study polyrhythms. One of the most common polyrhythms used today is the quarter-note triplet. To create a quarter-note triplet rhythm, begin with eighth-note triplets. In 4/4 time, play four groups of triplets with an accent on each beat starting with a right stick (Example 1A). Then change the accent pattern to every *second* triplet note; this will mean that every *right* stick will now play an accent (Example 1B). As you continue to play Example 1B, omit the unaccented left stick (or continue to play it off the head in the air); this results in you now playing Example 1C. You are now playing a quarter-note triplet, which is notated in Example 1D. Examples 1C and 1D are identical; they're simply two different ways to write the same rhythm.

TRACK 311

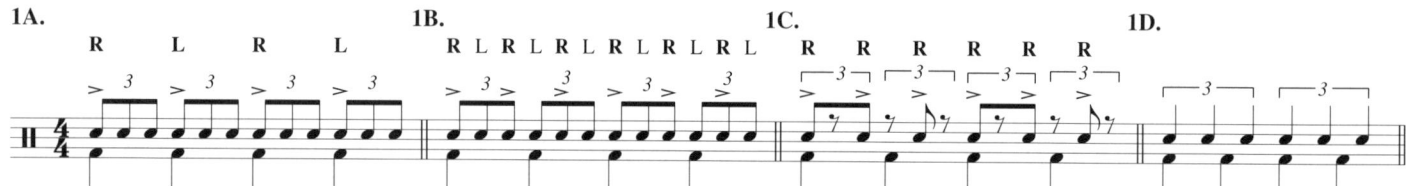

Another common polyrhythm is "4 against 3," also written as 4:3 or 4/3. The easiest way to learn this polyrhythm, and the meter in which it is most commonly found, is with 3/4 time. Begin by playing three groups of 16th notes with accents on each beat (Example 2A). Then accent the 16th notes in groups of three using an R-L-L sticking (Example 2B). Now omit the two unaccented left sticks (Example 2C), and the resulting rhythm is the "4 against 3" polyrhythm found in Example 2D.

TRACK 312

The method used to demonstrate 4 against 3 may be applied to any polyrhythm. Any polyrhythm may be deciphered by using this same method, which is similar to the *common denominator* process taught in math classes. If you understand the process of deciphering a polyrhythm, then you can work out *any* polyrhythm. For example, let's decipher 4 against 5 (4:5). This means that you want to play four notes over the span of five beats. The right number in this ratio is the number of beats in the polyrhythm. So, start with five beats in a bar, which means the time signature will be 5/4:

Now take the left number (4) of the ratio and divide each beat into four subdivisions, which means each beat will be divided into four 16th notes:

Using the right number (5), group each of the beat subdivisions in groups of five, using an accent on the beginning of each grouping:

If you listen to the accents, you'll hear just four accented notes over the span of five beats. To complete the process, omit any unaccented notes, and what you have left is 4 against 5 (or four notes over the span of five beats):

Using the same method, let's decipher another polyrhythm: 7 against 4 (7:4). This means that you want to play seven notes over the span of four beats. The right number (4) of the ratio is the number of beats in a bar, and the left number (7) is the number of subdivisions in each beat of the bar. So now you have four beats in a bar, with each beat divided into seven subdivisions (Example 7A). Use an accent to mark the beginning of each group of four (Example 7B). Then omit the unaccented notes to produce a 7:4 polyrhythm (Example 7C and 7D).

TRACK 313

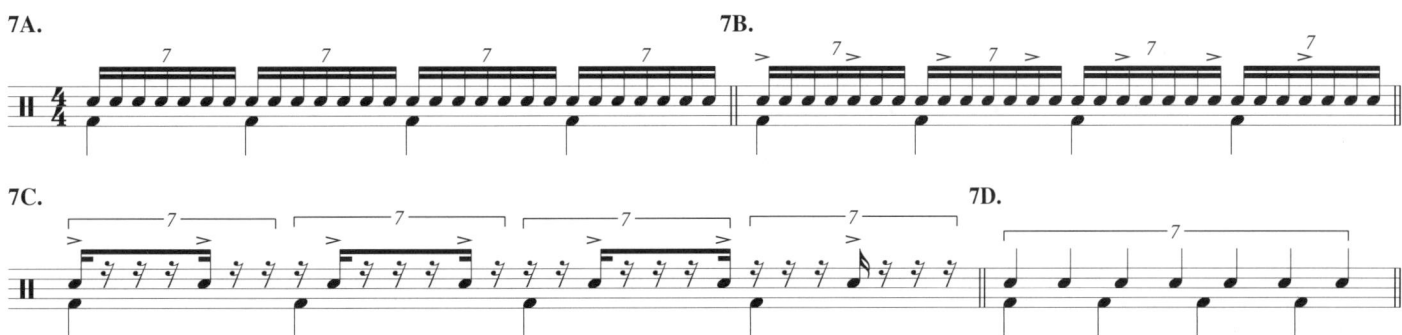

This method will work for any polyrhythm. Using this process, however, is based on your ability to play any beat subdivision, so you will have to develop that ability before attempting to decipher polyrhythms using beat subdivisions of two (eighth notes), three (triplets), four (16th notes), five (quintuplets), six (sextuplets), seven (septuplets), or any other odd number.

Lesson 96

Rock Drumset Solo #1

Rock Drumset Solo #1 is an intermediate-level drumset solo/audition piece that features some standard rock grooves (with 16th-note bass drum patterns), fills, rhythmic solo figures, and a 16-bar improvised solo section. The first four measures serve as an introduction to the main groove of the piece (that starts at measure 5). Measure 13 begins the solo section with a two-bar repeated eighth-note cymbal/snare drum motive. The cymbal groove then moves to the ride cymbal in measure 21, where the fills become more challenging. Another two-bar rhythmic solo motive appears in measure 29. An improvised drum solo takes place in measures 37–44 (which is played twice for a total of 16 bars). Measure 45 begins the repetition of the second main groove (now with more challenging fills) before the big fill that closes the solo.

ROCK DRUMSET SOLO #1 EXCERPT

TRACK 314

Lesson 97

Jazz Drumset Solo #1

Jazz Drumset Solo #1 is a solo/audition piece that includes many of the routine elements of a big band chart. Beginning with a traditional jazz open hi-hat pattern, it soon moves on to the ride cymbal with some background figures (which should be orchestrated on the snare drum or bass drum). An ensemble section that requires "setting up the figures" takes place from measure 13–20. Measure 14, 16, and 18 are intended to be played as "time" only. The drum solo (measures 21–24) should be in a swing style and repeated four times (16 measures in total). A rhythmically strong musical transition should be present as the solo moves into the ensemble figures (which should all be set up) at measure 25. Beat 2 of measure 33 is very important and should have a set-up on the downbeat. Measure 39 is the closing of the piece, so a strong, accurate fill should be used there. End with a short note (with snare, hi-hat/bass drum combination, or choked cymbal) on the downbeat of measure 40 and a fill starting on beat 3 of measure 40.

JAZZ DRUMSET SOLO #1 EXCERPT

TRACK 315

Lesson 98

Jazz Drumset Solo #2

Jazz Drumset Solo #2 is an intermediate-level jazz drum solo/audition work written in the style of a big band drum chart. Measures 1 and 3 are ensemble figures, followed by one-bar drum solos. Measures 5 and 6 feature some additional ensemble figures before a two-bar drum solo leads into the body of the chart. Measures 9–15 should be interpreted as background figures (on the snare drum or bass drum) while continuing to play time on the ride cymbal. A straight eighth-note fill is needed in measure 16 to make the transition into the bossa nova groove at measure 17. Measure 22 features some bossa nova ensemble figures before the transition back to swing in measure 24. Measures 25–32 are a typical big band "shout chorus," and the rhythmic figures should be orchestrated as such (i.e., set up each entrance of the band and solo around the figures). The drum solo in measures 33–36 is to be played eight times, using the opening rhythmic figure as a point of departure. It may or may not be played each time (at the player's discretion). More swing ensemble figures occur in measure 27–39. A straight eighth-note fill signals the transition back to bossa nova (measure 45). Measures 49–51 are a bossa style solo before the concluding unison figures in the last measure.

JAZZ DRUMSET SOLO #2 EXCERPT

TRACK 316

Lesson 99

Jazz Drumset Solo #3

Jazz Drumset Solo #3 is an advanced drumset solo/audition piece that features an open drum solo, changes of meter, and other elements found in most big band drum charts. The first measure is an open drum solo that is to be played *rubato* (without a steady tempo), so it can be shaped by each player as they see fit. Measure 2 is used to set the tempo (BPM = 200+) following the open drum solo. Measures 4–8 feature some standard jazz comping/background figures that should be played underneath the jazz ride pattern.

Measures 10–17 contain a series of figures that should be set up and executed like a big band ensemble section. Measure 18 begins a section in 3/4 time with some rhythmic figures that need to be orchestrated around the drums. There is a brief four-bar interlude (measures 34–37) that is followed by the eight-bar drum solo over a repeated rhythmic figure (measures 38–45). Measures 46–53 should be treated like a big band "shout chorus" with set-ups and fills before the two-bar pedal section (measures 54–55) and concluding figure.

JAZZ DRUMSET SOLO #3 EXCERPT

TRACK 317

Lesson 100

Jazz Drumset Solo #4

Jazz Drumset Solo #4 is an advanced drumset solo/audition piece that challenges the player to interpret swing/big band figures, play a mambo groove and execute rhythmic figures in that style, and solo (in either an Afro-Cuban or swing style). The eight-bar swing-style introduction (with figures) segues into a stop-time section in which the player only plays the indicated rhythms—no fills (measures 9–14). This leads into a mambo section with rhythmic shots and figures that need to be set up with fills (measures 20, 27, 29–30). The groove returns to a swing feel in measure 33 with some ensemble figures that require fills and set-ups. A 32-bar drum solo is next—in either a Latin or swing style. This leads into some more swing feel big band ensemble figures (similar to a "shout chorus") before the four-bar coda.

JAZZ DRUMSET SOLO #4 EXCERPT

TRACK 318

About the Author

Jazz drummer Terry O'Mahoney has appeared with such jazz greats as saxophonists Bud Shank and Phil Woods, pianists James Williams and Oliver Jones, guitarists John Abercrombie, Ed Bickert, Gene Bertoncini, Howard Alden, Lorne Lofsky, and Fred Hamilton, trumpeters Marvin Stamm and Terell Strafford, and trombonist Curtis Fuller. Aside from his work in the U.S., he's also performed in Japan and Brazil. His books, *Motivic Drumset Soloing* (2004) and *Jazz Drumming Transitions* (2010), are published by the Hal Leonard Corporation. He is currently Professor of Music at St. Francis Xavier University in Antigonish, Nova Scotia (Canada) where he teaches jazz and orchestral percussion, history, and coaches jazz ensembles. He has performed with the Louisville Orchestra (Kentucky, U.S.) and Symphony Nova Scotia (Halifax, N.S.). His education includes studies with jazz great Jeff Hamilton, a B.M. Ed. from the University of Louisville (KY), and a Master's degree from the University of Miami (FL). Terry's percussion ensemble compositions are published by Per-Mus Publications (Columbus, OH), and his articles on percussion have appeared in *Percussive Notes*, *Modern Drummer*, *Rhythm* (UK), and *Rhythm and Drums* (Japan) magazines. He was a presenter at the 2003 Percussive Arts Society International Conference (PASIC) in Louisville, KY. He was a contributing editor for *Percussive Notes* magazine and is active as a clinician and adjudicator at music festivals throughout the U.S. and Canada. He uses Crescent Cymbals and Vic Firth drumsticks exclusively.